Gender, Health, and History in Modern East Asia

Gender, Health, and History in Modern East Asia

Edited by
Angela Ki Che Leung and Izumi Nakayama

With an Introduction by Francesca Bray

HKU
PRESS
香港大學出版社

**Hong Kong Institute for the
Humanities and Social Sciences**
(Incorporating the Centre of Asian Studies)

This publication has been generously supported by the Hong Kong Institute for the Humanities and Social Sciences, and grows out of a conference convened by the East Asian Medicine, Science and Contemporary Public Health research group in the Institute's Inter-Asia Program.

Hong Kong University Press
The University of Hong Kong
Pokfulam Road
Hong Kong
www.hkupress.hku.hk

© 2017 Hong Kong University Press

ISBN 978-988-8390-90-8 (*Hardback*)

British Library Cataloguing-in-Publication Data
A catalogue record for this book is available from the British Library.

10 9 8 7 6 5 4 3 2 1

Printed and bound by Hang Tai Printing Co. Ltd., Hong Kong, China

Contents

Acknowledgments

The editors would like to thank the School of Modern Languages and Cultures, Faculty of Arts, at the University of Hong Kong for funding the workshop in 2009 where we and our colleagues brainstormed the series of conferences and workshops from which much of this volume originated. We have greatly benefitted their participation and contributions either as presenter or commentator in the 2011 conference "Making of East Asia: Gender and Health" and the 2013 workshop "Anatomical Modernity: Gender and Health in East Asia," in particular, Charlotte Furth, Sonja Kim, Jane Kim, Wen-hua Kuo, Yi-Ping Lin, Shao-hua Liu, Rayna Rapp, Azumi Tsuge, and Yi-li Wu.

We appreciate the wonderful staff of the Hong Kong Institute for the Humanities and Social Sciences for their logistical support, particularly Joan Cheng, our principal event coordinator. We are also grateful to Ruth Rogaski for her helpful comments and criticisms on an earlier version of the manuscript and to anonymous reviewers for their valuable feedback. We are indebted to the professional help of our copyeditor, Gershom Tse, and to Christopher Munn, who encouraged us to work with Hong Kong University Press. Last but not least, our thanks to Yuet Sang Leung and her colleagues at HKU Press for their help and support in the production of this book.

Illustrations

Figures

Tables

Introduction

Francesca Bray

This volume breaks new ground in the history of East Asian biopolitics, offering the first broad-based exploration of gender and health in the region during the long twentieth century. The core theme is the complex meshing of biology, body, and citizen that underpins projects of biological nation building and molds the forms of modern subjectivity. The nine case studies presented here, spanning Japan, Korea, China, Taiwan, and Hong Kong from the 1870s to the present, demonstrate just how tightly concerns with gender and health have been woven into the enterprise of modernization and nation building throughout the period. Colonial powers and medical associations, government bureaucrats, military personnel, and pharmaceutical companies as well as scientists, educators, and medical practitioners contributed to the legitimation and popularization of evolving scientific discourses and interpretations of the gendered body, sex, and reproductive health. As novel visions of the body and its possibilities took shape, new expressions of individuality, sociality, transgression or resistance, new desires, and fears emerged. Across the region and over the decades, norms and ideals, techniques, terminology, and forms of scientific or cultural authority circulated and converged, faded and resurfaced. In mapping such flows, influences, and reactions, the volume highlights the prominent role that the biopolitics of health and gender has played in knitting and shaping the East Asian region as we know it today.

These studies of biopolitics at work in non-Western contexts offer an excellent opportunity to test concepts that have become common currency in the historiography or social analysis of the biosciences. Critics note that Foucault's contrast between sovereign power and biopower derives from a scientific and political transition specific to early modern France,[1] and that terms like "biosociality"[2] and "biological citizenship"[3] likewise stem from

---

With many thanks to Izumi Nakayama for her significant contributions to this text.

1. Michel Foucault, *The History of Sexuality*, vol. 1 (New York: Vintage Books, 1978).
2. Paul Rabinow, *French DNA: Trouble in Purgatory* (Chicago: Chicago University Press, 1999).
3. Adriana Petryna, *Biological Citizenship: Science and the Politics of Health after Chernobyl* (Princeton: Princeton University Press, 2002); Nikolas Rose and Carlos Novas, "Biological

Western histories, institutions, and expectations. The question, then, is whether and how well such analytical tools travel and how we can best use them. Should we be thinking in terms of "biopolitics in Asia" or of "Asian biopolitics"?[4] If the latter, what is distinctive about Asian biopolitics, and what might that distinction tell us about the situated nature of biopolitics elsewhere, including societies like France or the United States, which are so often taken for granted as natural points of reference?

The book is divided into three parts. The first focuses on the biosciences of the body and the constitution of reproductive subjects; the second probes the agency of women as family health-carers, "household pharmacists," and consuming biocitizens; the third contrasts three cases of problematic virility, considered from the perspectives of medical etiology, sexual identity, and fertility. In this introduction I explore some significant themes that crosscut the book's three parts. I begin with some remarks on historiographical rationales for treating modern East Asia as a region. Then comes a critical reflection on how as historians we use such apparently natural concepts as health and gender, followed by discussions of biopower, nation building, and biological subjects; resistant bodies and modes of biocitizen agency; demographic control, imposed or embraced; and the national and personal challenges, respectively, of family planning and infertility. Low fertility levels were an essential factor in the economic "miracles" that have transformed East Asian nations into prosperous societies, and I briefly discuss the recent resurgence and rebrandings of "traditional" East Asian medicine that find growing appeal among middle-class families and professional women. I conclude with a discussion of the variants of biogovernance and biocitizenship revealed in the nine chapters.

East Asia: Taking a Regional Perspective

Several landmark studies of biopolitics and modernization in East Asian nations have appeared in recent years.[5] But research in this emerging field

---

Citizenship," in *Global Assemblages: Technology, Politics, and Ethics as Anthropological Problems*, ed. Aihwa Ong and Stephen J. Collier (New York: Blackwell, 2005), 439–63.

4. Nicolas Langlitz, "Is There an Asian Biopolitics?" *BioSocieties* 6 (2011): 487–500.

5. Key studies on the sciences of sexuality, eugenics, and race include Frank Dikötter's *The Discourse of Race in Modern China* (Stanford: Stanford University Press, 1992), and *Sex, Culture and Modernity in China: Medical Science and the Construction of Sexual Identities in the Early Republican Period* (Honolulu: University of Hawai'i Press, 1995) on late Qing and Republican China; and Sabine Frühstück, *Colonizing Sex: Sexology and Social Control in Modern Japan* (Berkeley: University of California Press, 2003) on Japan and its colonies. On the impact of hygiene and public health, see Ruth Rogaski, *Hygienic Modernity: Meanings of Health and Disease in Treaty-Port China* (Berkeley: University of California Press, 2004) on late Qing China; Dongwon Shin, "Hygiene, Medicine, and Modernity in Korea," *East Asian Science, Technology and Society: An International Journal* 3(1) (2009): 5–26, on Korea; Ka-che Yip, *Health and National Reconstruction in Nationalist China: The Development of Modern Health*

requires a confident grasp of difficult languages, extensive literatures, and complex histories as well as of the immediate geopolitical context, so it is hardly surprising that so far most studies, even those that are multiauthored, have focused on a single nation or its immediate zone of influence.[6] Although some nationally based studies address the regional networks within which their actors operate, typically the main focus is on the nation's relationship to the West. Even if many individual works differentiate between the agendas or contributions of particular Western scientific schools or institutions within a country, the cumulative effect of locally focused studies is to emphasize the significance of their most salient common factor, namely encounters and exchanges with what, by amalgamation, comes to appear as a broadly homogeneous, unitary Western science. Overall, this downplays or obscures the equally crucial circulation of local formulations of science and modernity, the flows and clashes of ideas and people, desires and values, institutions and practices, bacteria and commodities among localities, nations, or zones of influence within the East Asian region. It is important to acknowledge that for East Asians emulating or borrowing from the West is not always the first priority: even in the late nineteenth and early twentieth centuries, they were likely to first look to successful neighbors within the region for models.

Recognizing the serious problems intrinsic to taking the modern nation as a natural unit of analysis, compellingly laid out in the case of China by Prasenjit Duara,[7] there has recently been a surge of interest in "Asia as method" among science, technology, and society (STS) scholars and historians. The concept of "Asia as method" was first proposed in the 1940s and

---

Services, 1928–1937 (Ann Arbor: University of Michigan Association of Asian Studies, 1995) on Republican China; and Angela Ki Che Leung and Charlotte Furth, eds., *Health and Hygiene in Chinese East Asia: Policies and Publics in the Long Twentieth Century* (Durham, NC: Duke University Press, 2010) on the Chinese culture zone through the long twentieth century. There is also a substantial literature on Western medicine and modernity in East Asia. Important recent contributions include Hoi-eun Kim, *Doctors of Empire: Medical and Cultural Encounters between Imperial Germany and Meiji Japan* (Toronto: University of Toronto Press, 2014), which analyzes Meiji Japan's adaptation of German medicine for deployment as its own tool of empire; Michael Shiyung Liu, *Prescribing Colonization: The Role of Medical Practices and Policies in Japan-Ruled Taiwan, 1895–1945* (Ann Arbor, MI: Association for Asian Studies, 2009), which charts its applications in colonial Taiwan; and John P. DiMoia, *Reconstructing Bodies: Biomedicine, Health, and Nation Building in South Korea since 1945* (Stanford: Stanford University Press, 2013), which tracks the role of medical modernization in South Korea's nation-building project after its liberation from Japan. Bridie Andrews, *The Making of Modern Chinese Medicine* (Vancouver: University of British Columbia Press, 2014); and Sean Hsiang-lin Lei, *Neither Donkey nor Horse: Medicine in the Struggle over China's Modernity* (Chicago: University of Chicago Press, 2014) take a new approach to the complex relations between Western and indigenous medicine that unfolded in China between the 1890s and 1949, analyzing the two ostensibly irreconcilable forms of medicine in terms of coproduction or coevolution.

6. Luping Bu, Darwin H. Stapleton, and Ka-che Yip, *Science, Public Health and the State in Modern East Asia* (New York: Routledge, 2012) is a rare example of a cross-regional study.
7. Prasenjit Duara, *Rescuing History from the Nation* (Chicago: University of Chicago Press, 1995).

1950s by Takeuchi Yoshimi.[8] Takeuchi was a fierce critic of Japanese imperialism and what he considered its slavish embrace of the "best," adopted wholesale from an uncritically admired and supposedly coherent West. Takeuchi drew inspiration from the great Chinese writer and translator Lu Xun, who had trained as a biomedical doctor in Japan before returning to China to take up radical politics. Like the majority of his reformist and revolutionary contemporaries, Lu Xun was convinced that China's salvation depended upon replacing its "superstitions" (including indigenous medicine) with scientific rationality. But it was essential to cultivate a critical spirit and not to be blinded by uncritical adulation of the West's supposed perfections. Lu Xun therefore translated numerous "minor works" and resistance poetry by writers from small, oppressed nations in the Balkans or Central Europe, spotlighting the heterogeneity and fractures within "Western civilization" and drawing upon these expressions of resistance and despair to develop a critique of power both in Europe and in Asia.[9]

Takeuchi too rejected the facile East-West binaries that Japan's politicians and apologists had used to foment nationalist sentiment in favor of imperialist expansion and then, post-1945, to excuse defeat and claim the status of victim. Takeuchi argued that Asians must take full moral responsibility for themselves. Rather than using an idealized West to criticize Asia or to define its future goals, they should develop a critique of both the West and Asia that was firmly grounded in Asian conditions and experience, and that would support new forms of responsible agency. In an eloquent recent formulation by the Taiwanese activist-scholar Chen Kuan-hsing, "[U]sing Asia as an imaginary anchoring point can allow societies in Asia to become one another's reference points, so that understanding of the self can be transformed, and subjectivity rebuilt."[10] Yet while arguing for the value of "Asia as method," Takeuchi also cautioned against essentializing regions or nations, insisting upon the need to "fracture the singularity of Asia into a plurality with its own internal and variegated dynamics of colonialism and resistance."[11]

Three or four decades later, with the turn to postcolonial studies that began in the 1990s, Takeuchi's dual agenda was energetically revived: history must be rescued from the colonially rooted assumption that the modern nation was the natural unit of analysis, while the region must be rescued from the Cold War ideologies and epistemologies of area studies. As a field of organized, cross-disciplinary inquiry into the characteristics

8. Takeuchi Yoshimi, "Asia as Method" (1960), in *What Is Modernity? Writings of Takeuchi Yoshimi*, ed. and trans. Richard F. Calichman (New York: Columbia University Press, 2005), 149–66.
9. Shu-mei Shih, "Theory, Asia and the Sinophone," *Postcolonial Studies* 13(4) (2010): 473.
10. Kuan-Hsing Chen, *Asia as Method: Toward Deimperialization* (Durham, NC: Duke University Press, 2010), xv.
11. Shih, "Theory, Asia and the Sinophone," 472–73.

and potential of regions or areas identified as Africa, Latin America, the Middle East, and East, Southeast, South and Central Asia, area studies was vigorously promoted by the post–World War II US government as part of its project to stymie Communism and globalize American values and influence. The discipline of Area Studies came under intense fire as opposition to the Vietnam War grew across American campuses: critics tore to shreds the claimed ideological innocence and objectivity of researchers feeding information about America's "others" into a war machine.[12]

Many features of the Area Studies project justified its political and intellectual discrediting: the cultural coherence attributed to regions defined primarily by geopolitical strategy; the use of quantitative data to construct models that supposedly identified and explained profound cultural predispositions; the defining premise that America should lead the world and that American-style personal traits, social relations, and democratic institutions were values for which all should strive. But other, less strident branches of regional studies research had meanwhile persisted in the shape of regional journals or professional organizations, and the failure of Area Studies could not erase the value, empirical and analytical, of thinking about and with regions.[13] The region was debated, reconfigured, and mobilized by poststructural and postcolonial scholars,[14] becoming still more compelling as the concept of globalization infused the world of research, as regional economic alliances like ASEAN (Association of South-East Asian Nations), ECOWAS (Economic Community of West African States), OAS (Organization of American States), and CEPA (Comprehensive Economic Partnership Agreement) gathered strength and as the economic and cultural dominance of the United States and Western Europe became increasingly uncertain. In the face of these new geopolitical realities, scholars and teachers have sought ways to rework and democratize regional studies, to generate "Area Studies Inside-Out,"[15] starting from the viewpoint not of strategists in Washington but of local people.[16]

---

12. For a concise account of the foundations, goals, and techniques of area studies or regional science as it took shape in the post–World War II decades, see Trevor Barnes, "What Regional Studies Might Have Been: Cold War American Social Science," *Regional Studies* 47(3) (2013): 461–64. Terence Wesley-Smith and John Goss, eds., *Remaking Area Studies: Teaching and Learning across Asia and the Pacific* (Honolulu: University of Hawai'i Press, 2010) provides a very useful comparison of the US area studies project with other scholarly-political-economic regional studies programs, such as the Japanese government's investments in Southeast Asian studies.
13. Barnes, "What Regional Studies Might Have Been," 461–64.
14. For example, Martin Lewis and Kären Wigen, *The Myth of Continents: A Critique of Metageography* (Berkeley: University of California Press, 1997).
15. John Goss and Terence Wesley-Smith, introduction to Wesley-Smith and Goss, *Remaking Area Studies*, ix–xxvii.
16. One concrete example is *Teach 3.11*, "a collaborative online educational resource," initiated in response to the Fukushima nuclear disaster, "powered by volunteer students, teachers, and researchers who produce, translate, and share annotated citations of books, articles,

The question arises, of course, of how we identify a region and where (or whether) we draw its boundaries. Sometimes a region is defined primarily by what it is not (the classic case being Asia as not-Europe), sometimes it is defined as much by colonial history as by geography (sub-Saharan Africa or Latin America). Often what appears as a naturally dense lived coherence is in fact the result of considerable political effort and institutional investment (the European Community). Furthermore, the linkages that constitute a viable region need not be defined in rigidly territorial terms: Chinese Southeast Asia, Nanyang, is a good example of a fluid yet coherent region, its component territories determined at any historical point by where significant numbers of Chinese migrants worked or had settled. East Asia as conceived by the imperial Japanese state in the 1930s (Tō-a) comprises rather different territories or states from the "tributary" East Asian region that the historian Takeshi Hamashita sees as forming a self-conscious unit during the Qing dynasty.[17] In the immediate post–World War II period, the Communist and anti-Communist nations of East Asia had so little communication or exchange that they could legitimately be treated as independent zones. Today, however, they are all (even North Korea) tightly integrated into a region.

In a recent essay on the resurgence of Asia, Prasenjit Duara helpfully delineates the characteristic networks of trade, migration, capital flow, and political linkages that knit together a region known as Asia in successive historical eras: under colonialism, between the world wars, through the Cold War, and, in an unprecedentedly strong coalescence and cohesion, since the Asian financial crisis of 1997. Noting that Asia as a representation (external or internal) and Asia as an integrated social reality are by no means identical, Duara sees Takeuchi's Asia ("as method") as "a desired signifier of resistance . . . not [to] be confused with the more substantive goal of achieving regional sustainability by the critique of rampant capitalism and unyielding nationalism."[18]

I am not sure I can agree with Duara that the dizzyingly ambitious goal he formulates is indeed substantive. Most of us, as scholars or as citizens, will be satisfied with more modest aims. But the point is that taking Asia, or East Asia, seriously, whether as a signifier or as a field of action and experience,

films, and other educational resources to help advance knowledge and wisdom about disasters through the angle of the history of science and technology in Asia" (teach311.org).

17. Takeshi Hamashita, "Tribute and Treaties: Maritime Asia and Treaty-Port Networks in the Era of Negotiation: 1800–1900," in *The Resurgence of East Asia: 500, 150 and 50 Year Perspectives*, ed. Giovanni Arrighi, Takeshi Hamashita, and Mark Selden (London and New York: Routledge, 2003), 17–50.

18. Prasenjit Duara, "Asia Redux: Conceptualizing a Region for Our Times," *Journal of Asian Studies* 69(4) (2010): 1029. Duara perforce offers a sketch; for a more richly textured and rigorous (Marxist) analysis of cycles of regional cohesion and dispersion in East Asia since 1500, see Giovanni Arrighi et al., eds. *The Resurgence of East Asia: 500, 150 and 50 Year Perspectives* (London and New York: Routledge, 2003).

is at once a method and a political commitment. As a project for rethinking simultaneously the articulations of the world we live in and the tools we have devised to observe and analyze them, it resonates powerfully with unfolding concerns in history and philosophy of science. In the 1980s it was feminist theory that shook our certainties about the truth of science as we knew it, challenging the universalist claims of the Western scientific tradition, providing the analytical tools to expose how supposedly neutral truths were permeated by sexist, racist, and other power-laden assumptions.[19] In the 1990s critics like the feminist philosopher of science Sandra Harding took the next logical step, drawing upon non-Western and postcolonial science to challenge other forms of inequality and hegemony layered into the knowledge claims of Western science and into the associated values and institutions of modernity.[20]

It is doubtless no accident that the concern to take East Asia seriously as a catalyst of innovative analysis has been specially marked in the field of science studies, for in East Asia the links among STS scholarship, activism, and science policy are unusually close. Fu Daiwie, a philosopher of science and the founding editor of the international journal *East Asian Science, Technology and Society*, commissioned a series of reflections on why East Asia is good to think with in STS—and what "East Asia," with all its multiplicities and heterogeneities past and present, might mean in such a project.[21] As Warwick Anderson puts it, "Asia as method" in STS not only offers opportunities for a "fresh critique of technoscience" but constitutes "an ethical standpoint."[22] At one reflexive move further, what cultural values and power relations are built into our supposedly self-critical science studies, and how would "taking Asia as method" expose them? Anderson suggests that it "requires no negation or denial of Euro-American STS, but rather it allows us to treat this Western body of knowledge and practice as 'one cultural resource among many others.'"[23] Others might wish to argue for a more determined provincialization of Western STS and science studies.[24] In either

---

19. Sandra Harding, *The Science Question in Feminism* (Ithaca: Cornell University Press, 1986); Donna Haraway, "Situated Knowledges: The Science Question in Feminism and the Privilege of Partial Perspectives," *Feminist Studies* 14(3) (1988): 575–99; Londa Schiebinger, *Nature's Body: Gender in the Making of Modern Science* (Boston: Beacon Press, 1993).

20. Sandra Harding, *Is Science Multicultural? Postcolonialisms, Feminisms, and Epistemologies* (Bloomington: Indiana University Press, 1998).

21. Daiwie Fu, "How Far Can East Asian STS Go? A Position Paper," *East Asian Science, Technology and Society* 1(1) (2007): 1–14; Fa-ti Fan, "East Asian STS: Fox or Hedgehog?" *East Asian Science, Technology and Society* 1(4) (2007): 243–47; Warwick Anderson, "Asia as Method in Science and Technology Studies," *East Asian Science, Technology and Society* 6(4) (2013): 445–51.

22. Anderson, "Asia as Method," 445, 449.

23. Ibid., 448, quoting Kuan-Hsing Chen, *Asia as Method*, 233.

24. Langlitz, "Is There an Asian Biopolitics?"

case, however, it is clear that the two critical projects, science studies and Asia as method, can greatly benefit by joining forces.

This is the principle upon which the contributors to this volume proceed. While by no means dismissing the key importance of Western influence and power, their studies demonstrate that to understand the cultural and institutional resources and the worldviews that individuals, corporations, or states in modernizing or contemporary East Asia bring to decision making or policy, we need to give full weight to intraregional circulations, exchanges, and influence, and to factor in the imprint of common historical legacies. In the cases discussed in this volume, such shared experiences or preferences include the long-term impact of foreign colonialism, Japanese imperialism and Cold War alliances, repeated reformulations of "Confucian values" or "traditional medicine," and even long-standing brand loyalties.

Questions of Health and Gender

Health and gender are such everyday terms now, so deeply rooted as common currency in our personal lives, social institutions, and academic debates, that they appear quite straightforward topics for historical research. But, like sex and reproduction, or male and female, they are heavily loaded terms, denoting complicated concepts with vexed histories even in their native context. What happens when we transpose such terminology into another historical or geographical context? At this point we realize that we must treat these concepts not as natural facts but as what Raymond William calls keywords, terms denoting prominent features of our social experience that we use to explain our world and that we feel drawn to investigate and compare. We use words like culture or market, technology or environment, medicine, health, or gender as if they were obvious, universal, and unambivalent, yet as Williams notes they enfold complex histories and multiple, often inconsistent or contested meanings. Because they are polysemic they are rhetorically, analytically, and politically powerful—and also insidious.

Morally and philosophically loaded as it is, even the basic terminology of reproduction, sexuality, or gender, of health, normality, or deviance, did not (and still does not) translate easily among German, French, and English, let alone into or among Japanese, Chinese, or Korean. How should a scientist or author choose between competing terminological claims? Howard Chiang[25] tracks how Republican Chinese life scientists reached consensus on a terminology of male and female difference that would meet the requirements of the new biological science and its epistemologies. To denote biologically

---

25. Howard Hsueh-Hao Chiang, "The Conceptual Contours of Sex in the Chinese Life Sciences: Zhu Xi (1899–1962), Hermaphroditism, and the Biological Discourse of Ci and Xiong, 1920–1950," *East Asian Science, Technology and Society* 2(3) (2008): 401–30.

male and female (whether animal or human), they adopted *xiong* 雄 and *ci* 雌, terms traditionally used to designate male and female animals. For discussion of human norms and individual variants, they supplemented *xiong* and *ci* with the social terms *nan* 男 and *nü* 女 (man and woman). This new terminology put a very different ontological and epistemological spin on human sexual difference and gender from the evolving, mutually interdependent differentiation implied by yin and yang, the cosmologically rooted terms used traditionally (and still today) in Chinese medical theories of sex and sexual difference.[26]

So what are the challenges and rewards for historians of studying societies distant from our own in space or time through the lens of modern Western concepts like gender, health, or the paired term "gender and health," which in linking the two individual concepts implies strong forms of association between them? Is it legitimate, feasible, and fruitful to think of Al-Andalus, ancien régime France, or even Republican China or contemporary Japan in such terms? There is the risk that we shall distort the past by forcing it into modern categories that were not recognized in the language or lives of the historical actors, like gender, or that, like health, existed earlier in rough equivalents but were construed quite differently. Yet there is also the exhilarating promise of flinging open new windows not only onto the past but also onto the present, the process of critical comparison pushing us to probe the politics and assumptions of our research and of our broader society. The East Asian cases presented here are particularly illuminating, since they present the concepts of gender and health in motion. We see how new terms are coined and existing terms redefined, first in response to the introduction of concepts from the West and their filtering through East Asian communities of practice. Then, as time goes by, we are shown how keywords and clusters of association, ideals of healthy masculinity and femininity, shift in the face of new challenges and demands.

As mentioned earlier, there is now a sizeable body of research on the themes of medicine, medical services, and public health, in individual East Asian nations and occasionally also at regional level. But the science of gender and its historical unfolding, while central to state policies and profound in its personal impact, has hitherto received less explicit attention. Yet the nexus of gender and health is a compelling theme. Prominent in the earliest plans for modernization, it represents an area of private life and personal characteristics in which East Asian "developmental" states have actively and confidently intervened ever since. Yet, by the same token, in this arena of sexuality and gender where the personal is the political and the body encounters the state, the challenges of imposing scientific norms and propagating "healthy," "rational," or "responsible" practices and values

---

26. Ibid.

across space, class, and culture are particularly fraught. As in other parts of the world, among the nations of East Asia this has been a minefield of resistance, contestation, and radical claims over reproductive rights, definitions of normality, gender norms, and sexual identity. It is thus a richly documented field, yet so far it has received little attention outside the narrower context of birth-control programs.[27]

Biopower, Nation Building, and Biological Subjects

In focusing on the nexus of health and gender, this volume fills a significant gap in the literature.[28] It offers stimulating and often surprising new insights into the making of modern history in the vibrant region of East Asia, not least because this biopolitical arena has been regarded as vital by its governments, scientists, and citizens for more than a century.

> If sex was the "most secret quintessence of life" in the minds of European and North American biochemists and other scientists in the early twentieth century, issues of sexual characteristics and desire, gender roles and behavior, and heterosexual reproduction as well as marriage, love, passion, and how they relate to friendship and companionship similarly dominated the intellectual horizon of Chinese modernizing thinkers, including public intellectuals, university professors, scientists, physicians, self-appointed experts, etc. . . . Not only did they see sex as an important subject of scholarly inquiry, but they saw it as such precisely because of their conviction that the question of life was inextricably bound up with the question of sex.[29]

As Howard Chiang notes, for East Asian elites of that period the "question of life" was not merely a matter of intellectual or philosophical concern: the very survival of the nation was at stake.[30] This certainly applied to China, which, having endured several decades of Western encroachment on its sovereignty, experienced the culminating humiliation in 1895 when it was defeated by Japan, a former vassal state traditionally viewed as an inferior civilization.[31] The new biopolitics had begun to take shape even earlier in

---

27. On birth control see below, "To Whom Does My Body Belong?"
28. One important strand in the literature on gender and health not addressed in this volume is the gendering of the modern biomedical professions (doctors, nurses, and midwives) and the roles of these different professional groups as agents of modernization; pertinent studies include Aya Homei, "Midwives and the Medical Marketplace in Modern Japan," *Japanese Studies* 32(2) (2012): 275–93, on the introduction of the "new" midwifery in Meiji Japan; and Tina Phillips Johnson, *Childbirth in Republican China: Delivering Modernity* (Lanham, MD: Lexington Books, 2011) on the biomedicalization of midwifery in Republican China.
29. Chiang, "Conceptual Contours," 406.
30. So too was the very conception of modernity: could or should the "philosophy of life" be determined by the scientific method rather than by Confucian or other religious principles? See Lei, *Neither Donkey nor Horse*, 11.
31. Frank Dikötter pioneered historical scholarship in this field of East Asian studies, showing how physiological and sexual anxieties interwove in late Qing and Republican China to

Japan itself, where the traumatic "opening" of the country by Commodore Perry's battleships in 1853 launched a sustained inquiry into the roots of Japanese weakness and its potential for self-strengthening. Victory against its old Chinese rival in 1895 and against Russia just a few years later, as well as the annexation of colonies in Taiwan, Korea, and eventually Manchuria, prompted biological research into both the weaknesses and the strengths of the Japanese, as well as the sexual expression of racial hierarchies within East Asia.[32]

Since it was widely agreed that science played a significant part in the superiority of the Western powers, modernizers in East Asia, whether reformists or revolutionaries, viewed the implantation of modern science and technology as an essential step toward building up national strength. Engineering, physics, chemistry, and geology were valued not only as essential tools for building infrastructure and developing industrial and military capacity but also as intellectual and material disciplines for cultivating modern rationality and values. In the ruthless competition among late nineteenth- and early twentieth-century powers, building the health and strength of a nation was understood as an organic process, requiring far more thoroughgoing improvement than simply acquiring guns, establishing industries, and building up new forms of technical expertise. For an Asian nation to succeed on the world stage, it was not enough to foster an elite cadre of modern-minded professionals: the quality of the whole population, biological as well as behavioral, must be improved. To this end, the role of the state in regulating its population's health and reproductive practices was dramatically recast, as were the responsibilities of medical personnel, teachers, and ordinary citizens interpellated as responsible subjects embracing the imperatives of biogovernance.

As Izumi Nakayama recounts in her chapter, evolutionary science and comparative anatomy interpreted the "East Asian" body as being physically inferior to the "Western" body, and by extension its diminutive stature came to embody the failures of politics and civilizations.[33] Among Japanese elites

---

express fears of national, racial, or individual failure. See Dikötter, *Discourse of Race*, and *Sex, Culture and Modernity*.

32. See Frühstück, *Colonizing Sex* for an overview. One revealing example is the physician Yamazaki Masashige's indexing of the menstrual characteristics of different ethnic groups within the Japanese empire. See Yuki Terazawa, "Racializing Bodies through Science in Meiji Japan: The Rise of Race-Based Research in Gynecology," in *Building a Modern Japan: Science, Technology, and Medicine in the Meiji Era and Beyond*, ed. Morris Low (New York: Palgrave Macmillan, 2005), 83–102.

33. Let us not forget that Western elites and intellectuals were equally concerned with (moral and physical) degeneration among their own populations and the threat that this posed to national survival. During recruitment for the Boer War of 1899–1902, for instance, the British authorities realized with dismay that because of endemic poverty, poor diet, and poor health, "over one half of the Home army are unfit to carry a pack or to do a week's—I might perhaps say a day's—hard work in the field." Lord Wolseley, commander in chief of

and in aspiring middle-class households, Western furnishings, clothing, and posture were embraced as one way to remold the physique;[34] another way to build up adult strength was to eat beef, however disgusting the experience might be.[35] In the case of children, the science of school hygiene held that children must be exercised and trained so that their limbs would grow longer and they would grow taller. Masturbation triggered premature puberty, stunting growth and healthy maturation, so parents were given instructions on how to scrutinize and regulate their small children's most intimate behavior. Meanwhile in Republican China, as Jen-der Lee notes, in the 1930s the Ministry of Education introduced sex education textbooks for high-school children that instructed them in the details of male and female anatomy and the processes of sexual maturation—yet hardly touched upon sexual intercourse or reproduction. The textbooks emphasized male sexual hygiene and instructed boys in techniques to curb their desires, but girls, apparently construed as staid future wives with no inclination for premarital sex, were merely given cursory instructions for healthy exercise and washing.

In these and many similar instances, the biological turn marked a radical transformation in the scope and goals of governance in East Asia: hitherto disregarded as matters of public concern, the biological characteristics, gender identity, and reproductive behavior of individuals or families now became legitimate objects of official scrutiny, intervention, and management, essential components of broader programs to improve the "race," raise modern citizens, and strengthen the nation. Certainly the state or its representatives in precolonial China, Korea, and Japan had intervened in various ways in ordinary people's reproductive lives. There were laws regulating marriage or adoption practices; "unnatural" sexual liaisons were punished; persons deemed dangerously insane might be confined and thus, incidentally, prevented from reproducing. In late Edo Japan a vigorous pronatalist policy encouraged early marriage and outlawed abortion, while magistrates in some regions of China, horrified by the prevalence of female infanticide, attempted to stamp out the practice by providing small dowries to poor families. But such interventions in ordinary people's reproductive lives, identities, and choices were based on moral principle or political imperative, not rooted in any systematic classification of human quality or science of health, normality, deviance, or degeneracy. They were not knowledge-building projects, and while they supposed compliance from the population, they

the British army, quoted in Dennis Judd Dennis and Keith Terrance Surridge, *The Boer War: A History* (London: I. B. Tauris, 2013), 60.

34. Jordan Sand, *House and Home in Modern Japan* (Cambridge, MA: Harvard University Press, 2004).

35. Katarzyna J. Cwiertka, *Japanese Cuisine: Food, Power and National Identity* (London: Reaktion Books, 2006). As Buddhists the Japanese ate very little meat. Beef in particular was avoided, as also in much of China, because the ox or buffalo was considered such a valuable helper and friend to farming families.

did not aim to engage the common people as active contributors to programs of national improvement.

The late nineteenth century, thus, saw a key transformation in the place of reproduction in governance. The new biosciences of life opened up new political possibilities and imposed new responsibilities. It was now viewed as an essential political priority, as well as a national duty, for governments to nurture a vigorous, physically and mentally sound population, a new quality of citizenry. In East Asia as in Europe, modernizing elites turned from cosmology or religion to biology as the epistemological key to societal health, reframing the remit of "the state."[36] The biological sciences rendered bodies and behavior visible and manipulable in new ways. Physiology, genetics, epidemiology, medical and nutritional science, psychology, sexology, and statistics constituted a tool kit for identifying and classifying individual pathologies, abnormalities or weaknesses, unhealthy demographic trends, or perceived racial inferiority. Governments, scientists, and public intellectuals debated how best to enroll the public, whose bodily development, sexual behavior, educational responsibilities, and nutritional habits were now to be studied, improved, or corrected. Families were enlisted as well as schools and hospitals. As "stakeholders" in these national projects, as biocitizens expected to embrace, not to challenge, the findings of science, the roles assigned to ordinary members of the public were multiple: they were treated sometimes as lab rats, sometimes as lab assistants or even scientific collaborators, entrusted with collecting data on themselves or their children, sometimes as compliant patients and sometimes as trained experts, albeit in the domestic setting.

Needless to say, many people were unsettled by the demands of the new disciplinary regimes, often in unpredictable ways. Nakayama mentions, for instance, the cultural obstacles that Mishima Michiyoshi, the Japanese pioneer of school hygiene, encountered around the turn of the twentieth century while gathering physical data on schoolchildren. In seeking to master and apply the tools that the new biological sciences offered, scientists themselves, as well as policy makers and ordinary people, had to grapple with new concepts, epistemologies, and ideologies; new ways of perceiving, understanding, and acting upon the world; and new boundaries between public and private, legitimate and prurient. Jen-der Lee's study vividly

---

36. Lei, *Neither Donkey nor Horse*, 261. We should note also the vigor and rapidity of East Asian governments' incorporation of medical governance into their programs for modernizing the state. Not only was this strategy an internationally recognized badge of modernity; it also served to broaden their political base and strengthen their legitimacy at home. As Lei notes, "By 1928 the [Chinese] Nationalist government had committed itself to building an independent Ministry of Health—only one decade after Britain had established the world's first Ministry of Health in 1919" (9). In setting up rural health-care facilities, the Nationalist government "sought to connect with millions of poor and illiterate peasants whose lives no Chinese state had ever influenced directly before this time" (262).

illustrates the uncertainties attendant on locating boundaries. She traces the instability, the continuous shifts and differences in public and professional opinion in Republican China that informed whether "sex education" instruction should be restricted to the more abstract levels of anatomy and physiology, essentially treating humans as higher animals, or venture into the more intimately social dimensions of reproduction, discussing sexual intercourse, pregnancy, childbirth, or even female sexual desire.

Even today, in almost every country, authorities wishing to offer sex education in schools encounter some form of opposition: How can the naked physical facts of anatomy and physiology be reconciled with the moral or religious sensibilities of parents and teachers or with the embarrassment, derision, or pure disbelief of the children? As Lee shows, what was acceptable in one context might prove unacceptable in another, and officially produced sex-education textbooks in China usually offered rather different expressions of sexuality, sexual health, sexual difference, and gender roles from those found in commercially published books or women's magazines. The picture in Republican China was, in other words, extremely complex and continuously changing in response both to cultural change and to political agendas. There is no doubt that in this China was typical of worldwide experience, rather than exceptional.

A fascinating comparison between the gendering processes of biomedicine and those of East Asian medicines is the case of beriberi, explored by Angela Leung. Beriberi (*jiaoqi* in Chinese, *kakké* in Japanese) was a degenerative disease that became increasingly prevalent in colonial Asia through the nineteenth and into the twentieth century, affecting urban populations, soldiers, and overseas migrants throughout British India, the Nanyang region, and the burgeoning cities of China and Japan. Almost all those affected were young, vigorous men. The peak of the pandemic was reached in the decades around 1900. Biomedical scientists and practitioners of Chinese and Japanese (*kampō*, 漢方) medicine all sought ways to explain and cure this debilitating disease, viewed in all three systems as a very specifically male "disease of modernity." Initially, attention focused on sufferers who were young men of good families, who had left home to work in business or gone to town to study or enjoy life. Then attention shifted to a new and more numerous class of patients: poor migrant laborers leading hard and stressful lives. In addressing why rich young men contracted the disease, the Chinese and Japanese explanations emphasized weakness of the kidney, triggered by excessive sexual activity and high living, along with the problems of acclimatizing to a foreign and thus potentially poisonous environment. Once the disease became more closely associated with coolies, the latter explanation came to predominate. In both cases, a cure was most likely to be effected by having the patient return home, where reimmersion in his native *qi* 氣 would restore him to health.

Within the explanatory framework of the European biomedical sciences in the early twentieth century, a disease that had been rather baffling became transparent and manageable once the theory of deficiency disease had been elaborated. Beriberi was attributed to a deficiency of vitamin B1, due to the consumption of polished rice. Since beriberi was linked to a rice-centered diet, biomedical scientists considered it a distinctively Asian disease. But rice-eating was not a sufficient explanation: the biomedical scientists also had to account for the gendering of the disease, to explain why it affected men and not women. Initially it was proposed that wealthy young men were the most likely sufferers because they could afford to consume large amounts of white rice; later, the model was adapted to explain that coolies were especially vulnerable because white rice, albeit in small amounts, was all they could afford to eat.

It is interesting to note that both East Asian and Western medical theories were sufficiently flexible to accommodate changing epidemiological trends and that both saw beriberi as a disease catalyzed by the distinctively modern population flows of colonial migration and urbanization. Beyond that common ground, however, they offered quite incommensurable explanations of the gendered character of the disease.

Resistant Bodies and Consuming Citizens

The case of "China's first transsexual," discussed by Howard Chiang, likewise indicates how delicately we must tread the ground of proposing any simple "China-centered" or "East Asian" perspective when it comes to gender regimes. In 1953, Xie Jianshu, a 36-year-old soldier in the Taiwanese army, was discovered by doctors during a hospital examination for stomach cramps to be a hermaphrodite. After intensive negotiations among Xie, the doctors, and the army authorities, Xie declared that he wished to become a woman and the army paid for a sex-change operation. Chiang locates the passionate medical and public debates over Xie's sexuality and gender, and the huge media attention that Xie's case attracted, within a broader Cold War context. Ruling over a former Japanese colony, the GMD (Guomindang) in the Republic of China (Taiwan) was a government in exile, viewed by many of its subjects as an occupying force. It was also a committed American ally. The value assigned by Taiwanese scientists, politicians, media, and the public to Xie's right to choose his/her sex reflected a complicated braiding of science, democracy, legitimacy, and individual freedom echoed elsewhere in postcolonial East Asia. The GMD government's management of Xie's sex-change should be understood, Chiang believes, as part of a biopolitical drive to establish its sovereignty. Xie's case exemplifies "the emergence of transsexuality as a form of modern sexual embodiment in Chinese-speaking society," a form of subjectivity and entitlement far from identical with its equivalent in the US. The later feminist and gay and lesbian movements in Taiwan and other nations of East Asia, Chiang argues, must also be understood as having deep roots in this entangled postcolonial, post–Cold War regional heritage.

Health, like gender, is a highly malleable concept. In East Asia as elsewhere, politics have often dictated the desirable characteristics of health in a man or in a woman. In tracing the interwar history of Japanese proprietary tonics for women, marketed throughout the Japanese empire and its sphere of influence in East and Southeast Asia, Susan Burns shows a significant rupture in the ideals of female health portrayed. In the advertisements and advice columns of women's magazines in the 1920s and early 1930s, readers were invited to think of their health as an expression of personal vitality and independence, even glamour, as well as fulfilled motherhood. But in the later 1930s we see a shift: the elegant, tennis-playing "modern girls" faded away. As expressions of female health, the fit, smart, independent woman was largely, if not entirely, displaced by images of mothers with their infants. The priorities of female health shifted from general fitness to reproductive health, as gearing up for war increased the national need for manpower.

As Japan expanded its colonial reach and imperial ambitions, the female body became "the terrain the commodity culture was most eager to minister to, the government most anxious to control, and the consumer most hard pressed to defend."[37] The empire was hungry for manpower: it needed soldiers, farmers, and workers in its factories. Even before war began to loom in the mid-1930s, nationalist and colonial reformers throughout Japan and its colonies deplored what they saw as women's "deficient" bodies. Yet, through this earlier period, Burns notes, the commercial tonics offered women an alternative, more cheerful and individualistic, view of healthy womanhood: they "encouraged consumers to project themselves into new social identities, from fertile mother and happy wife, to erotic temptress and independent modern woman." The advertisements countered the strict racial and political hierarchies of Japanese bioscience with a more cosmopolitan message, asserting "that, like human feelings, 'medicine has no national boundaries' and that 'intelligent' foreign women use [the tonic] Chūjōtō to acquire their 'healthy beauty.'"

There was another, still more subversive, dimension to these products. Bearing brand names like "real mother pills," the female tonics derived from such long-established replenishing tonics as *siwutang* (four ingredients soup), a staple prescription for women in premodern (and contemporary) East Asian medicine. The advertisements promised relief of such symptoms as headache, cold sensitivity, back pain, infertility, frigidity, and nervous

---

37. Burns, quoting Thomas Richards, *The Commodity Culture of Victorian England: Advertisement and Spectacle, 1851–1914* (Stanford: Stanford University Press, 1990), 204.

disorders. The main health problem that all promised to cure, however, was menstrual irregularity—in other words, these pills, like *siwutang*, though framed as promoting fertility, could also be used as abortifacients,[38] a possibility of which women who purchased the pills were well aware. Just as condoms were advertised not as contraceptives but as preventives against sexually transmitted diseases,[39] the tonic pills were functional shape-shifters that niftily bypassed the laws that prohibited the marketing of contraceptives and outlawed abortion.

Noting the "tensions of empire" that such discrepancies between official and commercial images of healthy womanhood reveal, Burns reminds us that the primary goal for the medical capitalists who manufactured and marketed these medicines was to sell their products. If their targeted customers were likely to think of themselves as individualist consumers, then they used images of tennis-playing or glamourous women as well as loving mothers in their advertisements. But when patriotic obligations loomed larger, these companies, which had no inherent interest in undermining state policy, easily shifted to interpellating their customers as responsible patriots, eager to bear children for the Japanese empire.

To Whom Does My Body Belong? Demography and Economic Growth

"My mother only gives me my body, but the glory of the Party shines through my heart." This Cultural Revolution slogan eloquently conveys the utter commitment that the Chinese state then demanded from its citizens: they should gladly sacrifice their personal interests and emotions for the common cause, and the Communist Party claimed sovereignty over not only their actions but also their heart-minds, *xin* 心, and their bodies, *shen* 身.[40] In this context, where the prevailing moral code was premised on putting "politics in command" (another ubiquitous Maoist slogan), it became natural to feel that one's own desires, one's sexual and reproductive body, were first and foremost at the service of the collective. Yet the biopolitics of Maoism, which proclaimed the state's right to subordinate personal desire, sexuality, and reproductive choice to society's needs, was by no means an anomaly in the context of modern East Asia.

As we have just seen, until 1945, governments in East Asia by and large desired larger as well as healthier populations, but pronatalism was not

---

38. Francesca Bray, *Technology and Gender: Fabrics of Power in Late Imperial China* (Berkeley: University of California Press, 1997), 319–25; Sonja Kim, "'Limiting Birth': Birth Control in Colonial Korea," *East Asian Science, Technology and Society* 2(3) (2008): 349.
39. Sonja Kim, "Limiting Birth," 340.
40. Everett Yuehong Zhang, "Rethinking Sexual Repression in Maoist China: Ideology, Structure, and the Ownership of the Body," *Body and Society* 11(3) (2005): 6.

necessarily a philosophy that all their citizens accepted. Let us take as an example the case of Japan and its colony Korea. Starting in 1868 the Meiji government introduced a series of laws criminalizing abortion and infanticide.[41] Similar legislation was introduced in Taiwan and Korea when they were annexed as Japanese colonies.[42]

Where the Japanese imperial government saw population growth as a source of national strength, other constituencies, including social reformers in both Japan and Korea, saw Malthusian crowding and competition for scarce resources as a worrying trigger of class conflict and social strife.[43] The 1920s saw the emergence of public debates in the mainstream press, universities, political forums, and scientific publications, not only on eugenics[44] but also on birth control, with discussions of Margaret Sanger and her ideas and of Malthusian theories of overpopulation. Sonja Kim notes that these discussions of a "population problem" and of "limiting birth" were part of a transnational exchange of ideas, people, and markets that spanned the globe after the end of the 1914–1918 war.[45] Margaret Sanger, for example, was invited by Japanese proponents of birth control and received (reluctantly) official permission to visit the country in 1922. In 1924 the Japanese Birth Control Research Association was established in Tokyo, where Katō Shizue and her colleagues developed both a rhythm and a ring method of birth control. Family planning became a popular topic in women's magazines, and birth control clinics appeared in some Japanese cities.[46]

What did this mean for women? As Kim notes, the history of the birth control movement in Western countries at the same period emphasizes its feminist dimension. There were some early feminist attempts to popularize birth control as a form of female emancipation in East Asia, but most proponents, Kim shows, argued for birth control as a way to improve not the lives of women but the quality of the population, supporting healthy motherhood and the life chances of children. At first the articles that appeared in women's magazines on the advantages of small families or on how to use

---

41. Frühstück, Colonizing Sex, 120. Infanticide or "thinning" (mabiki), as in thinning out rice seedlings, was quite widespread among rural families in premodern Japan.
42. Sonja Kim, "Limiting Birth," 339.
43. Ibid., 341.
44. To give just one example, Osawa Kenji, an influential professor of physiology, proposed a eugenic program in which marriage (and permission to reproduce) would be restricted to women certified as healthy and normal. See Sumiko Otsubo, "The Female Body and Eugenic Thought in Meiji Japan," in Building a Modern Japan: Science, Technology and Medicine in the Meiji Era and Beyond, ed. Morris Low (New York: Palgrave Macmillan, 2005), 61–82. Startling as that seems today, let us note that Osawa's proposal echoed proposals by British eugenicists of the time.
45. Sonja Kim, "Limiting Birth," 337.
46. Institute for International Cooperation (IIC), Japan International Cooperation Agency (JICA), "Family Planning," in Japan's Experiences in Public Health and Medical Systems (Tokyo: JICA, 2005), 80.

a douche (acknowledged as being a very unreliable method) were almost all contributed by men. By the early 1930s, however, some voices, including those of several woman artists, were raised to argue for birth control in terms closer to those of the "New Woman," arguing for women's "rights to self-determination, sexual liberation, and development of one's talents."[47] In neither case have we any way of knowing how many of the women reading these exhortations felt encouraged to run out and buy a packet of condoms or to book an appointment at a birth control clinic—if a woman did want to limit her family, a box of "real mother pills" may have seemed a less outrageous and equally reliable alternative.

During the decade between Japan's declaration of war on China and the end of the Pacific War, the Japanese state stepped up its pronatalist measures. In 1938 all birth control clinics were closed. In 1941 contraception was prohibited, the age for marriage was lowered, and couples were urged to have at least five children.[48] But in a drastic reversal of wartime pronatalist priorities, in the early 1950s Japan completely overturned its policy. Like the other East Asian nations, postwar Japan vigorously promoted population control as part of the globally recognized path to successful economic modernization.

With the end of hostilities, repatriation from its former colonies and demobilization of its huge army, between 1945 and 1955 Japan experienced a baby boom and a sharp increase in population, from 72 to 91 million. The country was, however, still in ruins, poverty was severe, and there were shortages of food and housing. Abortion was still illegal, and many desperate women died or were permanently injured in their attempts to end a pregnancy. In 1948, the Diet legalized abortion; in 1955, a peak of 1,170,000 abortions was reached. In 1954, the Family Planning Federation of Japan was established to deliver contraceptive education and contraceptives, and already by 1960 contraception rates had reached 43 percent, overtaking abortion as the primary method of birth control. This transformation took place in the broader context of national policies to improve maternal and child welfare provision, along with the Ikeda cabinet's formulation in 1960 of a "National Income Doubling Plan."[49] The rest, of course, is history.

Political economists seeking to characterize the distinctive forms of East Asian macroeconomic development that took shape after 1945 coined the term "developmental state." The nations across the region were remarkable for the high degree of state intervention in macroeconomic planning and regulation—and although the concept was initially proposed as a particular model of capitalist development, its affinities with Soviet planning were clear from the outset. With hindsight and with the spectacular success of the 1980s economic reforms in the People's Republic of China (PRC) and Vietnam, it

---

47. Sonja Kim, "Limiting Birth," 344.
48. IIC, "Family Planning," 80.
49. IIC, "Family Planning."

now seems possible to think of the developmental state as a form of social contract that spans the socialist-capitalist divide throughout the East Asian region. One common feature across the region's nations has been their early and impressive demographic transition—prompted by active state intervention in demography, through family planning policy and provision, and variously negotiated with different constituencies of citizens.[50]

One of the tenets of post-1945 modernization theory and development economics was that nations could achieve sustained growth and prosperity, and raise general living standards, only if population growth rates fell to little more than replacement level. Birth control was considered an essential element of postwar aid packages to impoverished nations, and it is no coincidence that Japan was invited to the World Population Conference in Rome in 1954, as a representative of developing countries, and hosted the Fifth International Conference on Planned Parenthood, convened by the International Planned Parenthood Federation (IPPF), the very next year.[51] Taiwan's national family planning program in the 1960s to 1970s gained worldwide renown, with thousands of professionals flocking from around the globe to find out how it was done.[52]

Like Japan and Taiwan, South Korea responded quickly to postwar calls to reduce its birth rate.[53] Debates from the colonial period had already laid the groundwork: "Birth control appealed to Korean reformers because it promised a plan of action for the societal problems that worried them— rural poverty, abandonment of children, a population of perceived weak and inferior beings, unemployment, deterioration of national strength, etc. Thus, ideas on birth control were selectively integrated into the discourse."[54] Unlike in Japan or China, there was a sizeable Christian community in Korea. But although some opposed birth control, "there was no one Christian position."[55] What is particularly interesting in the Korean case is the government's decision to target men as sharing the responsibility for family planning.

John DiMoia shows us how Korean masculinities were refocused as part of the national development drive of the 1960s and 1970s. As a break with the conventional expectation that married men should try to father as many sons as possible, the government campaigned to persuade its soldiers

50. Gavin Jones, Paulin Tay Straughan, and Angelique Chan, eds., *Ultra-Low Fertility in Pacific Asia: Trends, Causes and Policy Issues* (London: Routledge, 2009).
51. IIC, "Family Planning," 82.
52. G. Cernada et al., "Taiwan's Population and Family Planning Efforts: An Historical Perspective," *International Quarterly of Community Health Education* 27(2) (2006): 99–120.
53. See Robert Repetto et al., *Economic Development, Population Policy, and Demographic Transition in the Republic of Korea* (Cambridge, MA: Harvard University Press, 1981); Sonja Kim, "Limiting Birth," 335–59; and DiMoia, *Reconstructing Bodies*, as well as the chapters by Ha and DiMoia in this volume.
54. Sonja Kim, "Limiting Birth," 344.
55. Ibid., 345.

to embrace a new form of paternal responsibility, limiting family size to increase available resources both for their own children and for the nation. Because potency was inextricably linked to male health in Korean medical theory and popular understanding, the campaign for voluntary vasectomy had to stress the complete safety of the operation and the absence of short- or long-term health effects. To further reassure volunteers, posters featured sex symbols like the singer Kim Yong Man proudly embracing his single child (a daughter, at that!). As a further inducement, volunteers were given priority on the waiting list for a modern apartment: the vasectomy was thus a stepping-stone for rural men and their families from the village to the town, and into modern middle-class life. In the decade following the introduction of the vasectomy program (1963–1973), between 15,000 and 20,000 men volunteered each year; the following five years the figures shot up, reaching 51,000 in 1977, and for the next decade they varied between 50,000 and 100,000 per year. Meanwhile the average age of acceptors fell from thirty-five to thirty-two.[56]

In Japan too men have shared a large part of the responsibility for limiting family size: since 1959, condom use has accounted for between 60 and 80 percent of contraception.[57] But nowhere outside Korea has male sterilization been an acceptable option. In China and Taiwan even male contraceptives have been generally rejected on the grounds that they would impair the user's potency and virility: neither government has succeeded, as the Korean government did, in reassuring men that a vasectomy would leave them healthy and sexually active.

How, then, was the "population problem" defined and addressed in a socialist East Asian state in the postwar period?[58] In the very early years of the PRC, population was viewed as a resource in its own right, and couples were not discouraged from having children. However, as part of the program to improve rural health, in the 1950s and 1960s birth control methods were made available to rural couples, who were encouraged to space their families for the sake of both mother's and children's health. The contraceptive technique of choice was usually intrauterine devices (IUDs) for women. Though Chinese researchers investigated several promising drugs for controlling male fertility, men in China as elsewhere were fearful that drugs or sterilization would damage their health and virility, so the burden of birth control fell almost entirely on women. At that time most women welcomed having the technological means to avoid frequent pregnancies. Meanwhile, improved standards of health and medical care meant that fewer infants and

56. Repetto et al., *Economic Development*, 641.
57. IIC, "Family Planning," 85, Table 4.2.
58. The following paragraphs are a somewhat revised version of Francesca Bray, "The Chinese Experience," in *Medicine in the Twentieth Century*, ed. John V. Pickstone and Roger Cooter (Amsterdam: Harwood Academic Publishers, 2000), 725–26.

children died, and adults lived longer, so even though the fertility rates of the 1960s were much lower than before, they nevertheless contributed to an inexorable swelling of the population.

From 1971 to 1978 the state encouraged a "later-longer-fewer" policy: couples should marry later, leave longer gaps between pregnancies, and have fewer children. Peasant couples were allowed three children in the early years of the policy, only two from 1977. Collective organization of production and administration made it relatively easy for the state to control reproductive behavior, refusing permission to underage couples to marry or imposing heavy fines on those who exceeded the norms of childbearing. Fertility fell dramatically in the course of the campaign, from six to just under three children per woman. Even so China's population grew from 540 million in 1949 to around a billion in 1979—a tribute to improvements in living standards and health care but a serious challenge to matching population and resources.

Official organizations like the National Women's Federation saw these early population control programs as benefiting women: they reduced the tolls of childbearing and freed women to work along with men and to participate as citizens. Women nevertheless bore the "double burden" of contributing to the collective while retaining responsibility for running the home. The burdens that were to come, at any rate for rural women, were far worse.

In 1979 the Chinese Communist Party introduced the one child family policy (OCFP), limiting each couple to a single child, whatever its sex.[59] The policy was formulated as a core element in a crash program designed to enrich families while raising GDP. As responsible biocitizens, families were called upon to sacrifice private fulfilment for the national good. Caught between the demands of the patriline and the state, women paid the price with their bodies. Highly controversial and in many instances shockingly coercive, the OCFP has received lavish attention. The program's scale and ambition; its complex and transformative demographic, economic, and social impact; its dramatic success; and above all its unashamedly intrusive and sometimes violent implementation have fascinated and often horrified outside observers, not least because the policy dramatically highlights the ambiguities of making women responsible for modernization through disciplining their own bodies.[60]

While China's OCFP is an extreme case of the state taking over women's bodies and redesigning the family, it fits with a region-wide acknowledgment

59. There were some exceptions, and the one-child rule did not apply to ethnic minorities, which resulted in an unprecedented rush of people wishing to sign up as minority rather than Han.
60. From a voluminous academic literature on this theme, let me cite the particularly interesting and perceptive work of Susan Greenhalgh, *Just One Child: Science and Policy in Deng's China* (Berkeley: University of California Press, 2008), and *Cultivating Global Citizens: Population in the Rise of China* (Cambridge, MA: Harvard University Press, 2010).

of the state's established right to intervene in reproduction and the deline-
ation of gender roles, in order to accelerate processes of national modernization and collective enrichment. Although men were also expected to
subordinate their sexual desires and paternal ambitions to national development, women were usually most directly affected. Still today we observe a
"general acceptance that women's bodies are to function foremost in their
reproductive and rearing capacities as mothers, often to meet national or
communal goals."[61]

Wealthy Nations and the Fertility Crisis

The East Asian states gained international renown for the success of their
postwar family planning programs and for the energetic push this demographic transition gave to economic growth and increased living standards.
As their populations normalized the disciplines and desires of modern
middle-class prosperity, however, it was not long before the "population
problem" in East Asian nations took a new and worrying turn.[62]

In China even today, poor families with access only to unskilled jobs
still stand to gain by adding children to their workforce. For them, as for
their ancestors, children are a source of wealth as well as of satisfaction. This
attitude still persists in much of China's rural hinterland, where hands are
needed to work the land and children who migrate to the cities for a factory
job send home remittances. Latterly, in recognition of these practical realities,
the authorities eased the OCFP rules in rural areas to allow families to try for
a son; now the government has announced that families should aim for two
children, not one. But China is no longer a nation of peasants. In 2014 for the
first time the urban population outnumbered the rural. The PRC now has a
solid claim to being a middle-class society like its neighbors. In China's burgeoning postsocialist economy, as elsewhere in East Asia, the typical family's
life is ruled by intense competition: for good jobs, for professional training,
for entrance to a good university or a good high school, or even for a place
in a good nursery school. For some time the majority of East Asian couples
have fully embraced the ideal of the small family as a condition for family
success and societal progress. Now, with costs of raising and educating even
a single child ballooning, many believe that they could not possibly afford
more than one child. Birth rates have fallen well below replacement level
throughout the region, while the greying of East Asia's population is accel-
erating. In this context infertility has replaced excess fertility as a matter of
public concern, as the chapters by Jung-ok Ha, John DiMoia, and Chia-ling
Wu make plain. This concern is so acute and so ubiquitously debated that we

---

61. Sonja Kim, "Limiting Birth," 356.
62. Jones et al., *Ultra-Low Fertility*.

might call it a moral panic. The twenty-first-century "population problem" has proved rather more intractable, however, than the previous challenge of lowering birth rates.[63]

As the recent U-turn by the Chinese government indicates, the new century has seen pronatalism reviving in East Asia, albeit in novel garb. One way in which today's governments may address the problem of low birth rates is through welfare provisions like increased child allowances or guaranteed nursery care, measures designed to induce fertile couples to expand their family size. These are costly items in the national budget, however. Another approach is to bring a greater number of people into the fold of the fertile by authorizing and promoting the biomedical fertility treatments collectively known as assisted reproductive technologies (ARTs). This costs a government rather little if patients pay for the services themselves, though there are frequent cases where a government is really worried about its birth rate or genuinely committed to reproductive rights for all, where the state picks up all or part of the tab.[64]

A socially neglected if personally tragic burden, infertility was not a matter of much concern to governments as long as reducing birth rates was their main goal. One might have thought that when societies were pressing their citizens to control or repress their reproductive urges, those who went childless whether by choice or necessity would have been given some appreciative recognition. This, however, never happens. In China at the height of the OCFP women suffered not only for being too fertile, but also for failing to be fertile, a problem that affected large numbers of couples even in the 1980s. In China, as elsewhere, male sterility was largely ignored. Social blame for childlessness, like medical treatment for infertility, targeted women almost exclusively. The OCFP's mechanisms, for instance, the recording of menstruation and issuing of birth permits by work units, brutally exposed intimate aspects of a woman's fertility or infertility to public view, adding, often unbearably, to private pressures and unhappiness. What was in reality an "everyone must have one child policy" pushed many "hens who can't lay eggs" into a desperate search for expensive and often inaccessible fertility treatments.[65]

---

63. The problem is not new but has only recently reached panic proportions. Already in the 1960s a marked drop in the Japanese birthrate, and concerns about the depopulation of rural villages, triggered rumblings of disquiet—and in consequence the state withdrew from family planning, leaving it to the private sector. The withdrawal of the Japanese state did little, however, to slow a steady drop in birthrates (IIC, "Family Planning").
64. French citizens are currently entitled to four free courses of IVF treatment.
65. Lisa Handwerker, "The Consequences of Modernity for Childless Women in China: Medicalization and Resistance," in *Pragmatic Women and Body Politics*, ed. Margaret Lock and Patricia A. Kaufert (Cambridge: Cambridge University Press, 1998), 178–205; "The Politics of Making Modern Babies in China: Reproductive Technologies and the 'New' Eugenics," in *Infertility around the Globe: New Thinking on Childlessness, Gender, and*

Once the demographic transition was achieved, however, state and society alike began to heed the laments of the childless and to document infertility, which showed some alarming patterns—including a regendering of the problem. Fertility levels were shown to be low and falling, not just for women but particularly for men—an uncomfortable reassignment of reproductive imperfection that has surfaced recently in most advanced economies. Though women's conception rates have fallen generally as a result of later marriage and delayed childbearing, there is also a worrying worldwide decline of men's fertility linked to falling sperm counts and low sperm motility rates. The rate of decline is particularly sharp in the PRC, where it is commonly attributed to high pollution. In what appears to be a widespread collapse in Chinese men's confidence in their masculinity, concerns about impotence have also reached epic proportions.[66]

In response to this perceived fertility crisis, East Asian governments began to authorize and promote an spectrum of ARTs, including treatments to promote ovulation or sperm motility, donor insemination (DI), in vitro fertilization (IVF), and even surrogacy. But each of these technologies presents complicated moral, social, and often legal challenges, requiring a rethinking of who is expected or entitled to become a parent and what the bonds between parent(s) and child would be under these new seminatural procedures. These Latourian hybrids of nature and society are also hybrids of old and new, entangling the latest formulations of biological science with ideas drawn from East Asian medical theory, and with deeper-rooted assumptions about health, family, and gender; about class, gender, or ethnic divisions of reproductive labor; and about the respective entitlements of the "biologically" versus the "socially" infertile.

Ever since surrogacy was made legal in the United States, feminist critics have pointed out that the American legal system generally considers the "true" mother to be the purchaser, not the provider, of such biological essentials as ovum or womb.[67] In debates over surrogacy in the PRC, opponents have argued that surrogacy constitutes a feudal exploitation of women, an equivalent to concubinage.[68] This moral-modernist argument against "renting a belly" resonated strongly enough with party and public to justify an official ban on offering surrogacy services in public hospitals,

Reproductive Technologies, ed. Marcia C. Inhorn and Frank van Balen (Berkeley: University of California Press, 2002), 298–314.

66. Everett Yuehong Zhang, "The Birth of *Nanke* (Men's Medicine) in China: The Making of the Subject of Desire," *American Ethnologist* 34(3) (2007): 491–508; *The Impotence Epidemic: Men's Medicine and Sexual Desire in Contemporary China* (Durham, NC: Duke University Press, 2015).

67. Katha Pollitt, "The Strange Case of Baby M," *Nation*, May 23, 1987.

68. Francesca Bray, "Becoming a Mother in Late Imperial China: Maternal Doubles and the Ambiguity of Fertility," in *Chinese Kinship: Contemporary Anthropological Perspectives*, ed. Susanne Brandstädter and Gonçalo D. Santos (London: Routledge: 2008), 181–203.

although profits in private clinics and agencies that provide commercial surrogacy services are booming. Another less revolutionary, more atavistic consideration comes into play when surrogacy or any other ART procedures are followed: the Chinese clinics always use, or claim to use, the husband's sperm so as not to threaten the still-potent principle of male descent. Insemination by donor is legal in China, but not at all popular. Women interviewed by Lisa Handwerker "would use an egg donor, as long as the egg was combined with their husband's sperm. The use of their husband's sperm was the most important factor in considering the child their own. On the other hand, women expressed great ambivalence about accepting sperm from an anonymous male donor out of [a well-founded] fear that their husbands or in-laws might reject the child."[69] Generally speaking, for most Chinese, including urban as well as rural families, it is still direct biological inheritance through the father's sperm that determines "natural" or real descent.

In the domain of sex and reproduction, new technologies always stir up moral trouble. When modern birth control technologies were first made available, whether in the United States and Europe or in the East Asian nations, their promoters were anxious to avoid any charge that they were encouraging promiscuity or undermining marriage. To gain social and legal support, they deliberately played down or denied the emancipatory potential of female contraception. Birth control was respectably packaged as a method for "family planning," to be made available not to all sexually active women but only to those who were married, often with the further stipulation that they should already have one or more children. This started to change only in the late 1960s, when the women's liberation movement claimed the right for any women to enjoy sex free from the fear of an unwanted pregnancy. Sometimes with a view to upholding women's rights, sometimes to minimize rates of teenage or unmarried pregnancy, various countries introduced legislation allowing doctors to prescribe contraception directly to new constituencies: unmarried women, widows, girls without parental consent . . . Conversely, sometimes what women have come to regard as a right to contraception is withdrawn from certain groups after a change of government or public opinion, or in response to pressure from religious groups.

Societal or legal decisions about who is entitled to use ARTs have followed a similarly checkered pattern. Not only do these new technologies enhance the prospects of conventional couples conceiving; they also offer the technical possibility of parenthood to those who are not in a heterosexual marriage. Single women, single men, gay and lesbian couples have all seen an opportunity here to fulfill cravings for a child who is biologically "theirs." Yet their claims that they are, like any human, naturally entitled to

---

69. Handwerker, "Politics of," 306, emphasis added.

be a parent are all too often rejected. As suggested earlier, the negotiations or confrontations over entitlement to conceive a child through ARTs reveal unexamined or latent ontologies of kinship, gender, sexuality, and status within a specific society, as well as the complex workings of heteronormativity, "the numerous ways in which heterosexual privilege is woven into the fabric of social life."[70]

Chia-ling Wu traces the "moral landscape" within which "the making of statutory regulation . . . and the less visible practices of access politics" combine to exclude the unmarried from ART services in Taiwan today. Since 1986 Taiwan has prohibited unmarried women and men from using ARTs (as does Japan). But for the last decade the Taiwan LGBT Family Rights Advocacy has mounted a lusty opposition, urging lesbians to self-inseminate with donated sperm, while several celebrities have publicized their trips abroad for legal (or sometimes illegal) ART treatment. Lobbying from such groups, joined by some sympathetic physicians, resulted in the legalization of surrogacy in 2005—yet it was restricted to heterosexual couples. A number of physicians came to support reproductive rights for single women, whom they typified as hardworking and responsible citizens, often well-off professionals or leaders of society, frustrated in their maternal urges and dutifully shouldering the support of their elderly parents, yet with no children to support them in their own old age. The physicians envisaged these worthy women as heterosexual, however, and lesbians found it necessary to masquerade as heterosexual in order to get treatment. This, Wu notes, is an interesting difference from Sweden or Britain, where "lesbian couples have been viewed as better parents than single women and thus more legitimate ART users." While ART access has not yet been officially liberalized in Taiwan, thanks to activism there has been a considerable shift in public support (40 percent in 2012) for "queer reproductive rights," and increasing numbers of Taiwanese women are foregoing marriage now they know they can have children now, or later, with the help of ART.

Family planning programs for reducing birth rates typically promise advantages for both maternal and infant health, and typically they deliver on these promises. When a nation discovers it is suffering from a fertility crisis, what is the likely health impact of publicly provided remedial programs? Jung-ok Ha sets out to examine the gender politics behind the state provision of ARTs in South Korea. After almost twenty years of steady decline from the replacement rate of 2.1, in 2005 South Korea found itself with the lowest total fertility rate in the world (1.076). In 2006 the Ministry of Health launched the Program, the First Basic Plan on Low Fertility and the Ageing Society. Over the next five years alone, it spent US$18 billion on providing ART services

---

70. Chia-ling Wu, quoting Stevi Jackson, "Gender, Sexuality, and Heterosexuality," *Feminist Theory* 7(1) (2008): 108.

to infertile couples, and since 2010 spending on the Program has accelerated. By 2012 the fertility rate had increased to a more respectable if hardly reassuring 1.300, and the total number of newborn babies had increased from 435,000 to 484,000.

Unfortunately, Ha tells us, the massive investment in the Program has had serious health repercussions. The Program measures success in birth numbers, not in maternal or infant morbidity, and these figures usefully veil a worrying rise in infant and maternal mortality, and in a range of other ob-gyn, general, and psychiatric health problems. The Program has been largely funded by taking money out of earlier programs for "improvement of maternal and child health," instead prioritizing "enlargement of subsidies for pregnancy and childbirth." Public funding for contraceptive interventions and provision has also been axed, along with money for building, maintaining, and staffing hospital delivery rooms. This dizzying pronatalist investment, in other words, has put women's and infants' health at severe risk. Moreover, Ha argues, the Program, which (unsurprisingly) restricts access to heterosexual couples, is seriously out of step with public sentiment. In the past ten years Korean attitudes toward reproduction have changed significantly. Marriage rates have declined and divorce rates have soared. In 1991 over 90 percent of respondents believed that a woman must have children, but by 2012 this had fallen to under 45 percent, while the number who thought a son was absolutely necessary fell from 40 percent to 8 percent. Furthermore, as John DiMoia notes, in another part of the government women are now being mobilized as valuable contributors to the workforce and offered childcare facilities to support them taking jobs outside the home. Korean mothers, and increasingly fathers too, also feel heavy pressure to engage and invest in their child's education. Under these circumstances it seems unlikely that the unimaginative Program, restricting its offer as it does to traditional heterosexual families, will succeed in its pronatalist goals.

Rebranding "Traditional" Bioscience

Let me finally turn to another curiosity of recent years, the resurgence of public enthusiasm for "traditional" East Asian medicine and therapies. Like the infertility crisis, this is closely linked to the achievement of development goals, a rise in prosperity and consumerism, and the prolongation of life. Of course, East Asian medicines, whether *guoyi* 國醫, *zhongyi* 中醫, or TCM (traditional Chinese medicine) in China, *kampō* in Japan, *dongŭi* 동의 or *hanŭi* 한의 in Korea, never disappeared even at times when social leaders were most eager to hasten the modernization of their country by stamping out indigenous medicine entirely. Nor should we think of these indigenous medicines as remaining dormant or simply surviving. To better understand the mutual fashioning of Chinese (or Japanese or Korean) medicine and the

Western medical systems with which they coexist, Bridie Andrews proposes the metaphor of two mirrors reflecting each other.[71] Sean Hsiang-lin Lei, for his part, emphasizes the surprising capacity of Chinese medicine over the decades to spawn vigorous "mongrels," syncretic, pragmatic, and effective combinations with the biomedicine of that time and place. These mongrels, Lei shows, give the lie to the supposed incompatibility or incommensurability with Western scientific rationality, most notably its "representationalist" conception of reality and its procedures for testing truth.[72]

Nevertheless, although these "traditions" would be unrecognizable to practitioners from a hundred years ago, and although in many of their instantiations they have adopted experimental, theoretical, or technical trappings modeled on or taken directly from biomedicine, a fundamental appeal of East Asian medicines to many patients, and an angle often argued by practitioners, is that they offer a "traditional" alternative or complement to modern Western medicine. They are said to deal with the root of the disorder rather than the superficial symptoms, to diagnose and treat the patient holistically, to use local ingredients and thus be specially suited to East Asian bodies and physiologies and to their characteristic disease manifestations. Above all, these East Asian traditional medicines promise help or relief where biomedicine admits its impotence, in the treatment of pain, of chronic disorders, and "diseases of modernity": stress, cancer, immune system disorders, inflammatory diseases, senility, impotence, and infertility.

This resurgence has been most intensively studied in the case of China. In the wake of the 1979 economic reforms the disbanding of the People's Communes and many other work units, along with the public health-care services they provided, pushed many individuals to seek new kinds of health care, and by the same token provided a hearty boost to entrepreneurialism both in biomedicine and in a thousand imaginative manifestations of "traditional medicine."[73] In an early study Judith Farquhar explained why many ordinary, low-income women suffering from infertility sought Chinese rather than biomedical diagnosis and treatment.[74] Everett Yuehong Zhang has followed the birth and flourishing of a completely new branch of Chinese medicine, *nanke* 男科, or male medicine,[75] that responds to the needs of post-Maoist masculinities, male desires, and insecurities.[76]

In premodern East Asia, while lower-class healers of both sexes offered all kinds of care and treatment ranging from midwifery and exorcisms to

71. Andrews, *Making of Modern Chinese Medicine*, 216.
72. Lei, *Neither Donkey nor Horse*.
73. Judith Farquhar, "Market Magic: Getting Rich and Getting Personal in Medicine after Mao," *American Ethnologist* 23(2) (1996): 239–57.
74. Judith Farquhar, "Objects, Processes, and Female Infertility in Chinese Medicine," *Medical Anthropology Quarterly* 5(4) (1991): 370–99.
75. By analogy with the centuries-old specialization of *fuke*, female medicine.
76. Zhang, "Rethinking Sexual Repression"; "Birth of *Nanke*"; *Impotence Epidemic*.

massages, acupuncture, and herbalism, reputable, literate physicians were almost exclusively male. The responsibility for diagnosing minor ailments or prescribing medicines within a well-off household sometimes fell to the master, sometimes to the mistress; in ordinary households these responsibilities fell to the wife. In modern East Asia, too, wives typically remain responsible for maintaining and supervising family health, often employing amalgams of indigenous and biomedical resources.

The brilliant career of Dr. Chuang Shu Chih (b. 1920), recounted by Sean Hsiang-lin Lei, illustrates the huge potential to be realized by the skillful reinvention of medical theory in an age of prosperity and professional employment for women. It also shows us "traditional" medicine in movement: Dr. Chuang develops a fusion of Chinese, Japanese, and biomedical concepts and practices, and builds authority for her unique formulations by strategic moves back and forth between Taiwan and Japan, between biomedicine and Chinese medicine (she has degrees both in Chinese medicine and pharmacology), and between the domestic and the scientific stage. In a series of best-selling recipe books, the first (*What Is the Healthiest Way to Eat?*) published in 1986, Chuang casts the Japanese and then the Taiwanese wife in the traditional role of family pharmacist. And yet, at least among Chuang's Taiwan devotees, this woman is likely to be a well-paid salary earner who spends far more time outside than inside the home. She does not repress her own desires and personal ambitions, and as a modern desiring subject she is not interested in moldering away at home as a slave to her infants or in growing old gracefully. As well as the means to safeguard her family's health, then, Dr. Chuang offers her a personal celebration of "women's three spring-times," puberty, pregnancy, and menopause, three privileged opportunities for bodily rejuvenation.

Dr. Chuang's regimen emphasizes the importance for a newly delivered woman of "doing the month" (*zuo yuezi*), an old, established practice for restoring postparturient health. Doing the month is definitely not part of the biomedical regime for postchildbirth recovery, and since most women in East Asia today give birth in a biomedical delivery ward the fortunes of doing the month went into decline for a while. But young professional mothers who gave birth in Chinese private hospitals found to their disgust that when they went home two or three days later their mother, or mother-in-law, would insist on feeding them large quantities of eggs, or meat, or no eggs, or no meat, forbidding them to take a shower or even brush their teeth or watch television until the month was over. And yet, these young women felt, there was something important about doing the month—if only it could be made a more pleasant practice![77] Dr. Chuang's prescriptions fulfill precisely this

---

77. Suzanne Zhang Gottschang, "Taking Patriarchy out of Post-partum Recovery," in *Transformations of Patriarchy in Contemporary China*, ed. Gonçalo Santos and Stevan Harrell (forthcoming).

need. Lei tells us how "in response to popular demand, Dr. Chuang's grand-daughters launched a commercial service that delivers cooked dishes made according to her recipes to families after childbirth. Partially helped by Dr. Chuang's reputation, 'sitting out the month' has returned as a huge business opportunity and distinctive feature of Taiwanese medical culture." Similar catering services are now thriving in the Shanghai region, where biomedical delivery clinics have integrated instruction on doing the month into their services.[78] So while Chuang Shu Chih is an altogether exceptional woman, she represents a rather typical recasting of the articulations between health and gender in East Asia today, in an age of prosperity and female agency.

Biogovernance and Biocitizens in East Asia

The chapters in this volume unfold a spectrum of biopolitics at work in East Asian history. Several cases (Nakayama, Lee, Ha, DiMoia) clearly illustrate the classic workings of biopower: the state or its agents determine biological and behavioral norms and impose them upon social groups or individuals, whether through coercion, regulation, or interpellation. Personal freedoms are constrained in the name of building a healthy nation. Such forms of top-down biopower seldom function purely through violence or coercion, as Western libertarians might like to claim. Rather than living in continual terror of retribution for illegal pregnancies, many Chinese families practiced contraception successfully and embraced the one child family policy as a necessary step toward greater prosperity for all. How different were their sentiments, motivations, loyalties to society, and sense of control over their own lives and bodies from those of the South Korean households where husbands underwent sterilization in order to gain access to a modern flat? Should we categorize such obedience to state expectations as victimhood or false consciousness, or as agency exercised within a field of shared expecta-tions? How fundamentally do the political or cultural forms of control over sexual and reproductive freedom exercised by East Asian governments, whether nationalist, fascist, communist, or "developmental," or the channels and expressions of contestation in those historical societies, differ from what seem to us like the "softer" regimes of biopower that since World War II have largely prevailed in the increasingly prosperous Western nations?

Chu Shuang Chih's reframing of the biological life cycle as something to be skillfully managed rather than suffered as inevitable fate, her celebra-tion of puberty, pregnancy, and menopause as "three spring-times" for reju-venation rather than successive phases of female imbalance and depletion, offered a bold challenge to medical wisdom and societal norms eagerly taken up by large numbers of women. Here, as with the LGBT activists in Taiwan

---

78. Ibid.

claiming the right to fertility treatment, we observe East Asian equivalents of the emancipatory rewriting of the script of healthy womanhood catalyzed in the United States by the 1971 publication of *Our Bodies, Ourselves* (*OBOS*). How should we categorize such East Asian cases of biocitizenship?

Composed by the Boston Women's Health Collective, *OBOS* was an unassuming, friendly, accessible, and affordable paperback. In plain, frank language and images, *OBOS* explained to women how to live with and understand their bodies as they grew and changed, flourished or ailed, loved, desired, or pined. The writers were feminist activists, not doctors or biologists. Their goal was to empower women to reclaim their own bodies against the patriarchal claims of biomedical experts, to explore and enjoy their true sexuality rather than numbly submit to rigid and often distorting or repressive concepts of what was "normal,"[79] and to reassure them of their right and capacity to choose not only in reproductive matters but also in matters of health and sickness, work and leisure, sexual and family relations and responsibilities.

OBOS literally put flesh on feminist assertions that the personal is political and that knowledge is power: we readers of the first edition felt the shock of recognition stir deep in our vitals. Even if we lived outside the United States, in societies with different health systems, social hierarchies, and stereotypes of femininity, we had only to consider our own everyday encounters and bodily experiences to confirm how deeply and insidiously the inequalities of class, race, and gender, the criteria for the normal and the pathological, were inscribed in medical science and practice in our own society and in our own understanding of health and illness, even in our most intimate bodily sensations.[80] By the same token, we realized that many new forms of liberation and agency were ours to grasp. Although the terms had not yet been coined, we now became conscious of the workings of biopower and resolved to challenge them by acting as biocitizens.

---

79. For example, without disparaging members of heterosexual partnerships, *OBOS* treated the sexual, social, and affective needs and desires of lesbians, single parents, and people who were disabled, old, or sick as normal and natural.

80. In the forty-odd years since it first appeared, *OBOS* has been translated into multiple languages and reissued in many editions. Although sometimes misunderstood or misrepresented by its translators, even—in the case of its Taiwanese translation in 1975—presented as an anodyne woman's manual rather than as a feminist manifesto (Hsiu-yun Wang, "How Did Our Bodies Become Your Body? Our Bodies Ourselves in Taiwan" [paper presented at the 12th meeting of the Taiwan Sociology Association, Tong-hai University, 2012]), more typically the work's pragmatic, action-oriented critique has, directly or indirectly, inspired groups all over the world (Kathy Davis, *The Making of "Our Bodies, Ourselves": How Feminism Travels across Borders* [Durham, NC: Duke University Press, 2007]), including various groups discussed in the contributions to this volume.

Biocitizenship,[81] and the related concept of biosociality,[82] are terms of quite recent coinage. Thanks to developments in genetics and the other biosciences and biotechnologies, our bodies have become newly transparent, their deficiencies newly malleable. New hopes and new fears have been born, old boundings of the individual body or family dissolved. Genetic mapping of diseases like diabetes or thalassemia, ARTs and sexual reassignation, nuclear fallout, the markets for transplant organs or reproductive materials that exploit the poor to rebuild the bodies or families of more fortunate individuals have generated new vulnerabilities and possibilities and conferred still greater malleability within and between bodies. Social scientists have noted the emergence during the past few decades of new forms of self-identification through shared pathologies, new expectations of survival and cure, new forms of claim upon state, bioscientists, corporations, and politicians to provide relief.

The form of collective action initially identified as biocitizenship was that of the victims of Chernobyl. They did not challenge the limits of medical science; rather, they worked together to gain official recognition of their disablement and of their entitlement as disabled citizens to state medical care and compensation.[83] Another register of biocitizenship is sometimes characterized as a mobilization of neoliberal values: the individual takes on the responsibility of self-care or self-cure in what Rose and Novas have termed an "economy of hope," Brekke and Sirnes an "economy of despair." As an example, Americans suffering from currently incurable diseases ranging from cancer to Parkinson's refuse to accept the practical and ethical limits to stem-cell research set by bioscientists as well as legislators. They urgently demand more stem-cell research as suffering individuals whose personal cure would bring a better future for others sharing their disorder.[84]

Another recent expression of biocitizenship, perhaps more characteristic of East Asia, is the spread of *yangsheng* 養生 (literally "nourishing life") in the PRC. *Yangsheng* refers to a spectrum of regimens of self-care typically including diet, exercise, breathing, and the like, widely practiced by retired Chinese to prolong active and healthy life. As China's population ages, public provision of health care dwindles and private health care increases in cost, *yangsheng* practices have exploded, supporting a booming industry of books, tonics, and other health aids. Here citizens self-identified as elderly and vulnerable are not demanding support from the state (as in the case of Chernobyl): they accept that public support is lacking and compensate by

---

81. Petryna, *Biological Citizenship*; Rose and Novas, "Biological Citizenship."
82. Rabinow, *French DNA*.
83. Petryna, *Biological Citizenship*.
84. Ole Andreas Brekke and Thorvald Sirnes, "Biosociality, Biocitizenship and the New Regime of Hope and Despair: Interpreting 'Portraits of Hope' and the 'Mehmet Case,'" *New Genetics and Society* 30(4) (2011): 347–74.

undertaking self-care. The spending power thus unleashed has built the *yangsheng* industry into "the fifth biggest sector in China's economy, following real estate, IT, automobiles and tourism."[85] Is *yangsheng* then a classic example of neoliberal biocitizenship, where individuals exercise biological agency and claims in their own interest, independently of the state, within an "economy of hope"? Is it rather, perhaps, an honorable complicity with the developmental state, a political commitment to pursuing solutions that will not undermine the social order? In this case might the Western concept of biocitizenship undermine the real emotional as well as bodily rewards of self-discipline in pursuit of improved health and longevity, and of the common good?[86]

Wu's chapter explores the dialectics of governance, citizen agency, and reproductive rights or entitlements in the debates about ARTs in postwar Taiwan. Some of her actors might be described as "neoliberal subjects"; others are better understood as "moral pioneers" actively producing new biological values. In the sex-change case that Chiang unfolds for us, should we think of the intersexed soldier, Xie Jianshun, as a moral pioneer or as a largely powerless victim object of GMD nation-building strategies? As Burns and Lei show, consumer choices offered Japanese and Taiwanese married women technologies of the self that sometimes encouraged the kinds of freedom and personal fulfilment that Western feminists regard as agency. In different political contexts, however, the same action confirmed their identity as "good wives and wise mothers," once more prompting us to ask whether social theories grounded in Western understandings of health and happiness, body and society, ethics and responsibility, governance and citizenship can adequately encompass East Asian experiences.

---

85. Wanning Sun, "Cultivating Self-Health Subjects: Yangsheng and Biocitizenship in Urban China," *Citizenship Studies* 19 (3–4) (2015): 286.
86. Judith Farquhar and Qicheng Zhang, *Ten Thousand Things: Nurturing Life in Contemporary Beijing* (New York: Zone Books, 2012).

Part I

Bodies beyond Boundaries: Evolving Physical Development and Reproductive Technologies

This section, containing chapters by Nakayama, Lee, Wu, and Ha, highlights processes that standardize gendered bodies in health and reproductive policies in modern and postcolonial East Asian states in face of changing demographic needs and realities. Nakayama and Lee zoom into Japan and China during the first half of the twentieth century, examining how the "standard" models of the body and physical growth were constructed by studies in child development and school textbooks. Theories of physical development, "Asian" or otherwise, shaped and were shaped by state anxieties over gender norms in imagined racial and civilizational hierarchies as well as "normative" familial relationships in a conflicted pursuit and construction of modernity. Shifting to postcolonial Taiwan and South Korea, Wu and Ha engage with the ongoing processes of forming and challenging gender norms through new reproductive technologies. In Taiwan, the controversy is over the state's policy to exclude assisted reproductive technologies (ARTs) based on the official narrative of normative "families." Meanwhile, South Korean laws have defined, redefined, and regulated gender norms and reproductive health by controlling legal and financial access to these new reproductive technologies.

1

Gender, Health, and the Problem of "Precocious Puberty" in Meiji Japan

Izumi Nakayama

Introduction[1]

Japanese children were precocious, and that was the problem. Not intellectually, per se, but physically. Mishima Michiyoshi 三島通良 (1866–1925), a pioneer of school hygiene (*gakkō eisei* 学校衛生), came to this conclusion after having gathered physical data from children all over Japan starting in 1892 to understand their physical development. In every stage of child development, Mishima meticulously compared notes with the data from his selected European counterparts and emphasized the sameness between Japan and the "West," as if the "West" was the original standard and Japan needed to match it. For Mishima, any variations between Japanese and Western data constituted a problem to be explained and resolved. Japanese boys and girls were experiencing puberty *too early* (and the European examples appeared to Mishima, to borrow the words of Goldilocks, "just right"). This deviation from the normative West was interpreted as a source of the inferiority of Japanese height and length of limbs, because, as Mishima noted, Japanese children kept pace with their Western counterparts at every stage of development until puberty.[2] After puberty, Japanese bodies stopped growing, he argued, remaining underdeveloped in comparison to Western children, resulting in shorter limbs and stature.

The Japanese body was under attack in the late nineteenth century during the period of Euro-American imperialism, unequal treaties, and the evolving new international order. It was too small, too short, too weak to compete with the imagined "Western body"; apparently, there was a lot for the Japanese elites to be anxious about. The revolutionary reforms

1. I would like to thank all the participants of the workshops and the two anonymous reviewers for their comments. I am also very grateful to Jan Kiely for his input and support.
2. Mishima Michiyoshi, *Nihon kentai shōni no hatsuikuron* [The theory of healthy Japanese children's development] (Tokyo: Dai nihon tosho, 1902), 247–48.

undertaken by the new Meiji government had resulted in the transformation of a once-isolated, resource-poor country into the most industrialized and militarily powerful nation-state in early twentieth-century East Asia. And yet Japan was compelled to conform to Western standards of "civilization" in order to rid itself of unequal treaties.[3] At the time, government officials and social critics made frequent and often obsessive comparisons between Japan and the Western "civilized" nations. The strength of the new nation was supposed to be demonstrated by the vitality, and more importantly, the physical stature of its people. The bodies of the Japanese people did, for many officials and intellectuals, represent a natural resource that had to be developed and marshaled in the new age of competition of races between nation-states. Yet as this historical examination will show, how intellectuals, government bureaucrats, school hygienists, and pediatric specialists of the Meiji period viewed and interpreted children's bodies and their physical growth illustrates the complex interactions between the ideals of civilization and its associated gendered norms.

The "precociousness" of Japanese girls and boys, measured not in absolute age but in relation to the idealized Western body, and the supposed resulting physical underdevelopment embodied significant gendered differences and interpretations.[4] For a girl, the timing of her menarche, deemed "early" or "late," was perceived by a wide range of male medical doctors and intellectuals to reveal the degree to which she was physiologically "civilized." As I have discussed elsewhere, these Japanese medical specialists in the Meiji period pushed forth a range of new interpretations of menstruation based on medical knowledge informed by ideas of a sociocultural and racial civilizational hierarchy, both domestic and international. In the last decades of the nineteenth century, menstruation was no longer a source of female impurity but a physiological phenomenon with serious consequences, and a foundation for the health of a woman, a family, and the nation.[5] Yet for Japanese boys, their condition was much less definite. Without a single, standardized indicator of puberty (like menarche), their physiological transformation was more opaque and wide ranging, including signs such as growth of pubic and facial hair, muscular development, coarsening of the voice, ability to have an erection, and nocturnal emissions. With this, medical specialists and social commentators focused on a physical act that represented, among other things, puberty: masturbation. While concerns

---

3. For a perspective taking international relations theory and ideas about the "European International Society" into account, see Shogo Suzuki, *Civilization and Empire: China and Japan's Encounter with European International Society* (London: Routledge, 2009).

4. For studies on actual cases of precocious puberty in the nineteenth century, see, for example, M. Jeanne Peterson, "Precocious Puberty in the Victorian Medical Gaze," *Nineteenth-Century Gender Studies* 4(2) (Summer 2008). http://www.ncgsjournal.com/issue42/peterson.htm.

5. For more details on these menstrual discourses, see chapter 2 in Izumi Nakayama, *Politics of Difference: Menstruation in Modern Japan* (manuscript in preparation).

over the assumed relationship among masturbation, neurasthenia, and the young male body was not unique to Japan within East Asia, the rationale for the civilized body differed in its interest for the delaying of puberty.[6]

Civilized Bodies

The idea of a child as a mnemonic device for the nation-state was, as Stefan Tanaka noted, integral to the development of the nation itself.[7] But even before the studies of child development, the links between the construction of a modern "civilization" and the national body had already been theorized in social Darwinist terms by some of the Meiji era's most important intellectuals. The relationship between ideas of civilization and the body was implied in the late nineteenth century by intellectuals theorizing on the changes not only of Japan as a nation-state but also its people. In 1875, Nishi Amane 西周 (1829–1897) wrote in the *Meiroku Zasshi*, "In the seven year period since the Meiji Restoration, people's bodies have transformed from their bones."[8] While Nishi most likely wanted to emphasize the dramatic political (as well as the resulting sociocultural) transformation of Japan since 1868, he also anticipated subsequent discussion of the body. His implication was that the major sociopolitical reforms required an equally dramatic transformation of Japanese bodies. Fukuzawa Yukichi 福澤諭吉 (1835–1901) commented, writing, "[Nishi] says that, during the seven years already passed since the Restoration, men, even physiologically, have fundamentally changed from the bones of their bodies and that it is indeed a fact that the enlightenment of society has invariably progressed during the subsequent days and months." However, for Fukuzawa, it was insufficient. He believed "[t]here has been

---

6. For examples in China, see Hugh Shapiro, "The Puzzle of Spermatorrhea in Republican China," *positions* 6(3) (Winter 1998): 551–95; and "Neurasthenia and the Assimilation of Nerves into China" (23rd International Symposium on the Comparative History of Medicine, Seoul, Korea, July 5–11, 1998). http://www.ihp.sinica.edu.tw/~medicine/conference/disease/shapiro.PDF, accessed January 1, 2016.
7. Stefan Tanaka, "Childhood: Naturalization of Development into a Japanese Space," in *Cultures of Scholarship*, ed. S. C. Humphreys (Ann Arbor: University of Michigan Press, 1998), 22–23.
8. Nishi Amane, "Naichi ryokō" [Domestic travels], *Meiroku zasshi* 23 (December, 1874). *Meiroku Zasshi* [Journal of the Japanese Enlightenment], trans. and with an introduction by William Reynolds Braisted, with the assistance of Adachi Yasushi and Kikuchi Yūji (Cambridge, MA: Harvard University Press, 1976). In the 1976 translation, the reference to "bones" is translated as the national body. I altered the translation to give more attention to the term "bones" of the human body. This is not the first discussion of human bones in relation to foreign relations for Japan. In the eighteenth century, Arai Hakuseki, in discussing the issue of foreign trade, likened Japan's natural resources to that of human bones— something essential that could not be replace or replenished. See notes on Sugi Kōji, "On Reforming Trade," in *Meiroku zasshi*, 307.

a renewal of the bone structure/quality during the last seven years, but the people's spirit undoubtedly remains as before."[9]

The problem of post–Meiji Restoration transformation of Japan for Fukuzawa was its superficiality, and yet he believed this had physical consequences as well. In his series of articles "On Japanese Women" published in 1885, Fukuzawa criticized Japanese society's long-standing "ill-treatment" of women that had left Japanese women weak and inferior, both physically and emotionally, and *so bearing weak children*.[10] He was equally critical of men's bodies. Japanese men, Fukuzawa held, had become effeminate and weak during the Tokugawa period. In times of peace, male bodies became weaker and smaller and were no longer able to support the suits of armor worn during the Warring States period. Male and female bodies were a fundamental reason for the nation's lagging behind in what he perceived as the global "civilizational" rankings.[11] Writing in the years prior to the termination of the unequal treaties and the Sino-Japanese War, Fukuzawa was very much concerned with not only the state of the physical body but the "barbaric" practices that rendered the Japanese body inferior in relation to the West. While he considered intermarriage with other races a benefit, Fukuzawa was initially optimistic, primarily arguing for a cultural transformation that would overcome the historical and social factors detrimental to the physique of the Japanese and, hence, to the country.

Even after Japan's military victories in the Sino-Japanese and Russo-Japanese Wars were perceived by many to have demonstrated the attainment of a certain level of "civilization," the former insecurities about the Japanese body remained. Okuma Shigenobu, a politician who later became

---

9.   Braisted, *Meiroku Zasshi*, 321. Here, Braisted's translation is "bone structure," although "bone quality" may be more appropriate. The major point of contention between Nishi and Fukuzawa was not the quality of Japanese bone mass or structure. The discussion centered on whether to allow foreigners to travel freely (*naichi ryokō*) within Japan prior to the elimination of the unequal treaties, particularly through the larger question of "mixed residences" (*naichi zakkyo*) or the legal restrictions concerning the travels, commerce, and residences of foreigners in Japan. Without the power of jurisdiction, litigation for foreigners' offenses was difficult for Japan, and Fukuzawa worried anxiously about injury to the "independence of the country." Fukuzawa's opinion opposing mixed residence was later indirectly supported in 1892 by Herbert Spencer, the English political and sociological theorist, but with a different rationale. Spencer weighed in on the question of Japanese mixed residence with foreigners (meaning Caucasian Americans and Europeans) and advocated keeping them away "as much as possible at arm's length" from the Japanese people. This physical separation, as argued by Spencer, was necessary for the survival of the Japanese, for intermarriage with a superior race would result in the decline of the inferior race. See letter to Kaneko Kentaro, in *The Life and Letters of Herbert Spencer*, ed. David Duncan (Methuen, 1908), vol. 2, 14–18, quoted in Kenneth Pyle, *The New Generation in Meiji Japan: Problems of Cultural Identity 1885–1895* (Stanford: Stanford University Press, 1969), 110.

10. Fukuzawa Yukichi, "Nihon fujin ron" [Theories on Japanese women], *Jijishimpō*, June 4–12, 1885, republished in *Fukuzawa Yukichi on Japanese Women: Selected Works*, trans. and ed. Eiichi Kiyooka (Tokyo: University of Tokyo Press, 1988), 6.

11. Fukuzawa, "Nihon fujin ron," 54.

prime minister, wrote in 1913 how he believed that the historical environment and sociocultural influences specific to Japan led to the "unnatural development" of the Japanese people. Okuma, unlike other intellectuals who focused on the physical frailty of Japanese women as the source of national weakness, argued that the "feudal class hierarchy" in recent Japanese history resulted in immense pressures from "above," causing lower-class individuals, particularly men, to bend over, walking while looking at the ground. This style of walking led to poor posture and shortness in stature and, in Okuma's opinion, to depression. And this further led to a subservient and pessimistic outlook. Such "ill" mind-sets and bodies, Okuma argued, made for a naturally inferior race compared to the Europeans, "who strode through the streets," unhindered by such historical pressures. These Europeans had excellent posture, walked with dignity, and, according to Okuma, had "fully and naturally developed." These "naturally developed" European bodies represented the physical standard, one deemed to be universal and imminent like Western civilization.[12] Okuma's assessment of Japanese poor posture was a kind of excuse for the physiological "inferiority" of the Japanese vis-à-vis the "naturally developed" bodies of the Europeans. Similar to the Chinese "natural feet" discussion examined by historian Dorothy Ko, the Japanese, according to Okuma, could have "naturally developed" had they not been crushed under the weight of the "feudal class hierarchy."[13] This historical sociocultural interpretation of Okuma, however, implied the potential for the Japanese body to improve and even catch up to, or surpass, the Europeans. Whether influenced by Confucian or Lamarckian perspectives on "soft inheritance," Okuma believed that this would all depend on whether the "uncivilized" norms and mind-sets could be changed. The Japanese race, Okuma held, was not inherently inferior but just a victim of history. Okuma's images of these superior "Western" bodies were based not on a particular nation-state (although most likely British, French, or German) or on a set of quantifiable data of physical measurements but, rather, on his impressions and ideals. As with the other discussions, references to "tradition" and "civilization" were made as part of an assumed linear narrative, in which Japan would have to shed unproductive practices from the past in order to join the universal, Western "civilization." The concept of the West was cultural, not

---

12. Okuma Shigenobu, *Taiyo* [The sun] (Hakubunkan, 1913), 413–14. Fukuzawa also criticized the ideal feminine physique endorsed by "tradition." "Willow waists" and "squash-seed face" may not sound attractive in English, but a thin-waisted woman with a pale, white oval face had been considered the ideal Japanese beauty. Yet critics argued such beauty standards elevated female frailty as an attractive characteristic to which women aspired, leading to the birth of frail Japanese children by frail mothers. Described as "geisha-like" or "the hysterical type," the transformation of Japanese women into healthier, robust beings was integral, as women were the medium for improving the Japanese body.

13. See Dorothy Ko, *Cinderella's Sisters: A Revisionist History of Footbinding* (Berkeley: University of California Press, 2005).

geographical, according to some optimistic believers, and whatever racial or religious prejudice may threaten Japan's trajectory, Japan could theoretically transform itself into attaining upward mobility and, finally, equality in the competition of civilizations. With this view of linear progression toward an assumed natural state (that was Western), perhaps it was not surprising that Japanese children were seen as the hope for the future; conflating the biological with the social, cultural, and political, Mishima viewed the physical growth of children as corresponding to the development of the nation.

The Japanese terms used to translate "development" in the late nineteenth century were many: seichō (成長), hatsuiku (発育), seiiku (生育), nenchō (年長), hattatsu (発達). In 1843, Rangaku scholar Horinouchi Sodō 堀内素堂 (1801–1854) translated selections of Christoph Wilhelm Hufeland's medical text as Yōyō seigi (幼幼精義), which became one of the earliest basic texts of pediatrics, and used the word hassei (発生) for the Dutch word ontwikkeling (development).[14] In another context, as educational historian Tanaka Masato has shown, the English word "development," as used in J. S. Mills On Liberty was translated as hattatsu (発達) by Nakamura Masanao 中村 正直 (1832–1891) in 1872. This, Tanaka argued, was not simply a matter of choice (using hattatsu over hassei or hasshutsu [発出]), but a deliberate understanding of a continual "developing" process. The "development" of virtue was understood as hassei, that of moral conduct as hasshutsu, and the culminating individual was hattatsu.[15] Maeda Akiko, an educational historian who examined a wide range of Dutch-Japanese and English-Japanese dictionaries from the late eighteenth to early twentieth centuries, explained that hattatsu was used to describe emotional and intellectual changes, while seichō was used more often to refer to physical transformations in the 1870s. However, there was a shift from hassei to the common use of hattatsu in the 1880s, which came to include ideas of emotional, intellectual, and physical development.[16]

---

14. The medical text was titled Bemerkungen über die natürlichen und impfen Blattern, verschiedene Kinderkrankheiten, und sowohl medizinische als diätetische Behandlung der Kinder (1798). Hufeland's text was translated into Dutch by J. A. Saxe, and Horinouchi worked from the Dutch text. See Tanaka Masato, "Rangaku ni okeru hattatsu no gainen no donyū ni tsuite (1–3)" [The introduction of the concept of development in Dutch studies], Kyōto daigaku kyoiku gakubu kiyō [Bulletin of the Faculty of Education, Kyoto University] 39–41 (1993–1994); and Maeda Akiko, "Seichōron ni okeru hon'yaku goro no yakuwari: Jūhachi, jūkyū seiki nihon no kosodate ron to shōni igaku ni chakumoku shite" [The role of translated terms in child development: Focusing on child raising and pediatrics in the eighteenth and nineteenth centuries in Japan], Hitsotsubashi ronsō 124(4) (Oct 2000): 547–53.

15. Tanaka Masato, "Bunmei kaikaki ni okeru hattatsu no gainen no donyū ni tsuite" [The introduction of the concept of development in the period of Bunmei kaika], Kyōto daigaku kyōiku gakubu kiyō 34 (1998): 116.

16. Maeda Akiko, "Kindai Nihon no hattatsu gainen ni okeru shintairon no kentō" [Education and the idea of development in modern Japan], Kagoshima daigaku kyōiku gakubu kenkyū kiyō kyōiku kagaku hen [Bulletin of the Faculty of Education, Kagoshima University, Studies in Education] 59 (March 2008): 283–95, 287.

The concern with physical development arose as a consequence of a "civilized" institution: the modern school system. In the first decades of the Meiji period, numerous Japanese medical doctors and hygiene specialists, out of fear that the modern education system and the physical structures of the schools themselves impacted and impeded the growth and vitality of young bodies, began scrutinizing the bodies of school children. They were not alone, as doctors and pediatricians in Germany, the United States, and England contemporaneously developed the field of school hygiene in the late nineteenth century, and, by 1904, the First International Congress for School Hygiene was held in Nuremberg. Japan was represented, along with the United States and numerous other European countries.[17]

The use of biometric data to decry the decline of children's health was a phenomenon shared in industrializing countries from the nineteenth century onward. Japanese concerns, tinged with a sense of inferiority to the imagined Western body and power, emerged in a period when the government attempted to get rid of unequal treaties and to gain equal standing in the international hierarchy. Richard Meckel, an American historian of public health, also pointed to the turbulent period between the US Civil War and World War I as the moment when American school hygiene became "the object of a discrete and significant discourse within the essentially urban public health movement."[18] His research demonstrated striking similarities to the Japanese case, when the rise of US public education raised new ideas and gendered concerns over mental overwork, physical development, and civilization, or, as expressed in the words of G. Stanley Hall, "[W]hat shall it profit a child if he gains the whole world of knowledge and loses his own health?"[19] Yet Americans also struggled with a different set of anxieties, categorized by additional domestic hierarchies based on race, religion, or even subregions.

In Japan, like elsewhere, school hygiene (*gakkō eisei*) was used to diagnose and cure those suffering from the "civilizing" effects of school through "school illness" (*gakkō byō* 学校病).[20] Yet the normative standard of a healthy body and development was an imagined perfect Western one, conveniently

17. See *Nature* 69 (1798) (April 14, 1904): 572, for details on the First International Congress for School Hygiene.

18. Richard Meckel, "Going to School, Getting Sick: The Social and Medical Construction of School Diseases in the Late Nineteenth Century," in *Formative Years: Children's Health in the United States, 1880–2000*, ed. Alexandra Minna Stern and Howard Merkel (Ann Arbor: University of Michigan Press, 2002), 187.

19. Ibid., 201.

20. See Izumi Nakayama, "Posturing for Modernity: Mishima Michiyoshi and School Hygiene in Meiji Japan," EASTS 6(3) (September 2012). Also, it is important to note that even before Mishima, there were opinions within the Ministry of Education, notably David Murrary (1830–1905), who pointed to the constrained seating arrangements and its detrimental effects on children of poor health. For a detailed account, see Kondō Mikio, "Meiji chūki ni okeru gakurei mimanji no shūgakukinshi tsūtatsu ni kansuru kentō" [Study on prohibition

overlooking the anxieties expressed by physicians in the United States and elsewhere. As government officials, medical doctors, and intellectuals of the nascent nation-state viewed the national body as weak and inferior in relation to the West, various ideas on how to "remedy" the situation emerged from these diverse groups, led foremost by Mishima Michiyoshi.

Mishima Michiyoshi and Child Development

"A pedophilic pervert" was what newspapers called Mishima for his interest in children's bodies. Some fanned suspicions that his physical examinations would "shorten lifespans."[21] On his way to pioneering school hygiene in Japan, Mishima was not bothered by such criticisms, nor did he question the scientific value of his studies. Having entered Tokyo Imperial University Faculty of Medicine in 1884 and in 1889 continuing on to its postgraduate program, Mishima chose to focus his research on pediatrics, examining the physical development of able-bodied children.[22] In 1891, the Ministry of Education commissioned Mishima, who was still a graduate student, to survey the state of elementary school hygiene throughout the country. Through this project, Mishima established himself as a leading school hygiene expert. He stayed on with the Ministry of Education to become the director for the School Hygiene Division in 1896, later traveling to study in Germany, England, and France in 1903.[23] He published widely on the topic of school hygiene, pre- and postnatal care, child development, and physical education, and translated numerous medical texts into Japanese.[24]

In 1892, Mishima began one of the first surveys focusing on the measurement of children's bodies ever to be conducted in Japan. Statistical surveys in Japan began around 1872, when Sugi Kōji 杉亨二 (1828–1917), a Dutch studies scholar turned Meiji bureaucrat, influenced by Dutch work on

---

of entering school notice for children pre-school age in the middle of the Meiji era], *Nagano-ken tanki daigaku kiyō* 60 (December 2005): 99–109.

21. Mishima, *Nihon kentai*, 10.

22. The term "able-bodied" is used as opposed to "disabled children." Sugiura Morikuni, *Wagakuni gakkō eisei no sōshisha Mishima Michiyoshi* (*jō*) [Mishima Michiyoshi, founder of our nation's school hygiene (part 1)] (self-published, 1971). In 1890, Mishima was one of the founding members of Mumeikai (無名会), the origins of the Japan Pediatric Society. In 1892, he founded the Imperial Vaccine Institute (Teikoku Tōbyōin 帝国痘苗院) with Numano Kōtarō 沼野孝太郎 to deal with the smallpox epidemic.

23. Upon his return, he resigned from his post at the Ministry of Education, because of bureaucratic redistributions and the closing of the School Hygiene division. For more, see Nakayama, "Posturing for Modernity."

24. While beyond the scope of this chapter, Mishima's works were introduced to Qing China soon after their publication in Japan. See Shō Taihō (Shang Dapeng), "Shinchō makki ni okeru shintaikan no keisei wo meguru Nihon no eikyō ni kansuru kenkyū" [Study of the Japanese impact on the formation of late Qing views of the body], *Heisei 17 nendo kenkyūhi hojokin kenkyū kekka hōkokusho* [2005 report for the research outcomes based on the grants-in-aid for research], March 28, 2006.

statistics, headed what is now known as the Statistics Bureau in the Ministry of Internal Affairs and Communications and began editing Japan's first national statistical handbook. In 1874, Mitsukuri Rinshō 箕作麟祥 (1846–1897), a French-educated Ministry of Education bureaucrat and legal scholar, translated *Eléments de statistique* by Alexandre Moreau de Jonnès (1778–1870) and coined the term *tōkei* (統計) as the Japanese equivalent for "statistics."[25] All these scholars, including Nishi Amane and Tsuda Mamichi 津田真道 (1829–1903), who studied with Simon Vissering at Leiden University, were involved in the influential Meiji 6 Society (Meirokusha), and their research interests and translations highlighted the significance of statistics and statistical surveys in the late nineteenth century.[26] In this vein, Mishima participated in the Japanese expectation that statistics could greatly benefit national interest through the collection of data.

Mishima began his 1892 commissioned study by first conducting a physical examination of more than 1,000 students attending Tokyo's elementary schools. Through this initial survey, Mishima came to believe that the new and modern education system in Japan was weakening the bodies of schoolchildren by enforcing long hours in the classroom without providing appropriate study environments. The complete national survey commissioned by the Ministry of Education, published in 1895 as *School Hygiene Investigative Report Conspectus*, covered regions from the southern island of Kyushu to the northern prefectures of Aomori and Akita. This report, reflecting Mishima's interests in addition to the commissioned assignment, first dealt with the physical structures of school buildings. The second half of the report was an investigation of student bodies and their development. This was Mishima's starting point for collecting data on the physical development of Japanese children.[27]

Mishima's *Developmental Theory of Japanese Able-Bodied Children* was based on his doctoral thesis, submitted to the Tokyo Imperial University in April 1902 for his degree four months before the publication of the book. The subject data he collected for this project was extensive: 9,609 boys and 7,467

25. The Dajōkan shōin seihyōka (太政官正院政表課), and the edited volume was titled *Nihon seihyō*. See Kaji Shigeo, *Sugi Kōji den* [Biography of Sugi Kōji] (Tokyo: Aoi shobō, 1960). Mitsukuri was the son of Dutch studies scholar Mitsukuri Genpo and educated in English, French, and German from a very young age. See Yoshi'i Tamio, "Seiō kindaihō no juyō to Mitsukuri Rinshō" [Mitsukuri Rinshō and the reception of European modern law], in *Meiroku zasshi to sono shūhen: Seiyō bunka no juyō, shisō to gengo* [Meiroku Journal and its environs: The reception, philosophy, and language of Western culture], ed. Kanagawa daigaku jimbungaku kenkyūjo (Tokyo: Ochanomizu bunko, 2004).

26. For the Dutch influence on the Japanese "statistical boom" in the late nineteenth century, see Okubo Takeharu, *Kindai nihon no seiji kōsō to oranda* [Modern Japanese political initiatives and Holland] (Tokyo: Tokyo University Press, 2010). For the Chinese example, see Tong Lam, *A Passion for Facts: Social Surveys and the Construction of the Chinese Nation-State 1900–1949* (Berkeley: University of California Press, 2011).

27. For details on this survey, see Nakayama, "Posturing for Modernity."

girls, totaling 17,076 Japanese children ranging from newborns to age fifteen. Newborns and infants up to the age of three were patients of the pediatric section of the Medical University, while the other children were examined in kindergartens and higher schools throughout Japan.[28] The lack of real statistical data, Mishima argued, was obstructing the progress of science in Japan and was an embarrassment.[29] He planned to remedy the situation, explaining how the development of school hygiene in Japan was not too far behind its European counterparts, referring to the 1877 publication of *Handbuch der Schul-Hygiene* by Adolf Baginski (Baginsky, 1843–1918) as the starting point. While Mishima did not completely dismiss the methodology or the conclusions arising from the works of Adolphe Quételet (1796–1874) and his idea of *l'homme moyen* ("the average man"), based on the mean values of measured variables, he also explained the rationale for his extensive survey by noting that while there were the translated studies and surveys by Quételet and Henry Pickering Bowditch (1840–1911), these works dealt with different races, climates, food, clothing, housing—all of little relevance to Japan.[30] Therefore, he began collecting data as his commissioned project for the Ministry of Education commenced and continued his research over the years, despite difficulties in gaining public support for these physical surveys. Such behavior, he felt, only proved to him the lack of "civilization" in Japan still, and its consequences for the body.[31] Nevertheless, Mishima lamented the uncooperative state of affairs in Japan and believed that his research would not rise to the accuracy of Euro-American standards.[32]

One of the original questions leading Mishima to this survey was why the Japanese were "a precocious race."[33] "Precociousness" and "precocious puberty" remain a modern medical term that describes a physical

---

28. He specifically noted the regions as "Tokyo, Kinai, Sanyō, Sanyin, Shikoku, Kyūshū, Ōba." The majority of the children aged four to six surveyed here attended kindergarten. The categorization by age was important, as he discovered in Kyūshū and elsewhere, for students began attending school at different ages. In one case, he found in one particular elementary school how the age difference between the youngest and oldest students in the same grade was more than eight years and six months. This and other discoveries led to his involvement in the debate of the appropriate age to start school. See Kondō Mikio, "Meiji chūki ni okeru shūgaku nenrei no giron ni kansuru ichi kōsatsu" [Study on prohibition of entering school notice for children pre-school age in the middle of the Meiji era], *Nagano-ken tanki daigaku kiyō* 59 (December 2004): 45–54.

29. Mishima, *Nihon kentai*, 3. The German title was *Das Wachstum des Kindes in Japan*.

30. See Adolphe Quételet, *Sur l'homme et le développement de ses facultés, ou Essai de physique sociale* (1835), 2 vols. Henry Pickering Bowditch, physiologist and dean of the Harvard Medical School, founder of the first physiological lab in the United States, taught Charles Sedgwick Mino and G. Stanley Hall, among others.

31. Mishima, *Nihon kentai*, 10.

32. Ibid., 3. In addition to being called a pedophile, other issues involved superstitious parents unwilling to divulge the exact birth date of their child or the unwillingness of girls to undo their tall hairdos and undress before measuring their height and weight.

33. Ibid., 1.

phenomenon that arrives earlier than generally expected.[34] But Mishima's use of the term was fundamentally different. He cited the works of Imperial Tokyo University professor Erwin von Baelz (Bälz, 1849–1913), and his reference to Baelz was likely not voluntary. According to one account, Inoue Kowashi (1844–1895), then Minister of Education, supposedly instructed Mishima to compare Japanese bodies with Western ones and introduced him to Baelz.[35] Baelz, reproducing popular European ideas regarding race and civilization, had deemed the Japanese a "precocious" race.[36] This notion of a precocious race was propagated widely by how, in the nineteenth and twentieth centuries, social Darwinists Francis Galton, Herbert Spence, and Thomas Huxley, among others, referred to those "less civilized," including the Japanese. According to them, such people were believed to mature early, hence "precocious," but with puberty came mental arrest, so their intellect would develop only to the level of an adolescent, hence they were describable as "child-like." Galton wrote in 1865 how "the savages seem incapable of progress after the first few years of their life. The average children of all races are much on a par." But, he argued, "as the years go by, the higher races continue to progress, while the lower ones gradually stop. They remain children in mind, with passions of grown men."[37] But even before Galton, others, most likely influenced by Charles Darwin's 1859 *On the Origin of Species by Means of Natural Selection*, explained the evolution of civilization in similar terms. For example, John Crawfurd, president of the Ethnological Society of London wrote in 1863, "[T]he vast superiority of the European over the other races of man, and especially over the precocious but soon stagnant races of Asia, need not be insisted on at length."[38] While he described the Japanese as "an example of the stationary character of the Eastern races carried to the last extremity,"[39] Crawfurd noted difference: "[T]he Japanese, although resembling in some respects the Chinese, must be considered a distinct race of man, both as to physical form and mental

---

34. For example, see J. C. Carel and Juliane Léger, "Precocious Puberty," *New England Journal of Medicine* 358 (2008): 2366.
35. This account is described in Sugiura Morikuni, "Mishima Michiyoshi 1–18," *Gakkō hoken kenkyū* 10(2)–12(12) (1968–1970). However, it seems rather bizarre for Inoue to assume that Mishima would not be familiar with Baelz's work, considering he had studied at the Tokyo Imperial University, and with the university president, Miyake Shū.
36. Mishima cites Baeltz's research on p. 240. The original work is Erwin Baeltz, *Die koerperlichen Eigenschaften der Japaner* [The physical properties of the Japanese] (Yokohama: Deutsche Gesellschaft für Natur- und Völkerkunde Ostasiens, 1882).
37. See Francis Galton, "Hereditary Talent and Character," *Macmillan's Magazine* 12 (1865): 157–66, 318–27.
38. John Crawfurd, "On the Connexion between Ethnology and Physical Geography," *Transaction of the Ethnological Society of London* 2 (1863): 4. "Man will be found savage, barbarous, or civilized, in proportion to the quality of the race to which he belongs, and to the physical character of the country in which his lot has been cast" (17).
39. John Crawfurd, "On the Physical and Mental Characteristics of the European and Asiatic Races of Man," *Transaction of the Ethnological Society of London* 5 (1867), 80.

capacity. . . . [T]heir civilization is not yet inferior, but different in kind from that of the Chinese."[40] For Mishima, the ideas of Baelz and Crawfurd were neither simplistic nor offensive; the ideas offered possibilities. While these European commentators fixated on the issue of mental arrest, Mishima was above all, throughout his investigation, concerned with the timing of child *physical* development in comparison with European counterparts. It appeared that he did not have one national model for comparison, partly due to the lack of comprehensive studies in any particular location. Instead, he seemed to have resorted to using any and every available survey and data on child development, resulting in the wide range of examples from France, England, Germany, and even Sweden.

Mishima thus organized his work in progressive developmental stages marked by physically notable characteristics: teething; first steps taken; the closing of the anterior fontanelle; weight and height of newborn; the development of a one-month-old baby; the weight, height, chest and head measurements of a suckling baby; and the weight, height, chest, and head measurements, span of arms, length of lower limbs, and timing of puberty of a child. He defined the stages of development to match the Western examples in the following way: the term "child" referred to anyone from a newborn until just prior to the time of puberty, which Mishima estimated to occur around age fifteen.[41] Within this were the subcategories of "infancy" (also referred to in the text as *infantia, enfance*) and "childhood" (*pueritia, jeunesse*). And "infancy" was further divided into two periods, the "suckling period" (*première enfance*) and "later infancy" (*seconde enfance*).

Initially, Mishima's data matched up well with the Western examples, with few anomalies. Comparing Japanese babies' teething periods with those studied in W. Henke's *Anatomie des Kindesalters*, Welcher's *Kramolog*, and the works of Philipp Biedert, Mishima developed the interpretation that Western incisors generally emerged after an average of seven months, with the earliest evidence around three months and the slowest around fourteen months.[42] On average, his Japanese results were comparable. At the same time, however, Mishima was alarmed by how precocious the female babies were, as, by the seventh month, over 50 percent of them were already showing their incisors; some were doing so as early as three or fourth months. If the boys were less precocious, still 49 percent were teething by seven months.[43]

---

40. Crawford, "On the Connexion," 15.
41. Mishima, *Nihon kentai*, 11–13.
42. Mishima cited M. Henke, *Anatomie des Kindesalters* (1881). Welcher is uncited. In Welcher's chart, the incisor (Schneidezahn), back tooth (Backzahn), and canine tooth (Eckzahn) are listed under deciduous or primary teeth, and the second section lists the permanent teeth with the additional molars (Molaris) and premolars (Proemolaris). Mishima cited Philipp Biedert, *Die Kinderernährung im Säuglingsalter* (1897).
43. Mishima, *Nihon kentai*, 28–30.

The start of walking followed a similar pattern. Walking began, at the earliest, around seven months for males and eight months for females, while the slowest began walking around twenty-six months for males and twenty-four months for females. Any later than two years was, according to Mishima, not necessarily abnormal. The taking of the first step on average around the thirteenth month for both male and female babies, Mishima noted with apparent relief, was "the same as the European examples."[44] Yet he also pointed out that while, on average, almost 60 percent of female babies were able to walk at twelve months, despite starting later (at eight months), only 55 percent of male babies were able to do so.

This pattern played out for the entirety of Mishima's project. In terms of the closing of the anterior fontanelle, he noted how his results were "exactly the same" as the selected cases from Europe, averaging around thirteen to fourteen months.[45] With regard to a newborn baby's weight, he detailed how both male and female babies averaged around 3,000 grams, after five to six months their weights doubled, and after twelve months tripled. By the fifth year, their weights had increased by five times and increased tenfold by ages twelve to thirteen, notably *earlier* for girls. Thus, despite the 200 gram difference in average weight between the Japanese and European data, Mishima concluded it was negligible. He wrote, "[I]t cannot be said that Japanese newborns weights are inferior to those of Europe."[46] He made similar observations with respect to comparisons of babies and infants' heights, chest, and head measurements.[47]

However, he identified problematic differences in data for the several years preceding puberty. His survey findings did not match up well with that of Axel Key's (1832–1901) Swedish school hygiene research on prepubescent weight, height, and timing of puberty.[48] While Key's research showed that boys generally surpassed girls in height between the ages of twelve and sixteen, in Mishima's results puberty arrived around the ages of twelve to fourteen. Key's data showed boys surpassing girls in weight between ages thirteen and sixteen, while Mishima's data showed the period to be between ages twelve and fifteen. Puberty for girls, according to Key, was experienced between ages twelve to fifteen, yet Mishima's data showed Japanese girls going through puberty between the ages of eleven to fourteen. Finally, the boys in Key's study underwent puberty between the ages of fourteen and seventeen, and Mishima's examples experienced puberty between the ages of twelve and sixteen. The comparisons revealed how Japanese boys and

---

44. Ibid., 33–34.
45. Ibid., 43.
46. For boys, it was at ages thirteen to fourteen when their weight increased tenfold. Ibid., 53.
47. Ibid., 54–131.
48. Axel Key, *Schulhygienische Untersuchungen* (1889), which was an abridged translation of the Swedish, *Redogörelse för den hygienska undersökningen*. Mishima also used Jean Quetelet's *Anthropométrie* (1835–1840), frequently in his work, although none is cited in this paper.

girls tended to experience and terminate all the key stages of development and puberty *earlier* than their supposed European counterparts and, often times, for shorter durations.

These results might have been read in various ways, but, for Mishima, variations from the European case studies proved that Japanese girls and boys were experiencing puberty *too early*; they were suffering from "precocious puberty." And this, to him, proved his view that the Japanese were a "precocious race." Mishima identified the impact of precocious puberty on the length of arms and lower limbs in Japanese children. In his nationwide survey of fifteen-year-olds, the children's arm spans were reported to be consistently less than the children's full height (which European theorists claimed it should be). The length of legs was also a deficiency, as it averaged 49.5 percent in relation to the full height, in contrast to the 50–55 percent of the European surveys. For Mishima, short arms and legs were evidence of a stunting or slowing of the natural development process that resulted from the premature puberty of Japanese children.[49]

Throughout his detailed survey, Mishima emphasized differences in development between the male and female subjects. In virtually all stages of his survey, female babies/infants/children were shown to develop at a faster rate than their male counterparts. From teething to the closing of the anterior fontanelle to the period of puberty, girls appeared to be the more precocious in development. Based on this, Mishima speculated that this was somehow related to girls outperforming boys in primary schools, but he was not certain. While some of his contemporaries might have used this data to further blame the weakness of Japanese children on the mother, he did not use it to theorize whether precocious girls gave birth to equally precocious babies. At this point, he appeared to be altogether unresolved about the import of the theory of the precocious race. He wondered, on the one hand, "whether this 'precocious maturity/precocious decline' would be advantageous or not" to Japan's competition with the other nations of the world. Yet, on the other, Mishima warned, "[W]e must research methods and borrow the power of science to develop equally to the peoples of Europe and America," fearing divergence from the Western "universal standard" bodies.[50]

Mishima exhibited great faith in the universalism of civilization, which he considered fully attainable. He identified causes of Japanese physical inferiority, which could be remedied by changing "uncivilized" customs and practices. In his discussion of height, he noted how the Japanese were "the shortest people in all of the world's known civilized countries," with a long torso and short legs. While he presented the positions of Broca and

49. Mishima, *Nihon kentai*, 189–94.
50. Ibid., 239. Considering how familiar he was with German scholarship, it is curious that he does not address or cite Carl Bergmann (1814–1865) and his ecogeographic principle, Bergmann's rule.

Boudius, who argued that height was an issue of heredity, not lifestyle, and Johannes Ranke's interpretation of "proportions," Mishima could not resist the occasion to expand on his theories.[51] Quoting a French scholar named Roberts, who apparently held that people who spent their time standing up were, on average, several centimeters taller than those who spent time lying down, Mishima postulated that Japanese "shortness" was related to the Japanese style of sitting on the floor from infancy. As opposed to the Western practice of sitting in a chair, the Japanese, through sitting, bent and obstructed their bodies, impeding the full development of their lower limbs. "The femur, or the shinbone, or the fibula would be crooked, and as a result, the length[s] of the lower limbs are shortened. Japanese people have, for over two thousand years, considered this sitting position to be propriety. . . . [T]his must be declared as absurdity."[52]

Mishima argued that, in Western countries, the social elites were taller than the rest of society, as they never experienced hardship and often exercised from a young age. So, likewise in Japan, Mishima argued that those in elite society were taller, but women were often weaker, as they lacked the "Western" habit of exercising. Yet since Gakushūin and Kazoku Girls' Schools, schools for children of the imperial lineage and nobility, had introduced physical education into their curriculum, Mishima approvingly reported that even the upper-class women so educated were healthier. He argued, furthermore, that the upper class and parts of the middle class were consistently taller than the lower classes, notably because of their adoption of new Western habits, sitting arrangements, and an improved diet. In theory, then, improved living standards and habits could make for taller Japanese children.

Mishima's work demonstrated a certain Meiji optimism that projected Japan's potential to overcome "race" through "civilization." He presented a scientific picture of a physical body with measurements of universal standards, attainable through the progression in the stages of civilization. Only if Japanese children did not experience puberty *too early* (in relation to that of a perfectly timed Westerner), they would have had similar measurements in height, weight, and arm and leg length. Mishima's desire to make all aspects of Japanese children's development match that of their Western counterparts featured the unscientific and unsubstantiated adulation and reverence of the idealized Western body. The value of height and long legs, in particular, was never questioned in scientific terms but revered as *the* physical standard and

---

51. Ibid.,197. Pierre Paul Broca (1824–1880): a French physician and anthropologist, known best for "Broca's area," an area in the frontal lobe. Boudious: perhaps Jules Boudou (Faculté de médecine de Montpellier, 1887) but not cited in Mishima. Johannes Ranke (1836–1916): anthropologist, brother of Heinrich von Ranke (1830–1909), professor of pediatrics at Munich University, father of Karl Ernst Ranke (1870–1926).
52. Ibid., 198–99. Also see Nakayama, "Posturing Modernity."

representation of "civilization" attained. The only question was how to slow down children's development so that they did not experience puberty too early.

Elsewhere, he had expanded on his theories about the Japanese as a precocious race:

> Whether it has been like this since ancient times, or a phenomenon arriving in recent years . . . the life span of precocious races is short and as health is difficult to maintain. . . . [I]n order to fulfill the one hundred year plan of the nation, it is an issue of extreme interest. It is difficult to find the root of the problem in the degree of education provided (and the period of its requirement), but this investigator believes that, over time, without too much difficulty, education will provide the way to naturally change "precocious" to "mature."[53]

Mishima did not elaborate further on what kind of education would provide such natural change to children's growth, except that it would teach "principles of hygiene." Part of what he meant could be found in educational songs like the "Hygiene Song," which called for washing hands and keeping bodies healthy for the sake of parents and the emperor. But he had more in mind than that.[54]

Puberty and Masturbation

"Puberty was a life-threatening time." This was the message that Takashima Heisaburō (1865–1946), a specialist on educational psychology and, later, editor of *Pediatric Research* (*Jidō kenkyū*), explained in his "Theories on Sexual Education," a chapter from his book *Principles of Physical Training* (*Taiiku genri*) (1904). Pay too little attention to a child undergoing puberty, and he or she may suffer drastic emotional and physical consequences later in youth. Takashima believed that, without proper guidance and education before and during puberty, young women would suffer from "hysteria" and "depression." Menstruating girls, Takashima declared, needed to take every precaution during their cycle, avoiding "stimulating" foods and not participating in physical activities. Female instructors should inform female students of the various "emotional and physical dispositions" prior to their menarche, and teach "proper hygienic methods" to deal with them. Otherwise, Takashima warned, girls may suffer many a "woman's illness" in the future, due to carelessness during this important time of their lives.[55]

---

53. Mishima Michiyoshi, *Gakkō eisei torishirabe fukumeisho tekiyō* [School hygiene investigative report conspectus] (Tokyo: Hakubunkan, 1895). Translated in Nakayama, "Posturing for Modernity."
54. See Nakayama, "Posturing for Modernity."
55. Takashima Heisaburō, *Taiiku genri* [Principles of physical education] (Tokyo: Ikueisha, 1904), 228–29.

For men, the consequences were more drastic and fatal, with Takashima warning that young men between the ages of twenty and twenty-four would die from a lack of proper guidance during puberty and its aftermath. Citing "authorities" such as the Austro-German psychiatrist Richard von Krafft-Ebing, Takashima highlighted how the highest percentages of men suffering from nervous breakdowns and committing suicide were between the ages of twenty and twenty-nine, which were "without a doubt, related to 'issues' of the reproductive organs." While Takashima advocated sex education before and during female puberty, he pointed to a postpubescent period for young men as equally significant. Sexual desires ruined one's character and, along with it, one's body. By teaching young men how to harness and repress sexual urges by taking cold showers every morning and exercising regularly, educators, Takashima concluded, could rehabilitate or even save their lives. This kind of knowledge, he added, may also delay puberty.[56] In this way, Takashima was similar to Mishima in looking for ways to delay puberty. While it may be difficult to "delay" puberty through external means, some scholars believed that it was possible to "not stimulate" its progression through different types of education. Several years after Mishima's treatise on child development, some attempted to educate the public on sex hygiene, including how not to promote puberty.

Kuroki Shizuya, a gynecologist, and Iida Senri, director of the Popular Hygiene Association (Tsūzoku eisei gakkai), in Sendagaya, Tokyo, published in 1906 their version of how to improve the Japanese body through knowledge of what they called "sexual hygiene" (shikijō eisei 色情衛生).[57] With laudatory words of endorsement from Morimoto Hirosaku and Arai Furuyoshi and the title lettering by Sakurai Ikujiro,[58] this book covered a wide range of topics from detailed explanation of male and female reproductive organs, "facts about sexual intercourse and pregnancy," "objectives for marriage," "venereal diseases," "important facts for pregnant women and how to raise a baby," "contraception," "erotomaniac" (shikijōkyō 色情狂), and "how to improve physique through love." In the twenty-some-pages-long section on "facts about sexual intercourse and pregnancy," the first seven pages are devoted to the importance of sex education for children. In a section sensationally titled "A Twelve-Year-Old Father and an Eleven-Year-Old

---

56. Ibid., 220–23.
57. Kuroki Shizuya and Iida Senri, Shikijō eisei tetsugaku: Jintai kairyō ron [Philosophy of sexual hygiene: Theories on improving the body] (Tokyo: Tsūzoku eisei gakkai, 1906).
58. Morimoto Hirosaku: former captain of Chiyodagata, the last of the Tokugawa bakufu's gunboat. Later captain of Karafuto-maru in Hokkaido and led the surveys of the Kuril Islands. Arai Furuyoshi: translated Albert S. G. Döderlein, Leitfaden für den geburtshilflichen Operationskurs (Sanka shujutsugaku, 産科手術学) and Friedrich Schauta, Lehrbuch der gesamten Gynäkologie (Sanka fujinka zenshū, 産科婦人科全集). Sakurai Ikujiro (1852–1915): professor of Tokyo Imperial University, established a midwifery school (Kōkyōjuku, 紅杏塾), founded the Research Group for Obstetrics and Gynecology in 1888.

Mother," Kuroki and Iida advised on avoiding the phenomenon of children "becoming parents" through guidance on avoiding precocious puberty. They pointed out six major characteristics that "promoted" puberty: warm climates, "barbarism," certain kinds of civilizations, immoral environments, luxury and gluttony, and masturbation. While recognizing that nothing could be done to change warm climates, they argued that girls in India were even more precocious, due to their "barbaric" practices and "civilization."[59] They also rather harshly criticized the "foolish" wealthy living in luxury and gluttony, arguing that exposing children to "disorder" (implying corruption of morals and illicit affairs) within the family would lead to precocious puberty. Hopes for such abrupt cultural change, however, were admittedly dim. But there was one impetus with a good chance of prevention—masturbation. Recommending that parents frequently and carefully examine their children's bodies, Kuroki and Iida explained how it was integral to pay particular attention to the reproductive organs. Infants, the authors noted, rub their reproductive organs without much awareness. If not taught properly how to wipe themselves after urinating, these areas may get itchy, leading children to scratch them. These practices "may lead to masturbation, and then they will experience precocious puberty without a doubt." Furthermore, the authors cautioned that masturbatory practices would damage the glans penis by inverting the foreskin for boys, and damage the external genital organs as well as causing catarrh (inflammation of mucous membranes) for girls. To avoid such traumatic incidents, they advised parents to supervise very closely until "the period of true intercourse" arrived. Furthermore, children ought to be informed about the "reproductive organs" and, as with cholera and tuberculosis, be taught about the ills of masturbation "until it [is] etched in their brain."[60]

Kuroki and Iida's views on masturbation were not unique, as other contemporary and subsequent sexology texts hinted at similar warnings of the physical ills of masturbation, not least of which was precocious puberty.[61] These views were not, similar to the discussions on school hygiene, restricted

---

59. The idea that climate, a category prominent in racial science, affects puberty was/is limited to women, usually focusing on their menarche. Other categories influencing menarche generally included ethnic origins, social status, urban or rural residence, and education, among others. See Nakayama, *Politics of Difference*.
60. Kuroki and Iida, *Shikijō eisei tetsugaku*, 36–38.
61. For example, Oda Shūzō, a medical doctor writing in 1930 on hygienic practices for daily matters at home and at school, devoted one section specifically to masturbation. "Such unnatural acts during the most important developmental stage of childhood," Oda explained, "would have serious emotional and physical consequences," citing seizures, precociousness, and other frightening consequences of masturbation for young girls and boys. See Oda Shūzo, *Gakkō katei tsūzoku eisei gaku* [Popular hygiene for home and school] (Osaka: Shinshindō shoten, 1930); Yūsei shoin henshūbu, ed., *Seinenki shōjo no kagakuteki kaibō* [Scientific dissection of a young woman] (Tokyo: Yūsei shoin, 1935), 273. Novels in particular are blamed for girls' masturbatory practices.

to Japan. As works by Joan Jacobs Brumberg and Heather Munro Prescott demonstrated, the shifting historical contexts and the new focus on children and the invention of "adolescence" propelled the American fascination with developmental and adolescent medicine from the nineteenth century onward, including concerns over precociousness for both genders.[62] Yet the American case appeared to focus more on precocity of the mind, with physicians warning middle-class families to shield their children from early exposure to the "temptations of the adult male world." Otherwise, physicians argued, "premature intellectual development could induce other disturbing forms of precocious behavior, most notably masturbation."[63]

Others took a more historical perspective to make their case. One of the few female authors on this topic, the nurse Matsumoto Yasuko, expanded in 1900 on the long history of masturbatory practices and objects in the court and elite societies since the Heian period, noting that the practice was largely confined to those who had already experienced puberty. Yet she also associated it with obstructing natural physical development:

> Without a way to restrain oneself, despite knowing its evils, [young people] with sudden increase in vigorous sexual desire engage in masturbation, harming their physical development that requires their full energy, unable to completely develop their sexual organs, subsumed by neurasthenia.[64]

Although the texts discussed here represent only a small sample of the countless publications on sexual hygiene, child-rearing, and domestic affairs that were scrutinized through the lens of science and medicine in the Meiji period, promoted as the new and modern "correct" knowledge of scientific specialists and Western authorities. Within a wide range of textbooks, guidebooks, and manuals on nutrition, health, and reproduction, the concern with masturbating children was evident.

These fears of masturbation propelling precocious puberty were expressed in translated works of sexology as early as 1879.[65] Later, in the Japanese translation of Frederick Hollick's *The Marriage Guide, or The Natural History of Generation* (1896), masturbation was described as "practiced frequently by children, and the damage of its ills and the accompanying

---

62. Joan Jacobs Brumberg, *The Body Project: An Intimate History of American Girls* (New York: Random House, 1997), Heather Munro Prescott, *A Doctor of Their Own: The History of Adolescent Medicine* (Cambridge, MA: Harvard University Press, 1998).
63. Prescott, *Doctor of Their Own*, 16.
64. Matsumoto Yasuko, *Danjo seishoku kenzen hō* [Healthy reproductive method for men and women] (Tokyo: Chūō kangofu kai, 1900), 94–95.
65. An article by a foreign scholar with the surname Meese, "The Bizarre Story of a Young Boy Engrossed in Masturbation," was translated and published in an 1879 issue of the *Tokyo Medical Journal*.

precocious puberty are great," explicitly referring to both boys and girls.[66] Notably, the terms used to describe masturbation were the German word *onanie*, "self-obscenity," and "hand-obscenity," the latter two believed to be early Meiji creations to problematize and medicalize the act.[67] The words used for masturbation in the early modern period varied greatly by region, but Edo-period "ditties" employed terms like *senzuri* (千摺り) with great frequency, also pointing to its relative social acceptance. Largely influenced by European sources (and some through Christianity), Japanese sexologists aimed to "educate" the populace about the impact of masturbation.[68] The difference was that they considered the primary detrimental consequence of masturbation to be the onset of precocious puberty. If masturbation brought about the early arrival of puberty, then the practice had to be eradicated for the sake of the nation. At once, the project to prohibit masturbation for the healthy development of the body went along with defining a normative sexual behavior, which, as in Mishima's work, was related to "improving" Japanese civilization.

Mishima, too, was concerned with masturbation. In his first speech after his departure from the Ministry of Education, which was at the First International World Conference on School Hygiene held in Nuremberg, Mishima elaborated on the need for informed, scientific sex education. Later published in the *Acta paediatrica Japonica* (児科雑誌 *Jika zasshi*, 1906) as "Issues on School Students' Sexual Desires," he argued that masturbation was preventable if students were properly taught sex education in schools.[69] At first glance, it might be surprising that Mishima, a school hygienist whose publications focused primarily on pre- and postnatal care, student posture, and overall hygiene in schools, would identify masturbation as a key issue

66. Frederick Hollick, *Seishoku shizen shi: Ichi mei kon'in no*, trans. Oki Keijirō and Ōnishi Naosaburo [The marriage guide, or The natural history of generation] (Tokyo: Shimamura Risuke, 1896), 304–5.

67. For the etymology of *onanie* in modern Japan, see Saitō, "'Onanie' kigō no keifu" [Genealogy of *onanie* sign], *Kyōto seika daigaku kiyō*, 31 (2006): 113–31.

68. The concerns over masturbation were introduced to Japan via translation of numerous medical texts from Europe. For studies in Europe, see Jean Stengers and Anne van Neck, *Masturbation: The History of a Great Terror* (New York: Palgrave, 2001), Thomas W. Laqueur, *Solitary Sex: A Cultural History of Masturbation* (New York and London: Zone Books, 2003); Paula Bennett and Vernon Rosario, eds., *Solitary Pleasures: The Historical, Literary and Artistic Discourses of Autoeroticism* (London: Routledge, 1995). For Tokugawa Japan, see Anne Walthall, "Masturbation and Discourse on Female Sexual Practices in Early Modern Japan," *Gender and History* 21(1) (April 2009): 1–18.

69. There are also interesting parallels with Jen-der Lee's illuminating chapter in this volume. Mishima Michiyoshi, "Gakkō seito no shikijō mondai" [The question of sexual desires in school students], *Jika zasshi* 70 (1906): 95–104. For a brief reference in English, see Frühstück, *Colonizing Sex*, 58. Mishima's views were further supported by an MOE school inspector, Ototake Iwazō, a Tokyo Higher Normal University professor sent to Europe by the MOE, in Ototake Iwazō, "Genji ōshū ni okeru seiyoku ni taisuru kyōiku oyobi inshu ni taisuru kyōiku no jōkyō ni kansuru hōkoku" [A report on contemporary European sex and alcohol education], *Kanpō* 7116 (1907): 566–68.

in the problem of precocious puberty. Yet perhaps it makes more sense if we take the theory of a historian of science and culture, Saitō Hikaru, into consideration. Saitō concluded, after years of examining the Japanese translations of Richard von Krafft-Ebing's *Psycopathia Sexualis* (*Sexual Psychopathy: A Clinical-Forensic Study*), that the Japanese translator (*tsukushi* 土筆子) of this important work that influenced understandings of sexual perversity, was none other than Mishima Michiyoshi.[70] Translated and published in serial form in *Legal Medicine*, a forensic medicine journal, the Japanese version of *Psycopathia Sexualis* was completed only eight years after its original publication. If Saitō's theory is correct, then Mishima's close reading and translation of this work may have well formed his views on masturbation.

Concluding Thoughts

This study began by exploring Mishima Michiyoshi's research on the physical development of Japanese children in a comparative framework with "Western" data. Among his most important findings were how Japanese children's bodies developed relatively similarly to their Western counterparts until they hit puberty. Then, he argued, the resulting comparatively small-limbed, short adult body was a consequence of "precocious puberty," which had arrested "full development" and "full potential." The timing of puberty, hence, was responsible for the smaller and weaker stature of the Japanese. Having identified the problem, Mishima believed the solution to be to delay "precocious puberty," a matter essential to the improvement of the national physique as well as the civilizational development of Japan. Around the same time, an emerging field of academic sexologists was similarly preoccupied with the problem of "precocious puberty." Influenced both by indigenous ideas and those from abroad, they identified masturbation as a principle factor in the initiation of "precocious puberty." In addition, they understood masturbation to be the source of physical and emotional problems for both men and women.[71] Their antimasturbation campaign was central to the project of trying to prevent "precocious puberty," which they, like Mishima, identified as crucial to the national development.

Much in the study of the early conceptualization of precocious puberty also relates to the formative history of medicalization and standardization

---

70. Saitō Hikaru, "Psychopathia Sexualis no hatsu hon'yaku ni tsuite: Hōyaku no genten wa gencho dai nanhan ka" [An original text of *Shikijōkyō hen* 色情狂編 1894], *Kyōto seika daigaku kiyō* 17 (1999): 72–91. I agree with Saitō's assessment.

71. For a particularly vivid example, in his *Popular Hygiene for Men and Women* (Tsūzoku danjo eiseiron, 1880), Fukujō Komatarō specifically warned women against the habit, for "masturbating or playing with the genital area may cause the fascia (the supporting muscle) to loosen, causing the uterus to be exposed outside the labia," describing an incident of female genital prolapse. Fukujō Komatarō, *Tsūzoku danjo eiseiron* (Tokyo: Tokyo shuppan kaisha, 1880), 34.

of female hygiene and menstruation, birth control, eugenics, and pronatalist movements, colonial medicine, and dominant discourses of sexual
health. For instance, the issue of precocious puberty appeared in the later
"sexual education" debates at the turn of the twentieth century, and "sexual
problems" debate of 1908, studied by Matsubara Yōko and Sabine Frühstück,
among others, which, in part, shifted the conception of masturbation as a
problem that spurred early puberty to one seen as harming postpubescent
men in physical and psychological ways. This contributed to the state and
medical professionals' medicalized and masculinized approach to treating
and preventing masturbation, as it was seen to cause sexual neurasthenia
leading to venereal diseases and insanity in men.[72] This shifting focus to male
masturbation served to deny and ignore female sexual desires, and to allow
medical specialists to engage in "menstrual-centric" discussions on women's
health. By equating the dangers of these two phenomena assigned to represent developmental transformation, these views abetted the internalization
of gendered sexualities and roles in twentieth-century Japanese society.

In its historical context, precocious puberty served as a convenient
explanation and rationalization for the perceived inequality (and thus,
"inferiority") of the size and length of the human body. The attractiveness of
such biological models and medical discourses, based on racially coded and
often class-specific "science," was the ability to reduce complex and different
populations into generic groupings as "men," "women," and "Japanese."
Certainly, these insecurities articulated by Mishima and others in Japan
were not unique or uncommon in the nineteenth and twentieth centuries, as
American and numerous Western European societies experienced contemporaneous crises of supposedly "lost" masculinities, femininities, and racial,
economic, and social (to name a few) identities in the flux of industrial capitalist transformations. The rise of school hygiene and other methods for the

---

72. Frühstück, *Colonizing Sex*, ch. 2. As Frühstück and others noted, sexuality was reduced to the
    pursuit of biological reproduction, and other manifestations of it were rendered abnormal.
    In this way, discussion of women's sexuality involved her reproductive organs (and all
    of its potential illnesses) and ignored, if not denied, her sexual desires. I am informed by
    Kawamura Kunimitsu's view on sexuality. See Kawamura Kunimitsu, "Onna no yamai,
    otoko no yamai" [Women's illness, men's illness], *Gendai shisō* 21(7) (1993): 88–109. To
    further support this, Tashiro Mieko has argued that, in her study of sex education from the
    1910s to the 1930s, female students studied elements of reproduction, namely menstrua-
    tion, pregnancy, and childbirth, not about sexual desires, whereas men were taught largely
    about repressing them. Tashiro Mieko, "Dansei no sekushuaritii to sei kyōiku—kindai
    nihon no seikyōiku ron ni okeru dansei to josei," in *Nihon no otoko wa dokokara kite, doko e
    ikunoka*, ed. Asai Haruo, Murase Yukihiro, and Itō Satoru (Tokyo: Jūgatsusha, 2001), 54–71.
    Yet there were (very) few exceptions, such as the widely circulated *General Sexology* (*Ippan
    seiyokugaku*) (Jitsugyō no nihonsha, 1920) by sexologist Habuto Eiji (1878–1929), where he
    elaborated on female bodies and sexual desires, alongside their male counterparts. His
    death, Saitō Hikaru has argued, resulted from suicide after a nervous breakdown. See Saitō
    Hikaru's commentary, *Hentai seiyoku non kenkyū: Kindai Nihon no sekushuaritii 3* [Sexuality in
    modern Japan: *Hentai* sexual desires and modern society] (Tokyo: Yumani shobō, 2006).

social analysis of the biological human reduced the body to depersonalized and decontextualized data sets, available for selective interpretation and manipulation to construct and to stabilize categories and markers.

The concern over precocious puberty shaped the invasive methods through which Japanese educational institutions measured and maintained records of students' physical development. In addition to measuring students' weight, height, and other categories as examined by Mishima, school doctors in state-run schools were required by the 1910s to identify the timing of puberty and so track when female students experienced menarche and monitor their menstrual cycles.[73] The national project for physical development was subsequently propelled as military officials in the 1910s increasingly intervened to strengthen the national surveillance of children's bodies through school hygiene and its physical examination system.[74] By 1930, a national competition (which continued annually until 1996) celebrated the most physically developed male and female sixth graders in Japan, and the *Asahi Newspaper*, a sponsor, reported how the first champions were more than twenty centimeters taller and weighed fifteen kilograms more than the national average; they were also noted for their exceptionally long arms and legs.[75] In 1935, the Japanese state introduced the measurement of "sitting height" (*zakō*) as one way to gauge the growth of limbs, one of the matters that had so concerned Mishima decades earlier. This practice, dreaded by many school children, is scheduled to be abolished in April 2016.[76]

As can be seen from the long-lasting existence of competitions and physical measurements, the concern with precocious puberty is, in some cases, still associated with Japanese shortness of stature and the desire for height and long limbs, even in the twenty-first century. Certain entrepreneurial medical doctors, such as Nukata Osamu, who operates a clinic in Kobe, have published several bestselling books promoting methods of helping "children grow taller," in part through a health regime aimed at forestalling precocious puberty. Nukata occasionally prescribes developmental hormones but emphasizes proper sleep habits, nutrition, and stable family and social situations that would provide the conditions for natural growth. Reminiscent of the work of Kuroki and Iida, for instance, Nukata has written, "If parents quarrel frequently, children become emotionally unstable, leading to poor distribution of developmental hormones. Furthermore, they feel

---

73. This practice was first followed sporadically, then later spread to even private schools. See Nakayama, *Politics of Difference*.
74. See Yamamoto Takuji, "Kokuminka to gakkō shintai kensa" [Nationalization and school physical examinations], *Ōhara shakai mondai kenkyūjo zasshi* [Journal for the Ohara Institute for Social Research] 488 (September 1999): 30–43.
75. Asahi shimbunsha, *Zen Nihon kara erabaretaru kenkō yūryōji sanbyakunin* [Three hundred healthy children selected from all over Japan] (Tokyo: Asahi shimbunsha, 1930).
76. The measurement of sitting height served to identify the length of one's legs. (Full standing height) – (sitting height) = (length of legs). Nakayama, "Posturing for Modernity."

danger, and instinctively try to mature quickly. In this way, if they quickly mature, their bones harden, and they stop growing."[77] Divorce, he further asserts, in line with the neoconservative political perspectives that blame the current crises of Japanese society and its economy on the breakdown of the patriarchal "family system," supposedly propelled by the increased female participation in the workplace, accelerates the onset of puberty by as much as six months, therefore impacting the growth of children. Precocious puberty, as conceptualized by Mishima and others, emerged during Japan's extraordinary transformation in late nineteenth and twentieth century. But it appears to have not yet been consigned to the past, for in this particular context in the twenty-first century, precocious puberty is viewed as a direct physical symptom of living in a society in crisis.

---

77. Nukata Clinic website, http://www.kobekids.net, accessed May 1, 2012. This claim is supported by work in child and developmental psychology, such as J. Belsky, "Family Experience and Pubertal Development in Evolutionary Perspective," *Journal of Adolescent Health* 48(5) (May 2011): 425–26; J. Belsky et al., "Infant Attachment Security and the Timing of Puberty: Testing an Evolutionary Hypothesis," *Psychological Science* 21(9) (September 2010): 1195–2011; J. Belsky et al., "Family Rearing Antecedents of Pubertal Timing," *Child Development* 78(4) (July 2007): 1302–21; Numata's own publications include Numata Osamu, *Kodomo no shinchō wo nobasutameni dekiru koto—shōnika senmoni ga oshieru shokuji to seikatsu shūkan* [How to increase a child's height—a pediatrician's diet and lifestyle] (Tokyo: PHP kenkyūjo, 2004).

2
Sex in School

Educating the Junior High Students in Early Republican China

Jen-der Lee

Introduction[1]

In the preface of his 1923 *Physiology and Hygiene Textbook for New Middle School*, Song Chongyi (宋崇義) stated:

> The section on reproduction, due to the nature of general education, was basically absent in earlier textbooks. But key organs are involved and how can we overlook them? Now that the world is promoting sex education, I therefore purposely add in such information here for the use of research.[2]

Song, a graduate of Peking University and former student of Lu Xun, dedicated Chapter 8 of his volume to the reproductive system and became the first to include sex in Chinese junior high textbooks. According to his statement, the reasons were twofold: reproduction was essential to the understanding of the human body, and the campaign for sex education deserved positive response.

It was the early twentieth century; what Song did was not peculiar. At the time, East Asian countries worried about the health of their youth and saw sexual hygiene as crucial to national strength. Research shows that Japanese students returning from Europe began to promote sex education toward the end of the nineteenth century. Concerned educators and medical professionals published essays and created journals that led to fervent debates in the newspapers since 1908, in regard to which were the right age groups, who were qualified instructors, and what were the appropriate contents for sex education. Several years later, activists eagerly initiated general surveys to

1. I would like to express my gratitude to librarians at the Textbook Library of National Academy for Educational Research in Taipei, Shanghai Lexicographical Publishing House, Beijing Normal University and People's Education Press for their generous support and assistance during my research there.
2. Song Chongyi, *Xinzhongxue jiaokeshu shengli weishengxue* [Physiology and hygiene textbook for new middle schools], 1923, 35th ed. (Shanghai: Zhonghua shuju, 1929).

find out the knowledge, attitudes, and behaviors of Japanese sexuality so that relevant and useful information could be introduced to students, preferably in primary schools.[3]

China lagged behind, but not much. Intellectuals at the turn of the twentieth century saw reproductive medicine as a branch of modern science and sexual identities a part of hygienic modernity.[4] Sex education was promoted in conjunction with a variety of movements ranging from women's liberation to population control, all geared toward a healthier and stronger nation.[5] Lu Xun, having returned from Japan in 1909, delivered lectures on Generatio to students at a southeast normal college before he transferred to the capital.[6] A pedagogical journal, supported by one of the pioneer publishers in Shanghai, printed a special issue on sex education in 1923, in which knowledge between the sexes was proposed for the younger generations not only for hygienic reasons but also as rational foundation to ensure girls' public education.[7]

Even though in the title of his chapter Song Chongyi used the word "reproduction" instead of "sex," what he did echoed his time. Many factors contributed to shaping the features of textbooks. Official directives laid out

---

3.   There were Japanese students returning from Europe that promoted sex education since the end of the nineteenth century. After the 1908 debates in *Yomiuri Shimbun*, Yamamoto Senji conducted a general survey of sex knowledge and attitudes among the Japanese population. See Sabine Frühstück, *Colonizing Sex: Sexology and Social Control in Modern Japan* (Berkeley: University of California Press, 2003), "Debating Sex Education," 55–82, and "Sexology for the Masses," 83–115.

4.   For the inspiring concept of hygienic modernity, see Ruth Rogaski, *Hygienic Modernity: Meanings of Health and Disease in Treaty-Port China* (Berkeley: University of California Press, 2004), introduction, 1–21. For its application to understanding East Asia, see Charlotte Furth, "Introduction: Hygienic Modernity in Chinese East Asia," in *Health and Hygiene in Chinese East Asia: Policies and Publics in the Long Twentieth Century*, ed. Angela Ki Che Leung and Charlotte Furth (Durham, NC: Duke University Press, 2010), 1–21. For reproductive medicine as a branch of Western science contingent to modernity, see Yō Ki, *Kindai Chūgoku no shussan to kokka, shakai: Ishi, josanshi, sesseiba* [Childbirth and the nation/society in modern China: Doctors, delivery assistants, and midwives] (Tokyo: Kenbun shuppan, 2011). For sexual identities of the youth and China's modernity, see Frank Dikötter, *Sex, Culture and Modernity in China: Medical Science and the Construction of Sexual Identities in the Early Republican Period* (Honolulu: University of Hawai'i Press, 1995), "The Cultural Construction of Youth," 146–79. For recent research on Chinese translation of sex and its intellectual as well as hygienic significance, see Leon Antonio Rocha, "Xing: The Discourse of Sex and Human Nature in Modern China," *Gender and History* 22(3) (2010): 603–28.

5.   Wang Xuefeng, *Jiaoyu zhuanxing zhijing: Ershi shiji shangban Zhongguo de xingjiaoyu sixiang yu shijian* [Mirror of the education paradigm shift: Theories and practices of sex education in China in the early twentieth century] (Beijing: Shehui kexue wenxian chubanshe, 2007).

6.   Lu Xun, *Rensheng xiangxiao* [Learning of the human body], in *Lu Xun yiwen quanji* [Complete collection of Lu Xun's lost works], ed. Liu Yunfeng (Beijing: Qunyan chubanshe, 2001), 100–258. All chapters of physiological systems in Lu Xun's text had Chinese titles; only the reproduction chapter was named in Latin. For Lu Xun and his two younger brothers' promotion of sex education, see Wang Xuefeng, *Jiaoyu zhuanxing zhijing*, 155–96.

7.   This was *Jiaoyu zazhi* [Education journal] 15, no. 8, published by Shanghai Commercial Press in 1923.

the basic format, but publishers' commercial concerns and authors' special interests might give weight to different subjects. Song's presentations of anatomical organs would later be revised by others, but his instructions on abstinence to ensure sexual hygiene would live on, albeit in various guises.

Teaching sex was never easy. The Meiji government, despite ardent contestation, had decided to exclude sex from general education, first because of morality concerns and, later, wartime ideology.[8] Chinese schools, however, took on the challenge early on, thanks partly to belief in modern science and that Republican education was meant for everyone. There were ramifications for teaching sexuality to novices: health policies and state building, norms of familial and social relations, perceptions of the body and individuality; all these drew intellectuals toward authoring textbooks; their products, however, have yet to be examined.

To date, research on textbooks of the early twentieth century has flourished around subjects directly related to national identities such as languages, history, and geography. Few have worked on the sciences in general education, not to mention physiology and hygiene, which under the Republican school system were categorized as physical education together with exercise and sports. While historians of women's education have introduced the emergence of girls' public schooling and its embedded gender prospects, neither sex- nor reproduction-related volumes are probed.[9] Recent scholarship lists curriculum guidelines of physiology and hygiene to prove that sex was finally incorporated into programs of general education, but the contents of course materials are not yet evaluated.

It is common knowledge that children do not come across sex only in school, and textbooks are not the primary source of information about their bodies. Nevertheless, sex as a part of general education, with its pledging nature and collective impact, has almost always created debates and sometimes controversies. Sex-related pedagogical materials reveal expectations of youths, as well as sociopolitical anxieties around them, and therefore deserve closer investigation.

This chapter explores the physiology and hygiene textbooks for Chinese junior high students in the first half of the twentieth century. More than

---

8. For the decisions of Meiji government, see Kubota Eisuke, "Kindai Nihon ni okeru kyōiku kara no 'seikyōyiku' haijo no kōzō—Meiji kōki no 'seiyaku kyōiku' ronsō to sono shakai haikei no bunkei wo tsūjite" [The removal of sex education in modern Japanese education—an analysis on the social background of late Meiji debates on sex education], *Gakujutsu kenkyū (kyōiku: shōgai kyōiku gakuhen)* 53 (February 2005): 55–69. It was not until after the war that the Japanese government instituted sex education in secondary schools.

9. For the emergence of girls' public education, see Paul J. Bailey, *Gender and Education in China: Gender Discourses and Women's Schooling in the Early Twentieth Century* (London and New York: Routledge, 2007). For female role models in textbooks, see Joan Judge, "Meng Mu meets the Modern: Female Exemplars in Early Twentieth Century Textbooks for Girls and Women," *Jindai Zhongguo funüshi yanjiu* [Research on women in modern Chinese history] 8 (2000): 129–77.

eighty different titles and nearly two hundred volumes are now collected mainly in libraries of textbook publishers and time-honored normal universities.[10] They are studied here to illuminate the intricacies in drawing the moral landscape pertinent to sex education. Extant ministerial guidelines will be quoted along the time line in the next two sections to provide a road map for further analysis in the following three sections. Both literal and pictorial contents will be examined to show contending appeals among, first, female reproduction and male sexuality, second, print capitalism and government authority, and, third, gender differences and egalitarian ideals.[11]

A few points can be highlighted here first. Frequent revisions of official directives testify to the fast-changing political and intellectual arenas of China. Shifted emphases between reproductive functions and puberty sexuality exemplify the professionals' uncertainties in getting to the early teens. Ambition for comprehensiveness first appeared in the early 1930s. An allegedly unified government braved constructing the base of a brand-new state. The Ministry of Education demanded different aspects of sex and reproduction be taught in each of the three years in junior highs. Pedagogical publication boomed, and writers experimented with both textual and visual materials.

A close observation finds the proximity between school instruction and the burgeoning New Life movement. Biomedicine was flagged as a door to learning one's own body as well as a whole new scientific world. But a healthier nation eventually relied on an individual's self-discipline not necessarily required of anatomical erudition. Unlike the dissected information of anatomy, secretion knowledge accessed the body from a holistic approach. It helped legitimize the gender division of social roles promoted by the authoritarian government. But, still, a young man would be allowed to take the central stage of humanity only after he won constant battles over destructive sexual drives throughout his puberty.

In a sense, girls were left out of the limelight of anxieties, but the need to secure their modesty reached beyond verbal representations. Their public significance grew alongside the ups and downs of the governments until motherhood became the sole focus of sex education during the war when China cried for nothing but a safe and strong posterity. I will begin with the late imperial efforts.

---

10. Wang Youpeng, ed., *Zhongguo jindai zhongxiaoxue jiaokeshu zongmu* [Contents of textbooks for primary and middle schools in modern China] (Shanghai: Shanghai cishu chubanshe, 2010), 753–61.

11. For print capitalism in China, see Christopher Reed, *Gutenberg in Shanghai: Chinese Print Capitalism, 1876–1937* (Vancouver: University of British Columbia Press, 2004).

Modern China: A New Curriculum for a New People

China's secondary education was initiated in late Qing but set off to full development only in the Republican period. From the beginning physiology was proposed as a major component of science education. The first imperial-sanctioned program for middle school appeared in 1902. Before the fall of the dynasty, it would twice be revised, but physiology remained in the curriculum.[12] Nevertheless, no course guidelines have been left to us to show the required contents of learning, and we see neither sex nor reproduction in physiology textbooks from this period, whether translated or composed by Chinese writers.

Age could be one reason for the omission. Qing-era middle schools admitted students over sixteen years old. By that age most would have been either engaged or married, so to keep a modesty-risk subject to the private domain seemed reasonable.[13] Another reason would be the source materials. Although the first few publications were translated from the West, more pedagogical information came from the East.[14] Four out of ten textbooks were translated directly from Japan, and those adopting diverse sources relied most heavily on Japanese publications. Since Japanese education kept silent on sex, we find no related contents being included by its Chinese counterpart either.

A Chinese author claimed in his 1908 volume that he drew materials from five Japanese, two English, and one German textbook. He was also the first writer to have included reproduction in the table of contents. However, when one turns to the page of that chapter, one sees nothing but a line noting that it was all right not to teach reproductive organs in a middle school program, so related information had been withheld for future supplementation.[15]

The policy to shy away from sex and the rhetoric to omit reproduction continued into the first Republican decade. In 1913, the Ministry of Education announced guidelines for secondary schooling, and physiology and hygiene courses were designed to teach human anatomy and personal

---

12. The program was revised in 1903 and 1909. Two hours were assigned to studying natural sciences, and the subject for the third year was physiology.
13. The Qing followed the Japanese system that allowed six-year-old boys to enter the four-year elementary schools. After that, there would be a three-year general primary and another three-year advanced primary schooling. Therefore, a young man would be at least sixteen years of age when attending middle school.
14. The earliest extant middle school textbook of physiology was translated and abridged from French by the Commercial Press in 1902. Both of the first two textbooks translated from English, published in 1902 and 1904, were authored by the prolific American education writer Joel Dorman Steele. Neither included information of sex and reproduction.
15. Chen Yongguan, *Shengli weishengxue* [Physiology], 1908 (Shanghai: Kexuehui bianjibu, 1911). In the preface, Chen mentioned that the book used materials from textbooks by Kure Shuzō, Ōmori Senzō, Hirai Genjirō, Oka Asajirō, and Ito Sakon from Japan, Huxley and Oestreich from Britain, and Kolliker from Germany.

and public hygiene, but reproductive system was not mentioned.[16] None of the sixteen extant pedagogical works of this period included sex. One of the most popular was a translation of middle school textbook by Mishima Michiyoshi, founder of Japanese school hygiene system who focused mainly on students' postures in assessing physiological development.[17] Another was by Wang Jianshan (王兼善), who followed the late Qing precedent to mention the reproductive system in the preface but removed it from the content proper.[18] Both books were published by the Commercial Press, the primary textbook provider in Shanghai.[19]

Sex was excluded not only from anatomical presentation. When talking about personal sanitation, Wang, like his contemporaries, focused on dietary control and household cleaning instead of sexual discipline. With regard to public hygiene, he listed only cholera, plague, malaria, and tuberculosis while completely ignoring syphilis and other sexually transmitted diseases. But that does not mean Wang had nothing to say regarding reproductive matters. He criticized breast vets and bound feet as unhygienic practices that would weaken women's physicality. In the midst of the antitradition campaigns, Wang, who held a bachelor of science and a master of arts from England, blamed Chinese mothers for their beliefs in "winds" and heavy clothes to protect their babies.[20]

In 1922, the Republican government abandoned the earlier Japanese model and shifted to the American school system. Primary education ended at twelve years of age. Six instead of four years were assigned to secondary schooling, which was again divided into two stages: junior high and high

---

16. A special revision for girls was issued in 1919. See Kecheng jiaocai yanjiusuo, ed., *Ershi shiji Zhongguo zhongxiaoxue kecheng biaozhun, jiaoxue dagang huibian* [Collection of curricula directives and teaching guidelines for primary and secondary education in twentieth-century China], vol. 1, *Kecheng jiaoxue jihua juan* [Planning for curricula and teaching] (Beijing: Renmin jiaoyu chubanshe, 2001), 102–4.

17. Mishima Michiyoshi authored, Sun Zuo translated, Du Yaquan and Du Jiutian reviewed, Ling Changhuan revised, *Shengli weisheng xin jiaokeshu* [New textbook for physiology and hygiene], 1911 (Shanghai: Commercial Press, 1923). Mishima did write about the bad influence of masturbation, but it appeared somewhat peripheral compared to most of his work. For Mishima's ideas and efforts and the earliest Chinese translation of his work, see Izumi Nakayama's chapter in this volume.

18. Wang Jianshan, *Shengli ji weishengxue* [Physiology and hygiene], 1914 (Shanghai: Commercial Press, 1927). In addition to this one, Wang wrote some of the earliest textbooks for Shanghai Commercial Press.

19. For textbook wars and the prominence of the Commercial Press in early twentieth-century Shanghai, see Reed, *Gutenberg in Shanghai*, "The Three Legs of the Tripod: Commercial Press, Zhonghua Books, and World Books, 1912–37," 203–56.

20. Wang Jianshan, *Shengli ji weishengxue*, 237. With regard to "wind" in traditional Chinese medical ideas, see Shigehisa Kuriyama, *The Expressiveness of the Body and the Divergence of Greek and Chinese Medicine* (New York: Zone Books, 1999), "Wind and Self," 233–70. For traditional Chinese medicine in modern health practices and policies, see Sean Hsiang-lin Lei, *Neither Donkey nor Horse: Medicine in the Struggle over China's Modernity* (Chicago: University of Chicago Press, 2014), introduction, 1–19.

school. Those between thirteen and fifteen were now put under the spotlight. Statistics in 1923 showed that there were roughly 100,000 males and
a little over 3,200 females in this new category of students.[21] Though a very
small fraction of the population, this group of boys and girls was growing
up together with the newly founded nation and expected to be leaders of
society. They still needed to study physiology and hygiene, among various
science and humanity programs.[22] What was different was that their bodily
transformation entered the realm of learning, and this was when sex first
appeared in Song Chongyi's work.

Song's textbook was published by Zhonghua shuju (Chinese Bookstore),
whose founder, Lubi Kui (陸費逵), was himself an enthusiastic promoter
of women's education. To counter the arguments that girls' public schooling would taint their purity, he wrote intensively, urging policy makers to
update their sexual knowledge.[23] In order to gain the upper hand in commercial competition, Chinese Bookstore not only printed textbooks with
generous illustrations but also produced sculptures for biomedical classes.

Song's chapter on reproduction contained three sections: the anatomy,
physiology, and hygiene of the sex organs. This order of presentation was
also used to introduce other systems and would be applied in physiology
and hygiene textbooks throughout most of the Republican era. As if reflecting the publisher's policy, Song's fascination with anatomical details was
unmistakable. He employed various expressions to elaborate on the shape,
color, and textures of the internal organs and introduced the external organs
with straightforward wordings. The testicles carried an elliptical shape, and
the penis was a diamond-like spongy tube. The womb had a pear figure
while the oviducts looked like trumpets. Detaching himself from traditional
concerns of chastity, Song described the hymen as a mechanism to protect

---

21. According to one statistic of 1923, there were 100,136 male and 3,249 female students in
    junior highs, and an extra 31,553 boys and 6,724 girls around the same ages went to normal
    schools that often used similar textbooks. In short, roughly 150,000 students fell into the
    category of our discussion when the new school system was established. See Chen Qitian,
    Jindai Zhongguo jiaoyushi [History of education in modern China] (Taipei: Zhonghua shuju,
    1970), 264–66, 306–8. For a further discussion on women students, see Bailey, *Gender and
    Education in China*, 86.
22. Physiology and hygiene, which used to belong to natural sciences, is now categorized
    anew to occupy four of the sixteen hours of physical education. See Lin Ben, "Woguo
    chuzhong kecheng zhi yanjin" [Development of junior high curricula in our country], in
    Jiaoyubu xiuding zhongxue kecheng biaozun cankao ziliao [Reference materials for revising sec-
    ondary school directives by the Ministry of Education], vol. 2, ed. Ministry of Education
    Department of Secondary Education (1960), 36–59, particularly the reference table on p. 42.
23. See Lubi Kui, "Seyu yu jiaoyu" [Appetence and education], *Education Journal* 3(9) (1911):
    75–78. Lubi Kui, "Nannü gongxue wenti" [Issue of coeducation], *Education Journal* 2(11)
    (1910): 5–7. Also Lubi Kui, *Funü wenti zatan* [Miscellaneous talks on women] (Shanghai:
    Zhonghua shuju, 1925). For Lubi's ideas and careers, see Yu Xiaoyao and Liu Yanjie, eds.,
    Lubi Kui yu Zhonghua shuju [Lubi Kui and the Chinese Bookstore] (Beijing: Zhonghua shuju,
    2002).

urine and dirty things from flowing into the vagina, and "the membrane will break and leave nothing but a vestige when the girl grows up."[24]

Song appended English originals after each translated Chinese technical term and inserted quite a few anatomical images along with the text. This made his chapter eye catching, but the pages had a mix of languages and looked somewhat muddled. He made every effort to keep with the biomedical line. Twice in the limited space he emphasized the importance of contemporary studies on locusts and mice to further knowledge on human embryology. Not referring to any traditional idea of female weakness or pollution, he depicted the mechanism of menstruation and professed that the monthly flow was indeed an indication of maturity.[25]

Although the first two sections appeared descriptive and value-free, Song changed to a didactic tone in the third one on sexual hygiene. He criticized youngsters for giving into sexual desires that corrupted not only their own body but also society. He advised on daily regimens of reading, exercise, and sleep, and alerted against prostitution that spread syphilis, gonorrhea, and chancroid. Those who indulged in sexual activities, including men and women, Song reproved, would damage their brain and cause bladder paralysis, irregular menstruation, uterine infections, spermatorrhea, impotence, and a range of psychosomatic problems. Of the three long paragraphs in the hygiene section, only one sentence talked about cleaning, but the phrase "swabbing one's body daily with cold water" reads more like a warning than instruction. His motto was clear: "The way of hygiene is nothing but to control one's desires with propriety and discretion," and the practice seemed to require none of the anatomical knowledge of the preceding sections.[26]

Still, no course guidelines were left from this period. Most of the eight extant textbooks of physiology and hygiene claimed that they were composed according to the new school system. Nonetheless, some might have briefly touched upon development from childhood to adulthood in a section titled "stages of human life," while others simply stayed silent on reproduction much like their predecessors. Only Guo Renyuan's (郭任遠) textbook, published six years after Song's, included information of sexuality. Guo's was published by Shijie shuju (World bookstore), the third leg of the so-called publication tripod in Republican Shanghai.[27] It focused on the physical changes of early teens, explaining the structure of reproductive

24. Song, Xinzhongxue jiaokeshu shengli weishengxue, 72.
25. Menarche indicated the ability to procreate, but menstruation carried the images both of women's weakness and polluting power in traditional Chinese medicine. See Jen-der Lee, "Gender and Medicine in Tang China," *Asia Major* 16(2) (2003): 1–23.
26. Song, Xinzhongxue jiaokeshu shengli weishengxue, 76.
27. Reed, Gutenberg in Shanghai, 241–53.

cells, apparatus of menstruation, and the process of conception as well as the development of a fetus.[28] Doubling Song's images, Guo's volume foretold the booming of pedagogical printings and epitomized the competition for attention between sexuality and reproduction in the coming era.

A Healthy Nation: Male Abstinence and Female Caretaking

Soon after the Nationalist government unified China, a set of temporary guidelines was issued, and, three years later, new directives for junior high education were announced. In the 1929 guidelines for physiology and hygiene, the only required chapter on sex was "sexual development, behaviors and responsibilities." Human reproduction, the main subject of Song Chongyi's textbook, was moved to the biology program and focused further on embryology and fetal development. In the 1932 directives, physiology and hygiene courses were required for all three years of junior high, and textbooks were supposed to include "physical changes in puberty," "problems of sexually transmitted diseases in our country," and "hygiene for mothers and children" in each of the respective years.[29]

This was after the unification and the Ministry of Education could for the first time claim as a national office, and it corresponded to the New Life movement promoted to create a new kind of citizen. More than ten different publishers joined the market and nearly sixty different "physiology and hygiene" textbooks for junior highs were available in this golden decade of state building. Some companies published not only textbooks but also comprehensive manuals for teachers.[30] In either form, these pedagogical materials displayed an unprecedented anxiety over young men's sexual desires.

Following Song Chongyi's pioneering chapter, abstinence was proposed for sexual hygiene, but the focus was overwhelmingly on boys. Authors used a lot of space to describe adolescent males transforming into sexually active beings and how their behavior would invite ailments.[31] Masturbation was repeatedly reprimanded, and spermatorrhea was listed as the major cause of nervous breakdown. One author claimed that syphilis was "the most horrible national disease," while another lamented that "sexually

---

28. Guo Renyuan, "Womende shenti zenme laide ne" [How did our body come about], in *Chuzhong ziran kexue* [Natural science for junior highs], vol. 2, *Shengli zhi bu* [Physiology], 1926 (Shanghai: Shijie shuju, 1930).

29. For the 1929 temporary guidelines and 1932 standard directives, see Kecheng jiaocai yanjiu-suo, *Ershi shiji Zhongguo*, vol. 11, *Shengwu juan* [Biology volume].

30. Nevertheless, not all textbooks followed the directives closely; some still forwent official requirement to teach sex without explanation.

31. Zhuang Weizhong and Gong Angyun, *Chuzhong shengli weishengxue* [Physiology and hygiene for junior highs], 1930 (Shanghai: Shijie shuju, 1933), 223–24.

transmitted diseases are all over our country!"[32] To counter these problems, most authors suggested washing the external organs with warm water to prevent "collection of dirty stuff stirring up one's sexual desires." Since self-cultivation was considered a major issue, not surprisingly, the most effective hygienic practice most authors proposed was to refrain from bad influences such as erotic novels, idle talk, staying up late, and visits to prostitutes.[33]

Anxiety over young men's sexual desires was not confined to the puberty chapter; morality was upheld in discussions of the secretion system, fatigue and sleep, domestic hygiene, and health care. A certain textbook, while explaining social hygiene, spent only one sentence to define each of the hereditary diseases but used nearly one hundred words to remind students of sexually transmitted diseases' lasting impact on posterity.[34] Most wording on the connections between reproductive organs and sexual hygiene, however, was abstract and opaque, in a way that conveyed an over-whelmingly threatening power.

Girls, of course, should have been aware of dangers too, but they appeared not to alarm textbook authors. One stated clearly that women by nature did not as easily give in to sexual yearnings.[35] Oftentimes only one or two sentences were reserved for girls, advising them to exercise regularly to prevent menstrual disorders and to wash off vaginal discharge daily. Only one writer took pains to elaborate on unwarranted sexual activities for young women, but it was not in the context of desire. The writer was Cheng Hanzhang (程瀚章), who warned against intercourse during menstruation and pregnancy because "excitement at those times will cause gallstones, which may hinder conception later in life."[36]

Cheng's three volumes were published by the Commercial Press in 1933 and showed prevailing interest in reproductive hygiene over male absti-nence. He did not follow the official directives to break down the subjects of puberty, STD, and maternal care into three volumes. Rather, he introduced the anatomy, physiology, and diseases of the sex organs in the first two volumes and dedicated an independent chapter to women's health in the third. While all other textbooks would focus on maternal-infant mortality and preschool nursing in a chapter titled "Hygiene for Mothers and Children," Cheng began his book with health care for little girls, followed by hygienic practices during menstruation, pregnancy, delivery, postpartum, and menopause. His

---

32. See Gu Shoubai, *Kaiming shengli weishengxue jiaoben* [Physiology and hygiene textbooks from Kaiming Bookstore] (Shanghai: Kaiming shudian, 1932), 178. Cheng Hanzhang, *Weishengxue* [Hygiene] (Shanghai: Commercial Press, 1933), vol. 2, 104–5.
33. To treat coed girls as sisters was also among popular advice. See Wei Chunzhi, ed., *Shengli weishengxue* [Physiology and hygiene], rev. Jing Libin (Beijing: Zhuzhe shudian, 1932), 108–9.
34. Zhuang and Gong, *Chuzhong shengli weishengxue*, 223–24.
35. Ibid.
36. Cheng Hanzhang, *Weishengxue*, vol. 2, 96–97.

concern was obviously lifelong health care for women, and infant mortality was mentioned only at the end. By pushing official directives of infant protection back to its origin in motherhood, Cheng taught teenage girls about their body and well-being in the context of reproduction.

Cheng encouraged girls to exercise, albeit only mildly for fear of hurting their reproductive ability. He assured adolescent women with menstrual discomforts, claiming that abdominal pain, headache, and frequent urination were all normal. He was the first to teach his readers to make menstrual belts with underwear, linen, and cotton. Peculiarly enough, he was also the first among textbook writers to treat menstruation as a dreadful state that would influence young women's sentiments and lead to criminal behavior, instead of as a celebration of maturity. Unfortunately, in Cheng's assessment, to stop menstruating was also considered physically terrible. Menopause was portrayed as causing severe mental disorders, obesity, womb cancer, and endometritis. He suggested that Chinese women learn from their Euro-American sisters, to go to the doctor for checkups and get advice from medical specialists in this period of life.[37]

Cheng Hanzhang practiced gynecology in Shanghai and served on the editorial board of *Ladies' Journal*, published by the Commercial Press. He was invited to host the special column of "Advice on Medicine and Hygiene" since 1926 and wrote for each issue since 1930 on domestic medicine and women's physiology. An advocate for women's health care, Cheng set his priorities rather clearly. He advised against traditional Chinese medicine and over-the-counter drugs, and he changed the column's editorial policy from earlier interest in sexuality to nursing knowledge.[38] Cheng's instructions on sanitary belts paralleled advertisement of Kotex napkins in the magazine, and his negative views of menopause echoed American medical discourse of the time.[39] His interest in women's health went beyond the official directives,

---

37. Cheng, *Weishengxue*, vol. 3, 85–86. Cheng's ideas about menopause were not shared by his contemporary textbook writers but were inherited by many authors in postwar Taiwan. For more discussion, see Lee Jen-der, "Taiwan shengli weisheng jiaoyu zhong de xing, shengzhi yu xingbie (1945–1968)" [Sex and reproduction in physiology and hygiene textbooks of postwar Taiwan], *Research on Women in Modern Chinese History* 22 (2013): 64–125.
38. The *Ladies' Journal* (1915–1931), *Education Journal* (1909–1948), and *Eastern Journal* (1904–1948) were the three pioneer publications by Commercial Press in early twentieth-century Shanghai. Both the *Ladies' Journal* and *Eastern Journal* contained columns on medical advice. For Cheng Hanzhang's role and style when in charge of the column, see Chang Chechia, "Funü zazhi zhong de yishi weisheng guwen" [The medical advisory column in the *Ladies' Journal*], *Research on Women in Modern Chinese History* 12 (2004): 145–68.
39. For discussion on the configuration of modern menstrual care, ideas of women's health, and consumerism in Republican Shanghai, see Shing-ting Lin, "'Scientific' Menstruation: The Popularisation and Commodification of Female Hygiene in Republican China, 1910s–1930s," *Gender and History* 25(2) (2013): 294–316. For American medical development on menopause in the twentieth century, see Judith A. Houck, *Hot and Bothered: Women, Medicine and Menopause in Modern America* (Cambridge, MA: Harvard University Press,

but it was obvious that he saw a woman's reproductive years as the prime time of her life.

Men were supposed to practice abstinence to avoid STDs, and women were expected to learn to care for their reproductive body.[40] Such was the different sexual hygiene required of adolescent males and females. However, partly due to the breakdown of subjects into three volumes, no extant textbooks showed efforts to establish theoretical connections between anatomical knowledge and hygienic practices. It was not until right before the New Life movement that we see a holistic explanation of differences that put men and women on diverse ladders not only of social advancement but also in the civilizing process.

Sexual Difference as Reproductive Knowledge

Sexual differences were a given in physiology and hygiene education. Even textbooks without a chapter on reproduction would have listed physiological distinctions between the sexes. A man's smaller pelvis, lower level of fat, slower pulse, broader vocal cords, hence lower pitch, greater volumes of respiration, perspiration, and urination were always mentioned. Most textbooks would also point out that men breathe with the abdomen while women breathe with their chest, and some noted that men had bigger brains than women.[41]

Textbooks that followed the official directives to include sex would depict different developments in puberty. Men grew beards, and women, breasts. Boys were aggressive, and girls, shy and quiet. They would encounter various health issues because of their different bodily functions.[42] But most of these dissimilarities were listed separately in chapters on various systems and were not presented in relation to an overarching mechanism. One popular textbook writer, uniquely, started with the secretion system and argued for sexual differences in an essentialist manner.

2006), "'Endocrine Perverts' and 'Derailed Menopausics': Gender Transgressions and Mental Disturbances, 1897–1937," 40–57.

40. Cheng Hanzhang wrote several textbooks for different publishers, and his stress on reproductive hygiene was followed by some textbook writers. For instance, see Liu Huaizhu ed., *Chuzhong weishengxue*, emended by Zhou Zhongqi [Hygiene for junior highs] (Shanghai: Beixin shuju, 1933).

41. Song, Xinzhongxue jiaokeshu shengli weishengxue, 78.

42. For instance, see Zheng Mian, Gu Zhonghua, and Hua Fuxi, eds., *Chuzhong weisheng* [Junior high hygiene], rev. Hua Jucheng (Shanghai: Zhonghua shuju, 1933–1934), vol. 1, 83–84. In the book, the authors described men as strong in masculine buildup, perceptive abilities, pursuing long-term goals, and making friends, while women were weak in muscles, good at memory, full of compassion, and interested in cleaning.

Extant materials show that Xue Deyü (薛德焴) helped edit at least three textbooks and composed three more sets.[43] The long prefaces of his textbooks indicated that he taught at various institutes, including Zhejiang University, and was a recognized science educator in the lower Yangtze area. In one preface he claimed to have tested his drafts in several schools before sending the final version to print.[44] He attached a four-page preface in his first *Physiology and Hygiene for Junior Highs*, explaining his longtime concerns of science education and nearly three-year preparation for this set. He professed to have investigated the classroom environment, evaluated students' learning, and collected multiple materials before finalizing his publication.[45]

Xue's chapter on reproduction was highly structured, and the secretion system was proposed from the beginning to explain the following physiological, psychological, and pathological differences between the sexes. According to Xue, the internal secretion transformed a girl into a woman, and her bodily structures developed from that point to fulfill her reproductive function. Her chest was narrow but her breasts were big. She had short legs that would lower her center of gravity and make her stable. She was hence tranquil, if not motionless, fit for pregnancy and childbirth. Her social role should have adapted to her biological structures so that she could accomplish her responsibilities as a human being. A man was different. With a big face, broad shoulders, and long legs, he was built to be active and fit to fight and defend. Therefore, Xue concluded, "it is most suitable for a man to be the center of society, while a woman, the center of family."[46]

To support his argument on the gender division of labor, Xue described men with mostly upfront and positive terminology, such as strong bones and mighty muscles. Although women also needed strength to undertake the burden of reproduction, Xue did not portray them as "strong." Instead, he claimed that women's muscles were weak and they were prone to fatigue, painting an image sharply in contrast to the sturdy and fully developed chests, lungs, stomachs, tonsils, and mouths of men.

The strong and weak contrast was also depicted with regard to mental and pathological states, albeit in an "absentee" way of comparison. In presenting

43. Xue became a biology professor of East China Normal University in the 1950s. In addition to the textbook of Zhuang and Gong, published by the World Bookstore, Xue also edited two publications for Chen Yucang. See Chen Yucang, ed., *Chuzhong weisheng* [Hygiene for junior highs], rev. Xue Deyu (Shanghai and Nanjing: Zhengzhong shuju, 1935); Chen Yucang, ed., *Chuji zhongxue shengli weishengxue*, rev. Xue Deyu [Physiology and hygiene for junior highs] (Nanjing and Ganzhou: Zhengzhong shuju, 1936). The former based on the 1932 directives has three volumes and the latter based on the 1936 revised guidelines has only one volume.
44. Xue Deyu, *Beixin shengli weisheng* [Physiology and hygiene of Beixin Bookstore] (Shanghai: Beixin shuju, 1933).
45. Xue Deyu, *Chuzhong shengli weisheng* [Physiology and hygiene for junior highs] (Shanghai: Xinya shudian, 1932).
46. Ibid., 91–94.

mental features, Xue mentioned only the good and bad of women. After describing her incompetency with perception, application, and planning, her tendency to be emotional, her weak willpower but tenacity in subjective opinions, Xue stated that women were made for domestic activities. He did not analyze men's abilities, therefore giving an impression that there was not a thing that men were not good at or could not do and, as a matter of course, were fit to be the center of society. While presenting pathological differences, Xue provided conditional backgrounds for men's disorders but did not put women's diseases into social contexts and simply stated that women were easily subject to hysteria and tuberculosis, hence giving an impression that women were weak by constitution.

Xue Deyü's emphasis on male strength and female fragility was unparalleled. His was the first junior high textbook to argue for social roles from biology.[47] The paragraph on the gender division of labor was dropped in another set of three volumes that he published the following year, but he maintained his strategy to lead the narrative with the secretion system, which was central to the sexual differences. To strengthen his arguments, Xue emphasized that women were slower than men in physiological development. Their big head and broad forehead, soft muscles and fine skin, less frequent pulses and higher body temperature, and many other conditions were portrayed as evidence that women preserved more physiological features from childhood than men.[48]

The discussion of developmental lag echoed some earlier textbooks. Gu Shoubai (顧壽白), who returned from Japan with a medical doctor degree, published different sets of junior high *Physiology and Hygiene* in the 1920s.[49] None included a chapter on reproduction—not abiding by the official directives—but all elaborated on diverse characteristics of the sexes. Gu pointed out that animals had a keener sense of smell than humans, but "among humans, children had the keenest sense of smell, followed by women, while men were least sharp."[50] This statement had not appeared in textbooks before his but was copied by later work, and one author explained that the sense of smell differed with sexes, ages, and degrees of civilization: "Usually

---

47. Similar arguments were present in some contemporary publications on sex education. For instance, Zhou Jianren, the younger brother of Lu Xun, once talked about the gender division of labor from the onset of sperm, eggs, and conception in his book *Xing Jiaoyu* [Sex education] (Shanghai: Commercial Press, 1931). For discussions, see Dikötter, *Sex, Culture and Modernity*, "The Passive Sex: The Naturalization of Gender Distinctions," 14–61.

48. Xue Deyu, *Chuzhong weisheng* [Junior high hygiene] (Shanghai: Xinya shuju, 1933), "Physiological changes in puberty," 113–16.

49. Gu Shoubai, *Xiandai chuzhong jiaokeshu shengli weishengxue* [Modern junior high textbook of physiology and hygiene] (Shanghai: Commercial Press, 1923); and Gu Shoubai, *Xinzhuan chujizhongxue jiaokeshu shengli weishengxue* [New composition of junior high physiology and hygiene textbook] (Shanghai: Commercial Press, 1926).

50. Gu Shoubai, Xiandai chuzhong jiaokeshu, 143.

children are keener than adults, while women keener than men, and the savages keener than civilized people."[51]

To affiliate women with a more primitive or underdeveloped human stage corresponded with Xue Deyü's viewpoint. In addition to smell, Xue enlisted methods of breathing to show the difference between the savage and the civilized, claiming that, "among the civilized people, women breathe with the upper part of the lungs, while men breathe with the lower part. But there is no such difference among the savages." As for the reason for men and women to breathe differently, he referred to women's reproductive functions, explaining that "once pregnant, a woman's abdomen will inflate to press the diaphragm and cause difficulties in respiration." Since her chest was not as firm as a man's, "thoracic breathing—rib breathing is most suitable for her."[52]

Xue's essentialist perception led him to overlook the fact that savage women also reproduced, hence women were in general depicted as slower in advancing the civilizing process. Not all pedagogical writers subscribed to these biological overtones. To prevent readers from misunderstanding, one textbook reminded readers that men and women had no hierarchy in their intellectual power even though their brain capacity might differ.[53] Reinforcing the statements in the textbook, the accompanying teachers' manual cited J. B. Watson, founder of psychological school of behaviorism, to attribute women's seemingly underachievement in society to their marital choices and domestic responsibilities instead of any physiological or mental orientations.[54] Similar sociological explanations were followed up by several writers. Biological differences and gender equality, like the other pair of sexual anxiety and reproductive anatomy, existed in constant competition in junior high textbooks until the official directives set in again to remove all of them.

The reason given by the government was to lighten the heavy load on teenage students, but it also had the effect of lifting from publishers the burden of multivolume textbooks. The Ministry of Education revised the curricular guidelines twice before the end of the anti-Japanese war. Physiology and hygiene were reduced to one-third of their earlier capacity and were later extended again to a two-year program. Except that STDs were mentioned in the section of social hygiene, no knowledge on puberty development or reproductive organs was required. Embryology was touched upon slightly in the 1936 directives, and in 1941, well into the war, the section on

---

51. Zheng, Gu, and Hua, *Chuzhong weisheng*, vol. 1, 80.
52. Xue, Beixin shengli weisheng, 49.
53. Zhuang and Gong, *Chuzhong shengli weishengxue*, 223–24.
54. Ji Sihua, *Chuzhong shengli weisheng zhidaoshu* [Teachers' manual for junior high physiology and hygiene] (Shanghai: Shijie shuju, 1933), 223–24.

maternal and infant care was resumed, and a new one on "national hygiene" was implemented.[55]

At first, new publications still amounted to more than ten sets, but the numbers dropped visibly after Shanghai fell into Japanese hands.[56] Most textbooks faithfully kept silent on sex and reproduction. A few continued earlier interest in sexual differences, but the arguments were put in the context of national welfare, asking young men and women to take care of their health to fulfill their respective responsibilities.[57] The focus was no longer on puberty sexuality but on preserving posterity. This was perhaps the first time since the creation of secondary education in China that commercial print houses complied so closely with official directives with regard to sex education.

Commercial Presses Following Official Norms—or Not

Politics affected business, including print houses, and government support was crucial to textbook publication in many aspects. A Chinese student in Tokyo once filed an application to the Qing authority for copyright protection. This student, who later became president of Peking University, was at the time working with friends to translate science textbooks for the surfacing middle school program and found no stronger help other than from the court.[58] The Shanghai Commercial Press, established in 1897, gained imperial favor not only for its pioneering technology but also for its sympathy with monarchical ideology.[59] When it stumbled over the establishment of the Republic, the Chinese Bookstore, founded in 1912, became a powerful rival. The latter's founder, Lubi Kui, an advocate for revolutionary education, made clear more than once that profitable Chinese print capitalism required the presence of the state. Lacking the resources available to its predecessors,

---

55. The first revision in 1936 came shortly before the Nationalist government pulled out completely from Shanghai, and another one in 1941 announced right before the Pacific War broke out. For curriculum guidelines and course descriptions of these two directives, see Kecheng jiaocai yanjiusuo, *Ershi shiji Zhongguo*, vol. 1, 105–7.
56. Before Japan declared war against the West in December 1941, Shanghai relied on the Concession Authorities and enjoyed certain prosperity as an "isolated island" for about four years.
57. See Yuan Shunda, *Chuzhong xin shengli weisheng* [New physiology and hygiene for junior highs] (Shanghai: Shijie shuju, 1936), 89–96. And Mao Zhengwei, *Weishengxue* [Hygiene] (Shanghai: Commercial Press, 1936) went further to include a section on maternal and infant care before the official directives required it in 1941.
58. This was Ho Yushi, who led a student society in Tokyo to translate both Euro-American and Japanese scientific materials for Chinese secondary schools. Their application was granted, and Ho printed the official copyright letter on the first pages of his textbook. See Joel Dorman Steele, *Zhongxue shengli jiaokeshu* [Physiology for middle schools], trans. Ho Yushi (Tokyo: Kyōkasho henyakusha, 1902).
59. For a short introduction of the Shanghai Commercial Press, see Dai Ren (Jean-Pierre Drege), *Shanghai Shangwu Yinshuguan, 1897–1949* [La commercial press de Shanghai 1897–1949], trans. Li Tongshi (Beijing: Commercial Press, 2000).

the World Bookstore, which started in 1921, emerged as a third competitor in the Shanghai textbook war through strategies including printing Nationalist propaganda.[60]

But the Chinese state was not always strong, and recognition of its authority differed in levels and formats. None of the earliest Republican directives were left to us, but there must have been some basic requirements because a few textbooks confirmed in their prefaces that they "adopted the three-system arrangement from official prescriptions."[61] Others would state in the editorial notes that the press followed the ministry's guidelines to set the sequences by adding practical, however brief, hygiene information to each chapter of various physiological systems.[62] Some publishers would print official reviews on the back cover to show their legitimacy, particularly for textbooks revised from late Qing editions.[63]

The Shanghai Commercial Press, to stay on top of the competition, did just that. Mishima Michiyoshi's textbook was first translated into Chinese in the very last year of the Qing dynasty, and the revised twenty-second edition came out when the new school system was just implemented. To validate its authority across different regimes, the Commercial Press printed the latest comments from the Ministry of Education, assuring that "[a]ll the revisions are appropriate. The publisher displays cautious devotion and should be complimented. This textbook is approved to be continuously used for middle and normal schools."[64]

Such practices were dropped later in the Nanjing decade. Instead, up to two-thirds of the textbooks acknowledged in the editorial notes that the contents were written according to official standards, confirming the norm of government directives. Growing authority of the education office can also be seen in the use of nomenclature. Earlier authors struggled with translation of technical terminology; many inserted original English or French for verification. Some even put horizontal Latin terms in the vertically printed

60. For the textbook war in Shanghai and the different policies of the three presses, see Reed, *Gutenberg in Shanghai*, 203–56, particularly pp. 215, 252, and 255.
61. For instance, Gu Shusen, ed., *Xinzhi shenglixue jiaoben* [Physiology textbook for new school system], reviewed Wu Jiaxu (Shanghai: Zhonghua shuju, 1917), editorial notes.
62. Hua Wenqi ed., *Zhonghua zhongxue shengli jiaokeshu* [Chinese Bookstore's physiology and hygiene textbook for junior highs], reviewed Dai Kedun, Yao Hanzhang, and Lubi Kui, 1913 (Shanghai: Zhonghua shuju, 1921). Quotes from the extant 18th edition. Also see Wang Jianshan, *Shengli ji weishengxue*, editorial notes.
63. For instance, to advertise for its 10th edition in 1912, Wenming shuju printed the official comments, "This book has correct forms and clear translation, therefore is approved as textbook for middle and normal schools" for Kure Shuzo, *Zhongxue shengli weisheng jiaokeshu* [Physiology and hygiene textbook for middle schools], trans. Hua Shenqi and Hua Wenqi, 1906 (Shanghai: Wenming shuju, 1912).
64. Others such as Du Yaquan and Ling Changhuan, eds., *Gongheguo jiaokeshu shenglixue* [Physiology textbook for the Republic], 1914 (Shanghai: Commercial Press, 1923), also printed official approval in its copyright page for legitimacy and for advertisement.

Chinese texts, which made the pages looked rather disordered.[65] Others
used either a glossary or comparison tables but still felt compelled to explain
time and again their choices of words.[66] In the 1930s, most of these practices
were gone. Authors like Xue Deyü took pride in their erudite preparation;
Xue noted that he consulted Cousland's *English-Chinese Medical Lexicon* in
addition to suggestions from the ministerial office. Others would simply
apply nomenclature finalized by the official review board without additional
references.[67]

Even in the 1930s, however, not all official norms were carefully followed,
and the most obvious discrepancy was the authors' ignoring the regulation
to teach sex. Some completely omitted the subject,[68] another mentioned the
importance of reproduction in passing without concrete content, while others
did provide a chapter for reproductive physiology but deleted all of the
required information on puberty.[69] This could have reflected certain authors'
peculiar positions and professions. For prolific writers who published
with more than one company, it could also have been marketing strategy
to attract readers of diverse interest and concerns. Take Cheng Hanzhang,
for example. In addition to the idiosyncratic textbooks mentioned earlier, he
wrote another three volumes the same year for Dadong Bookstore. Unlike

---

65. For instance, see Wu Bingxin, ed., *Shiyong jiaokeshu shengli weishengxue* [Practical textbook
    of physiology and hygiene], emended by Ling Changhuan, 1915 (Shanghai: Commercial
    Press, 1926).
66. For instance, Xie Honglai, a prolific Christian translator, started with an apologetic legend
    to demonstrate his knowledge base and to explain his reasons to follow Japanese precedent
    seiri to render "physiology" into the Chinese *shengli*. He appended a table of glossary at
    the end of his textbook. See Joel Dorman Steele, *Shenglixue* [Physiology], trans. Xie Honglai
    (Shanghai: Commercial Press, 1904), preface. For recent research on terminology, see Yuan
    Yuan, *Jindai shenglixue zai Zhongguo* [Modern physiology in China, 1851–1926] (Shanghai:
    Renmin chubanshe, 2010), 153–70, on translation of physiological nomenclature.
67. See Xue, *Chuzhong shengli weisheng*, 4. In his 1933 set of three volumes, Xue actually dropped
    Cousland's title and stuck only to the terminologies announced by the official review board.
    But still, for fear that some of the nomenclatures were not well known enough, he appended
    a glossary at the end of his books. See Xue, *Chuzhong weisheng*, 2. For P. B. Cousland's effort
    and contribution to Chinese translation of physiological terms, see Zhang Daqing, "P. B.
    Cousland—a Promoter for the Standardization of Medical Nomenclature," *China Historical
    Materials of Science and Technology* 22(4) (2001): 324–30.
68. For instance, Mi Zanzhi coedited two different textbooks with Hua Wenqi in 1930; neither
    contained a reproductive chapter. Their volumes, however, listed quite a few physiology
    works from Europe, the United States, and Japan. Several Japanese textbooks quoted by Mi
    and Hua were also used in colonial Taiwan, and they too did not include any information
    about sexuality and reproduction.
69. Some did include a few reproductive information but did not follow the official guidelines,
    see, for instance, Cheng Shijie, *Shengli weisheng* [Physiology and hygiene] (Tianjin: Baicheng
    shuju, 1932); and Zhu Maoting, *Renti shengli weishengxue* [Physiology and hygiene of the
    human body] (Nanjing: Nanjing shudian, 1932).

the former set, Cheng arranged this one with an order and contents exactly following the official directives.[70]

It is noteworthy that the founders of Dadong and World Bookstores were members of the same family. Both had official affiliations, and Dadong printed currency for the Nationalist government.[71] We do not know for sure whether Cheng stuck to official norms to comply with the company's policy, but the increasing pressure of governmental influence was identifiable. In 1930, the Nationalist bureaucrats required all Shanghai publishers to join the comprehensive government-directed trade association, and in 1933 the government-run Zhengzhong Bookstore was created to compete with independent Shanghai publishers.[72]

This was right before the inception of the New Life movement, in which habituating hygienic practices was integrated into a moral revolution project and individual regimens were perceived as reflecting a person's public virtues.[73] This was also a time when Euro-American governments were calling their female citizens back to domestic responsibilities, and the Chinese intellectuals enthusiastically argued about such ideas. To deploy human resources for more effective control, the Nationalist government promoted "new virtuous wives and good mothers" in response and created even further debates on women's sociopolitical roles.[74]

Amid this antifeminist rhetoric, Xue Deyü may have considered the gendered division of labor a way to maximize societal strength, particularly if founded on physiological differences. His proposal was included in the 1932 Xinya textbook; although the specific paragraph was dropped in the 1933 version, its biological reasoning remained. However, neither of these

---

70. Cheng Hanzhang, *Chuzhong weisheng jiaoben* [Junior high hygiene textbook] (Shanghai: Dadong shuju, 1933).
71. The World Bookstore was created by Shen Zhifang, a former Commercial Press and Zhonghua employee. His nephew Shen Junsheng was a founder and board member of Dadong shuju, established in 1916. See Reed, *Gutenberg in Shanghai*, 244, 283.
72. For ramifications after the Nationalist set up government in Nanjing in 1928, see Reed, *Gutenberg in Shanghai*, 223–24. Zhengzhong shuju remained an important textbook publisher throughout the war and also after the Nationalist government moved to Taiwan in 1949.
73. For personal discipline as hygienic practice in the New Life movement, see Hsiang-lin Lei, "Habituating the Four Virtues: Ethics, Family and the Body in the Anti-tuberculosis Campaigns and the New Life Movement," *Bulletin of the Institute of Modern History, Academia Sinica* 74 (2011): 133–77.
74. For Euro-American promotion of women's domesticity between the wars and during the Great Depression, see Anne-Marie Sohn, "Between the Wars in France and England," trans. Arthur Goldhammer, in *A History of Women in the West*, ed. Françoise Thébaud et al. (Cambridge, MA: Harvard University Press, 1996), 92–119. For Chinese intellectuals' debates on women's roles and the Nationalist government's policies, see Xu Huiqi, "Guoxinshenghuo, zuoxinnüxin: Xunzheng shiqi guomin zhengfu dui shidai nüxin xingxiang de suzao" [Living a new life, being a new woman: The image-making of the modern ideal woman by the KMT government in the Nanjing decade], *Taidai Wenshizhe xuebao* [Humanitas Taiwanica] 62 (2005): 277–320.

was printed in his 1933 Beixin textbook.[75] Two speculations come to mind. As Xue claimed that he ran several test teachings for the Beixin edition before finalizing its contents, one suspects that his views on gender, though corresponding with governmental policy, may not have been wholeheartedly welcomed by his trial readers. Meanwhile, since Xinya was a government-affiliated press, whereas Beixin was famous for its printing of Lu Xun's works and for advocating New Culture ideals, one wonders whether the latter took an interest in sustaining the cause of women's liberation to the extent that it affected the layout of junior high textbooks.[76]

Whichever is the case, a general survey suggests that commercial presses followed official directives inadvertently and accepted Nationalist propaganda eclectically. To continue their business, profits were their primary concern. Ministerial recognition was important advertisement, but diverse components to attract different readers seemed also to be at work. Among various strategies to balance between governmental requirements and social expectations with regard to scientific knowledge, illustration was another field of extrapolation for textbook competition.

Visualizing Gendered Physiology

Pictorial presentations were considered essential to teach Chinese students a whole set of body knowledge coming from the West. A late Qing author recommended microscopes for observing muscles and tissues but was practical enough to suggest quality paper models of the human body as substitutes. To make it easier for instructors, he included in his textbook information of traders and prices as well as latest Japanese productions in Shanghai.[77]

Quite a few authors took pride in their chosen images, and publishers bragged about their best prints. The Shanghai Commercial Press boasted of the value of Mishima's translation, with more than seventy illustrations. Wang Jianshan inserted a number of visual genres including microscopic images of cells and germs, anatomical depictions of internal organs, line drawings for emergency rescue, and photographs showing the New York City government handling public sanitation.[78]

Shanghai's Chinese Bookstore was also proud of its pedagogical materials such as maps, pictures, and sculptures. On the back page of Song Chongyi's book, the publisher announced a project to produce human and

---

75. See Xue, *Chuzhong shengli weisheng*, 91–94; Xue, *Chuzhong weisheng*, "Physiological changes in puberty," 113–16. Also Xue, *Beixin shengli weisheng*.

76. Xinya bookstore, established around 1925, published educational aids, primary and secondary school science textbooks, and semiofficial Nationalist Party publications. Beixin Bookstore, established in 1924 in Beijing, was forced out and relocated in Shanghai in 1926. See Reed, *Gutenberg in Shanghai*, 282, 287.

77. Steele, *Shenglixue*, teaching notes, 7–8.

78. Wang Jianshan, Shengli ji weishengxue.

animal physiology replicas. It claimed to have sent a team to Germany, the most advanced country in modern medicine, to buy and bring back the latest models. The team then disassembled the models, learned all the details, and made revised, less expensive ones in China for educational, medical, and domestic uses.[79] Such was the advertisement to show the resources and technology of the Chinese Bookstore. Unfortunately, we do not have any three-dimensional teaching apparatus from this period, so do not know whether these models included the reproductive system.

Fortunately, Song Chongyi did include six images in his reproductive chapter. He did not provide citations, but, from references of similar images in other publications, we know that they were borrowed from Euro-American textbooks for medical colleges.[80] Echoing Song's balanced treatment of men and women in the texts, the six images were also equally divided between the sexes. This was not necessarily the case for later writers, who, although caught in an anxiety of male sexuality, would use many more pictures to explain the female reproductive system. However, all of Song's illustrations were of cells and organs, corresponding to his, and perhaps the publisher's, interest in anatomy. This style was actually followed by most junior high textbooks of physiology and hygiene, thus rendering visual representation of sex education almost identical with reproductive biology.

In addition to images cited from Western publications, a few authors seemed to have prepared their own illustrations. Different drawings of the dissected penis, womb, and breasts were printed.[81] Many were not referenced nor seen in other textbooks. Only Xue Deyü bothered to thank his illustrator friend for helping with the drawings, confirming local support for visual materials.[82]

Xue's observation also provides us with some reality of the teaching fields amid the boasts of quality images. He described the shabby classrooms with neither human models nor hanging diagrams and criticized students'

79. Song, *Xinzhongxue jiaokeshu shengli weishengxue*.
80. Guo Renyuan included similar images in his textbook published by World Bookstore in 1929 and provided original references. See Guo Renyuan, "Womende shenti senme laide ne," in *Chuzhong ziran kexue*. The ones from Karl Joseph Eberth (1835–1926) and Stihr-Tewis were copied by later writers such as Zhuang Weizhong, Gong Angyun, and Liu Huaizhu. Other Western medical college textbooks excerpted by early Republican writers include Edwin Grant Conklin (1863–1952), *Heredity and Environment in the Development of Men* (Princeton: Princeton University Press, 1915); and James Clifton Edger (1859–1939), *The Practice of Obstetrics, Designed for the Use of the Students of Medicine and Practitioners* (Philadelphia: P. Blakiston's Son, 1903).
81. See Zhu Maoting, *Renti shengli weishengxue*; and Cheng Hanzhang, *Weishengxue*. In addition to Zhu and Cheng, Cao Fei and Wei Chunzhi also provided unprecedented and unreferenced images. See Cao Fei, ed., *Chuzhong shiyong shengli weishengxue* [Practical physiology and hygiene for junior highs], reviewed Chen Lieguan, 1928 (Changsha: Fenfengguan, 1948). See also Wei, *Shengli weishengxue*.
82. This is noted in a later edition of his textbooks. See Xue Deyu, *Chuzhong shengli weishengxue* [Junior high physiology and hygiene] (Shanghai: Zhongguo kexue tushu yiqi gongsi, 1949).

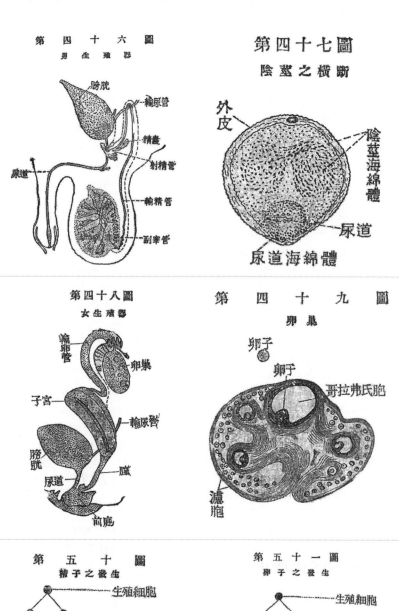
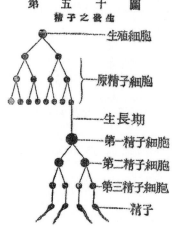
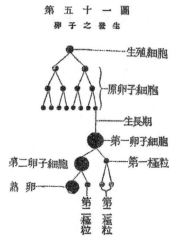

Figure 2.1
Song Chongyi's illustrations (1923)

inability to point out the positions of internal organs. To relieve learners from poor, small pictures in the textbooks, Xue made a separate pamphlet in which he not only expanded sketches of bones, muscles, and different organs but also "tried to connect them with each other as in reality." The brochure was sold alongside the textbook in hopes that students would read them at their convenience and "unwittingly remember the parts and names of the anatomical body."[83]

Regrettably, the pamphlet was not left in any of the extant collections, and we can only guess from a much later version what Xue had provided for his readers. In a 1949 textbook, he explained that due to time pressure he had had to reduce the text to its utmost simplicity but made every effort to include the latest, most correct, and meaningful images to substantiate the texts. In this single volume of fewer than one hundred pages, Xue spent eight pages to introduce the reproductive system and inserted ten illustrations.[84]

Among the ten, only three exhibited the male systems. A woman's body, instead of a man's, was illustrated to show the location of internal organs. This presentation echoed Xue's earlier evaluation of how students learned and confirmed his emphasis on women's reproductive responsibilities. Another unprecedented picture was a maturing breast, showing decisive changes between the ages of eleven and sixteen, further demonstrating his concerns with puberty as a life stage that transformed men and women into different beings.

Xue's presentation carried on the pictorial tradition since Song Chongyi. Eight out of his ten images depicted anatomical details of the reproductive organs, none relating to sexual hygiene. It was not until the Nationalist government moved to Taiwan after the war that we see cartoons and other visual categories used to present gender relations and concerning behaviors in junior high textbooks.[85] For early Republican writers, to focus on internal organs and to refrain from relational portrayals appeared to serve their purpose better.

Xue's illustrations of the female torso, however, signaled another creative teaching method in the 1930s. We do not know whether his separate pamphlet included nude figures, but a few contemporary writers did provide such images for students to either locate or to memorize bones, muscles, and internal organs of the body.[86] Guo Renyuan, who usually listed

---

83. This pair of book and pictures was published by Xinya in 1932. See Xue, *Chuzhong shengli weisheng*, preface, 2–3. But Xue mentioned the problems of images in his other textbooks as well. See also Xue, *Chuzhong weisheng*, "Guidelines," 1.
84. Xue, *Chuzhong shengli weishengxue*.
85. See Lee Jen-der, "Taiwan shengli weisheng jiaoyu zhong de xing, shengzhi yu xingbie," 109–13.
86. For nudity in China as legitimate presentation of human body through arts and sciences, see discussion by Wu Fang-cheng, "Luode liyou: Ershi shiji chuqi Zhongguo renti xiesheng

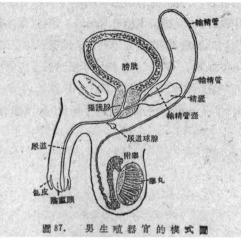

圖87. 男生殖器官的模式圖

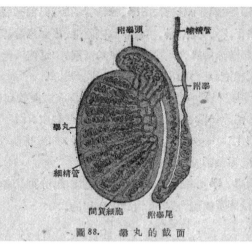

圖88. 睾丸的截面

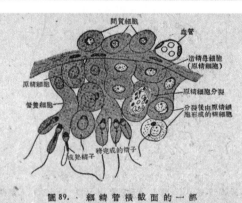

圖89. 細精管橫截面的一部

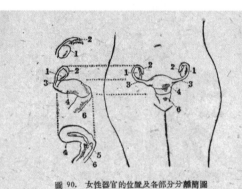

圖90. 女性器官的位置及各部分分離簡圖
1.卵巢 2.輸卵管的開口 3.輸卵管 4.子宮 5.子宮口 6.陰道

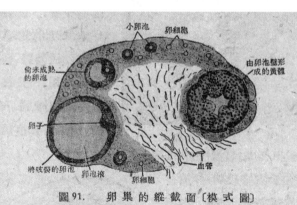

圖91. 卵巢的縱截面〔模式圖〕

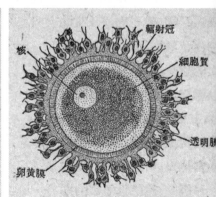

圖92. 卵子〔圍於許多卵泡細胞〕

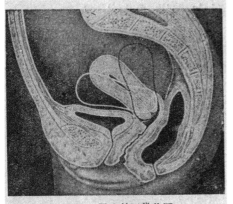

圖 93. 子宮的正常位置
〔白線是前傾，黑線是後傾，都不正常．〕

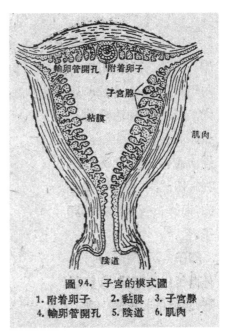

圖 94. 子宮的模式圖
1. 附着卵子　　2. 黏膜　　3. 子宮腺
4. 輸卵管開孔　5. 陰道　　6. 肌肉

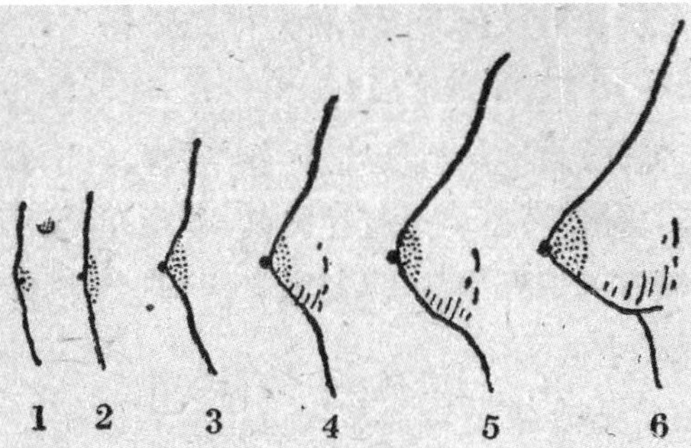

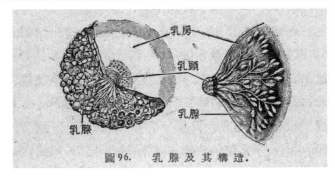

圖 95. 女子乳房發育的輪廓.
1. 四個月　2. 五歲　3. 十歲　4. 十一歲　5. 十六歲　6. 成人

圖 96. 乳腺及其構造.

Figure 2.2

Xue Deyü's illustrations (1949)

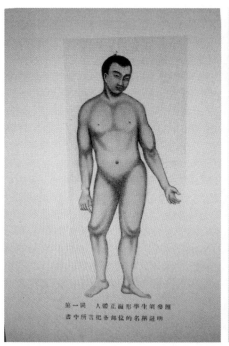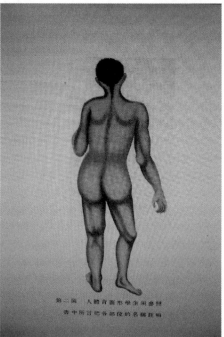

Figure 2.3
Guo Renyuan's pair of nude figures (1929 / 1930)

Western references for his illustrations, included a pair in his textbook, only this time without citations.

Zhuang Weizhong (莊畏仲) and Gong Angyun (龔昂雲), who used mostly the same images as Guo, applied another pair of nude figures in their first pages. This pair was not given original references either but was copied three year later in yet another volume.[87] All three textbooks were published by the World Bookstore, and the authors noted that nudity was useful to provide space for marking down body parts.

Learning through nude figures was not the only way, however, and the practice of not giving credits ran across publishers who competed over pedagogical innovations. Gu Shoubai, who took pride in his generous use of illustrations, offered in his textbook more than 160 black-and-white images as well as several big color ones.[88] One of his experimental devices was to attach a set of two photos, showing the front and back of a nude man. He then covered the photos with transparent papers and marked the names of muscles across the figure. When readers opened the textbook and flattened

---

wentide taolun" [Questions concerning nude figure drawing in China at the beginning of the twentieth century], *Xinshixue* [New History] 15(2) (2004): 55–113.

87. Yuan Shunda, *Chuzhong xin shengli weisheng.*

88. Gu Shoubai, *Kaiming shengli weishengxue jiaoben.*

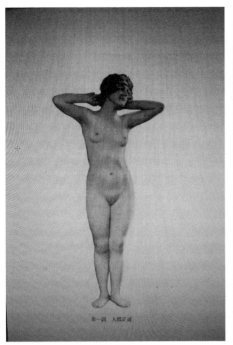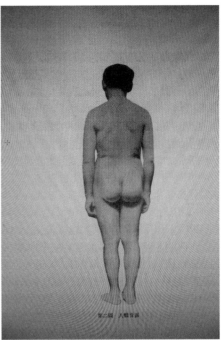

Figure 2.4
Zhuang Weizhong and Gong Angyun, pair of nude figures (1933)

the transparent paper from the left to the right, they could easily check the corresponding muscles with the photos. Such creative method and materials had not been seen thus far and were not inherited as a whole set by later publications. Instead, a simplified line-drawing appeared three years later; the clear, nude Caucasian male was deleted, with no credit given to Gu's original.[89]

To put all these images together, the deliberate choice to show nudity with both gender and ethnicity is fascinating. To take Guo Renyuan's pair, for example, the front image appeared to be an Asian man, but his genitals were intentionally made opaque. Since Guo did include anatomical images in his reproductive chapter, one wonders whether the blurring was done not to withhold sexual information but to preserve a kind of decency. If that was the concern, then decency may have been reserved only for Asian figures, particularly for Chinese women.

In fact, most Asian or Chinese women in the textbook illustrations were well dressed, even wearing cheongsam in some cases. If a woman's chests

---

89. Chen Yucang used Gu Shoubai's figures twice, in 1936 and in 1949, but neither presented the whole set nor provided reference or a credit line. See Chen, *Chuji zhongxue shengli weishengxue*; and Chen Yucang ed., *Shengli weisheng* [Physiology and hygiene], rev. Zhou Jianren, 2nd ed. (Changchun: Northeast Xinhua bookstore, 1949).

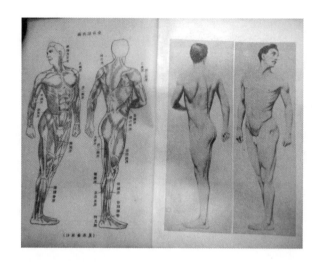

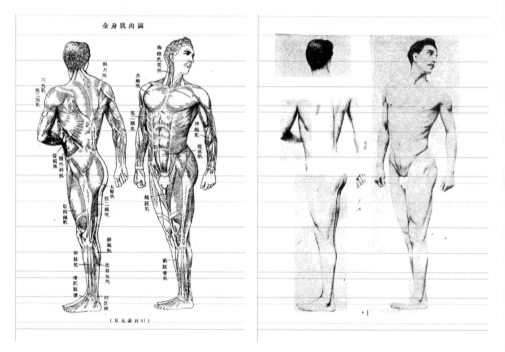

Figure 2.5
Gu Shoubai's photographic illustrations of a nude man and muscles

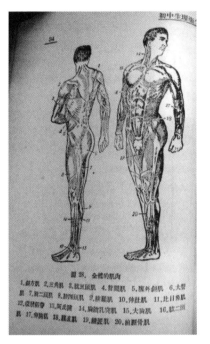

Figure 2.6
Chen Yucang and Xue Deyü, simplified
image of muscles

or abdomen was needed to depict the damage of breast-binding, the respiration system, or in Xue Deyü's case to locate the reproductive organs, only
the torso but not the face would be shown.[90] Male nudity, with some reserva-
tions, was all right for Asians, but female nudity, with no exception, could
be represented only by Caucasians. In the borrowing and appropriation of
visual materials between rivals, gendered physiology accompanied ethnic
choices of presentations.

Conclusion

Many have researched sex and sexuality of Republican China, but few have
touched upon related education in schools. Historians have studied textbooks, but none have investigated those designed to teach teenagers about
sexuality and their bodies. This chapter delves into the course materials of
physiology and hygiene of junior highs and identifies the contents of sex
education in early twentieth-century China. A number of features can be
found after our preliminary survey, and the most obvious would be the competition for attention between sexuality and reproduction throughout the
setting up and revisions of official directives and textbook publications.

---

90. For instance, Zheng Mian's illustrations "Breathing Styles" and "Postures in Sitting,
    Standing and Walking," in Zheng, Gu, and Hua, *Chuzhong weisheng*. Also Zhuang Weizhong
    and Gong Angyun's illustrations "Comparison of Chest and Organs" and "Correct Posture
    in Walking," in Zhuang and Gong, *Chuzhong shengli weishengxue*.

After the establishment of a new school system in 1922, an independent chapter on reproduction was required in junior high physiology and hygiene textbooks. The official directives were revised several times, in 1929, 1932, 1936, and 1941. Although the physiology part remained focused on the reproductive organs, the hygiene sections shifted between puberty behaviors and postpartum care.

To read in the context of physiological systems, one would expect a chapter on reproduction to include at least conception, pregnancy, and delivery. But neither the official directives nor available textbooks were comprehensive in that regard. Instead, discussion of puberty often aimed at curtailing desires, and syphilis instead of infant mortality was lamented as a national disaster in junior high learning. Sex education was thus directed toward abstinence in the name of reproductive knowledge, but the sheer emphasis on self-restraint somehow rendered detailed anatomical presentations irrelevant to sexual hygiene.

Tan Sitong, the nineteenth-century revolutionary, emphasized the importance of visual materials in curtailing wax human model, with its revealing nature, would help the purposes even further, Tan confirmed.[91] Using not only prints but also stereoscopic presentations, Tan seemed to have heralded an ideal sex education, but early Republican writers apparently did not go along with his approach of abstinence. Their illustrations on reproduction portrayed mostly separate, dissected organs, with more associated with female than male. The limited nude figures for memorizing body parts were of Caucasians, more men than women.

This ran across the wide spectrum of writers and publishers: college professors, practicing gynecologists, normal school teachers, journalists, and Christian writers returning from England, the United States, Germany, and Japan with both science and nonscience degrees devoted themselves to writings on physiology and hygiene. After the unification of the Nationalist government, pioneering Shanghai publishers, Shangwu, Zhonghua, and Shijie, were joined by many other companies as well as science communities in big cities to compete for textbook business.[92]

Quite a few authors accepted invitations from various presses, and, to distinguish their own work from others, they arranged contents differently, often based on their professional interests to the effect of not abiding with the ministerial directives. Gynecology-oriented authors focused on women's lifelong health, downplaying the official prescription on adolescent sexuality. A biology professor found the secretion system more useful than anatomical information to integrate physiology, psychology, and pathology into

---

91. Tan Sitong, *Renxue* [On humanity] (Taipei: Taiwan Xuesheng shuju, 1998).
92. Among the extant eighty-some sets, quite a few were published by bookstores, journal companies, and science communities in Nanjing, Peking, Tianjin, Chongqing, Changsha, and Ganzhou. See Wang Youpeng, *Zhongguo jindai zhongxiaoxue*, 753–61.

the mechanism of sexual differences, so much so that a gendered division of labor was proposed to fulfill both personal responsibilities and to echo contemporary political rhetoric. Not all textbook writers endorsed such elaboration despite governmental promotions, and the zigzag between sexual differences and gender equality became a noteworthy parallel to the tug-of-war between sexuality and reproduction.

3
From Single Motherhood to Queer Reproduction

Access Politics of Assisted Conception in Taiwan

Chia-ling Wu

Introduction

Precisely who can become a parent through assisted reproductive technology (ART)? ARTs such as in vitro fertilization (IVF), donor insemination (DI), and surrogacy separate procreation from sexuality and thus create new possibilities for building unconventional kinship and family, as well as new gender orders and relationships. As feminist scholarship has pointed out, the practice and use of ART shed light on how society imagines and enables the creation of the family and of the next generation, all of which is deeply intertwined with the politics of gender, sexuality, and heteronormativity.[1] Many countries have been faced with making a policy decision on who should have access to ART, and they have often based their decision on discrete and exclusive categories such as marital status and sexual orientation.[2] Such selection policies are a fertile entry point when it comes to assessing the characteristics of sociality that govern ART.

Globally, the regulations addressing access to ART are moving toward liberalization, and increasing numbers of countries do not restrict its use to married, heterosexual couples alone. However, after the Muslim world, (South)East Asia is the second–most prominent region where ART eligibility criteria are based strictly on marital status. According to the latest survey by the International Federation of Fertility Societies (IFFS), among the sixty-two

---

1. See Faye. D. Ginsburg and Rayna Rapp, eds., *Conceiving the New World Order: The Global Politics of Reproduction* (Berkeley: University of California Press, 1995); Sarah Franklin, *Embodied Progress: A Cultural Account of Assisted Conception* (London: Routledge, 1997); Marcia C. Inhorn, *Local Babies, Global Science: Gender, Religion, and In-vitro Fertilization in Egypt* (New York: Routledge, 2003); Charis Thompson, *Making Parents: The Ontological Choreography of Reproductive Technologies* (Cambridge, MA: MIT Press, 2005); Marcia C. Inhorn and Daphna Birenbaum-Carmeli, "Assisted Reproductive Technologies and Culture Change," *Annual Review of Anthropology* 37 (2008): 177–96.
2. Ken Daniels and Karyn Taylor, "Formulating Selection Policies for Assisted Reproduction," *Social Science and Medicine* 37(12) (1993): 1473–80.

countries and regions surveyed, only fourteen countries specify married couples as the only eligible treatment group. The IFFS thus concludes that the "[s]trict requirement of marriage is reported to be present in a small number of countries, mainly Islamic and Southeast Asian,"[3] the Asian countries or regions include China, Hong Kong, Japan, South Korea, Taiwan, the Philippines, and Singapore. Whereas there is a rich scholarship examining ART regulation in the Muslim world,[4] little has been done to explore this Asian phenomenon.[5] To bridge the gap, this chapter takes Taiwan as a case study and investigates the regulatory trajectory of ART eligibility there.

Taiwan's dynamic political scene provides fertile ground when it comes to examining the debate over access to ART. Taiwan has, from the first ethical guidelines in 1986 to the Human Reproduction Law in 2007, continued to prohibit unmarried women and men from using ART. While state regulation seems to legitimize the privileges accorded to heterosexual marriage, the Taiwan LGBT Family Rights Advocacy has, since the mid-2000s, openly advocated the self-insemination by lesbians of donated sperm. Their 2010 publication *Building a Family: Childbearing Guidebook for Lesbians* was the first such book ever to be published in an East Asian country. The coexistence of strict state regulation and this kind of radical ART advocacy in Taiwan enriches our understanding of the interplay of gender, sexuality, and heterosexuality throughout the regulatory trajectory of access to ART.

The tension between the conventional statute and the practices of "gender outlaws,"[6] those who break the gendered order of institutional norms, also reminds us to take a "technoscientific governance" approach instead of the tradition policy analysis approach. Traditional policy study usually limits its scope to formal policy making and policy makers. By comparison, technoscientific governance emphasizes the broader spectrum of

---

3. Steven J. Ory and Paul Devroey, ed., *IFFS Surveillance 2013* (International Federation of Fertility Societies, 2013), 31, accessed February 24, 2014, http://c.ymcdn.com/sites/www. iffs-reproduction.org/resource/resmgr/iffs_surveillance_09-19-13.pdf.

4. Inhorn, *Local Babies, Global Science*; Marcia C. Inhorn, "'He Won't Be My Son': Middle Eastern Muslim Men's Discourses of Adoption and Gamete Donation," *Medical Anthropology Quarterly* 20(1) (2006): 94–120; Marcia C. Inhorn, "Making Muslim Babies: IVF and Gamete Donation in Sunni and Shi'a Islam," *Culture, Medicine, and Psychiatry* 30 (2006): 427–50; Marcia C. Inhorn, *Cosmopolitan Conceptions: IVF Sojourns in Global Dubai* (Durham, NC: Duke University Press, 2015).

5. For a few exceptions, see Azumi Tsuge, "How Society Responds to Desires of Childless Couples: Japan's Position on Donor Conception," *Meijigakuin Daigakuin Shakaigakubu Fuzokukenkyusho Nenpo* [Bulletin of Institute of Sociology and Social Work, Meiji Gakuin University] 35 (2005): 21–34; Chia-Ling Wu, "Managing Multiple Masculinities in Donor Insemination: Doctors Configuring Infertile Men and Sperm Donors in Taiwan," *Sociology of Health and Illness* 33(1) (2011): 96–113.

6. Kate Bornstein, *Gender Outlaw: On Men, Women, and the Rest of Us* (New York: Routledge, 1994).

regulatory mechanisms, wider relevant actors, and more specific pathways.[7] In terms of ART regulation, Robert Blank offers a framework to include a spectrum of regulatory mechanisms—ranging from individual clinicians' own criteria, to professional association guidelines, and to governmental guidelines on statutory regulations—and thus avoids confining "regulation" within a narrow, legal definition.[8] Inhorn further extends the regulatory actors from experts (such as medical professionals, bioethics experts, and governmental officials) to the general public. She argues that we must consider "non-official" moral practice in the local moral world if we are to fully capture the moral landscape.[9] This is particularly important in analyzing the case of Taiwan, where civil society has challenged state regulation and practiced civil disobedience.

This chapter therefore examines both the making of statutory regulation so as to exclude the unmarried and the less visible practice of access politics in other parts of the moral landscape. How do state and society define who are the "appropriate" users of ART? What are their rationales? How do these diverse governing activities validate, challenge, or shape the social relationships that, I will argue, feature at the intersection of gender, sexuality, and heteronormativity?

The Intersection of Gender, Sexuality, and Heteronormativity

Feminist scholarship examines the politics of access to ART first of all from a gender perspective. Longer-established ART techniques such as DI had the potential to threaten the patriarchal gender order:[10] with DI, women can conceive with donated sperm, without having sexual intercourse with men—DI disrupted the triangular association among sex, marriage, and reproduction.[11] Some of the strategies arose in response to DI to help to safeguard those threatened hegemonic masculinities.

The extreme example of this would be the prohibition of DI under all circumstances, including for infertile married couples, since reproduction absent of a husband's sexuality could be argued to violate the husband's

---

7. Alan Irwin, "STS Perspectives on Scientific Governance," in *The Handbook of Science and Technology Studies*, ed. Edward J. Hackett, Olga Amsterdamska, Michael Lynch, and Judy Wajcman, 3rd ed. (Cambridge, MA: MIT Press, 2008), 583–607.

8. Robert Blank, "Regulation of Donor Insemination," in *Donor Insemination: International Social Science Perspectives*, ed. Ken Daniels and Erica Haimes (Cambridge: Cambridge University Press, 1998), 131–50.

9. Inhorn, *Local Babies, Global Science*.

10. Patricia Spallone, *Beyond Conception: The New Politics of Reproduction* (London: Macmillan, 1989).

11. Erica Haimes, "Recreating the Family? Policy Considerations Relating to the 'New Reproductive Technologies,'" in *The New Reproductive Technologies*, ed. Maureen McNeil, Ian Varcoe, and Steven Yearley (New York: St. Martin's Press, 1990), 154–72.

patriarchy and blood-based patrilineage.[12] If DI is allowed, it is first limited to married couples, with doctors and policy makers adjusting the image and procedures of DI so as to guarantee the rights of infertile husbands.[13] Discourse on the importance of fatherhood is often mobilized against family formation where a male is lacking. For example, some legislators in the Australian Parliament in the early 2000s asked that gender equity law be decoupled from regulation of access to ART and proposed removing the right of single women and lesbians to use ART.[14] The main debate centered on the needs and the rights of unborn children to have "natural parents," de facto meaning a loving father.

While the protection of fatherhood often means placing limits on access, debates over motherhood often broaden the possibilities of ART usage. Women's reproductive rights are the most important force for some feminist and lesbian movements, who promote ART as a new reproductive resource for women. The spirit of the women's health movement in the United States and United Kingdom, which emphasizes rights, empowerment, and self-help, has had spillover effects in advocating women's right to ART.[15] Women's groups themselves, sometimes with supportive medical personnel, have developed several routes to ART. One is the so-called turkey-baster method, where single women and lesbians took advantage of the easiest DI technique and developed their own networks for self-insemination. Some women's groups established sperm banks to offer DI resources to single women and lesbians.[16] Some activists have also fought for the formal inclusion of unmarried women in access to ART through social policy.[17] However, advocacy of women's reproductive rights in the sphere of ART is not necessarily linked with the feminist movement in other societies. Kahn argues that it is the ideology of motherhood—that having children is the ultimate goal for women—that has led to the unrestricted use of ART in Israel, including

---

12. Inhorn, *Local Babies, Global Science*.
13. Yoram S. Carmeli and Dapnha Birenbaum-Carmeli, "Ritualizing the 'Natural Family': Secrecy in Israeli Donor Insemination," *Science as Culture* 9(3) (2000): 301–24; Tsuge, "How Society Responds to Desires of Childless Couples"; Inhorn, *Local Babies, Global Science*; Chia-Ling Wu, "Managing Multiple Masculinities in Donor Insemination."
14. Jennifer Lynne Smith, "'Suitable Mothers': Lesbian and Single Women and the 'Unborn' in Australian Parliamentary Discourse," *Critical Social Policy* 23(1) (2003): 63–88; Rachel Thorpe, Samantha Croy, Kerry Petersen, and Marian Pitts, "In the Best Interests of the Child? Regulating Assisted Reproductive Technologies and the Well-Being of Offspring in Three Australian States," *International Journal of Law, Policy and the Family* 26(3) (2012): 259–77.
15. Daniel Wikler and Norma J. Wikler, "Turkey-Baster Babies: The Demedicalization of Artificial Insemination," *Milbank Quarterly* 69(1) (1991): 5–40. Lisa Jean Moore, *Sperm Counts: Overcome by Man's Most Precious Fluid* (New York: New York University Press, 2007).
16. Ibid.
17. Stine Willum Adrian, "Sperm Stories: Policies and Practices of Sperm Banking in Denmark and Sweden," *European Journal of Women's Studies* 17(4) (2010): 393–411.

single women's use of surrogacy.[18] In the Israeli context, realizing mother-hood outweighs marriage as the arbiter of social inclusion of ART.

Next to gender, some of the literature highlights the importance of a hier-archy of *sexuality* in the access debate. One of the early voices raised against ART is its "unnaturalness": it is reproduction through medical interven-tion rather than through sexual intercourse. Thus, the sexual hierarchy that privileges sex as a means of reproduction is challenged by new reproductive technology. It is the fear of "adultery" from third-party donation that leads some countries to allow only married couples to use ART.[19] ART regulation centers upon the stratification of sexuality: natural versus artificial, within marriage versus outside, heterosexual versus others. Sexuality stands out as having its own unique order, and this affects how ART is thought about, but some of these binary contrasts are essentially gendered. For example, the British debate over "virgin motherhood" through DI demonstrates that it is women's reproduction without sexuality that can lie at the root of agitation.[20] The fact that gay fatherhood is more stigmatized than lesbian motherhood reveals the gendered norm on parenthood for sexual minorities.[21]

Heated debates on the use of ART by lesbians and gays further broaden the analytical scope to incorporate *heteronormativity* as a separate frame. Heteronormativity—"the numerous ways in which heterosexual privilege is woven into the fabric of social life"[22]—used to be discussed within the sexuality literature. However, as Jackson argues, heteronormativity is not only about sexuality but also about other social arrangements, including the gendered division of reproductive labor and parenthood.[23] The claim that the ideal family consists of a father and a mother is one of the most commonly encountered reasons for negotiating the idea that a "normal" family can be founded upon ART. Gender complementarity during chil-drearing rather than child making becomes the main issue over the so-called "natural family" or "the child's best interests." In addition, when it comes to using ART, a hierarchy of respectability and recognized citizenship exists among heterosexuals: single, heterosexual women are less legitimate users than are women who are in a "stable relationship" with a man. By compari-son, single, heterosexual men are almost never the imagined users of ART, demonstrating a gendered heteronormativity in the field of reproduction.

---

18. Susan Martha Kahn, *Reproducing Jews: A Cultural Account of Assisted Conception in Israel* (Durham, NC: Duke University Press, 2000).
19. Inhorn, *Local Babies, Global Science.*
20. Davina Cooper, *Power in Struggle: Feminism, Sexuality and the State* (Buckingham: Open University Press, 1995); Sandra Barney, "Accessing Medicalized Donor Sperm in the US and Britain: An Historical Narrative," *Sexualities* 8 (2005): 205–20.
21. Judith Stacey, *Unhitched: Love, Marriage and Family Values from West Hollywood to Western China* (New York: New York University Press, 2011).
22. Stevi Jackson, "Gender, Sexuality, and Heterosexuality," *Feminist Theory* 7(1) (2008): 108.
23. Ibid., 105–21.

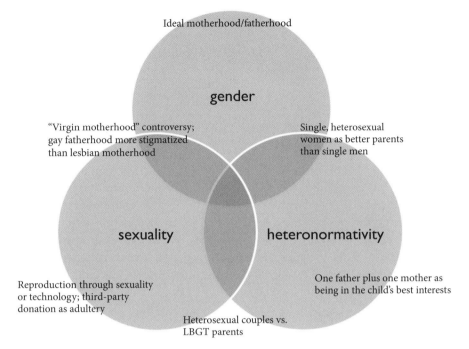

Ideal motherhood/fatherhood

gender

"Virgin motherhood" controversy;
gay fatherhood more stigmatized
than lesbian motherhood

Single, heterosexual
women as better parents
than single men

sexuality   heteronormativity

Reproduction through sexuality
or technology; third-party
donation as adultery

One father plus one mother as
being in the child's best interests

Heterosexual couples vs.
LBGT parents

Figure 3.1

The intersection of gender, sexuality, and heteronormativity in access to ART

Figure 3.1 shows a conceptual framework of the triangular intersection of gender, sexuality, and heteronormativity that can be used to analyze the major social relationships that shape the politics of access to ART. Each circle indicates a major organizing principle that may guide the governance of access within society. Each rectangle, both for the major circles and their overlapping areas, offers an exemplar concept or phenomenon that has been discussed in the literature. We can use this graph as a framework to examine the specific rationales behind governance. In addition, the boom in gay parenthood through surrogacy has become a new arrival in the debate over access to ART.[24] To understand the legitimacy of gay parents' access to ART, it is the major organizing principles of sexuality, gender, and heteronormativity that underlie the obstacles. This triangular framework thus suitably captures the changing debate over access.

The technoscientific governing approach reminds us to follow diverse stakeholders to see how discourse and practices of gender-sexuality-heteronormativity triangulation may change. For example, the British case demonstrates a great transformation of the politics of access through the interaction of the state, legislators, medical professionals, activists, and ART users. There, in 1984, the Warnock Report into how to regulate ART stressed the importance of children being born into "a loving stable, heterosexual relationship," prioritizing heteronormativity as the principle of inclusion and exclusion.[25] Following Warnock, the UK passed the Human Fertilisation and Embryology Act 1990, one of the world's earliest formal regulations of ART.[26] Although the act did not specify marital status as a requirement for using ART, it stated that treatment providers should take into account the welfare of any child affected by ART, including "the need of that child for a father,"[27] and specified the importance of fatherhood in family formation. The Human Fertilisation and Embryology Authority (HFEA), the UK's regulator of fertility services, has continued to emphasize taking proper account of children's welfare and gave licensed clinics the right to decide on appropriate users. The media frenzy over "virgin births" in 1991 revealed that even though only a few clinics offered DI to single women, such noncoital reproduction received attacks from the medical community, newspaper columnists, and conservative legislators.[28] A majority of infertility experts working under the National Health Service refused to offer DI to single women and lesbians,[29] forcing them to turn to private clinics.[30] Gay and lesbian groups called such regulation "discriminatory," and by the 2000s they had joined other LGBT movements (such as that for civil partnerships) in using a discourse of gender and sexual-minority rights, as well as quality of health provision, to challenge the HFEA's bias. In the mid-2000s the HFEA formed an equality and diversity working group to ensure that single women and lesbian couples received safe and appropriate services. To incorporate diverse opinions over ART, the HFEA actively sought evaluation and suggestions from lesbians and single women, and the revised HFE Act changed the 1990 wording on the need for a father to "the need . . . for supportive parenting." The UK case reminds us how the state, market, medical providers, activists, and users all shape the network of ART use.

Building upon this rich existing literature, I propose to investigate the regulatory trajectory of access through examining the making of identities, institutions, discourse, and representations during the process, all of which may demonstrate the specific intersections of gender, sexuality, and

---

25. Ellie Lee, Jan Macvarish, and Sally Sheldon, "Assessing Child Welfare under the Human Fertilisation and Embryology Act 2008: A Case Study in Medicalization?" *Sociology of Health and Illness* 36 (2014): 500–15.

26. Warnock, "Report of the Committee of Inquiry into Human Fertilisation and Embryology." London: Her Majesty's Stationery Office, 1984. Human Fertilisation and Embryology Act (HFEA), accessed March 1, 2014, http://www.legislation.gov.uk/ukpga/1990/37/contents.

27. Ibid.

28. Cooper, *Power in Struggle*.

29. Lisa Saffron, "Can Fertility Service Providers Justify Discrimination against Lesbians?" *Human Fertility* 5(2) (2002): 42–46.

30. Barney, "Accessing Medicalized Donor Sperm in the US and Britain."

heteronormativity. In following the governance approach, I incorporate not only official policy makers, medical professionals, women's organizations, and pressure groups, but also lay users—and not only advisory committee meetings and congressional hearings but also clinical encounters—in order to reveal the wider hinterland that feeds into the governance of ART. Examining such technoscientific governance in action may better reveal the coevolution of ART on the one hand and, on the other, gender, sexuality, and heteronormativity in Taiwan.

Data and Method

The research design was born of a broadly based project on IVF.[31] I conducted three waves of research on IVF development in Taiwan, in 1999–2001, 2006–2008, and again in 2010–2015. In the first wave I conducted field work in infertility clinics in Taipei and interviewed married couples about their infertility treatment experiences. I also interviewed gays and lesbians about their reproductive wishes, since, although none of them had used ART, they did have many opinions on the access to it.[32] My understanding of ART access policy grew with this IVF project. I began focusing in 2010 on access and exclusion in Taiwan.

The data for the following analysis includes archives, in-depth interviews, and some preliminary field work. Combining these methods, I adopted multisite ethnography to trace various actors' governing activities,[33] including relevant actors' opinions of media releases, public education, arguments and testimony during public hearings, discussion during regulatory meetings, processes of negotiating with other actors, and clinical encounters between medical professionals and users. Since governing activities occur at different sites, I followed these activities through different methods. Archival data that I used to follow these activities included newspaper databanks, newsletters of related organizations, conference discussions, academic research, and governmental documents. I interviewed twenty-five relevant actors about their practices with regard to ART and their participation in debates and negotiation with regard to access. The interviewees included three government officials, fourteen IVF specialists and technicians, two nongovernmental organization activists, one legislator, one journalist, and

---

31. Chia-Ling Wu, "Managing Multiple Masculinities in Donor Insemination."
32. Wu Chia-Ling, "Shou wuming de xingbie, xingbiehua de wuming: Cong Taiwan 'buyun' nannü chujing fenxi wuming de xingbie zhengzhi [Stigmatized gender and gendered stigma: The "infertile" men and women in Taiwan]," *Taiwan shehui xuekan* [Taiwanese Journal of Sociology] 29 (2002): 127–79.
33. Rayna Rapp, "One New Reproductive Technology, Multiple Sites: How Feminist Methodology Bleeds into Everyday Life," in *Revisioning Women, Health and Healing: Feminist, Cultural and Technoscience Perspectives*, ed. Adele E. Clarke and Virginia L. Olesen (New York: Routledge, 1999), 119–35.

two scholars of bioethics. Four of them served on the Taiwan Society for Reproductive Medicine (TSRM) advisory committee, and three were TSRM presidents. I also attended conferences, annual meetings, and continuing education programs held by the TSRM, along with some activists' meetings (such as those of the Lesbian Mothers' Alliance), to learn how the medical community and activist groups discussed this controversial issue. I participated in events and conferences on ARTs held by LGBT groups. Through snowballing sampling, I tried to reach "excluded" users—singles, lesbians, and gays—who used ART. I also used archival data to construct profiles for each ART user. In addition to media reports, some reveal their experiences in detail on their blogs or Facebook pages. So far, I have established twenty profiles of these excluded users.

Heterosexual, Married, Infertile Couples as Default Users

In introducing DI to Taiwan, physicians were primary gatekeepers in deciding who could have access, and they took married couples to be its "legitimate" users. The pioneering doctors in the 1950s claimed DI as the only useful treatment for serious male infertility. They quickly realized its potential threat to an infertile husband, however, since his biological link with the DI baby was broken. Doctors used several strategies to mitigate the absence of biological fatherhood for these infertile husbands.[34] First, they mixed donors' and husbands' sperm. Second, donors remained anonymous so that biological fatherhood would not threaten social fatherhood. Third, they tried their best to find donors from among medical students and young doctors who matched the infertile husbands' biological features (blood type, race, and body type) and sometimes even some social characteristics (general appearance and style). The clinical procedures of DI were modified to maintain the infertile husbands' biological fatherhood to some extent: the sperm-mixing procedure obscured whether their sperm might still work, the biological father remained unknown, and the DI child's resemblance to the husband was maximized. Sperm mixing was later abandoned and only the anonymity policy remained. In the early 1980s, doctors successfully promoted third-party donation in Taiwan, but the requirement that the woman be married did not change.

Legal experts began to discuss formal regulation of ART only after the birth of the first test-tube baby, born in Britain in 1978. IVF provoked a tremendous amount of discussion on the regulation of ART around the world, even though DI had been in practice for a much longer time. It was the discussion in the English-speaking world, rather than local clinical practice, that triggered Taiwanese legal experts' attention. As latecomers to both ART

---

34. Chia-Ling Wu, "Managing Multiple Masculinities in Donor Insemination."

and legal regulation, Taiwanese legal scholars tended to consider the trends in familiar countries, such as in this case the United States, Britain, and Germany. Most Taiwanese legal experts assumed that ART should be used for married couples, in accordance with most international legal scholars at the time. Only one leading expert briefly mentioned the use of ART by single women in some Western societies, dubbing it "a side effect of the women's movement."[35]

A year after the birth of the first Taiwanese test-tube baby in 1985, the Ethical Guidelines for Practising ART was promulgated in Taiwan. The government followed the pattern of family planning practiced in Taiwan since the 1960s and started policy formation by establishing an advisory committee under the Ministry of Health. The first committee was composed of eleven members, six of whom were doctors and all of whom were men. Although these guidelines aimed to regulate IVF, they also incorporated DI, which had remained almost unregulated in Taiwan for more than thirty years. The ethical guidelines clearly stated that ART was to be used by married couples with infertility problems and prohibited single and widowed people from using it. This restriction was not based on any controversial practices or real cases in Taiwan; rather, it was simply the norm that the advisory committee intended to enforce. When I asked one advisory committee member why the guidelines specified the exclusion of singles, he replied, "In 1985, you simply didn't come across movie stars wanting to have kids out of wedlock. By default, we limited the use of ART to married couples."[36]

In my interviews, celebrities from the world of entertainment often emerged in Taiwan as individuals who challenged ideas of "conventional" reproduction. Called "moral pioneers," by Rayna Rapp,[37] they built a new public image of single motherhood and later highlighted the potential use of ART for their own reproductive needs. As this advisory committee member recalled, in 1985 no such pioneers had emerged as possible challengers to the restrictions on ART access. Being married was treated as the default requirement for users of ART.

Voluntary Single Motherhood: Celebrities as Moral Pioneers

Single motherhood went through significant change during this period. Before the mid-1980s, when Taiwan began to formally regulate ART, single motherhood in Taiwan was either invisible or was portrayed as the tragic

---

35. Li Hong-hsi, "Rengong shoujing de 'falu houyizheng': Cong shiguan ying'er tanqi (3) youshengxue guan yu nuquan yundongzhi 'fuzuoyong'" [Legal "after effects" of artificial insemination: Eugenics and women's movement's "side effect"], *Dangdai yixue* [Contemporary medicine] 12 (1979): 96–102.
36. Interview with Professor R, May 31, 2011.
37. Rayna Rapp, "One New Reproductive Technology, Multiple Sites."

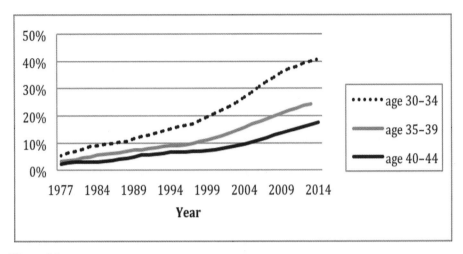

Figure 3.2

Trend of percentage of never-married women in Taiwan, 1977–2014

result of innocent young women being forced to engage in sex. At the same time, women started to delay marriage, mostly because of their increasing attendance at institutions of higher education. A local clothing brand called Single Noble (Dushen Guizu) was established in 1979, reflecting women's newfound pride in remaining single and delaying marriage. By 1990, an unprecedented 6.0 percent of women aged thirty-five through thirty-nine had never married; the figure was higher than in South Korea (2.4 percent), but lower than in Singapore (14.8 percent), Hong Kong (10.2 percent), and Japan (7.5 percent).[38] The image of voluntary single motherhood started to emerge only in the late 1980s, when several Taiwan- and Hong Kong–based celebrities became pregnant without the fathers' names being revealed (at least for a while). This paved the way for other single female celebrities going abroad in the late 1990s to seek sperm banks to fulfill their reproductive desires.

In a country where ART is not available to unmarried women, going abroad to access it can become an openly discussed option. Scholars term this "reproductive exile," rather than "reproductive tourism," to emphasize the constraints that force members of the excluded minority to go abroad.[39] By the late 1990s, DI had become more openly available to single women in several Western countries.[40] Some well-known celebrities in Taiwan revealed

38. Gavin W. Jones, "Changing Marriage Patterns in Asia," Asia Research Institute Working Paper Series 131, accessed July 28, 2015, http://www.ari.nus.edu.sg/docs/wps/wps.htm. See also Figure 2.
39. Marcia C. Inhorn and Pasquale Patrizio, "Rethinking Reproductive 'Tourism' as Reproductive 'Exile,'" *Fertility and Sterility* 92(3) (2009): 904–6.
40. Moore, *Sperm Counts*.

frankly to the public that they had gone to Japan or the United States for ART treatment, though none of them had succeeded in becoming pregnant. The United States allowed access to sperm banks for singles, but Japan prohibited nonmarried couples from using ART, and those celebrities who went to Japan preferred to mobilize their rich social networks to access illicit DI there rather than trigger controversy at home in Taiwan.

Through broad media coverage, these celebrities successfully publicized the option of DI for single women. However, these gender outlaws did not challenge the law. Some revealed their personal stories to the media, often describing the pain and suffering of undergoing DI, but they did not openly criticize the legal limitations in Taiwan. They thus presented their new identities as women who intended to become mothers without a male partner but did not engage in discourse about reproductive rights or structural constraints. One governmental official explained to me:

> I've met Bai Bing-bing [白冰冰, an entertainment celebrity who became famous for going abroad to seek DI treatment from the late 1990s] several times. She is a very understanding person. She knows that regulation has to follow the social norm, and that [the government] should not be forced to change it.[41]

Although these moral pioneers created a new image of ART users, they managed to make it one of individual effort. They neither translated their actions into a challenge to official regulations nor created a new discourse on ART use; this was down to the power of local "social norms."

What exactly was the social norm in Bai's mind that prevented an unpartnered celebrity like her from publicly arguing for her reproductive rights? Comparing this example with the case of surrogacy might shed some light on this question. Surrogacy had been prohibited in Taiwan ever since the establishment of the ethical guidelines in 1986. Women who suffered from a malformed uterus or repeated miscarriages could only possibly have their own offspring with the help of a surrogate. Beginning in the mid-1990s, some of these infertile women went abroad to contract a surrogate, just as single celebrities went abroad to use ART. The difference was that these infertile women—who were married—not only made efforts to fulfill their own reproductive needs but also demanded local legal reform. They gained open support and sympathy from some well-known medical doctors, and together they lobbied for the legalization of surrogacy in Taiwan. This prompted continuing media coverage, several public hearings, and debates among members of the advisory committee. Finally, the Ministry of Health held a consensus conference and decided to conditionally legalize surrogacy in 2005. Over the same period, single women never enjoyed similar collective mobilization or strong public support for their access to ART.

---

41. Interview with Governmental Official Q, April 13, 2011.

This contrast illustrates the gradated support of the "clinically infertile" versus the "socially infertile."[42] Married women who needed surrogacy were deemed to be socially acceptable mothers since they were married women desiring children. In addition, their physical infertility fitted in with the mainstream definition of infertility. Single women with healthy reproductive systems who were unwilling or unable to achieve procreation through heterosexual intercourse intended to build an unconventional family, and they did not accord with the cognitive picture of infertility. A hierarchy existed among heterosexual women insofar as their desire for ART was perceived as legitimate or not. However, doctors as clinical gatekeepers gradually became insiders who were willing to speak up for these socially infertile women.

Unmarried CEOs as ART Users: TSRM's Inclusion of Singles

The first political mobilization for the inclusion of unmarried women in ART regulation came from the Taiwan Society for Reproductive Medicine (TSRM), the leading medical association for infertility experts. In 2001, the TSRM surveyed various groups' opinions on ART regulation, including the legalization of surrogacy and the inclusion of single women in access to ART. Although only one-third of 200 doctors responded to the questionnaire, this was the first significant attempt by the TSRM to systematically seek the viewpoints of ART providers. Fifty-nine percent of doctors who responded to the survey supported surrogacy, but only 26 percent said yes to giving unmarried women access to ART. By comparison, 67 percent of respondents in feminist groups surveyed supported the legitimacy of access to ART for unmarried women. However, it was the TSRM that moved ahead of feminist groups by holding a press conference in 2001 to promote the inclusion of unmarried women in access to ART.

At the press conference, the TSRM argued that a variety of unmarried women needed ART. They shared their clinical experiences of certain women coming for infertility treatment: singles, feminists, cohabiting couples, and women who had been divorced due to infertility and who could remarry only if they succeeded in becoming pregnant. This was the first time that the ART access policy debate had been based on clinical cases from the general public, rather than on hypothetical situations or high-profile celebrities. Doctors, as the gatekeepers of DI, were front-runners in meeting these legally excluded groups, and they gradually became their spokespersons in expressing their needs.

The 1986 ethical guidelines had prohibited single women from using ART, but some doctors at least had nevertheless provided some services

---

42. M. M. Peterson, "Assisted Reproductive Technologies and Equity of Access Issues," *Law, Ethics and Medicine* 31 (2005): 280–85.

to single women and had grown more aware of their needs. In my field-work, I met a single mother, Hsiao-Yi, who gave birth to twins through DI in 1985; this was the earliest case that I could find of a single woman fulfilling her reproductive needs through DI. Hsiao-Yi had once been an activist in Taiwan's budding democracy and women's rights movements in the late 1970s, and she later developed a successful business career. Daring to take an unconventional route, she had wanted to become a mother without marriage when she reached her early thirties. To her disappointment, she first found that as a single woman she would encounter great difficulty in adopting a child. This attractive woman thought about getting pregnant through a one-night stand, but, according to her, none of her admirers supported the idea. She then met a sympathetic doctor who recommended DI, which she had never previously considered. The doctor arranged a sperm donor, and she gave birth to twins.

Doctors did gradually meet single women in their clinics who requested access to DI. Doctors I interviewed explained how they evolved their moral world to handle these gender outlaws. First of all, some acted on the basis that the 1986 ethical guidelines and the regulations of 1995 were not statutes and that they would not face any sanctions if they ignored them; before the Human Reproduction Law in 2007, assisting unmarried women did not put doctors at risk of violating the law. They admitted, however, that, after 2007, the registry system strictly required ART centers to upload patients' identification documents along with their marriage certificates and that they faced greater risks if they assisted the unmarried. Second, they often presented themselves as value-neutral technicians maximizing the utility of technology; they downplayed the ideological debates, treated ART as a value-neutral tool, and offered their services at their patients' request. These doctors' swearing of the Hippocratic oath justified their efforts to help the socially infertile in the spirit of altruism. Ho found that, in the 2000s at least, some doctors, mostly infertility experts working in private clinics, managed to offer DI to single women; others, though, still limited DI to the treatment of serious male infertility alone, not that of the unmarried.[43] Doctors I interviewed told me that, for medical centers and public hospitals, bureaucratic surveillance imposed extra pressure to obey the official regulations. By comparison, private clinicians had more room for negotiation.

From one perspective, Hsiao-Yi represented a type of woman whom the TSRM most wished to exemplify and support in expanding the provision of DI: women of high socioeconomic status yet with no prospect of marriage. Ambitious career women, labeled "strong women" by the media, became a

---

43. Ho Szu-Ying, "'Feifa' qingjing xia de kuer shengzhi: Taiwan nütongzhi de rengongshengzhi keji shizuo" [Queering reproduction in a prohibited context: Assisted reproductive technologies as utilized by Taiwan's lesbians], *Nüxue xuezhi funu yu xingbie yanjiu* [Journal of women and gender studies] 12 (2014): 53–122.

conventional image for the public and, sometimes, a role model. This was the type of woman the TSRM most often presented when striving to provide access to ART for single women. In the TSRM report, Dr. Ming-Yang Chang 張明揚 explains:

> Some of these single women are their parents' only breadwinners. Plenty of them are CEOs or active leaders in our society. They were too busy to have an opportunity to find the right man and get married. Should we deprive them of their reproductive rights?[44]

Dr. Chang further stresses that, with coresident parents and financial resources, these women had both the right and the capacity to raise children well. Equally important, Dr. Chang points out that these women were "involuntarily single" and so deserved reproductive rights. Although the TSRM press conference presented diverse types of women who required access to ART and even mentioned "feminists" as a category, it supported mostly those women who were unable, rather than unwilling (like Hsiao-Yi), to enter into marriage. Dr. Chang also highlights the importance of a family's only daughter bearing offspring for the sake of family lineage, a reason effectively unknown in Western society.

Overall, it was single women of high socioeconomic status who desired but were unable to get married who mostly won doctors' support. By comparison, lesbians, another group of active DI users, tended to be discriminated against by doctors. As Ho finds, lesbians had started to approach doctors for DI in the mid-1990s, quickly discovering that if they revealed their sexual orientation in an infertility clinic, they ran the risk of being discriminated against.[45] They strategically presented themselves as single heterosexuals and were more likely to gain their doctors' support.

In public, the TSRM has as a whole since early 2001 framed the access debate in terms of "women's reproductive rights" during its lobbying for the Human Reproduction Law. It initially supported a statute proposal that stated that women's reproductive rights legitimized single women's access to ART:

> Based on equal rights, ART should not be limited to married women. In 1949, the Geneva Convention ensured the protection of reproductive rights, this protection not being limited to married women.

In other countries, it has often been feminists rather than medical professionals who have adopted such a position to argue for liberalization of access to ART. As I will soon discuss, women's groups in Taiwan had other

---

44. Zhang Ming Yang, "Shehui dazhong dui rengong shengzhi fa de zhengyi xinghua ti diaocha jieguo fenxi" [The responses of the public toward the controversy of assisted reproduction law: Survey results], *Zhonghua Minguo neimoyiweizheng funu xiehui huikan* [Taiwan Endometriosis Association Journal] 8(4) (2001): 3–8.
45. Ho Szu-Ying, "'Feifa' qingjing xia de kuer shengzhi."

reform agendas on their mind and did not expend much effort on this particular issue.

The TSRM did not, however, aggressively insist upon this appeal to equality, since support from the medical profession was relatively low compared with the surrogacy issue, and opposition from the general public remained high. The TSRM decided that "we'd better compromise with the social trend."[46] One former TSRM president believed that the time for reform would soon come around.[47] It was Doctor N's view that, so long as the percentage of women in the affected categories continued to increase, society would in time have to accept the expansion of ART provision. Indeed, the increasing tendency to remain single continued; in 2014, one-quarter of women aged thirty-five through thirty-nine were never married, another historical high.[48] Although the TSRM only passively proposed the inclusion of unmarried women, it pushed the issue from individual request to public debate. Nevertheless, it was still one unmarried woman's strongly worded request rather than the TSRM's lobbying that made the access issue a widely publicized national event.

The "Lee Case" and the Dead Father

The "Lee case" in Taiwan, like that of Baby M in the United States or the Nahmani case in Israel,[49] provoked a huge societal debate on ART regulation and became a fruitful opportunity for negotiating hierarchies of gender, sexuality, and heteronormativity in relation to ART. In 2005, a Taiwanese army lieutenant died in a tank accident. His fiancée, Hsing-Yu Lee (李幸育), with the assistance of the high-profile infertility expert Dr. Mao-Sheng Lee (李茂盛), asked for posthumous sperm harvesting to undergo artificial insemination and bear the lieutenant's child. The Ministry of Health at first declined this request, claiming that, according to the regulations then in force, ART was restricted to infertility treatment. The media covered the story intensively, portraying Lee's strong love for her fiancé and her passionate desire to have his biological child. Facing criticism for not being flexible enough, the prime minister agreed to allow the sperm to be retrieved, leaving the question of whether Lee would be permitted to undergo artificial insemination to be decided later. Vast numbers of people expressed their opinions, from the vice president, legislators, and experts to activists and bloggers, both supporting and objecting to the use of posthumous sperm for Lee's insemination. The Ministry of Health formed a special committee, composed of various experts, to decide whether the frozen sperm could be used. Legislators also fastened

46. Interview with Doctor X, July 18, 2001.
47. Interview with Doctor N, April 18, 2011.
48. See Figure 3.2.
49. Susan Martha Kahn, *Reproducing Jews*.

a delayed stipulation onto the Human Reproduction Law to give this case a formal legal status. The debate around the Lee case became a window on how Taiwanese society responded to this proposed unconventional use of ART.

Expressions of support were based on diverse and even contrasting discourses. The most prevalent opinion was that this was a much-to-be-respected romantic love, since Lee was ready to go to such lengths to bear her fiancé's child even though he himself had perished. Several legislators negotiated with the prime minister to have the sperm retrieved and then made efforts to grant the Lee case a legal foundation. Other supporters used a rights discourse to support Lee. One well-known activist for surrogate motherhood argued that women's reproductive agency should be respected and protected. Taking celebrity cases of single motherhood as examples, one legislator stated that Taiwanese society had made significant progress and that the law should follow suit to fulfill this new need.

Paradoxically, objections to the idea came from both traditional family ideology and progressive women's liberation. The leading legal expert on ART, Professor Dongxiong Dai (戴東雄) of National Taiwan University, stated that the government should not encourage nonmarital births. Whenever people praised Lee's devoted love, legal experts in Taiwan tended to argue that being engaged to marry was not the same as being legally married, and hence that engaged couples did not enjoy certain rights, including access to ART. Lee and her late fiancé's family maintained that the two had already been like a married couple and even proposed having a posthumous "ghost marriage," but legal experts stressed that unless all the administrative procedures had been fulfilled, Lee was not entitled to the rights of a married person. A new discourse also emerged for the first time—namely, objections to Lee's case on the basis of the absence of a father for her potential child. Minister of Health Shui-Sheng Hou claimed that the mutually supportive institutions of family and marriage should be maintained. One of his key arguments was the need to consider the child's welfare. Deliberately raising a child without a father was portrayed as being against the child's best interests. One leading IVF expert used a DI case in the United States to suggest that children growing up without fathers might develop deviant behavior. A number of letters to the editors of Taiwanese newspapers also revealed that some members of the public believed it might not be the best arrangement for a child to be born without a father.

Not only did the absence of a father become a new concern, but too many donations to sperm banks by the same donor emerged as a new, if hypothetical, problem. In Congress, the legislator Shui-Sheng Hou (侯水盛) offered an image of modern women's use of DI in Taiwan:

> The new generation does not regard marriage as important. . . . Our law does not prohibit birth out of wedlock. Therefore, if some single women

want to raise a child to relieve their work pressure, because as long as they see children who look like movie stars, they feel happy and fulfilled, how can we reject it? . . . Possibly, a whole street full of girls would like to get hold of Bae Yong Joon's sperm![50]

Bae Yong Joon (裴勇俊) was a Korean film and TV actor who was tremendously popular in Taiwan at that time. Though Legislator Hou was presenting an image of crazy fans who might want to become the mothers of his children, the scenario was impossible under the administrative guidelines in force at the time, which specified that donors had to be anonymous and also limited the number of live births per donor to just one.[51] However, Hou's words introduced the idea of a hitherto unimagined kind of single woman into the ART access debate: not the devoted Ms. Lee but the irrational modern woman who would reject marriage in favor of bearing the child of a movie idol. The inclusion of such single women in access to ART was presented as bringing chaos to society, especially if many children might be fathered by the one donor.

Feminists also joined in the objections to the Lee case by way of the discourse against compulsory motherhood and for women's best interests. Feminist legislator Shu-Ying Huang (黃淑英) suggested that it was a patriarchal value to extend patrilineage through posthumous insemination. Vice President Hsiu-Lien Lü (呂秀蓮), a pioneering feminist in Taiwan's women's movement, also encouraged Lee to give up her birth plans and start a new life. These feminists worried that the compulsion to bear her fiancé's child might hinder Lee's life opportunities, suggesting that she cool down and then make a decision. In this context they saw ART less as a resource to fulfill women's reproductive desires than as a tool with which to reinforce traditional patriarchal values.

Indeed, in the second wave of the women's movement in the United States and the United Kingdom since the 1960s, feminists and lesbians had rewritten the script regarding DI and used it to build families without men. By comparison, the budding women's movement in Taiwan during the same time period had just started its first wave, aiming to promote women's rights to education, work, and political participation.[52] In the field of reproduction, women claimed the right not to be confined to the roles of wife and mother. Under such circumstances, motherhood was the target problem, not the

---

50. The Legislative Yuan, Congress Library Publication in Gazette: Social Welfare and Environmental Hygiene Committee and Judiciary and Organic Laws and Statutes Committee, 6th, session 2, October 6, 2005 (pp. 63–88). Taipei: The Legislative Yuan of Republic of China.

51. Charlotte Wang, Miao-Yu Tsai, Mei-Hsien Lee, Su-Yun Huang, Chen-Hung Kao, Nong-Nerng Ho, and Chuhsing Kate Hsiao, "Maximum Number of Live Births per Donor in Artificial Insemination," *Human Reproduction* 22(5) (2007): 1363–72.

52. Yenlin Ku, "The Changing Status of Women in Taiwan: A Conscious and Collective Struggle Toward Equality," *Women's Studies International Forum* 11(3) (1988): 179–86.

primary interest. As for other reproductive technologies, mainstream feminists supported abortion and opposed surrogacy, implying that the rejection of involuntary motherhood was more a part of the feminist agenda than were alternative ways to motherhood. Legislator Huang and Vice President Lu, demonstrating the legacy of the women's movement against compulsory motherhood, did not support Lee's ART-mediated motherhood plans.

The Lee story ended with a change of mind on the part of the lieutenant's family. In a patriarchal legal hierarchy, his father had the right to decide what to do with the sperm. According to media reports, the family became disturbed by Lee's requests for child-raising funds and sought a peaceful family life by destroying all the frozen sperm. The Human Reproduction Law, which was passed as a result of the Lee case, continued to prohibit singles from using ART. Although unmarried women's reproductive rights were discussed by some legislators, no one insisted on them, including TSRM members and the feminist legislator Shu-Ying Huang. No women's groups lobbied for the inclusion of singles, though they had often lobbied for the Gender Equity Law, the Gender Education Law, and civil law reform. In 2007, the Human Reproduction Law was passed, and Taiwan continued to exclude unmarried people from having access to ART. Without continuous lobbying and support from medical professionals and women's groups, discourse on women's reproductive rights was not translated into legal reform on access.

Lesbian Mothers' Alliance

It was only after the 2007 enactment of the Human Reproduction Law that an organization formed by excluded users became directly involved: the Lesbian Mothers' Alliance. Taiwan's gay and lesbian movement had boomed in the early 1990s and soon took on a leading role in Asia,[53] but parenthood remained a marginal issue, partly due to echoes from the women's movement agenda against compulsory motherhood. As one lesbian feminist observed, "[T]he benefit of being a lesbian was not to enter motherhood; we did not think of having children through DI."[54] The Lesbian Mothers' Alliance has broadened the appeal of the lesbian movement in recent years. It was first formed as a support group in 2005 and then transformed in 2007 into the activist Taiwan LGBT Family Rights Advocacy. A number of young student activists from the gay and lesbian rights movement initiated the group and invited lesbian mothers to talk about their experiences. Most of these mothers had children from a previous heterosexual marriage. One mother, "Vicky,"

---

53. Stevi Jackson, Jieyu Liu, and Juhyun Woo, eds., *East Asian Sexualities: Modernity, Gender and New Sexual Cultures* (New York: Zed Books, 2008).
54. Interview with Ms. A, October 11, 2000.

was a rare case of a woman who had given birth to two children through ART, one via DI in Japan and the other through self-insemination in Taiwan. Student activists soon found that lesbian motherhood through ART was an important item on the social reform agenda and promoted this strategy for the lesbian community. The Taiwan LGBT Family Rights Advocacy now shares information on self-insemination for lesbian couples, and it advocates removing all legal, social, and cultural discrimination against LGBT families. Reforming the Human Reproduction Law has become its latest goal.

Self-insemination, a token women's health movement in some Western countries since the 1970s, was first promoted among lesbians in Taiwan in the late 2000s. The practice was popular in the United States and the United Kingdom in the 1970s among feminists and lesbians who wanted to become mothers without men and without medical intervention.[55] Although equally technically feasible in Taiwan, it seems it was never advocated or even mentioned among feminist groups there. When self-insemination started to develop its local network, it was strongly associated with lesbians. The Lesbian Mothers' Alliance first searched for detailed information in English on websites, published information about the technique in its newsletter, and later added personal experiences to enrich the discussion with tips and know-how. It became included in their self-help book *Building a Family: Childbearing Guidebook for Lesbians* and has recently become the topic of island-wide workshops. In a series of information-sharing sessions and discussions, detailed procedures are set out: you should ask the donor to have a medical examination first; determine the timing of your ovulation; invite the donor to provide a fresh sperm sample in a clean container; put it into a 10 ml sterile plastic disposable needleless syringe, easily bought in a drugstore; lie on a bed, put a pillow under your hips; put the syringe into your vagina to dispense the semen, either yourself or with the assistance of your partner; and remain recumbent for ten minutes. Legal issues were clarified during this promotion of self-insemination. Activists point out that from a legal perspective self-insemination is similar to a one-night stand, which of course does not violate legal regulations regarding ART. To prevent the donor from claiming fatherhood, women are advised to either search for an anonymous donor or ask the donor to sign an agreement.

Vicky, who is a sort of ad hoc spokesperson for self-insemination, has become a mediator to help provide insemination services to other women. As already mentioned, she had DI in Japan to conceive her first child. She then practiced self-insemination, with a friend as the sperm donor, and bore a second. After joining the support group and witnessing the increasing needs of lesbian couples, she became a mediator in the spirit of community service. In the ten cases that she shared with me during the interview, she

---

55. Wikler and Wikler, "Turkey-Baster Babies."

said that for sperm donors she mostly found single, Caucasian men who were working in Taiwan as English teachers. She claimed that this type of donor had the advantages of desirable characteristics and anonymity (since they would leave Taiwan eventually). Although it is difficult to know how prevalent this practice was and is, activists' promotion of self-insemination does democratize the use of ART by extending it to these legally excluded persons through sharing simple technology. Still, self-insemination is narrowly associated with lesbians and does not extend to heterosexual single women or feminists in general.

Some lesbian couples have instead chosen to go abroad, where they have rights to access ART. One Taiwanese lesbian couple wrote a blog about their ART experiences in Canada in the mid-2000s, and this became a rich source of information for the lesbian community. So far they have guided dozens of lesbian couples toward ART in Canada. Another lesbian couple offered detailed information on their Facebook page as to how they considered international sperm banks, finally ordered sperm from Denmark, and then traveled to an infertility clinic in Thailand, where there were no specific laws to prevent them accessing ART;[56] their story has become just the latest resource for the lesbian community in Taiwan. Such women, with high cultural capital and financial stability, are demonstrating their ability to organize diverse resources into a workable ensemble and form a global assemblage of self-replicating cells, information, regulation, and expertise. Behaviors such as the cross-border use of ART often prompt Taiwanese citizens to reflect on their country's strict regulations, and the cross-national comparison of regulations has become a reference point for evaluating access policy in Taiwan.

The limitation of ART to heterosexual married couples faced serious challenge at a 2012 consensus conference on surrogate motherhood sponsored by the Ministry of Health in Taiwan. In the preparatory meetings, invited civic group representatives and feminist scholars objected to the fact that the theme of the conference was limited to married heterosexual couples and received wide media coverage on the point; when a similar meeting was held in 2004, the marriage-based status limitation had not been raised as an issue. The rights of singles, lesbians, and even gays to become parents through ART have now gained unprecedented attention. In the final report of the 2012 consensus conference, participants (including lay citizens) emphasized that "marriage is not the only basis for establishing a family" and that "cohabiting couples, same-sex couples and even singles should have reproductive rights" and expressed a wish for their future incorporation into ART access.

---

56. Andrea Whittaker, *Thai in Vitro: Gender, Culture and Assisted Reproduction* (New York: Berghahn, 2015).

This report has, perhaps unintentionally, extended the access debate to gay men, who have never before been mentioned in this context in Taiwan. Among the legally excluded groups, single women and lesbians can use DI to fulfill their reproductive needs. But when surrogacy is discussed, gay men emerge as potential users to achieve biological fatherhood. In the wake of the 2012 conference report, the lesbian-centered LGBT Family Rights Advocacy held workshops for gay men to discuss gay fatherhood. A gay family, a Taiwanese-American, and an American who raised a boy through gestational surrogacy all shared their experiences of paternity with the participants: lesbians were guiding gays on becoming parents. Overall, lesbians, who were the least-represented ART users in earlier access debates, have now become the most powerful network builders for a possible rewriting of the script of ART use in Taiwan.

Conclusion

Does Taiwan continue to restrict ART eligibility to married couples? In terms of legal regulation, the answer is yes, but not really in the clinics or in activists' forums. The governance approach reminds us to move beyond formal policy making and include other governing activities in other loci. Individuals have practiced DI secretly in Taiwan and openly abroad. Doctors, the gatekeepers who initially decided who would have access to ART in Taiwan, have nevertheless practiced DI with legally excluded women. Lesbians such as Vicky have organized self-insemination services as alternatives. Although Taiwan is listed as one of the fourteen countries among the sixty-two countries and regions above in the IFFS report to have conservative limitations on access, these practices show that society is nevertheless managing to provide ART to excluded users and thereby demonstrating its own social order on ART use.

How does the governing trajectory reveal the features of gender, sexuality, and heteronormativity in Taiwan? From Hsiao-Yi in 1985 to Lee in 2005, it seems that, among excluded users, single heterosexual women who lack the chances to enter into marriage have won the most sympathy and support. This differs from the situation in Sweden and Britain, where lesbian couples have been viewed as better parents than single women and thus more legitimate ART users.[57] I would argue that single heterosexual women, particularly those with high socioeconomic status and resource-rich family support, come closest to married women as the ideal of motherhood in Taiwan. Medical doctors focused on these singles' desire for motherhood—an acclaimed femininity—rather than on their challenge to heterosexuality or to the institution of marriage, as the rationale for granting all women

---

57. Adrian, "Sperm Stories"; Lee, Macvarish, and Sheldon, "Assessing Child Welfare under the Human Fertilisation and Embryology Act 2008."

access to ART. By comparison, the stratification of sexuality made lesbian users invisible, unthinkable, and undesirable until the passing of the Human Reproduction Law.

The tension between gender and sexuality regimes also reveals various manifestations of collective resistance to access regulation. The lack of involvement by the women's movement in Taiwan needs to be understood within the country's specific social and cultural contexts. The agenda against compulsory motherhood has made feminists groups in Taiwan actively promote abortion rights but hesitate to support the right to procreate. Feminist critics of the medicalization of women's bodies are implicitly prevented from viewing medically intrusive ART as being a useful resource.

The women's liberation movement did help create an identity for women who chose to have DI and raise children without men, and such women's seeking of medical help triggered doctors' support and lobbying. Still, these moral pioneers' actions remained mostly individual efforts rather than a matter of collective reform. Compared with feminists groups, the Lesbian Mothers' Alliance embraces motherhood in the first place and then asks for reproductive rights as an extension of the LGBT movement's broader discourse of rights, thus seeking better links with ART reform. These two different agendas—with women's groups aiming to reshape the gender order (against compulsory motherhood) and lesbians' groups aiming to reorder the sexuality hierarchy (asking for reproductive rights)—has led to Taiwan's challenge to heteronormativity and to the privileges of marriage being done at the hands of lesbians rather than feminists.

Such a paradoxical trajectory to liberalizing ART access has had ironic consequences. In 2015, the percentage of women remaining unmarried at age forty to forty-four was 17.6 percent, not only a historical high but one of the highest in Asia. No organization has been formed specifically to lobby for the inclusion of singles in access to ART. The latest ART trick from the world of celebrities is for women to freeze their eggs before reaching the age of forty, an expensive and medically intrusive method, and to wait for Mr. Right to come along; they are not asking for a change of policy over ART access. To become included in access to ART through the route of policy debate has become almost exclusively an issue for lesbians, and occasionally for gay men. Some recent surveys show that around 40 percent of the general public supports the rights of lesbians and gays to reproduce or adopt children,[58] indicating growing support for nonconventional family formation in Taiwan. "Queer reproduction," not long ago invisible and almost unthinkable in Taiwan, has in rather a dramatic fashion become the strongest force in reconfiguring the politics of access to ART.

---

58. United Marketing Research, "Survey on Same-Sex Marriage," *United Daily*, December 3, 2012, p. 1; Ying-Hua Chang, Tu Hsu-Hao, and Lia Pei-Shan, *Taiwan Social Change Survey 2012* (Taipei: Academia Sinica, 2013).

4

Solving Low Fertility Rate with Technology?

Jung-ok Ha

Introduction

South Korea's total fertility rate (TFR) was 1.08 in 2005 (it was 1.15 in 2009 and 1.21 in 2014), and it was the world's lowest. This TFR has continued to fall steadily, in fact, since the country's population reached a replacement level of 2.1 in 1983 (Table 4.1). In the five years between 2006 and 2010, the South Korean government invested a total of 19.7 trillion won (US$18 billion) of public funds in an attempt to tackle low fertility.

Among all related governmental initiatives was the launch of the National Support Program for Infertile Couples ("the Program") in 2006, through which expenditures for a range of assisted reproductive technologies (ARTs) such as in vitro fertilization (IVF) and intrauterine insemination (IUI) are subsidized.

Table 4.1
Total fertility rate in Korea (1980–2014)

										(Unit: thousand persons, per reproductive woman)
Year	**1980**	**1983**	**1986**	**1989**	**1992**	**1995**	**1998**	**2001**	**2003**	**2004**
No. of total newborn babies	863.0	769.0	636.0	639.0	731.0	715.0	635.0	554.9	490.5	472.8
TFR	2.820	2.060	1.580	1.560	1.760	1.634	1.448	1.297	1.180	1.154
Year	**2005**	**2006**	**2007**	**2008**	**2009**	**2010**	**2011**	**2012**	**2013**	**2014**
No. of total newborn babies	435.0	448.2	493.2	465.9	444.8	470.2	471.3	484.6	436.5	435.4
TFR	1.076	1.123	1.250	1.192	1.149	1.226	1.244	1.297	1.187	1.205

Source: Statistics Korea, *Final Results of Birth Statistics in 2014.*

The Program has been called "very successful," and its budget has been increased as a result. In fact, no other programs have produced such a visible effect: the high number of babies born as a result of the Program has been considered proof enough of its success. For the past ten years since its implementation, research has focused on the number of infertile couples who have benefited from government medical subsidies through the Program, with most emphasis placed on the number of newborns. However, any assessments should not end there; they should continue with "*but . . .* "

This chapter examines three issues in the context of gender politics—low fertility and ARTs, norms and practices related to family and gender, and national policies on women's health. Specifically, this study seeks answers to these research questions:

First, how do the Program's two variables, low fertility and ARTs, interact? Now, ten years since the Program began, state support for ARTs seems natural. However, prior to the Program's introduction, ARTs had been considered in an entirely different light. Indeed, it was the launching of the Program that resulted in low fertility and ARTs being associated with one another, the latter being a solution to the former. The two variables appropriated how each other was understood.

The second question deals with the wider context in which the Program is situated: Does the Program adequately reflect changes in the Korean society, in particular, those related to the norms and practices of family and gender? Or does it rather act as an encumbrance? This chapter argues that the Program has thus far failed to keep up with changes in the areas of family and gender, and that this failure is found not only in the Program itself but in South Korea's family-related laws and policies as well.

Third, what impact has the Program had on the regulation of ARTs in South Korea? As the scale of the Program increased, approximately 60 percent of all IVF treatments were subsidized by the government. The Program's expansion saw newly introduced standards and guidelines, which brought about significant changes in the governance of ARTs in South Korea.

Finally, what impact does the Program have on women's health policies? This question is related to how the implementation of the Program has strengthened connection between ARTs and low fertility and how this connection was granted legitimacy. Before the Program, ARTs were perceived as a strictly private practice, and there was scant state support for and few regulations of both ART research and treatments. The introduction of the Program, however, changed things. Government subsidies legitimized ARTs as a response to low fertility, and the national policy on reproductive health began to reorganize around the Program. The government's first priority was population growth. Consequently, women's reproductive health was given a narrower redefinition that included only pregnancy and childbirth but excluded contraception and safe abortion—a redefinition to support the government's policies that focused on women's childbearing role.

This study attempts to answer these questions by examining Program-related government documents and national policies on women's health, with particular reference to changes made to the amended Maternal and Child Health Act (which took effect in 2009) and to Maternal and Child Health Services. In-depth analyses of the establishment and actual implementation processes of national policies were carried out through interviews with the main agents of the Program and its beneficiaries (the infertile couple self-help community).

The structure of the chapter is as follows:

First, I review the general implications of low fertility and ARTs, the issues behind the launch of the Program, and the impact the Program has had on gender politics in South Korea. Second, I present a general review of the Program, including project scale, budget changes, and the procedures required to receive subsidies. The third section examines whether the Program adequately reflects changes occurring in the Korean society, particularly those related to family and gender norms and practices. Finally, I examine how the Program has affected government policies on women's health in South Korea.

Multiple Realities

Launched in 2006, the Program is the intersection of two variables: low fertility and technological intervention in reproduction. Before we discuss the Program in more detail, it is valuable to review possible scenarios in which gender politics are affected by the two variables.

The "population problem" and gender politics

As terms like "population explosion" and "low birth rate crisis" imply a huge population problem, such issues have come to connote massive, even decisive impact on society at large. Their resolution has come to be seen as an overwhelming priority, but what are the gender politics of this? A simple conclusion on this matter cannot be drawn easily, as well indicated by political history.

On the one hand, as the "population problem" comes to be seen as a society-wide issue of pivotal importance, its speedy resolution can become an opportunity for women's empowerment. Historically, with the emergence of the eugenics movement, many feminists perceived genetics as a potentially useful vehicle for the realization of feminist political interests and actively engaged with it.[1] The goal of eugenics, so-called better breeding, was, after all, reproduction—an event that happens in women's bodies. It was this fact that led feminists to believe that the movement would contribute to elevating the status of women. Margaret Sanger (1879–1966), leader of the first birth control movement that sought to assert woman's right to choose reproduction or not, is well known to have taken much interest in eugenics later in her life.

Moreover, over the past forty years, the UN-backed International Population Conference and World Women's Forum have demonstrated a shared role in transforming views on matters related to women and population.[2] The most representative examples in this regard are the 1994 Cairo International Conference on Population and Development and the 1995 Beijing World Women's Forum. At the former, "population" was redefined as an issue of women's health and empowerment from its previous definition as an issue of development. Meanwhile, at the latter, women's rights were advocated as a gender-mainstreaming strategy as opposed to a mere matter of development. The 1974 Bucharest World Population Conference advocated an economic development first strategy, contrary to what had hitherto been the dominant view; the conference argued that economic development would lead to population control.[3] In the following year, during the First World Women's Forum in Mexico City, the UN's Women's Decade was launched together with the Women in Development approach, which emphasized the role of women in development. This marked the beginning of the written history of feminist women's policies. Outside of these institutions, the 1992 Rio UN Conference on Environment and Development and the 1993 Vienna World Conference on Human Rights quoted the expansion of women's participation and the ending of discrimination as their core priorities.

This discussion of "population issues" means that a space has opened where women's rights have to be considered, even if only in an instrumental sense, and feminism has actively entered this space and appropriated it for its own interests.[4]

---

1. Greta Jones, "Women and Eugenics in Britain: The Case of Mary Scharlieb, Elizabeth Sloan Chesser, and Stella Browne," *Annals of Science* 52(5) (1995): 481–502.
2. The International Population Conference meets every ten years, while the World Women's Forum meets every five, but they have been held in consecutive years several times. The Population Conference of 1974 in Bucharest was followed by the Women's Forum meeting in 1975 in Mexico City, while the 1984 meeting of the Population Conference in Mexico City was followed by the Women's Forum of 1985 in Nairobi, and the Cairo Population Conference of 1994 was followed by the 1995 Beijing Women's Forum.
3. L. P. Freedman and S. L. Isaacs, "Human Rights and Reproductive Choice," *Studies in Family Planning* 24(1) (1993): 18–30.
4. Of course, although both the Women's Forum and the Population Conference used the terms "development" and "rights," this does not mean that they departed from the same premises. For instance, with respect to reproductive rights, using the expression "a right to

Another element of problematizing population is the direct connection of reproduction in a population with its viability. Such a connection leads to repressive consequences for women. Reproduction has always been a field for political struggle. According to Ginsburg and Rapp, "[R]eproduction provides a terrain for imagining new cultural futures and transformation," and the imagination itself involves "the deepest aspirations and the sense of survival" of diverse groups.[5] It is for these reasons that, historically, women have not always had the opportunity to exercise their reproductive rights; rather, reproduction has figured hugely in the ideological struggles of states, with women barely considered during such struggles.

It is widely known that the Rhee Syng-man government (1948–1960) banned the import of contraceptive pills and devices into Korea to strengthen national power in preparation for the South to invade the North and the two Koreas to unite. Similarly, the Ceausescu government in Romania forbade any forms of abortion in order to maintain the power of state.[6]

Moreover, control over the reproductive capabilities of women can easily become intertwined with moral constraints on female sexuality. The Act for the Suppression of Trade in, and Circulation of, Obscene Literature and Articles of Immoral Use (US Congress, 1873), commonly known as the [Anthony] Comstock Law, was introduced to regulate the spread of contraception (both knowledge and methods) in the United States and was enforced until the early twentieth century. The law equated control over the capacity to reproduce with moral constraints over sexuality,[7] and moral conservatism continues to make use of similar rhetorical devices.

Korean population policies have always seen women as the object of state control. This was not just population control policies, but also policies introduced subsequent to the TFR falling below population replacement levels. A government research institute report published in 1989 (and supported by the United Nations Fund for Population Activities) discloses that even after the TFR reached the population replacement rate of 2.06

---

freely and responsibly decide," they are opposed to the compromise sought by feminists with respect to population control policies. However, in normal dialogue, especially within the context of the UN governance (expansion) dialogue, the radical opposition of feminists can be covered up by the "consensus" over codes of conduct. Furthermore, in the arena of actual politics, concepts of "development" and "security" in population control policies can form an opposing structure to religious fundamentalism (as opposed to population "crisis"). In this area, among the wide variety of feminists, those that link their goals with discourses of "development" in international politics and its discourse when opposing religious fundamentalism have sometimes been successful in realizing their goals.

5. Faye D. Ginsburg and Rayna Rapp, eds., *Conceiving the New World Order: The Global Politics of Reproduction* (Berkeley: University of California Press, 1995), 2.

6. Lesley Doyal, *What Makes Women Sick: Gender and the Political Economy of Health* (New Brunswick, NJ: Rutgers University Press, 1995).

7. L. J. Kaplan and R. Tong, *Controlling Our Reproductive Destiny: A Technological and Philosophical Perspective* (Cambridge, MA: MIT Press, 1994).

in 1983, the population policy–related portions of the Sixth Five Year Plan were implemented up until 1991.[8] The plan states that the goal was to "reduce TFR from 2.1 in 1985 to 1.75 by 1995." However, by 1987 the TFR was already around 1.6, thus population policies had no need to affect any further reduction in birth rates. Yet, interestingly, as the plan had reached its target ahead of schedule, a new rationale for the plan suddenly and unexpectedly emerged, not as a response to population shrinkage or a call for a sober analysis of the causes of rapid declines in population growth, but as an idea of controlling sexuality. In the 1989 interim assessment report, the new purpose of South Korea's population policy was described as "to respond to the sexual problems between unmarried people as well as the high levels of going off birth control, abortion and continued gender imbalance by broadening the parameters and targeted groups of the policy [to include not only married but also unmarried people]." While gender is not explicitly mentioned, control of female sexuality is clearly implied. It was only in 1996 that the Korean government officially ended its policy of population control; until 1996, the aforementioned policy that sought to control sexuality had remained in effect.

Low fertility and negotiated outcome

The so-called low fertility response national policy, which included the Program, was proposed in earnest in 2006 as the First Basic Plan on Low Fertility and the Aging Society. The government, rather than presenting its population policies as based on the results of in-depth analyses and rational assumptions, instead used "crisis" and "fear" and effectively sent the public into a state of panic.[9] This prevalent sense of crisis was the impetus behind the government's prioritizing "low fertility response" in its policy agenda. Since the First Basic Plan, "low fertility response" was used as powerful rhetoric to justify the arguments not only in the official documents of government officials and policy researchers, but also in conversations among

8.   Nam-Hun Jo, Il-Hyeon Kim, Mun-Hee Seo, and Yeong-Sik Jang, *Choigeuneoi ingoojeongchaeck donghyanggwa jeonmang: Je 6 Cha 5 Gaenyeon Gaeheockeul Joongseemeuroo* [Contemporary trends and prospects for population policy: The Sixth Five-Year Plan] (Seoul: Korean Population and Public Health Research Center, 1989).
9.   According to the Second Basic Plan on Low Fertility and the Aging Society drafted by the Korean government in 2010, one of the major outcomes of the First Basic Plan was the "creation of a national agreement" on the necessity of solving the problem. See Republic of Korea Government, *Second Basic Plan on Low Fertility and the Ageing Society in Korea, 2011– 2015: Rolling Plan 2015* (2010), 35. The Second Basic Plan also cited surveys conducted under the First Basic Plan in which most of those questioned (64.3 percent) were shown to take the problems of low fertility and the aging population very seriously and were worried about the impacts these issues might have on their own lives. Thus policy makers of the Second Basic Plan preposterously presented the public's concerns as "national agreement," fortifying this point with reference to the term "population" and by emphasizing "the problem."

regular people. Infertile couples, who had been strongly lobbying the government for subsidies to finance the medical expenses of ART, also appropriated this rhetoric, to significant effect.

With the growing prevalence of ARTs, beginning with IVF, within South Korea, from the 1990s, the infertile have separately requested that the National Health Insurance cover IVF treatments. A self-help community called Agaya (아가야 in Korean, *aga* refers to a baby and *ya* is a vocative postposition) was founded in 2003 (renamed the Korean Federation of Subfertile Families [KFSF] in March 2013) and in May 2005 conducted a signature drive in support of National Health Insurance coverage of IVF. The group collected the signatures of 8,540 infertile people from fertility clinics nationwide during a one-month period. The petition was delivered to the Ministry of Health and Welfare (MOHW), only to receive a disinterested and negative response, with lack of money cited as the reason for IVF's exclusion from National Health Insurance coverage.

> We continue giving our petitions to the MOHW, and every time we do, they respond like this: "because this is an issue for the individual, the individual is responsible, not the state. It is also not serious or potentially life-threatening, thus it should be solved at the individual level."[10]

The group then appealed to lawmakers from the Health and Welfare Committee of the National Assembly and, along with fourteen lawmakers, petitioned the National Assembly for medical subsidies on July 15, 2005. At the time, the KFSF and lawmakers upheld the phrase "low fertility response" as a means of claiming the legitimacy of medical subsidies for IVF. Up until then, a phrase that emphasized the legitimacy of subsidizing "the suffering and rights of infertile couples" had been used.

In a petition put forth in 2005, a rephrasing and reappropriation was undertaken by the MOHW when it promoted the Program as its low fertility policy. When the Program was launched in 2006, the MOHW officially stated that the petition by infertile couples had served as a foundation for the Program. An interesting point is that in the Program's literature, the term "National Health Insurance" has been replaced with "state aid." Thus, the KFSF's request for National Health Insurance coverage and the MOHW's political interests (to distinguish its low fertility policy from those of other departments) have found common ground in the Program.

The Program has been promoted as a "countermeasure to low fertility" in statistical terms, which means that the Program project can be withdrawn whenever the need—low fertility response—is eliminated. Infertile couples are also well aware of that fact.

---

10. Excerpt from an interview with the president of the KFSF at the KFSF office, October 7, 2011.

The government has instituted the Program to expand the population, rather than to protect the rights of infertile couples to have babies and live happy lives. . . . I wish the government would respect the desires and rights of these couples to have babies. . . . We need an empathic approach instead of a statistical approach, as is so often adopted by the government, in order to satisfy the rights of human beings and better the lives of infertile couples.[11]

Requests for government subsidies to finance the high medical expenses of IVF treatment began in the 1990s, with no response from the government. Things have changed dramatically since then, with the government now investing massive amounts of funds to solve Korea's low fertility issue. This new investment, however, should not be viewed as a positive answer to the long-awaited requests made by infertile couples but rather as merely a short-term policy to tackle low fertility.

Overview of the Program

Size and budget transition

The shifts in the annual goals and budgets of the Program are shown in Table 4.2.

Table 4.2
Transition of annual Program goals and budgets (2006–2015)

(Unit: Cases/1,000 won)

| | Program size | Budgets | | |
		Total	State subsidies	Local subsidies
2006	16,426	46,488,600	21,300,000	25,188,600
2007	11,694	31,509,461	14,180,268	17,329,193
	(−28.8%)	(−32.2%)	(−33.4%)	(−31.2%)
2008	17,900	26,851,407	12,042,999	14,808,407
	(53.1%)	(−14.8%)	(−15.1%)	(−14.5%)
2009	17,539	26,255,888	12,073,000	14,182,888
	(−2.0%)	(−2.2%)	(0.2%)	(−4.2%)
2010	62,412	55,272,070	25,401,000	29,871,070
	(255.8%)	(110.5%)	(110.4%)	(110.6%)
2011	66,784	65,542,697	30,121,000	35,421,697
	(7.0%)	(18.6%)	(18.6%)	(18.6%)
2012	65,100	64,741,563	28,309,000	36,432,563
	(−2.5%)	(−1.2%)	(−6.0%)	(2.9%)

(continued on p. 123)

---

11. Excerpt from an interview with the president of the KFSF at the KFSF office, October 7, 2011.

Table 4.2 (continued)

	Program size	Budgets		
		Total	State subsidies	Local subsidies
2013	67,020	75,798,162	34,466,000	41,332,162
	(2.9%)	(17.1%)	(21.7%)	(13.4%)
2014	77,000	85,743,725	38,908,000	46,835,725
	(14.9%)	(13.1%)	(12.9%)	(13.3%)
2015	76,185	89,572,000	40,679,000	48,893,000
	(2.9%)	(4.5%)	(4.6%)	(4.4%)

* Figures in brackets are year-on-year percentage changes.

Sources: MOHW, *Guidelines for the National Support Program for Infertile Couples*, 2006, 2007; *Guidelines for the Maternal and Child Health Services*, 2008, 2009, 2013, 2014, 2015; *Guidelines for the Family Health Services*, 2010, 2011, 2012, recomposed.

In 2006 when the Program was first launched, over 46 billion won (about US$4.3 million) was put toward financing 16,500 cases; the number declined gradually until 2009 but then abruptly surged in 2010 with over 55 billion won given in subsidies. The Program's budget was increased more than twofold in 2010 from the preceding year, the standards for subsidies were eased (from less than 130 percent of the average income of urban laborers to less than 150 percent of the national average household income, or less than 4.8 million won for a two-member household as of 2010), and subsidies that had been granted for IVF treatment were extended to IUI. In addition, in the case of dual-income households, just 50 percent of the income of the lower income earner was considered since 2010. This meant that the range of subsidies was greatly enlarged.

The types and amounts of treatments and the subsidies supporting them have all steadily increased over the years. In 2006 when the Program started, subjects were entitled to two treatment cycles and a 1.5 million won subsidy per cycle. The number increased to three cycles in 2009, and four cycles in 2011. Also in 2011 the subsidy was raised to 1.8 million won per cycle for three cycles with the exception of 1 million won for the fourth cycle.

The Program has been evaluated as a very successful one among the various government-initiated low fertility policies.

> The Program has been very successful, even compared with other low fertility policies; the budget for it was also relatively large. The Program has shown visible outcomes in terms of the number of newborn babies, so the MOHW itself and the government overall are pretty satisfied with the results.[12]

---

12. Excerpt from an interview with an MOHW official in charge of the Program at the MOHW office, September 30, 2013.

The budget for the Program has been steadily increasing. The MOHW official in charge of the Program expressed how, "even though it was not easy to operate such a big project smoothly, it went well with all the budget spent."[13] Thus, the Program is lauded as a successful project not just by the MOHW but by other government departments as well. However, there is a need for a more detached analysis of whether it is indeed a good thing that more women have experienced the program.

> What we call today the "[IVF] procedure market" is receiving a huge amount of government assistance, so there are a lot of people who think "you would be an idiot not to take the money." IVF subsidies are in the region of 1.8 million won, so many see no harm in giving the procedure a go. Even people who can conceive naturally often see no reason why they shouldn't go the IVF route anyway. I am worried that as government subsidies become ever larger, the amount of unnecessary procedures will rise even further.[14]

What is at stake here is not just the efficient use of public resources but also the health of women. We will look at this in more detail in the part "The Program's Effects."

Application process and eligibility requirements

Subsidy applicants go through various complex procedures. There is no "one-stop administrative system" in place, forcing applicants to make repeated visits to various administrative agencies and clinics. First, applicants must obtain a diagnosis of infertility from a fertility clinic. Second, they must submit the required documents to the local public health center and apply for subsidies. Third, selected patients receive a notice of determination, which must be submitted to a fertility clinic. Last, the patients receive IVF or IUI treatment at a fertility clinic and pay any costs not covered by the Program grant, which later go to the fertility clinic through the local public health center.

Only couples in legal marriages are eligible to apply for the subsidy, and a diagnosis of infertility from their doctor is essential. As mentioned previously, the applicant's financial situation is one of the considerations, so income-related documents are also required.

Limiting subsidy eligibility to legally married couples was a first in the history of ART governance in Korea. The Bioethics and Safety Act, a major plank in ART-related regulation, enacted in 2004 and implemented from 2005, did not specify regulations on marital status as part of eligibility for ART.[15] Few hospitals requested a marriage certificate, however, since their

---

13. Ibid.
14. Ibid.
15. This was not because the Bioethics and Safety Act respected couples out of wedlock or treated them equally with legally married couples, but because the embryo was the main

goal was to increase profits by treating as many patients as possible; there was no need to ask for a document that might get in the way of that goal.

The Program restricts eligibility to couples in a legal marriage even though people's ideas and practices about marriage and childbirth have changed. In other words, the Program is lagging behind, failing to reflect the changing norms and practices of Korea's modern reality. The problem is laws and institutions are failing to keep up with such social changes.[16] For instance, it was only in 2005 that the patriarchal family system (*hojuje* 戶主制) was finally and officially abolished in Korea, at least from the perspective of Korean civil law.

Even until the mid-1990s, almost everyone got married; most married couples had babies, and most of them were born in wedlock.[17] Since the 2000s, however, the number of unmarried people between twenty and thirty-nine has sharply risen along with the divorce rate. The number of people in their thirties not married has risen dramatically. There are seven times as many men unmarried as of 2010 (3.5 percent) as there were in 1970 (0.5 percent), while the number of women unmarried in their thirties is twenty times larger, rising from a mere 0.1 percent in 1970 to 2 percent in 2010.[18] Public opinion also reflects the change. In a survey on marriage conducted in the late 1990s, 33.6 percent of the participants agreed with the statement "You must get married," while 23.8 percent agreed with "You don't neces-sarily have to get married." The same survey conducted in 2014 showed reversed results: 15.2 percent for the first statement and 38.8 percent for the second (Table 4.3).

The gap is particularly wide among female respondents and the unmar-ried group. In 2014, only 13.5 percent of female respondents agreed with the first statement while 43.2 percent agreed with the second. Among the unmarried group, the ratio was 8.1 percent to 47.6 percent.[19]

---

issue of the act since the "respect for the embryo verses technological advances (and the economic benefits gained from them)" was the dominant discourse during the enact-ment process of the act. The act also contained the following clause: (in the order of) "The creation of embryos—use in treatment—supply to research—storage and disposal," and even referred to fertility clinics as "embryo producing medical institutions."

16. Seon-Young Park, Keuk-Kyoung Yoon, Bok-Soon Park, and Hye-Kyung Kim, *Gajockeui day-anghwaaei tareeun gwanyeonbeopjae jeongbee yeongoo: Yeoseong yieengwon bojang meet chabyeol-haesoreul weehan gwanyeonbeopjae jeongbee yeongoo (II)* [A study on the law for women's rights and elimination of discrimination (II): Focusing on the family] (Seoul: Korean Women's Development Institute, 2008).

17. T. H. Kwon, T. H. Kim, D. S. Kim, K. H. Jun, and K. S. Eun, *Hangook Choolsanyock Byeoncheoneui Yeehae* [Understanding Korea's demographic transition] (Seoul: Ilshinsa, 1997).

18. Y.-K. Kim, M.-J. Jin, Y.-J. Song, and G.-H. Kim, *Gagoo gajeockeui byeondonggwa jeongchaeckje-ock daeungbangan yeongoo* [Changes in family and household structures and social welfare policies] (Seoul: Korea Institute for Health and Social Affairs, 2013).

19. Statistics Korea, *2014 sahwaejosa bogoseo* [The 2014 report on the social survey], accessed May 25, 2015, http://kosis.kr/ups/ups_01List01.jsp?pubcode=KN.

Table 4.3
Opinions on marriage (2002–2014)

	Must get married	Prefer to get married	Impartial	Prefer not to get married	Must not get married	No opinion	Total
1998	33.6	39.9	23.8	1.1	0.2	1.4	100.0
2002	25.6	43.5	27.2	1.7	0.2	1.8	100.0
2006	25.7	42.0	27.5	1.8	0.4	2.6	100.0
2008	23.6	44.4	27.7	2.4	0.5	1.4	100.0
2010	21.7	43.0	30.7	2.8	0.5	1.3	100.0
2012	20.6	42.4	33.4	1.5	0.3	1.8	100.0
2014	15.2	42.1	38.8	1.6	0.4	2.0	100.0

Sources: Kim et al., *Changes in Family and Household Structures and Social Welfare Policies*, 2013; Statistics Korea, *Report on the Social Survey*, 2008, 2010, 2012, 2014, recomposed.

Female respondents in their thirties exhibited the most extreme results in 2014: 5.7 percent for the first statement and 57.7 percent for the second. Another poll conducted in 2013 indicated a similar trend: 46.1 percent of respondents agreed with the statement "A couple does not necessarily have to marry to live together."[20]

Public opinion on childbirth has also changed. Until 1991, the ratio of "You must have children" versus "You don't necessarily have to have children" among married women was overwhelming toward the first statement, with 90.3 percent agreeing with it, and only 8.5 percent agreeing with the second. In 2012, the same poll showed reversed results: 46.3 percent agreed with the first, and 54.5 percent with the second.[21]

The most dramatic change can be found in the answer to the question of the "necessity of sons." Much governmental effort was made to change the traditional preference for sons beginning in the mid-1970s when the National Family Planning Program (NFPP) was implemented, with little success made into the mid-1990s.[22] But even this figure changed in the 2000s. For instance, the number of married female respondents who responded "Not necessarily" to the question of whether sons were a necessity increased more than twofold, to 58.3 percent in 2012 from 28.0 percent in 1991. Meanwhile, the percentage of married female respondents responding "Absolutely" to that question plummeted to 8.2 percent in 2012 from 40.5 percent in 1991 (Table 4.4).

---

20. Kim et al., *Gagoo gajeockeui byeondonggwa jeongchaeckjeock daeungbangan yeongoo*.
21. Ibid.
22. Kwon et al., *Hangook Choolsanyock Byeoncheoneui Yeehae*.

Table 4.4
Changes in the perceived necessity of sons among married women aged fifteen to forty-four (1991–2012)

(Unit: %, persons)

Year	Must have	Prefer to have	Impartial	No opinion	Total	Number of respondents
1991	40.5	30.7	28.0	0.8	100.0	7,448
1994	26.3	34.3	38.9	0.5	100.0	5,175
1997	24.8	35.0	39.4	0.8	100.0	5,409
2000	16.2	43.2	39.5	1.1	100.0	6,350
2003	14.1	41.8	43.3	0.8	100.0	6,599
2006	10.2	39.3	49.8	0.7	100.0	5,386
2009	8.9	39.2	51.8	0.1	100.0	4,868
2012	8.2	33.0	58.3	0.5	100.0	4,535

Sources: Kim et al., *2012 National Survey on Fertility, Family Health, and Welfare in Korea*, 2012; KIHASA, *2010 National Survey on Fertility, Family Health, and Welfare in Korea*, 2010, recomposed.

Births outside marriage also increased significantly in the 2000s (Figure 4.1), from a flat 1.0 percent throughout the 1980s and 1990s to 2.1 percent in 2012.

Such changes led one report to conclude that "the reproductive function of the family has been reduced in Korea."[23] If that is true, then pregnancy and childbirth require much stronger and proactive decision making now compared with the mid-1990s.

The Program's Effects

A policy that increases demand for the policy

As stated above, it is necessary to receive a diagnosis of infertility to apply for Program benefits. The requirement of infertility diagnosis has resulted in an increase in the number of men and women diagnosed with infertility (Table 4.5). However, the word "diagnosed" is frequently omitted, and the number is used as an indication of a rise in the "infertile population," hence a justification for the Program.[24]

While trends vis-à-vis the total population remain relatively constant, the number of infertile women and men is increasing every year to an

---

23. Park et al., *Gajockeui dayanghwaaei tareeun gwanyeonbeopjae jeongbee yeongoo (II)*.
24. Nami Hwang, "The Status and Performances of the National Support Program for Infertile Couples," *Health and Welfare Issue and Focus* 192 (2013): 1–8.

Figure 4.1
The rates of births outside marriage among total births in Korea (1981–2014)

(Unit: %)

Source: Statistics Korea, *Final Results of Birth Statistics in 2014.*

unreasonable degree. Especially in 2006, the first year of the Program, the number of women diagnosed with infertility increased by 14.1 percent from the previous year; in 2010, when IUI treatment was included in the Program, the number of men diagnosed with infertility showed a 27.7 percent increase from 2009.

These increases do not represent an actual increase in the size of the infertile population. The increases result from rises in the number of those going to the hospital with the intention of being diagnosed as infertile in order to receive government aid. Additionally, in an analysis of the results of this policy, 62.1 percent of those who received financial aid were deemed infertile for "causes unknown," much higher than "fallopian issues" (11.2 percent) or "issues with male fertility" (9.0 percent). Such "inconclusive" numbers have remained basically the same over the lifespan of this policy.[25]

---

25. M.-H. Kim, H.-C. Kwon, S.-J. Paik, C.-S. Park, and G.-H. Lee, *Naneembooboo jeewonsaeup gaeseonbangan yeongoo* [A study for the improvement of sub-fertility couple supporting program] (Seoul: Ministry of Health and Welfare, 2013), 29.

Table 4.5
The number of women and men diagnosed as infertile compared to total population
(2004–2011)

	Woman (Unit: person)		Man (Unit: person)		Total population (Unit: 1,000 people)		Woman	Man
		Year-on-year variation		Year-on-year variation		Year-on-year variation*		
2004	104,699		22,166		48,584		24,221	24,363
2005	110,248	5.3%	20,747	–6.4%	48,782	0.4%	24,326	24,456
2006	125,793	14.1%	23,576	13.6%	48,992	0.4%	24,435	24,557
2007	134,318	6.8%	26,184	11.1%	49,269	0.6%	24,578	24,691
2008	133,883	–0.3%	26,314	0.5%	49,540	0.6%	24,717	24,823
2009	135,749	1.4%	27,804	5.7%	49,773	0.5%	24,843	24,930
2010	148,551	9.4%	35,506	27.7%	50,516	1.5%	25,205	25,310
2011	151,006	1.7%	40,199	13.2%	50,734	0.4%	25,327	25,407
2012	148,472	–1.7%	41,407	3.0%	50,948	0.4%	25,444	25,504
2013	147,078	–0.9%	42,858	3.5%	51,141	0.4%	25,553	25,588
Increase from 2004 to 2013		40.5%		93.4%	Increase from 2004 to 2013	5.3%		

* The increase in total population was calculated with use of the original population figures, not in increments of 1,000 persons.

Sources: National Health Insurance Service, *National Health Insurance Statistics*, 2005–2015; Statistics Korea, *Population Statistics Based on Resident Registration in 2013*, 2014, recomposed.

The higher rises in the number of people wishing to receive infertility treatment than the increase in actual instances is a phenomenon common worldwide.[26] Indeed, "infertility prevalence" is a figure that includes those "who wish to be pregnant." Although "not becoming pregnant after a year without the use of birth control" may be the medical definition of infertility, unless one wishes to get pregnant and seeks a medical diagnosis, one is not included in infertility prevalence figures. Hence, in an article that compares infertility prevalence figures for the year 1990 with those of the year 2010, it is concluded that "[a]lthough there were no statistically significant changes in the prevalence of infertility, . . . reduced child-seeking behavior resulted in a reduction of primary infertility among all women from 1.6% to 1.5% . . . from 1990 to 2010."[27]

---

26. Kaplan and Tong, *Controlling Our Reproductive Destiny*, 187.
27. M. N. Mascarenhas, T. Boerma, S. Vanderpoel, and G. A. Stevens, "National, Regional, and Global Trends in Infertility Prevalence since 1990: A Systematic Analysis of 277 Health Surveys," *PLOS Medicine* 9(12) (2012): 1.

Table 4.6
Total cycles of IVF in Korea, cycles of the Program (1992–2010)

Year	Total cycles of ART* (a)	Year-on-year variation	Cycles of the PROGRAM (b)	(b)/(a)
1992	6,838			
1993	7,687	12.4%		
1994	10,818	40.7%		
1995	8,700	–19.6%		
1996	8,694	–0.1%		
1997	16,286	87.3%		
1998	13,380	–17.8%		
1999	17,073	27.6%		
2000	15,386	–9.9%		
2001	14,436	–6.2%		
2002	17,996	24.7%		
2003	16,753	–6.9%		
2004	17,375	3.7%		
2005	18,941	9.0%		
2006	29,531	55.9%	19,137	64.8%
2007	26,935	–8.8%	14,700	54.6%
2008	27,819	3.3%	13,267	47.7%
2009	27,756	–0.2%	17,691	63.7%
2010	30,571	10.1%	24,452	80.0%

* This table includes only the type of ART treatments supported by the Program. Oocyte donation is not included here.

Sources: ACIC-KSOG, "Current Status of ART in Korea," for the years 1994–2004; AC-KSOG, "Current Status of ART in Korea," for the years 2005–2008; CA-KSOG, "Current State of ART in Korea, 2009"; RMC-KSOG 1995; Choi et al., "Analysis and evaluation of the result of national supporting program of infertile couples in 2010"; Lee et al., "Current Status of ART in Korea, 2010," recomposed.

Rise in the scale of ARTs

The changes in attitudes toward marriage and childbirth discussed above and the general low fertility trends in Korean society have had a huge impact on the IVF industry, which saw a drop in IVF treatments in the 2000s, a shock from the upward curve it had experienced until the 1990s. However, government policies have resulted in a rapid rise in the number of cases of IVF treatment in South Korea today.

According to the "Current Status of ART in Korea," an annual report published by the Korean Society of Obstetrics and Gynecology (KSOG), the number of IVF cycles across the nation steadily increased throughout the 1990s. Reaching a peak of 17,073 cycles in 1999, it continuously declined during the early 2000s.

However, in 2006, the year the Program was introduced, the number of cycles jumped by 55.3 percent to 29,733 from the 18,941 recorded in the previous year (Table 4.6) and remained at around 30,000 cycles thereafter (according to the most recent report of 2010 published in 2015). Approximately 60 percent of the total IVF cycles conducted between 2006 and 2010 were supported by the Program.

As a result of this change in government policy, the number of IVF treatments has increased, and the numbers of oocyte donations and cases of IVF surrogacy have also increased as a consequence. I have been a member of an institutional review board at an infertility clinic (with more than 1,000 cases of IVF each year) in Seoul since 2007, and cases of IVF surrogacy reviewed by the board have continued to increase this year. It makes sense that due to government policies, the number of IVF cases has increased, and among those that have failed to conceive as a result of IVF, some would resort to IVF surrogacy. The number of oocyte donation cases reviewed by the board also continues to rise this year.

The rise of IVF procedures, indeed the exponential rise in the number of procedures performed, has had negative side effects. *Health Statistics* published by the National Health Insurance Service includes a detailed breakdown of health insurance funding allocations by disease. Complications related to ARTs have become one of the top 500 causes of hospitalization since 2006. Indeed, since the introduction of the Program, 1,000 women on average have been admitted to the hospital annually due to complications arising from ARTs, and they stay for an average of ten days. Treatment for complications costs around 700 million won a year, with the National Health Insurance Service paying out around 400–600 million won annually in disbursements for treatment.

ARTs are also endangering the health of the infants. The proportion of twins and multiple pregnancies as a percentage of all births has risen from 2.0 percent in 2003 to 3.5 percent in 2014. Similarly, the instances of premature birth have risen from 4.5 percent of all births in 2003 to 6.7 percent in 2014, and the number of low birth weight babies has gone up from 4.1 percent in 2003 to 5.7 percent in 2014.

The increasing utilization of ARTs and concomitant rise in the number of instances of ART-related complications, as well as rises in multiple pregnancies, premature births, and low birth weight can be termed "iatrogenic diseases." Financial pressures on state budgets combined with fears of the impact on female and infant health have led many states to urge patients to first utilize less invasive procedures before attempting the use of ARTs.[28]

Stunted and deformed policy on women's health

The Program supported expenditures for ARTs and, at the same time, impacted national policies on women's health. This section examines how the introduction of the Program affected Maternal and Child Health Services (MCHS) by making women's health an instrument for ensuring women's reproduction and higher fertility rates.

The MCHS is the only national program focused on women's health. This fact reflects a general bias toward reducing women's health to reproductive health. A great deal of feminist literature on women's health levels shows strong criticism against this bias and women's health policies devised in the context of maternal and child health services or family planning projects.[29] Women's health policies for a long time were not treated separately from maternal and child health services or family planning projects, though the recent introduction of gender mainstreaming has made inroads in positioning women's health in its own context.

The MCHS has not developed alongside an understanding and consideration of women's health but instead is viewed purely as being an element to be managed within the context of the "population problem." Until the 1960s, the MCHS was a titular project; it was the NFPP that provided practical services for women. The MCHS gained momentum later on due to the enactment (1973) and revision (1986) of the Maternal and Child Health Act (MCH Act) but lost steam during the 1990s with the abolishment of the NFPP. In 2006 the MCHS was revitalized again with the launch of the Program, albeit for the opposite reason: conception, not contraception. The Program's influence on the MCHS has been significant: it has literally changed concepts of maternal and child health.

The Program doubled the size of the MCHS: the budget for the MCHS, which had been between 2.6 and seven billion won before the launch of the Program, surged to between 25 and 48 billion won in 2006. The 48.5 billion won budget granted to the MCHS in 2010 was nineteen times that given in

---

28. Jung-Ok Ha, "Risk Disparities in the Globalization of Assisted Reproductive Technology: The Case of Asia," *Global Public Health: An International Journal for Research, Policy and Practice* 8(8) (2013): 904–25.

29. Tracy Johnson and Elizabeth Fee, "Women's Participation in Clinical Research: From Protection to Access," in *Women and Health Research: Ethical and Legal Issues of Including Women in Clinical Studies*, ed. Anna C. Mastroianni, Ruth Faden, and Daniel Federman (Washington DC: National Academy Press, 1994); Nacy Krieger and Elizabeth Fee, "Man-Made Medicine and Women's Health: The Biopolitics of Sex/Gender and Race/Ethnicity," in *Women's Health, Politics, and Power: Essays on Sex/Gender, Medicine, and Public Health*, ed. Elizabeth Fee and Nancy Krieger (New York: Baywood, 1994), 11–29.

2003 (2.6 billion won) and seven times that given in 2005 (7 billion won). This increased budget expanded the size of the MCHS as well. In 2009 and 2010, the budget for the Program rose by 13.328 billion won, which accounted for 91.6 percent of the total budget increment of 14.547 billion won. These numbers reflect not only the Program's importance but also the Program-centeredness of the MCHS and the resulting deformation and reduction of the concept of maternal and child health.

The Program-centeredness of the MCHS gained legal ground with the extensive revision of the MCH Act in 2009. While its revision in 1973 was to support the NFPP, the 2009 revision was aimed at placing the Program in a subcategory of the MCHS. This ultimately resulted in reversing MCHS aims from contraception in the NFPP era to conception in the Program era.

In the amended MCH Act, which was passed in the National Assembly in December 2008 and went into effect in July 2009, provisions for sterilization and contraceptive surgeries—which were subsidized by the government and once considered essential measures for maternal and child health—were deleted,[30] and in their place a clause was inserted to "support pregnancy, childbirth and child rearing." Such provisions laid the legal foundation for the Program to become a part of the MCHS.

The concept of contraceptive operations was completely erased from all provisions and replaced with other concepts such as "reproductive health management and healthcare program development for women at reproductive age." In the 2012 revision, the MCH Act came to include even the provision "preventing artificial abortions."

The Program-centeredness of the MCHS is also reflected in the "[b]asic goals and policy approaches" of *The Guidelines for Maternal and Child Health Services* published every year by the MOHW. Until 2005, "[i]mprovement of maternal and child health" took precedence in the guideline, but in 2006, when the Program first began, the focus shifted to "[e]nlargement of subsidies for pregnancy and childbirth for infertile couples and mothers."[31] Since 2008, "[i]mprovement of the reproductive health of women in reproductive age" has taken a central position,[32] which the guideline explains should be achieved through such initiatives as operating more reproductive health centers for college students, promoting the prevention of artificial abortions, and opening a portal site for information about pregnancy, childbirth, and childrearing. This means that Korean women can now receive public subsidies for conception instead of contraception, which had been subsidized

---

30. The range of contraception was also drastically reduced; the concepts of "contraceptive operation and contraceptive pills" were changed to "contraceptive pills, etc." or "contraceptive pills or contraceptive devices." Provisions on abortion doctor qualifications or state subsidies were also deleted.
31. Ministry of Health and Welfare (MOHW), *Nyeondo moja bogeon saeop annae* [Guidelines for the maternal and child health services] (2004, 2005, 2006, 2007).
32. MOHW, *2008 nyeondo moja bogeon saeop annae.*

in the past, but still receive none for the protection of their physical, mental, and social health.

An irony is that, despite this focus of women's health policies on conception, the most basic of reproductive services have deteriorated because of a disinterested government and profit-seeking hospitals. For instance, nowadays, it is not uncommon for a university hospital to be without a delivery room. This justification is that maintaining a delivery room for less than ten deliveries per month is a waste of money. If university hospitals are like this, it is not surprising to find local clinics with even worse conditions. According to a recent report, forty-seven cities among the nation's 164 cities (*si*), counties (*gun*), and districts (*gu*) lack obstetrics and gynecology hospitals.[33] Gangwon province is particularly bad, with a combined total of only thirty-five beds in all of its delivery rooms. This is astounding considering that the number of pregnant women in that area in 2011 was 11,612.[34]

Furthermore, midwife-assisted births, either at birthing centers or at home, are not an option for many. Thus 98.2 percent of Korean women gave birth in hospitals in 2010, and 99.0 percent in 2014.[35]

The maternal mortality ratio (MMR) in Korea was 17.2 in 2011, twice the Organisation for Economic Co-operation and Development average of 9.3 (Figure 4.2). Again, needless to say, the MMR figures show huge regional variations. For example, Gangwon province had an MMR of 32.1 in 2012, more than three times that of Seoul in the same year.[36]

Conclusion

The Program was the negotiated outcome of the overlapping interests of two groups: the government (more specifically, the MOHW), which felt pressured to come up with a policy to reverse fertility decline, and infertile couples, who had lobbied the National Health Insurance for years to support the expenses associated with ARTs. Having once been indifferent to each other's interests, the two parties have appropriated and reappropriated each other's interests since the launch of the Program.

Owing to the increased number of newborn babies, the Program is regarded as a highly successful policy to tackle low fertility, and its size and budget have continuously increased. The huge budget allocated to the

---

33. "Chungcheong 11 gae jidgaechae sanbooingwa boonmanseal eopseo" [There is no delivery room in 11 Chungcheong counties], *Daejonilbo*, October 18, 2013.
34. "Gangwon Yeemsanboo Samangbee 32.1 Myeong, Jeongook Si Do Choigoo" [The maternal mortality ratio of Gangwon province is 32.1, the highest among all Korean counties] *Yonhap News*, October 9, 2013.
35. Statistics Korea, *2010 nyeon choolsaengtonggae* [Final results of birth statistics in 2010] (2011), accessed January 8, 2014; and Statistics Korea, *2014 nyeon choolsaengtonggae* [Final results of birth statistics in 2014] (2015), accessed November 24, 2015, http://kostat.go.kr.
36. "Gangwon Yeemsanboo Samangbee 32.1 Myeong, Jeongook Si Do Choigoo."

Figure 4.2
Comparison of maternal mortality ratio in Korea and OECD averages

(Unit: number of maternal deaths per 100,000 live births)

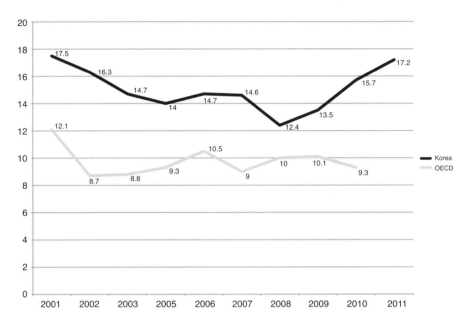

Source: MOHW, *Guidelines for the Maternal and Child Health Services 2013.*

Program has not only changed the aims of the MCHS but entire policies with respect to women's health, so that excessive focus has been placed on conception.

Nevertheless, it is hard to agree that conception-focused policies to tackle low fertility have actually produced desirable outcomes when we look at the disturbing reality of deteriorated ob-gyn services. There has been much mutual recrimination between the government and medical circles because of this situation, but worsened MMR rates and neonatal indexes speak for themselves.[37]

Furthermore, the Program has failed to reflect changes in society and public sentiment regarding families and communities, choosing instead to concentrate on figures. Limiting eligibility for subsidies to legally married couples tellingly demonstrates how the Program is lagging behind, failing to account for the changing norms and practices.

Most of the literature discussing "low fertility" in South Korea starts with astonishment over the numbers' (TFR equals 6.0 in 1960, 2.8 in 1980, and 1.2 in 2010) massive, indeed, seismic drops in just a few decades. Attitudes

---

37. Ha, "Risk Disparities in the Globalization of Assisted Reproductive Technology."

toward women, however, have by and large remained the same: they have statistical, not human, significance.

South Korea's NFPP was brought in by the Park Chung-hee government, which emphasized the value of the "modern family," specifically, "Modernization of the Fatherland," as part of the 1970s economic development. The low fertility rate that South Korea is now facing is considered a national crisis, and the Program represents the government's attempt at a medical technology–based solution. However, the bodies of women are still considered objects in TFR statistics, much as they were in the 1970s when the government aggressively pursued its family planning agenda. This has led to a situation in which the health and even the lives of women are being endangered once again.

Acknowledgments

This work was supported by a grant from the National Research Foundation of Korea funded by the Korean government (Grant No. NRF-2013S1A3A2054579).

Part II

Women Producing and Consuming Health Knowledge: Embracing Drugs, Vitamins, and Food

Though not unique to East Asia, maintaining the health of the family (and hence the nation) was a responsibility shouldered mainly by women, yet the production and consumption of health knowledge through the management of patent drugs, vitamins, and food, as discussed by Burns and Lei in this section, demonstrate specifically the East Asian modern and postcolonial tensions and struggles over legitimacy, authority, and authenticity. Burns explores modern Japan's pharmaceutical interest in and competition over women's bodies in the 1920s and 1930s, analyzing how patent drugs as "medical commodities" promoted multiple and competing representations of health and femininity not only to citizens but also to colonial subjects. Lei's study, in contrast, unpacks the theories of postcolonial Taiwan's Dr. Zhuang Shuqi, who commercialized health knowledge and products repackaged in the language of traditional "Asian" dietary therapy, with the female consumer of her theories and products cast as a "housewife" cum "family pharmacist." Facilitated by growing consumer and media cultures, the marketing of health and medical products and knowledge not only competed with the state over the formation of gender and body norms and roles, but allowed for selective production and consumption by women themselves.

5

The Japanese Patent Medicine Trade in East Asia

Women's Medicines and the Tensions of Empire

Susan L. Burns

On September 27, 1922, a large advertisement appeared on page 3 of the *East Asia Daily* (*Tonga ilbo* 東亜日報), a Korean-language newspaper. The advertisement in question (Figure 5.1) featured a line drawing of the head and shoulders of a so-called modern girl with a short haircut and a beaded headband, a figure popular in East Asia no less than in the United States and Europe.[1] In large bold print, the copy declared, "[H]uman feelings have no national boundaries." This was an advertisement for a Japanese patent drug called Chūjōtō (中将湯). An herbal medicine for women widely sold throughout East Asia, Chūjōtō was described by its manufacturer as efficacious for a wide range of female ills, from menstrual difficulties and "uterine disease," to prenatal and post-natal problems, to a more diffuse set of apparently gender-specific complaints such as cold sensitivity and "hysteria." Although the advertisement noted that Chūjōtō was manufactured in Japan, it also declared that, like human feelings, "medicine has no national boundaries" and that "intelligent" foreign women use Chūjōtō to acquire their "healthy beauty."

The visual and rhetorical logic of this advertisement hints at the complicated meanings that were attached to health within the expanding market of medical commodities in the Japanese Empire. It links female health with cosmopolitan modernity and physical beauty, while also implying the existence of shared sentiment on the part of all consumers, colonial, ethnic, and national divisions notwithstanding. The large and growing literature on medicine in East Asia has examined topics such as the rise of biomedicine, the formulation of medical and public health policy, the forging of new professional identities, and the establishment of educational and clinical institutions. While this body of research has demonstrated that medicine was shaped by

---

1. On the international history of the modern girl, see the essays in Alys Eve Weinbaum et al., *The Modern Girl around the World: Consumption, Modernity, and Globalization* (Durham: Duke University Press, 2008).

and subject to the politics of nationalism and empire, the implications of market capitalism in East Asia for ideas about health and the body has yet to be thoroughly explored. This chapter, like Sean Hsiang-lin Lei's contribution to this volume, argues that medical consumerism needs to be considered as a central part of medical culture. In this regard, Thomas Richards' work on "therapeutic commodities" in late nineteenth-century Britain is suggestive. By examining the discourse surrounding patent drugs and other health-related products, Richards exposed how the human body became the site of contestation because it was "the terrain the commodity culture was most eager to minister to, the government most anxious to control, and the consumer most hard pressed to defend."[2]

Nikolas Rose and Carlos Novas have also drawn our attention to medical consumerism. They argue that what they term the "the market economy of health" is a crucial part of the "regulated political economy of health." The state apparatus, medical professionals, commercial enterprises, and individuals are all involved in creating channels through which medical

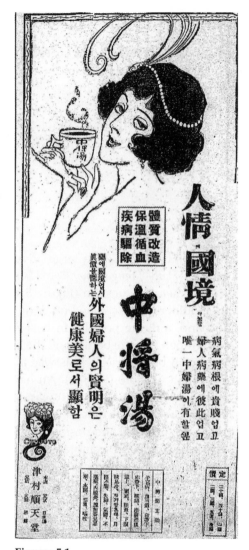

Figures 5.1

East Asia Daily, September 27, 1922

information, in various and competing forms, flows.[3] Significantly, commercial enterprises such as pharmaceutical companies often present themselves as speaking directly to consumers, encouraging them to understand

---

2.   Thomas Richards, *The Commodity Culture of Victorian England: Advertisement and Spectacle, 1851–1914* (Stanford: Stanford University Press, 1990), 204.

3.   Nikolas Rose and Carlos Novas, "Biological Citizenship," in *Global Assemblages: Technology, Politics, and Ethics as Anthropological Problems*, ed. Aihwa Ong and Stephen J. Collier (Malden, MA: Blackwell Publisher, 2005), 455.

themselves in biological terms but also calling upon them to question bio-medical authority that encourages "passive and compliant" patienthood.[4]

Prompted by the work of Richard, Rose, and Novas, in this chapter I explore how medical commodities became implicated in a struggle over the care of the body and the meaning of bodily health in the Japanese Empire of the 1920s and 1930s. I focus specifically on the marketing of so-called women's medicines. Among the most profitable of the many patent drugs that flowed from the metropole to the colonies, products for women such as Chūjōtō, Kitani Jitsubosan (喜谷実母散, "Kitani's real mother pills"), and Inochi no Haha (命の母, "Mother of life") were heavily advertised via news-papers, magazines, posters, and signboards.[5] Sold by large and small retail shops, by mail order, and by itinerant peddlers, they were widely available throughout the colonies and beyond. In his study of German advertising and empire, David Ciarlo has argued for the significance of commercial culture for understanding "the colonial," stating, "[C]ommercial culture, with its diffuse points of origin, offers a new opportunity. It resists investiga-tion through institutional or organizational lenses, but this very dispersal can offer an entry point into a broader view of society."[6] My project differs from that of Ciarlo. While he examined the uses of colonial imagery to sell products to German consumers, I am interested in the marketing of Japanese products to Japanese colonial subjects. But his point that the consideration of consumer culture can complicate our understanding of empire is perhaps even more pertinent in this context. In marketing their products, Japanese manufacturers and retailers of medical commodities did not simply confirm the gendered biopolitics of the Japanese state. Rather, they appealed to the desires and aspirations of colonial consumers and promoted multiple and contesting images of health and femininity.

Medical Modernization and Patent Drugs

Japan's modern patent drug industry took form after 1890, and the products that appeared and became profitable in this era reflected a profound recon-figuring of Japan's medical culture. Beginning in the 1870s, the recently founded Meiji government made medical modernization one of its many goals and began to promote the institutionalization of Western biomedi-cine and the disestablishment of traditional Sino-Japanese medicine. New schools to train doctors, midwives, and pharmacists were established, licens-ing procedures were put into place, and public health policies that sought to

---

4. Ibid., 448.
5. Throughout this chapter, I use the term "patent drugs" as a translation for the Japanese term *baiyaku* (literally, "sold medicines").
6. David Ciarlo, *Advertising Empire: Race and Visual Culture in Imperial Germany* (Cambridge, MA: Harvard University Press, 2011), 13.

control infectious disease were promulgated. As the plan for medical modernization unfolded, the trade in packaged medicines (*baiyaku* 売薬) came under new scrutiny. Prepared herbal compounds, sold in single doses, had a long history in Japan, appearing as early as the mid-seventeenth century.[7] Advertisements for prepared medicines, in the form of handbills, date from the 1680s, making medicines one of the first products to be marketed in this way, a development that probably reflected the large number of producers and the intense competition for customers.[8] By the late eighteenth century, major cities such as Edo (later renamed Tokyo) and Osaka had hundreds of "medicine shops" (*kusuriya*) that manufactured and sold prepared medicines.

The first attempt to control the patent drug trade came in 1870 when the Japanese government issued the Rules for the Regulation of Patent Drugs (*Baiyaku torishimari kisoku* 売薬取締規則). It required that all patent drugs be evaluated by the newly established government medical school to ensure that they were in fact effective and also addressed the advertising conventions of the early modern period. References to the divine origin of medicines, to "secret recipes," and "secret family formula" were all forbidden. However, the requirement for testing quickly proved untenable when the medical school was flooded by requests from medicine producers to examine and approve their product.[9] In 1875 a new law was promulgated which made "harmlessness" rather than efficacy the standard for prepared medicines: it required testing only when a complaint was filed. This was followed in 1877 and 1882 by more regulations, which established stiff new taxes and licensing fees for producers and retailers, as well as a stamp tax on the products themselves.[10] In the eyes of the Japanese government, patent drugs were akin to alcohol and tobacco: they were wasteful indulgences rather than legitimate medicines. In this same period journalists and civil reformers also began to rail against the medicine trade, arguing that manufacturers encouraged consumers to squander their money on ineffective, even dangerous, nostrums, when they would do better to visit a modern physician.[11]

The new regulations proved disastrous for many well-known medicine producers whose once-prosperous businesses declined under the financial requirements of the new laws.[12] The new pharmacies that emerged after

---

7. Yoshioka Shin, *Edo no kigusuriya* [A pharmacy in Edo] (Tokyo: Seiaibō, 1995), 16.
8. Masuda Tajirō, *Hikifuda ebira no fūzoku shi* [Fūzoku history of advertisements and posters] (Tokyo: Seiaibō, 1981), 199–200.
9. Shimizu Tōtarō, *Nihon yakugakushi* [History of Japanese pharmacology] (Tokyo: Nanzandō, 1949), 99.
10. Ibid., 200.
11. For a discussion of criticism of patent drugs, see Susan L. Burns, "Marketing Health and Beauty: Advertising, Medicine, and the Modern Body in Meiji-Taisho Japan," in *East Asian Visual Culture from the Treaty Ports to World War II*, ed. Hans Thomsen and Jennifer Purtle (Chicago: Center for the Art of East Asia, The University of Chicago, 2009), 175–96.
12. On the impact of the Meiji regulations, see Tamagawa Shinmei, *Hangontan no bunkashi: Etchū Toyama no kusuriuri* [The cultural history of Hangontan: Medicine seller in Etchū Toyama]

1890 succeeded by carefully negotiating the new medical culture of the day. Some of the most successful new medicines capitalized on governmental and popular concern for infectious diseases. Morita Jihei marketed Hōtan, a medicine for diarrhea, as a cure for cholera, the great scourge of the nineteenth century, while Morishita Hiroshi's pharmacy Nanyōdō, which manufactured the famous "revitalizer" Jintan, also produced Dokumetsu (Poison extinguisher), a syphilis cure. Nōgan (Brain pills) and Kennōgan (Health brain pills) were both advertised as effective treatments for "brain disease," headaches, and nervousness, disorders that were believed to result from the stress of modern life.[13]

Not surprisingly given the dangers of childbirth for women before the rise of modern obstetrics, medicines for pregnancy, birth, and postpartum problems were a vital part of both the old and new medical trade. Kitani Jitsubosan, a combination of botanicals that included angelica root, cnidium rhizome, scutelleria root, saussurea root, and cassia bark, was first sold in the early eighteenth century in Edo and proved to be immensely profitable, earning a fortune for the Kitani family, who manufactured it.[14] Similar medicines were produced around the country; some were called Jitsubosan in emulation of the famous Edo product, while others had names such as Anzantō (安産湯, "Safe birth decoction") and Soseitō (蘇生湯, "Life-renewing decoction") that suggested their desired effect. Many of these medicines survived the reform era—evidence of their popularity—but none was more successful than Kitani Jitsubosan, in part because the Kitani family quickly adapted to the new commercial culture, adopting a trademark and using the new newspapers to advertise their product.

In contrast, Chūjōtō and Inochi no Haha are both examples of the new patent drugs of this era: while based on traditional Sino-Japanese pharmacology, they were aggressively marketed in terms that stressed their affinity with biomedicine. Chūjōtō was manufactured by Tsumura Juntendō, a pharmacy founded in Tokyo by Tsumura Kanekichi in 1893. To name his product and explain its origin, Kanekichi referenced the well-known story of the Chūjō princess, the subject of both Nō and Kabuki plays. The daughter of a nobleman in eighth-century Japan, she was said to have been tormented by her stepmother, who plotted to kill her, but was saved when she managed to take refuge in a nunnery outside the old imperial capital of Nara. According to Tsumura Kanekichi's version of the story, his distant relation aided the

---

(Tokyo: Shōbunsha, 1979); and Suzuki Akira, *Nihon no denshōyaku* [Japanese folk medicine] (Tokyo: Yakuji nippōsha, 2005), especially ch. 6.

13. Other well-known and still popular patent drugs that date from this era include Seirōgan (正露丸, a diarrhea remedy), Asadaame (浅田飴, a throat lozenge), and Rōto meiyaku (ロート目薬) and Daigaku meiyaku (大学目薬), two brands of eye drops.

14. I discuss the history of Kitani Jitsubosan in Susan L. Burns, "Marketing Women's Medicines: Gender, OTC Herbal Medicines and Medical Culture in Modern Japan," *Asian Medicine* 5 (2009): 146–72.

princess in making her escape, and she rewarded him with the formula for a miraculous drug for women. This formula, Tsumura claimed, was then passed down secretly within his family until he decided to manufacture and market it for the benefit of all women. By 1893, regulations for pharmaceutical producers specifically forbade the use of such "origin tales" in advertisements, but Tsumura Kanekichi circumvented the law by making the image of the princess his trademark. This nod to tradition notwithstanding, Tsumura Juntendō promoted the "modern" nature of its product: early ads incorporated the language of biomedicine, displayed endorsements by well-known physicians, and celebrated the joys of female reproductive health by featuring pictures of attractive and prosperous bourgeois families.

Inochi no Haha was manufactured by Sasaoka Shōzō, who, like Tsumura Kanekichi, was a native of Nara, a region famous for the production of medicinal botanicals. The grandson of a doctor, Sasaoka is said to have been inspired to develop his medicine by his mother, who suffered from lifelong poor health following his birth. He developed Inochi no Haha by combining elements of four traditional *kampō* formulas. Inochi no Haha entered the market in 1903, long after Kitani Jitsubosan and a decade later than Chūjōtō. Sasaoka's innovation was to sell his product largely through mail order, a business model he helped pioneer and one that allowed him access to consumers who were unable or unwilling to purchase medicines at drugstores.[15] In addition to newspaper and magazine ads, in 1910, Sasaoka partnered with the prominent obstetrician Kitabatake Takao to produce a work called *Knowledge for Sufferers of Women's Diseases: Home Treatments for Uterine Disease and Other Female Problems*, which was in essence an extended advertisement for Sasaoka's product.[16] Readers were encouraged to order a two-, five-, or ten-week supply of Inochi no Haha, the cost of which included shipping fees. This was a notable departure from the practice of Tsumura Juntendō and the Kitani Company, both of which sold their medicines in single-dose packets (as well as in larger quantities), making them available to even those with little cash on hand.

While the emergence and popularity of products such as Chūjōtō and Inochi no Haha might seem to reflect the pronatalist policies of the Japanese state, their advertisements linked fertility and fecundity to personal rather than national aspirations. Reproductive health was portrayed as the key to a happy, productive, and prosperous life. One long-running Chūjōtō ad featured a series of before-and-after pictures that contrasted the life of a sick, unmarried, and impoverished woman with that of the consumer of

15. Sōda Hajime, *Nihon no dentōyaku: "Furusa" ga ima, totemo shinsen* [Traditional medicine of Japan: "Old" is now, very fresh] (Tokyo: Shufu no tomo sha, 1989), 14–15.
16. Sasaoka Shōzō and Kitabataki Takao, *Fujinbyōsha no kokoroe: Shikyūbyō chi no michi jitaku hō* [Knowledge for those with women's diseases: Home remedies for the way of blood uterine disease] (Tokyo: Sasaoka Shōzō, 1910).

Chūjōtō, the epitome of a happy bourgeois housewife and mother. The text-heavy Inochi no Haha advertisements often included stories of women who were threatened with divorce because of their infertility, until their use of Sasaoka's product brought them motherhood and marital harmony. Other medicines for women overtly challenged official reproductive policies. Patent drugs with names such as Tsukiyaku (Monthlies), Ryūkeigan (Regular flow pills), Tsukiyaku oroshi (Make the monthlies start pills), and Chōkeigan (Menstruation regulation pills) began to be widely advertised beginning in the 1890s first in daily newspapers and then in the new women's magazines. These were so-called menstrual regulators, which responded to women's anxiety over amenorrhea. "Menstrual stagnation" was regarded as a cause of female ill health when it was not a symptom of pregnancy. The print ads for these products featured coy promises that the pills were effective "no matter the cause, no matter the length" of the failure to menstruate, language that clearly implied that these products would be effective as abortifacients.[17] These menstrual regulators appeared on the market as the government criminalized abortion in a series of laws promulgated in 1873, 1880, and 1904, each of which increased the severity of the punishment for women found guilty of the offense. Although a target of frequent criticism for promoting immorality, menstrual regulators continued to be openly advertised until the late 1930s, when magazines began to refuse to print such ads in response to increasing government pressure.[18]

The export trade in patent drugs

If regulation and taxes propelled the reorganization of the domestic medical trade, it also pushed producers to explore overseas markets. In 1886, manufacturers in Toyama, one of the most famous medicine-producing regions, dispatched a representative to Hawai'i, and by the mid-1890s Toyama products were being sold in Taiwan and China.[19] As the patent drug trade recovered and expanded, the export trade exploded. "Prepared medicines" first became a category within official foreign trade records in 1904, and over the course of the next twenty years the value of patent drugs exports to China, Hong Kong, South and Southeast Asia, and Hawai'i increased by almost 3,000 percent.[20] But it was in Japan's new colonies of Taiwan and Korea that Japanese medicines had their most profound impact. Unlike its

17. Burns, "Marketing Women's Medicines," 162.
18. Miki Hiroko, "Josei zasshi ni okeru baiyaku kōkoku" [Pharmaceutical ads in women's magazines] *Mediashi kenkyū* 13 (2002): 110–29.
19. Murakami Seizō, *Toyama-shi yakugyō shi* [Pharmaceutical history of Toyama] (Toyama: Toyama-shi shōkōrōdōbu yakugyō kakari, 1975).
20. Trade statistics are available in *Dai Nihon bōeki nenpyō* (Annual return of the foreign trade of the empire of Japan), a serial publication of Ōkurashō (Ministry of Finance) from 1882. Here and in the discussion that follows the calculation of the increase of trade is my own.

counterpart in Korea, the Taiwan Governor-General's Office did not keep
separate records of patent drug imports and instead grouped these products
with raw drugs and chemical compounds, but even so the figures are suggestive: between 1898 and 1925, the value of the medical and chemical
products trade increased by 5,800 percent.[21] Korea proved to be an equally
lucrative market for Japanese patent drug producers. In 1904, the year before
it became a Japanese protectorate, the value of patent drug exports to Korea
was only about ¥24,000, but by 1925 that figure had grown to just under ¥1
million.[22]

Initially, in both Taiwan and Korea, itinerant peddlers or small retail
establishments ("general stores" that sold stationery and other sundries)
were largely responsible for the growth of the retail trade. In Taiwan, in 1897,
there were forty medicine dealers with most clustered in Taipei; by 1925 that
number had risen to 3,274, although this figure includes a diverse range of
businesses including both traditional Chinese drugstores and those that sold
mass manufactured patent drugs and modern over-the-counter medicines
such as aspirin.[23] Japanese wholesale drug sellers established shops in Korea
around the turn of the century. When Korea became a protectorate in 1905,
there were already Japanese-owned pharmacies in Hanyang (later known
as Keijō and now Seoul), Pusan, Daegu, Inch'ŏn, and P'yŏngyang. By 1906,
there were fifteen Japanese-owned pharmacies in Keijō alone.[24]

The proprietors of these establishments entered the colonial market
through a variety of routes. Arai Kotarō (b. 1867), the founder of a medicine
shop called Arai Yakubō, was an employee in the Osaka Tax Bureau before
he entered the medicine trade. The district known as Dōshōmachi in Osaka
had been the center of raw medicine trade from the early modern period, and
several of the new patent drug pharmacies of the Meiji period were located
here. As part of his responsibilities at the Tax Bureau, Arai was charged with
the collection of the stamp tax on patent drugs, and this brought him into
contact with the proprietors of these pharmacies. He eventually quit his job

21. Trade statistics are from *Taiwan bōeki nenpyō* (Annual return of the foreign trade of Taiwan),
    serial publication of the Taiwan sōtokufu saimukyoku seimuka (Taiwan governor-general,
    Financial Affairs Division, Revenue Division) from 1898 to 1945.
22. Trade statistics are from *Chōsen bōeki nenpyō* (Chōsen table of shipping and trade), serial
    publication of the Chōsen sōtokufu (Korea governor-general) from 1910 to 1945. The 1904
    figure is from *Dai Nihon bōeki nenpyō*.
23. *Taiwan Sheng xingzheng zhangguan gongshu tongji shi, ed., Taiwan Sheng wushiyi nian lai
    tongji tiyao* [Taiwan 51-year statistical summary] (Taipei, 1946), 1250. This is a compilation
    of colonial government statistics by the Chinese nationalist government. On the compli-
    cated nature of the medicine trade in colonial Taiwan, see Michael Shiyung Liu, *Prescribing
    Colonization: The Role of Medical Practices and Policies in Japan-Ruled Taiwan, 1895–1945* (Ann
    Arbor, MI: Association for Asian Studies, 2009), 107–10.
24. Hong Hyŏn-o, *Korea History of Pharmacy* (Seoul: Handok Yakŏp Chusikhoesa, 1972), 158.
    Quoted in Soyoung Suh, "Korean Medicine between the Local and the Universal" (PhD
    diss., University of California at Los Angeles, 2006), 201.

at the Tax Bureau and made his way to Korea, where—with the backing of Osaka manufacturers—he established himself as a wholesaler in Inch'ŏn, dealing initially in soap, toothpaste, and patent drugs and later in pharmaceuticals and medical instruments as well. In 1909, Arai moved his business to Keijō. His shop on Nandaemon Street became something of a landmark— the two-story structure featured an illuminated sign for Jintan on its roof, while large signs for famous patent drugs decorated the storefront.[25]

Like Arai, Yamagishi Yūtarō (1868–1927) established his shop Yamagishi Tenyūdō, later the largest retail drug store in Keijō, in the period before annexation. Yamagishi Yūtarō was born into a samurai family in Kanazawa. From the age of sixteen he worked for a dealer in raw medicines there, until at twenty-two he left for Tokyo, where he found employment with the pharmacy Shiseidō, before moving on to work in a company that dealt in medicines and medical supplies. Then at age twenty-nine he founded a wholesale medicine shop, but the business failed to prosper. In 1906, at the age of thirty-eight, Yamagishi set off to make his fortune in Korea, accompanied by seven family members and two employees.[26] The success of the pharmacy he founded on Honmachi, said to be "the most prosperous Japanese street in Keijō," was in part attributable to his many years of experience in the medicine trade, but other factors came into play as well.[27] According to Yamagishi Kenji (1892–1961), Yūtarō's adopted son, the time before annexation was something of a golden age when "there were no laws for doctors or pharmacists, no regulation of pharmaceuticals, no edicts of any kind, and we could do whatever we wanted."[28] Doing "whatever we want" apparently included the sale of alcohol-based preparations, morphine, and cocaine, all substances banned in patent drugs in Japan.[29]

Given this situation, it is not surprising that the colonial governments quickly moved to crack down on the booming new market in medical commodities. In 1912, both the Taiwan governor-general and the Chōsen governor-general independently promulgated regulations for the manufacture and sale of pharmaceuticals in their respective jurisdictions. Many regulations replicated those in place in Japan, but others were entirely new. The regulations for Korea included a provision that packages display fixed prices and forbade retailers from charging more than this price. Most controversial

---

25. Kubo Kan, "Arai Kotarō ryakuden" [An abbreviated biography of Arai Kotarō] in *Zaisen Nihonjin yakugyō kaiko shi* [History of Japanese pharmaceutical industry in Korea] (Zaisen Nihonjin yakugyō kaikoshi hensankai, 1961), 377–80.
26. Yamagishi Kenji, "Kaiko 50-nen" [Reviewing fifty years], in *Zaisen Nihonjin yakugyō kaiko shi*, 200–202.
27. Nayoung Aimee Kwon, "Translated Encounters and Empire: Colonial Korea and the Literature of Exile" (PhD diss., University of California, Los Angeles, 2008), 89.
28. Yamagishi, "Kaiko 50-nen," in *Zaisen Nihonjin yakugyō kaiko shi*, 184.
29. Sogabe Takao, "Dainikigoro no omoide" [Memories of the second period], in *Zaisen Nihonjin yakugyō kaiko shi*, 373. Sogabe was an employee of the Tenyūdō.

of all were the requirement that producers and retailers submit detailed lists of the ingredients and preparation methods of their products to the colonial police office, which was charged with supervision of the industry, and open up their facilities to government inspection upon request.[30] The regulations in both Taiwan and Korea reflected concern that the retail medicine trade might impact the progress of medical modernization: patent drug retailers were explicitly prohibited from criticizing doctors or implying their treatments were ineffective. Significantly for my topic, both sets of regulations explicitly forbade the marketing of any product as an abortifacient or a contraceptive.

The 1912 colonial regulations in fact anticipated developments in Japan proper, evidence of the intertwined nature of metropolitan and colonial policies. In 1914, the Japanese government promulgated a new Patent Medicine Law (*Baiyakuhō* 売薬法) that attempted to tighten controls on both the manufacture and marketing of medical commodities. As in the colonies, one of the aims of the law was to ensure that patent drugs did not challenge the authority of licensed practitioners of biomedicine. The law required manufacturers to employ a physician or pharmacist on their staff and to open their factories to government inspectors upon request. It also imposed new restrictions on the advertisement of medicines, making it illegal to criticize physicians or to imply that medical treatments were effective. Additional articles addressed advertisements and forbade the use of the exaggerated claims, fraudulent evidence, and illustrations or language designed to frighten consumers. And as in the colonies, the 1914 law made it illegal to advertise any product as an abortifacient or contraceptive.

The new restrictions notwithstanding, the patent drug trade continued to prosper in the colonies. In 1935, the Hygiene Bureau (Eiseika) of Taiwan's governor-general published a report titled *Taiwan no eisei* (Hygiene in Taiwan) that included a discussion of the patent drug trade. According to the report, in 1934 there were 6,783 retailers and 6,352 peddlers of patent medicines. The authors of the report expressed dismay that while Taiwanese had abandoned their traditional practice of seeking healing by visiting temples and shrines, they had not embraced the care of modern medical professionals. Instead, they chose to dose themselves with patent medicines.[31] In Korea, the value of Japanese patent drug exports rose steadily over the course of the

---

30. The Regulations for the Enforcement of Laws for Medicinal Products and the Medicinal Product Businesses (Yakuhin oyobi yakuhin eigyō torishimari shikō kisoku) are available in Chōsen sōtokufu, ed., *Chōsen hōrei shūran* [Select collection of Chōsen laws] (Gansho shoten, 1915). The Rules for the Regulation of the Patent Drug Businesses in Taiwan (Taiwan baiyaku eigyō torishimari kisoku) are included in Taiwan sōtokufu, *Taiwan hōrei shūran* [Collection of Taiwan laws and ordinances] (Teikoku chihō gyōsei gakkai, 1918), section 8: *Eisei keisatsu* [Health police], 10–11.

31. Taiwan sōtokufu keimusho eiseika, *Taiwan no eisei* [Hygiene of Taiwan] (Taipei: Taiwan sōtokufu, 1935), 72–73.

colonial period, reaching ¥3.6 million in 1939. The popularity of manufactured medicines transformed Korea's medical culture, all but destroying the trade in traditional herbal remedies. In 1910, there were 2,551 Korean-owned medicine shops selling herbal compounds. A decade and a half later, that number had fallen to 142, while the number of Japanese drug stores was about 300 in 1910 and grew to almost 500 by 1925.[32]

Some Korean entrepreneurs managed to survive in the new and competitive medical market by emulating the products and practices of Japanese manufacturers and retailers. The most successful was Yi Ŭng-Sŏn, who founded a pharmacy called Hwapyŏngdang in 1904. Born in 1897, Yi was apprenticed to a traditional medical shop at the age of nine. When he was sixteen, he opened his own pharmacy in Inch'ŏn and became one of the first Korean dealers in Western medicines before he turned to manufacturing his own products.[33] The Hwapyŏngdang manufactured and sold several patent medicines, but the most famous was a medicine for women called T'ae'yangjogyŏnghwan (胎養調経丸, "Fetus-nurturing menstruation-regulating pills"). The reference to menstrual regulation notwithstanding, T'ae'yangjogyŏnghwan was, like Chūjōtō and its competitors, advertised as a reproductive aid that promoted fertility and cured all manner of gynecological ills. In the 1920s, other Korean manufacturers began to produce similar medicines. The Samyongbang Pharmacy, operated by one Cho Byŏng-Sŏn, sold a medicine called Pu'injogyŏnghwan (婦人調経丸, "Women's menstruation-regulating pills"), but like T'ae'yangjogyŏnghwan, its ads too contain none of the euphemistic language hinting at abortion that was so common in the ads for Japanese products. It is unclear whether this reflected a more vigorous regime of censorship on the part of colonial officials. Although Japanese manufacturers of Tsukiyaku and Ryūkeigan do not seem to have sold their products in the colonies, publications with titles such as *Contraceptive Research: How to Have a Child When You Want To* were openly advertised in Korea throughout the 1920s.[34]

---

32. Chōsen sōtokufu, ed., *Chōsen Sōtokufu tōkei nenpō* [Korea governor-general annual report and statistics] (Seoul: Chōsen sōtokufu, 1936), 365. By the 1920s the proliferation of Japanese-owned drug stores had become an object of concern on the part of men like Arai and Yamagishi, who had arrived in Korea before it became a colony. They took the lead in founding an organization known as the Chōsen Yakuyūkai (Korean Friends of Medicine Association), which aimed to "prevent pointless competition" and "to unify prices," policies designed to protect their dominant position in the Korean market. See "Nakada Kōsaburō shi wo kakonde" [A discussion with Nakada Kōsaburō], in *Zaisen Nihonjin yakugyō kaiko shi*, 14–15.

33. Obituary of Yi Ŭng-Sŏn, *Tonga ilbo*, June 3, 1927.

34. A pamphlet with this title authored by "sexologist" Tsuda Junjirō was advertised almost daily in the *Tonga ilbo* in the 1920s and early 1930s. See, for example, the ad in *Tonga ilbo*, February 22, 1925, p. 4.

Marketing Women's Medicines in the Colonies: Consumer Desire and Imperial Biopolitics

The appearance of these Korean-made products reflected not only the booming sales of their Japanese counterparts but also a new concern for reproductive health throughout the Japanese Empire. In both the metropole and colonies, medical discourse and policy linked female reproductive health to the strength and well-being of the nation and empire. Fu Daiwie, Wu Chia-ling, Theodore Yoo, Jin-kyung Park, and Sonja Kim have all explored colonial medical policies for women in Taiwan and Korea.[35] Like Fujime Yuki, whose groundbreaking work argued that the Japanese state's concern for population drove the articulation of new policies toward reproduction, prostitution, and venereal disease, these scholar argue that colonial medical policy too was profoundly shaped by the belief that population growth was necessary for the expansion, strength, and vitality of the empire.[36] As a result, the colonial governments not only put in place pronatalist policies that sought to improve the health of both mothers and infants, including sponsoring educational campaigns that attacked customary practices and establishing midwifery schools and obstetrical clinics; they also tried to limit recourse to abortion and contraception through criminal and censorship laws.[37]

Within Japan's imperial biopolitics, women, whether Japanese, Korean, or Taiwanese, were similarly positioned: their reproductive potential was vital to the empire while their poor health threatened to undermine it. This is not to say that colonial relations of power played no role in the formulation

---

35. Fu Daiwie, *Yaxiya de xinshenti: Xingbie, yiliao yu jindai Taiwan* [Assembling the new body: Gender/Sexuality, medicine, and modern Taiwan] (Taipei: Socio Publishing, 2005); Wu Chia-ling, "Have Someone Cut the Umbilical Cord: Women's Birthing Networks, Knowledge, and Skills in Colonial Korea," in *Health and Hygiene in Chinese East Asia*, ed. Angela Ki Che Leung and Charlotte Furth (Durham, NC: Duke University Press, 2010), 160–80; Theodore Jun Yoo, *The Politics of Gender in Colonial Korea: Education, Labor, and Health* (Berkeley: University of California Press, 2008), esp. chapter 5, "The Colonized Body"; Sonja Kim, "'Limiting Birth': Birth Control in Colonial Korea," East Asian Science, Technology, and Society: An International Journal 2(3) (2008): 335–59; Sonja Kim, "Contesting Bodies: Managing Population, Birthing, and Medicine in Korea, 1876–1945" (PhD diss., University of California, Los Angeles, 2008); Jin-Kyung Park, "Corporal Colonialism: Medicine, Reproduction, and Race in Colonial Korea" (PhD diss., University of Illinois at Urbana-Champaign, 2008).

36. Fujime Yuki, *Sei no rekishigaku: Kōshō seido, dataizai taisei kara baishun bōshihō, yūsei hogohō taisei e* [History of sexuality: From the licensed prostitution and illegal abortion system to the Prostitution Prevention Act and the Eugenic Protection Act system] (Tokyo: Fuji Shuppan, 1997), 87–100.

37. On the "modernization" of childbirth in Japan, see Aya Homei, "Birth Attendants in Meiji Japan: The Rise of the Biomedical Birth Model and a New Division of Labour," Social History of Medicine 19(3) (2006): 407–24; and Julie Rousseau, "Enduring Labors: The 'New Midwife' and the Modern Culture of Childbearing in Early Twentieth Century Japan" (PhD diss., Columbia University, 1998). For a discussion of modern obstetrics, see Yuki Terazawa, "Gender, Knowledge, and Power: Reproductive Medicine in Japan, 1790–1930" (PhD diss., University of California at Los Angeles, 2001).

of public health and medical policy in the colonies. In fact, a chorus of voices insisted that colonial bodies were, in fact, both different and inferior. According to Wu Chia-ling, officials in Taiwan adopted a "deficiency model" to explain the high rates of infant and maternal mortality, casting colonial women as backward, ignorant, and conservative and arguing that their flawed practices undermined their own health and that of their children. Similarly, Park has described the efforts of Japanese physicians to demonstrate the deleterious effects of Confucian patriarchy on the health of Korean women through research on gynecological disorders and female criminality.[38] At the same time, the discourse on "deficient" women did not neatly track along the colonizer-colonized divide. As Theodore Yoo has noted, Korean reformers, educated men of the new middle class motivated by nationalism, too, argued that the health of the Korean women was weakened by flawed customs such as early marriage and primitive childbirth practices.[39]

Within this literature, only Park has addressed the significance of medical commodities within the colonial marketplace. She argues that the colonial medical discourse on deficiency shaped the commercial realm: advertisements for women's medicines asserted the effectiveness of Japanese-manufactured patent drugs to "redeem" or "salvage" the diseased and weakened bodies of Korean women.[40] This view, however, overly simplifies the relationship between the official and commercial interests. As Japanese patent medicines flooded into Taiwan and Korea in the 1910s and 1920s, manufacturers and retailers were less interested in echoing colonial policy than in cultivating consumer demand. The print advertisements for women's medicines that appeared in two newspapers, the *Taiwan Daily News* (台湾日々新報, *Taiwan nichi nichi shinpō*) and the *East Asia Daily* (*Tonga ilbo*) reveal how Japanese involved in the medicine trade negotiated the politicized terrain of women's health. Published between 1898 and 1944, the *Taiwan Daily News* had the largest readership and the most advertisement content of any of the newspapers published in Taiwan in the colonial era. While it has been characterized as the "official" newspaper of the colonial state, the *Taiwan Daily News* was not just a mouthpiece for the governor-general: the

---

38. Wu Chia-Ling, "Shou wuming de xingbie, xingbiehua de wuming: Cong Taiwan 'buyun' nannü chujing fenxi wuming de xingbie zhengzhi" [Stigmatized gender and gendered stigma: The "infertile" men and women in Taiwan], *Taiwan shehui xuekan* [Taiwanese Journal of Sociology] 29 (2002): 161; Jin-kyung Park, "Corporal Colonialism," 139–48.

39. Yoo, *Politics of Gender in Colonial Korea*, 172.

40. Ibid., 2–4, 120–32. In addition to Park's work on Korea, several scholars have written on the marketing of Japanese "women's medicines" in China. See Barbara Mittler, *A Newspaper for China? Power, Identity, and Change in Shanghai's News Media, 1872–1912* (Cambridge, MA: Harvard University Asia Center, 2004), 259–68; Sylvia Li-Chun Lin, "Pink Pills and Black Hands: Women and Hygiene in Republican China," *China Review* 4(1) (Spring 2004): 201–27; Tina Phillips Johnson, *Childbirth in Republican China: Delivering Modernity* (Lanham, MD: Lexington Books, 2011), 42–48.

paper was at times harshly critical of colonial policy.[41] The *East Asia Daily* was founded in 1920, one of several Korean vernacular newspapers established in the wake of the declaration of the new policy of "cultural rule" that loosened press and other restrictions. It quickly became a powerful organ of Korean nationalism, with the result that publication was suspended on four occasions until in 1940 it was forced to cease operation.[42]

As in the Japanese newspapers, patent medicine advertisements predominated in the *Taiwan Daily News* and the *East Asia Daily*. According to one source, medicine-related ads occupied 30 percent of advertisement space in *East Asia Daily* in 1923 and 50 percent by 1938.[43] Both colonial newspapers typically had twelve horizontal rows of print on each page. On pages 1 and 2, advertisements were usually limited to the lowest two rows. In the inner pages, however, the percentage of news space devoted advertisements was far greater: it was not uncommon for ads to fill the lower third or half of an inner page. By the mid-1920s large and illustrated advertisements were common, with a single ad sometimes filling an eighth of a page or more.

While medicine ads were ubiquitous, gauging their influence and their readership is not easy. In Taiwan, high rates of attendance at so-called common schools, which promoted Japanese language instruction, meant that by the 1920s literacy rates were quite high.[44] In contrast, in Korea, literacy rates in both Korean and Japanese were comparatively low, especially among women. According to a Chōsen governor-general report from 1930, roughly 55 percent of men between the ages of twenty and thirty-nine were able to read han'gul in contrast to only 10–16 percent of women in the same age range. There was, however, significant regional variation, with those in the cities of the South having far higher rates of literacy.[45] Even so, it may well have been that in Korea men were the primary readers of the newspapers and their medicine ads.

Concern for popularizing their products clearly drove these intense marketing efforts. Japanese manufacturers and retailers of medical products believed that consumer demand in the colonies lagged far behind that in the

---

41. Liao Ping-hui, "Print Culture and the Emergent Public Sphere in Colonial Taiwan, 1895–1945," in *Taiwan under Japanese Colonial Rule, 1895–1945*, ed. Liao Ping-hui and David Der-Wei Wang (New York: Columbia University Press, 2006), 84, 88.

42. Mark E. Caprio, "Assimilation Rejected: The Tong'a ilbo's Challenge to Japan's Colonial Policy in Korea," in *Imperial Japan and National Identities in Asia, 1895–1945*, ed. Li Narangoa and Robert Cribb (London: Routledge, 2003), 129–45.

43. Shin In Sup and Shin Kie Hyuk, *Advertising in Korea* (Seoul: Communication Books, 2004), 44.

44. E. Patricia Tsurumi, *Japanese Colonial Education in Taiwan, 1895–1945* (Cambridge, MA: Harvard University Press, 1977). For a chart on school attendance rates, see Taiwan Kyōikukai, ed., *Taiwan kyōiku enkakushi* [Historical background of Taiwanese education], 1939 (Tokyo: Seishisha, 1983), 408–10, 984–86.

45. Chōsen Sōtokufu, *Showa 5-nen Kokuzei Chōsa* [1930 national census], vol. 1 (Keijō: Chōsen sōtokufu, 1931), 82–83.

metropole, although estimates of the size of the gap varied. According to one source, Korean spending on patent medicines was less than 10 percent of their metropolitan counterparts, while another source suggested that it was closer to 30 percent.[46] The question of whether consumers in the colonies could easily afford to purchase Japanese patent drugs is another knotty issue. In the 1920s a single dose of Chūjōtō, the least expensive of the major Japanese women's medicines, sold for twenty Korean sen, while a single dose of T'ae'yangjogyǒnghwan sold for only five sen, evidence that Korean pharmacies may have used competitive pricing to undercut their Japanese counterparts. This price disparity notwithstanding, the exponential growth of medicine exports to the colonies suggests that consumer demand for Japanese goods grew over the course of the colonial era. Additional evidence of rising demand comes from the work of economic historian Terasaki Yasuhiro on the standard of living in the colonies. Terasaki's analysis suggests that, in both Taiwan and Korea, spending on medicine and hygiene products grew steadily over the colonial period, on average at an annual rate of close to 0.7 percent.[47]

Advertisements are complicated and cryptic visual and verbal configurations, and every historian of consumer culture confronts the problem of how to analyze them. Do they reflect consumer desire or mold it? In answer to this conundrum, Roland Marchand, in his study of American advertisements, famously termed advertising "a fun house mirror" that selects from but also distorts the larger cultural milieu.[48] In other words, Marchand argues for a dialogical relationship between advertisement discourse and the larger culture, in which advertisers draw upon specific aspects of the culture but manipulate them to promote their products. The analysis of women's medicine advertisements that follows identifies the motifs that came to constitute the commercial vernacular of women's medicines and traces their evolution over time. While no analysis of marketing strategies can reveal the motives that shaped any single purchase on the part of any individual consumer, the "imagined consumer" that the ads discursively constructed and to which they appealed offers insight into the conceptions of gender and health that circulated within the colonial marketplaces of Taiwan and Korea.

46. Ibid., 16.
47. Terasaki Yasuhiro, "Shokuminchi-jidai no Chōsen ni okeru kojin shohi shishutsu to suikei, 1913–1937" [Individual consumption expenditures and estimates in Colonial Korea], *Nagasaki Daigaku Kyōyō Gakubu Kiyō* 24 (January 1984): 61–95; Terasaki Yasuhiro, "Taiwan Chōsen no shohi suijun," in *Kyu Nihon shokuminchi keizai tokei: Suikei to bunseki* [Economic statistics from the former Japanese colonies: Estimates and analyses], ed. Toshiyuki Mizoguchi and Mataji Umemura (Tokyo: Toyo Keizai Shinposha, 1988).
48. Roland Marchand, *Advertising the American Dream: Making Way for Modernity, 1920–1940* (Berkeley: University of California Press, 1985), xvii. Quoted in Sheldon Cochran, *Chinese Medicine Men: Consumer Culture in China and Southeast Asia* (Cambridge, MA: Harvard University Press, 2006), 38.

The advertisement in Figure 5.2 for Chūjōtō appeared in the *East Asia Daily* in May 1925, three years after the ad described in the introduction to this essay. It features an image of three women with serious, even pensive, expressions: a habited Catholic nun, a Japanese woman in kimono, and a "modern girl," whose nationality and ethnicity are unclear. The text of the ad, in large bold print, states "even though our ideas [思想, *shisō*] and circumstances [境遇, *kyōgū*] are different, there is one daily practice we have in common." That daily practice is of course their shared liking for Chūjōtō, which is said to be the source not only of a "healthy body and glowing complexion" but also "womanly pride." What is striking about the ad is not only the absence of a figure who can be identified specifically as "Korean," the depiction of which might be expected given the readership of the newspaper, but also the charged political valences of the terms *shisō* and *kyōgū*. While I have translated the former as "ideas," it can also mean "thought" or "ideology," and it appears in terms such as "thought crime" (思想犯 *shisōhan*) and "freedom of thought" (思想の自由 *shisō no jiyū*), a vocabulary that would have resonated with politically minded Koreans. "Circumstances" is equally fraught: it was used to reference the differences in lifestyle that resulted from class, education, and other social divisions, and, within the empire, status as colonizer or colonized. The absence of a woman explicitly marked as "Korean" perhaps deflected the highly politicized language of the ad, but its message is clear nonetheless: in spite of differences in nationality, religion, ethnicity, all women are essentially the same "under the skin," vulnerable to the same gynecological disorders, a lengthy list of which was featured in this and almost every ad.

The appeal to female consumers in the ads in Figures 5.1 and 5.2 based upon their shared corporality, became one of the most important motifs ordering the marketing of "women's medicines" in the colonies and metropole alike. In Japan, patent medicine producers were often quick to capitalize upon popular pride in Japanese expansion to sell their products. No one did this better than Morishita Hiroshi, the manufacturer of Jintan.[49] Emblematic of his use of the culture of imperialism to market his products was the "Jintan is here too" campaign. Begun in the 1910s, it took the form of the issuance of a series of collectable picture postcards of sites throughout East Asia. Each scene included a billboard or sign with the trademark of Jintan, the famous mustachioed figure in a military uniform. Figure 5.3, a postcard from the mid-1930s, shows the Manchurian city of Andong with a Jintan billboard conveniently indicated with a large red arrow that has been superimposed on the photograph. The campaign thus inserted Morishita's products into an imperial landscape and simultaneously celebrated his company's expansion and that of the Japanese empire.

---

49. On the marketing of Jintan in China, see Cochran, *Chinese Medicine Men*, 44–46.

Figure 5.2

East Asia Daily, May 11, 1925

Figure 5.3

Advertisement postcard for Jintan

Figure 5.5 (above)

Chūjōtō advertisement, *Taiwan Daily News*, January 20, 1922

Figure 5.4 (left)

Chūjōtō advertisement, 1916

Manufacturers of "women's medicines," however, for the most part eschewed this approach for one that foregrounded the shared appeal of their products for all women. The Chūjōtō ad in Figure 5.4, which appeared in a Japanese newspaper in 1916 is suggestive of this strategy: it depicts women of varying ethnicities under a banner that states, "[F]amous throughout the world . . . today it is widely used throughout the East and West." The copy went on to declare, "[I]n female society of every country everyone agrees it is the best." This was also the approach that manufacturers used in marketing their products in Taiwan and Korea in the 1920s. The advertisement in Figure 5.5 appeared in the *Taiwan Daily News* in January 1922. It featured a Western woman sealing an oversized envelope with the headline, "I'm recommending Chūjōtō to all my friends in foreign countries!" The remaining copy, the text of her letter, stated, "after I came to Japan my body improved very much. This is completely due to the woman's medicine called Chūjōtō. I've recovered from my tendency to feel cold, the vaginal discharges have stopped, and my face and skin color are much improved." Here we see again the assertion that all women suffered from a set of similar gynecological ills and had a similar desire for health and attractiveness, an implicit rejection of one major motif of medical discourse in the imperial age—the anxiety about the perceived superiority of Western bodies over those of racialized "others." The advertisement implied that European women, no less than those of Taiwan and Japan, are prone to gynecological disorders that render them weak, uncomfortable, and unattractive.

This is not to say that explicit attempts at "localizing" products for the Taiwanese or Korean markets did not occur. As Figure 5.6 from the *Taiwan Daily News* (December 18, 1932) and Figure 5.7 from the *East Asia Daily* (September 12, 1933) reveal, advertisers at times incorporated images of women explicitly marked as Korean or Chinese by their clothing and hairstyles. However, when encountered within the pages of the newspapers, as presumably a regular reader would have, even these attempts at localization seem to suggest the cosmopolitan nature of the "women's medicines," whose consumers were one day represented as Korean or Taiwanese but the next day as European or Japanese. A different kind of localization shaped the medical language of the advertisement copy. Although manufacturers stressed the modern and scientific nature of their products, they also incorporated concepts that originated in Chinese medicine: terms such as "the way of blood" (血の道, *chi no michi*), "blood *qi*" (血気, *kekki*), and *senki* (疝気, abdominal pain said to be the result of *qi* stagnation) are but a few examples. Moreover, in both Taiwan and Korea, advertisers tended to stress the "Asian" nature of the products, usually by describing them as a "Sino-Japanese medicine."

While the text of advertisements invariably included lengthy descriptions of the myriad ailments to which all women were prone, illustrations

Figure 5.6

Chūjōtō advertisement, *Taiwan Daily News* (Kanbun edition), December 18, 1932

Figure 5.7

Chūjōtō advertisement, *East Asia Daily*, September 12, 1933

focused on depicting the benefits of the good health that the medicines promised. Not surprisingly, pictures of happy mothers with their infants were a common motif. Indeed, advertisements for Inochi no Haha focused almost exclusively on the joys of maternity even though the medicine promised relief for a variety of symptoms, including stiff shoulders and headache, that were not necessarily related to reproduction. Advertisers were quick to incorporate photographs of actual satisfied customers (in the form of engravings, a costly and therefore uncommon element in newspaper ads until the 1930s). Figure 5.8, which appeared in the *Taiwan Daily News* in 1920 included pictures of four infants along with the surnames of their (Japanese) parents and their hometowns. Figure 5.9, from the *East Asia Daily*, featured the photograph of a woman who was cured of the uterine disease that had plagued her for twenty years after she began taking Inochi no Haha, with the

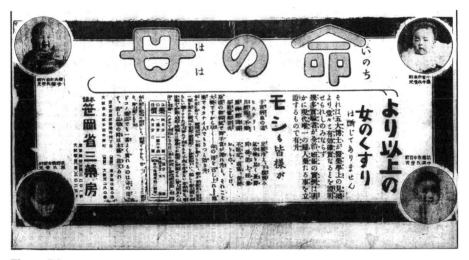

Figure 5.8
Inochi no Haha, *Taiwan Daily News*, February 21, 1920

Figure 5.9
Inochi no Haha advertisement, *East Asia Daily*, July 29, 1927

Figure 5.10
Jitsubosan advertisement, *East Asia Daily*, March 24, 1930

result that she gave birth to a healthy boy. Readers of this and other ads were offered a free copy of a pamphlet on "how to cure uterine disease at home" so that they could achieve the same happy result. Jitsubosan advertisements also depicted mothers and babies, but the ads more explicitly addressed the social and personal value of maternity, describing it as the key to a "happy home." Significantly this "home" was described with the neologism *katei* (家庭), which was used to describe the nuclear family of husband and wife, but not the extended patriarchal family (Figure 5.10). Until the beginning of the Second Sino-Japanese War in 1937, in the colonies as in the metropole, advertisers promoted reproductive health for the personal benefits it would bring—motherhood and conjugal happiness—not for the national or imperial good.

But maternity was not depicted as the only or most important benefit of reproductive health. From the mid-1920s through the early 1930s, those in the medical trade also utilized images of female sexuality to market their products. Figure 5.11 is an advertisement for Chūjōtō that appeared in the *East Asia Daily* in 1927. The text above the figure of the nude woman describes the effects of Chūjōtō—glowing and flexible skin, energy, and beauty. In the mid-1920s, advertisements for Inochi no Haha too made use of the eroticized female body—a notable departure from the photographs of happy mothers and babies and the triumphant narratives of overcoming infertility. Figure 5.12 is an advertisement from 1926 that features a partially draped female figure with one breast exposed, while the text promises that use of Inochi no Haha will rejuvenate the female body, making it as youthful and fresh "as a virgin." Others advertisements featured women lying in bed, emerging from a bath, or seemingly "caught" in the midst of undressing. While these ads may well have been designed to capture the attention of male readers, they linked female health to sexuality and beauty rather than to motherhood and marriage.

Significantly, these ads appeared amid others that promoted commodities that addressed sex and sexuality. Beginning about 1925, the pages of the *East Asia Daily* were filed with advertisements for books with titles such as *The Sexual Lives of Virgins and Wives* (*Shojo oyobi tsuma no sei seitaku*), *Sexual Love* (*Seiai*), *New Research on Male and Female Sexual Desire and Sexual*

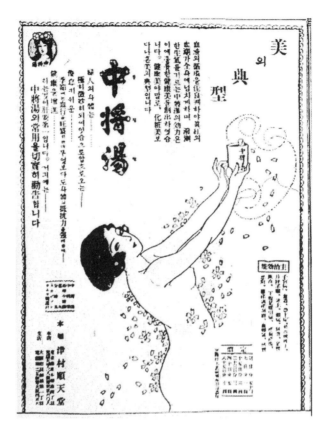

Figure 5.11
Chūjōtō advertisement, *East Asia Daily*, April 26, 1927

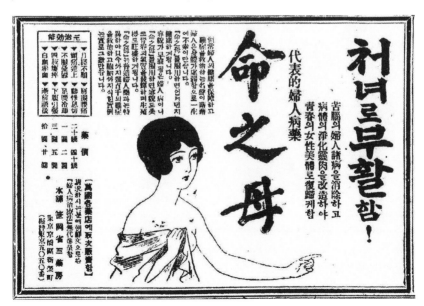

Figure 5.12
Inochi no Haha advertisement, *East Asia Daily*, October 5, 1926

Intercourse (*Danjo seiai oyobi seikō no shinkenkyū*), products of Japanese sexo-logical discourse that were actively promoted by their Japanese publishers in the colony.[50] Did such ads implicitly play upon the sexual anxieties of colo-nized male subjects? It seems unlikely, given that both the Japanese origin of these products and their avid readership in the metropole were explicitly referenced. Instead, both these works and the erotic bodies on display in the medicine ads point to a new vision of bodily health that promoted sexual desire, knowledge, and expression.

In the 1930s, a new series of ads for Chūjōtō appeared at roughly the same time in both the *Taiwan Daily News* and the *East Asia Daily*. This long-running campaign featured photographic images of smartly dressed women in poses that project a confident sexuality (Figures 5.13–5.15), but one that was no longer transparently configured to appeal to the male gaze. The women in question are represented as modern professionals who take Chūjōtō to promote a healthy vitality. While this campaign depicted youthful East Asian women, it provided no clues to their culture of origin or their marital or maternal status. The women in the ads are represented not as wives and mothers but as modern women for whom good health has brought a life of enviable independence, prosperity, and leisure. Moreover, this new vision of cosmopolitan East Asian womanhood no longer relied upon the evocation of

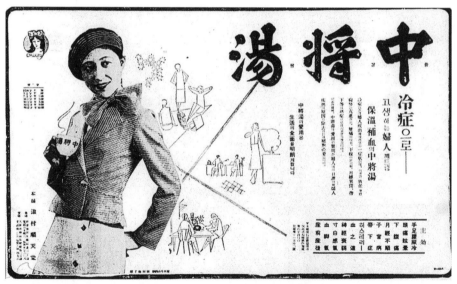

Figure 5.13
Chūjōtō advertisement, *East Asia Daily*, November 29, 1933

---

50. Sabine Frühstück, *Colonizing Sex: Sexology and Social Control in Japan* (Berkeley: University of California Press, 2003).

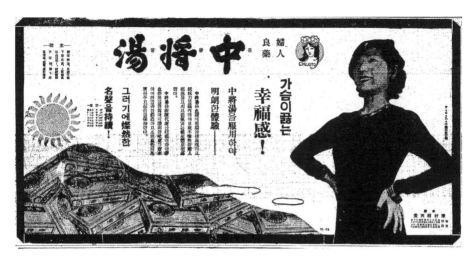

Figure 5.14
Chūjōtō advertisement, *East Asia Daily*, February 21, 1935

Figure 5.15
Chūjōtō advertisement, *Taiwan Daily News*, December 18, 1935

the shared pathology of the female body, and far from promoting imperial biopolitics, these ads celebrate the agency of female consumers who pursue health for their own benefit.

The outbreak of war in 1937 marked the end of what, following Rose and Novas, might be termed the "political economy of hope" that ordered patent drug advertisements.[51] The commercial vernacular of sexy bodies, upward mobility, and happy families quickly disappeared, as the manufacturers of Chūjōtō and other products began to link their products to the war effort. Typical of the ads in this period is a 1941 print advertisement for Chūjōtō that incorporated both the timely military term "advance" (as on the battlefield) and the wartime slogan "give birth and multiply," which encouraged women to do their best to produce children to people the expanding empire. It featured a serious-looking woman holding a box of the product accompanied by copy that read, "Let's advance one step at a time by giving birth and multiplying. A strong maternal body produces a strong baby!"[52] The use of this language was at this time voluntary, but in 1943 a change in the pharmaceutical law required pharmaceutical companies to "cooperate with the national policy of improving the physical strength of the people" and allowed censorships of ads that failed to comply with this directive.[53]

Conclusion

Patent medicines were an essential aspect in the modern medical culture of Japan and its colonies. Sold by peddlers and retailers, large and small, these products and the ads that promoted them circulated throughout the empire, reaching those who might have had only tenuous or occasional contact with modern medical professionals or institutions. As we have seen, in both the metropole and the colonies, officials were concerned about the potential of the patent drug industry to subvert the state-supported program of medical modernization and its pronatalist gender ideology. They responded by attempting to police the industry and limit its influence. In spite of these efforts, in marketing their products, medical capitalists did not simply or uniformly confirm the biopolitics, gender ideology, or colonial divisions authorized by the imperial state. In advertisements for "women's medicines," the "deficient" body of the Korean and Taiwanese woman that both nationalist and colonial reformers bemoaned rarely appeared. Instead, the manufacturers and retailers of medical commodities offered alternative images of health and the body, and encouraged consumers to project themselves into new social identities, from fertile mother and happy wife, to erotic temptress and

51. Rose and Novas, "Biological Citizenship," 451.
52. *Yomiuri Shimbun*, May 29, 1941 (evening edition), p. 4.
53. Sugaya Akira, *Nihon iryō seidoshi* [History of Japanese medical policies] (Tokyo: Hara shobō, 1976), 290–93.

independent modern woman. However, the ease with which the manufacturers of "women's medicines" shifted course from one strategy to another and their willingness after 1937 to embrace the state policy of "give birth and multiply" exposes the unsurprising fact that Japanese pharmaceutical companies had no inherent interest in undermining the policies of the imperial state. They merely sought to sell their products, and so we are left to ponder the long-term significance of a discourse on health that was driven by concerns about market share and profits, rather than the imperatives of empire.

6
Housewives as Kitchen Pharmacists

Dr. Chuang Shu Chih, Gendered Identity, and Traditional Medicine in East Asia

Sean Hsiang-lin Lei

Introduction[1]

It is well known that any health care–related surveys revealing a gender disparity invariably show that women use alternative medicine more frequently than do men.[2] Very little is known, however, about the reasons for this strong correlation between gender and alternative medicine use. To understand this phenomenon, the legendary career of Dr. Chuang Shu Chih (Shukuki Soo

1. I would like to gratefully acknowledge the many helpful suggestions and comments that I received from Francesca Bray, Chen Yuan-peng 陳元朋, Fu Daiwie 傅大為, Charlotte Furth, Jin Jungwon 陳姃湲, Kuo Wen-hua 郭文華, Pi Guoli 皮國立, Wu Chia-ling 吳嘉苓, Yeh Wen-shin 葉文心, and especially Jen-der Lee 李貞德 when we cotaught a class in the spring of 2015. Linda Barnes, Angela Leung 梁其姿, Izumi Nakayama 中山 和泉, Ruth Rogaski, Françoise Sabban, and Hue-Tam Ho Tai have greatly improved my work with their helpful written comments. Thanks also to Hsu Hsueh-chi 許雪姬, Komiya Yukiko 小宮 有紀子, Lin Yi-ping 林宜平, Liu Yan 劉焱, and Tsai Wei-li 蔡偉立 for sending me valuable documents and references. As always, I would like to thank Sabine Wilms for her excellent editorial work and helpful suggestions.

    Right before I finalized this article, I had an in-depth exchange with Dr. Chuang's daughter, Dr. Chuang Jin Funn and some of her friends. They closely read an earlier draft of this chapter, shared with me many valuable details, insights, and criticisms, and later sent me two extensive written comments. Precisely because they might still disagree with some aspects of my revised article, I would like to express my gratitude for having that honest and friendly exchange. The interaction with these warm, sincere, and professional ladies, as they shared with me their loving memories about Dr. Chuang, allowed me once again to understand the deep admiration her followers have for her and her work.

    Finally, I would like to announce (albeit a bit prematurely) some great news: Dr. Chuang Jin Funn 莊靜芬 has graciously decided to donate Dr. Chuang Shu Chih's archival materials, around 180 boxes in total, to the public. Thanks to the generous support from Jen-der Lee, then deputy director of the Institute of History and Philology (IHP) at Academia Sinica, and Hsi-yuan Chen 陳熙遠, head of IHP's Archival Center, IHP will be the new home for these precious materials. It is my hope that the present article can help generate interest in Dr. Chuang's work and attract more scholars to make use of these archival materials in their research.

2. Mary Ruggie, *Marginal to Mainstream: Alternative Medicine in America* (Cambridge: Cambridge University Press, 2004), 58.

in her English academic articles and Zhuang Shuqi in Chinese pinyin) 莊
淑旂 (1920–2015), a female Taiwanese practitioner of traditional medicine,
might provide some helpful insights. Dr. Chuang emerged as a successful
and prolific author of health-related books while living in Japan in the 1970s
and 1980s, moved back to Taiwan in the late 1980s, and subsequently became
arguably the most popular author of books on traditional medicine in contemporary Taiwan. Her career and medical doctrines can shed light on three
related questions about gender and traditional medicine in contemporary
East Asia.

First of all, as gender was essential to Dr. Chuang's identity and work,
they in turn carry a highly unusual gender significance. In light of the fact
that the vast majority of famous practitioners of traditional medicine in
China and Taiwan were—and still are—male, her achievements and popularity are no less than phenomenal. Instead of downplaying her gender,
moreover, she foregrounded it in her public persona, presenting herself as a
caring female physician, a filial daughter, a beloved wife, and—during her
stay in Japan—a gentle mother of five children. Most importantly, she successfully summoned and inspired housewives (*zhufu* 主婦 in Chinese and
shufu in Japanese) to serve as the agents of her regimen. Given that the social
role of housewife is a modern creation in East Asia as well as in the world
in general,[3] Dr. Chuang's success in building an alliance between traditional
medicine and the modern housewife represents a novel development for
both the history of traditional medicine and the history of gender in East
Asia. Her phenomenal success makes one wonder, What factors made this
novel alliance possible? And how did this alliance conversely influence her
doctrine of traditional medicine and the role of the housewife in East Asia?

Second, the traditional medical practice that Dr. Chuang drew on in
creating this alliance is dietary therapy (*shiliao* 食療), the traditional practice
of using food as medicine. Her strategic use of dietary therapy again represents an unusual development in the twentieth-century history of traditional
medicine in the following sense: When reformers of Chinese medicine in
the first half of the twentieth century endeavored to make Chinese medicine
more similar to a real "medicine," as defined by modern biomedicine, they
strove not only to distance Chinese medicine from semireligious practices but
also to downplay the connection between medicine and food. In opposition
to this historical trend, aimed at creating the officially sanctioned modern
profession of Chinese medicine, Dr. Chuang endeavored to convince many
of her followers that food can serve as a powerful tool for coping with illnesses as formidable as cancer. Regrettably, medical historians know very
little about what has happened to the practice of dietary therapy ever since

---

3.   Emiko Ochiai, *The Japanese Family System in Transition: A Sociological Analysis of Family
      Change in Postwar Japan* (Tokyo: LTCB International Library Foundation, 1996).

East Asian governments legalized the division between food and medicine with regulations in the twentieth century. The prominent case of Dr. Chuang thus provides a valuable entry point from which to investigate an intriguing question: Why and how do so many people in East Asia still enthusiastically embrace food as an effective form of medicine, in spite of the lack of validation by the medical establishment?

The third question concerns the conflicting consequences of the gendered identities that Dr. Chuang created with the help of dietary therapy. On the one hand, it appears that her teachings on dietary therapy empower women as providers of health care. Feminist studies of health have criticized the biomedical establishment for "constituting women as patients while subordinating those occupations which are dominated by women."[4] These suppressive measures sometimes extended to preventing women from fulfilling active roles in the production of health.[5] In sharp contrast, Dr. Chuang's teachings on dietary therapy equate food preparation to medical treatment and thereby significantly raise the value of women's labor and knowledge in producing health.

On the other hand, however, Dr. Chuang urged married women to acquire knowledge about dietary therapy so as to serve as an educated "female master of the family" (the literal meaning of *zhufu* in Chinese). As such, her strategy of empowerment ran the risk of reinforcing the tired patriarchal ideology of confining women to housework. This is a much-contested strategy because it was for the sake of liberating women from such confinement that American feminists launched the first modern anticooking movement in the late 1890s.[6] In a similar vein, the issue of housewife and housework had provoked three rounds of intensive public debates in postwar Japan.[7] While the notion of the housewife has never been a focus of such public debates in Taiwan, the implied gender division of labor has been criticized repeatedly in the past decades and recently has been regarded as one of the root causes of Taiwan's alarmingly low marriage and birth rates. In light of this political context, Dr. Chuang's teachings on dietary therapy constituted not only medical knowledge for coping with health problems but also a moral framework for reconfiguring the contested role of housewife, and by extension gender relations in general. Instead of taking the role of housewife for granted, this paper investigates Dr. Chuang's contributions to the struggle over the social role, moral responsibility, and self-identity of the housewife in contemporary East Asia. The findings presented here will

---

4. Bryan S. Turner, *Medical Power and Social Knowledge*, 2nd ed. (London: Sage Publication, 1998), 130.
5. Adele Clarke and Virginia Olesen, "Revising, Diffracting, Acting," in *Revisioning Women, Health, and Healing*, ed. Adele Clarke and Virginia Olesen (New York: Routledge, 1999), 3.
6. Harvey Levenstein, *Revolution at the Table: The Transformation of the American Diet* (Berkeley: University of California Press, 2003), 68.
7. Ochiai, *Japanese Family System in Transition*, 24–27.

help to explore the question, To what extent do these East Asian "female masters of the family" differ from housewives in other parts of the world?

From Laundrywoman to "Mother of the Anticancer Campaign"

Even Taiwanese who pay little attention to traditional medicine have most likely heard the popular story about the rise of Dr. Chuang Shu Chih to become a renowned physician. It is an inspiring story, almost too remarkable to be credible. Born in 1920 in Japanese-ruled Taiwan, the young Chuang Shu Chih lived a life not dissimilar to that of the average Taiwanese housewife during the colonial period. This all changed abruptly when a series of family tragedies took place. Her father, an herbalist and practitioner of Chinese medicine, died of rectal cancer when she was nineteen; seven years later she unexpectedly lost her beloved husband to lung cancer. At the time she was widowed (1945) at the age of twenty-six, Chuang was already a mother of four children and three months pregnant with a fifth. To protect her children from mistreatment, she rejected all proposals for remarriage. Instead, she made a living by doing laundry for well-off families while collecting semi-spoiled cabbage from the market to feed her family.

Driven by the fear that her children would also become future cancer victims, the devastated mother started to seriously study traditional medicine. As an assistant in her father's drugstore since the age of ten, she had become familiar with the various drug prescriptions and related medical knowledge. In 1950, Chuang Shu Chih became the first woman to pass the national qualifying examination for traditional Chinese medicine, even though the practice had been suppressed during Japanese colonial rule.

One important legacy of Japanese colonial rule was the creation of a modern public health infrastructure and a system of state medicine. The Japanese colonial government substantially reduced the infant mortality rate, while at the same time establishing a new socioeconomic class of Taiwanese elites largely centered on modern professions such as medicine and law.[8] To reduce the influence of traditional medicine, the colonial government offered a one-time registration exam for traditional practitioners in 1901. While there had been almost 2,000 traditional practitioners when Japan took over Taiwan in 1895, by the 1940s the number of registered practitioners had dropped to under 100. As a revealing contrast, the number of herbalists, who were not required to pass a strict test, actually rose from about 700 to more than 3,000. It appears that because the Japanese government had outlawed the practice of traditional medicine, these specialists began practicing covertly under the guise of herbalists. In fact, Chuang's father

---

8.   Michael Shiyung Liu, *Prescribing Colonization: The Role of Medical Practices and Policies in Japan-Ruled Taiwan, 1985–1945* (Ann Arbor, MI: Association for Asian Studies, 2009).

was one such herbalist who continued to practice traditional medicine in semisecrecy. After the Nationalists' defeat on the Mainland and their subsequent move to Taiwan, a new medical standard was introduced, and the first national license examination for traditional Chinese medicine was held in 1950. Among a few hundred people who took the exam, only Chuang and one mainlander passed.[9]

Once she started practicing medicine, Dr. Chuang gained the name of *zamou xianxin*, literally "female doctor."[10] While this nickname reveals that female practitioners of traditional medicine were perhaps uncommon in postcolonial Taiwan, a tradition of female medical practitioners had previously existed in imperial China. Just as in Dr. Chuang's case, women had learned medicine from their male relatives, often by working closely with their fathers. Texts such as *Xunnu yixue* (Medical learning for teaching daughters) were produced specifically for this purpose.[11] However, by Chuang's time it was becoming increasingly popular for Taiwanese women to take on the professions of medicine or nursing. Although the Taipei Medical College did not accept female medical students, more than 200 women went to Japan for medical education during the colonial period, often studying at schools designed specifically for women.[12] Despite these female pioneers, we could argue that no other female medical practitioner, whether in premodern China or in modern Taiwan, ever achieved a level of respectability and visibility comparable to that of Dr. Chuang.

Given that Chuang Shu Chih's formal education had ended with grade school, it is hard to imagine how she managed to overcome all sorts of daunting obstacles to realize her dream of studying medicine in Japan. Nevertheless, in 1956 she formally registered at the medical school of the prestigious Keio University. According to her autobiography, Professor Abe Katsuma 阿部勝馬 (1892–1968), head of Keio's medical school and later her advisor, decided to accept her application on the basis of the fact that she was a licensed practitioner of Chinese medicine.[13] After five years of hard work, Chuang Shu Chih received a PhD in pharmacology from Keio University in 1961. During the three decades that she stayed in Japan, the medical health regimen she developed became well received in Japanese society. Her first book, penned in Japanese and titled *A Youth-Preserving Lifestyle and Diet*, sold

---

9.   Chuang Shu Chih, *Zhuang Shuqi huiyilu* [Memoir of Chuang Shu Chih] (Taipei: Yuanliu chubanshe, 2001), 108.
10. Xu Fangju, "Zhuang Shuqi: Daziran de nü'er" [Chuang Shu Chih: Daughter of mother nature], *Kangjian zazhi* [Common Health Magazine] 41 (2002): 109.
11. Angela K. C. Leung, "Women Practicing Medicine in Pre-modern China," in *Chinese Women in the Imperial Past: New Perspectives*, ed. H. Zurndorfer (Leiden: Brill Academic Publishers, 1999), 126.
12. Fu Daiwie, *Yaxiya de xinshenti: Xingbie, yiliao yu jindai Taiwan* [Assembling the new body: Gender/sexuality, medicine, and modern Taiwan] (Taipei: Socio Publishing, 2005).
13. Chuang, *Zhuang Shuqi huiyilu*, 145.

more than 2 million copies within the first year of its publication in 1970.[14] Besides authoring numerous books during her three decades in Japan, she also founded the International Family Cancer Prevention Association.

In the middle of the 1980s, Dr. Chuang shifted the focus of her activities from Japan to Taiwan with immediate success. Her first book in Chinese, *What Is the Healthiest Way to Eat?*,[15] has already been printed more than 200 times, representing about 400,000 copies sold.

Dr. Chuang's immediate success owed much to the testimony of her celebrity patients. For example, Wang Yongqing 王永慶 (1917–2008), the president of the Taiwan Plastics Corporation, then the largest private company in Taiwan, openly vouched for the special physical exercise regimen that she had designed, which she called Cosmic Gymnastics (*yuzhou ticao* 宇宙體操), as being beneficial for his own health. To show his appreciation and support, Wang allowed Dr. Chuang to include in her book a picture of him practicing the exercise with her trademark towel.[16] It has been suggested that the health benefits he personally enjoyed from Dr. Chuang's treatments and exercise regimen caused Wang to enthusiastically offer his support to traditional medicine in Taiwan, founding the Traditional Chinese Medicine Branch at his Chang Geng Memorial Hospital in 1996. In addition to the support Dr. Chuang received from social elites, a popular movement emerged in which thousands of Taiwanese started practicing Cosmic Gymnastics in local parks and grade-school playgrounds. In 2001, her inspiring memoir received a book award from a major local newspaper. Before she passed away in February 2015, she was a much-admired icon, being honored with numerous interviews and reports from the media, as well as being praised by some as the "mother of the anticancer campaign."

Qi and Taste

Any cancer patient who wanted to consult Dr. Chuang had to first fill out a health questionnaire that began with an unusual question: What is your body type? One cannot help but wonder why body type is so crucial for coping with cancer and exactly what these body types mean for Dr. Chuang.

According to her own account, her classification into four body types is derived from two distinct sources. On the one hand, it is based on a survey that she herself conducted on more than 30,000 Japanese cancer patients. On

---

14. Ibid., 207.
15. For two reasons, I consider Chuang Shu Chih the author of this book, even though her daughter, Dr. Chuang Jin Funn 莊靜芬, a pediatrician, wrote the text of this book. First, her daughter makes it clear that the book is based on her mother's teachings and that she is just summarizing the doctrines of her mother. Second, the fame and charisma of Chuang Shu Chih simply overshadow that of her daughter at that time.
16. Chuang Shu Chih, *Zenyang shenghuo bu shengqi* [How to live without generating *qi*] (Taipei: Zhongyang ribao she, 1990), 178.

the basis of that survey, she classified human bodies into four types: (1) pro-truding upper abdomen, (2) protruding lower abdomen, (3) hunchback, and (4) standard, as represented in Figure 6.1. On the other hand, she claimed that her fourfold typology of the human body is rooted in traditional Chinese medicine. She explained that her conception of body types draws on the idea of constitution (*tizhi* 體質), which was first articulated in the great Chinese medical classic, *Treatise on Cold Damage Disorders* (*Shanghanlun* 傷寒論), from around 200 CE. Given this supposed East Asian origin, Dr. Chuang empha-sized that these four body types refer not to different distributions of muscle and fat but to four patterns of *qi* storage within the body. By juxtaposing two frameworks for classifying body types, she thus linked the findings of modern medical surveys with the concept of *qi* in traditional East Asian medicine.

While in modern Chinese language the concept of *qi* includes the specific meaning of air, in the English-speaking world it is closely associated with Chinese medicine and with *qigong*, and therefore is widely understood as a distinctively Chinese concept for which no Western equivalent exists. For one thing, *qi* and *xue* (blood) have a paired relation just like the one between *yin* and *yang*. During the Republican period, when practitioners of Chinese medicine debated the validity of their medical paradigm with bio-medical physicians, they often defended the concept of *qi* by claiming that *qi* transformation was beyond the gaze of Western anatomists. Nevertheless, Chuang's conception of *qi* is neither the self-claimed invisible, immaterial *qi* of Republican China nor the notion of "life-energy" nowadays widely asso-ciated with the term *qi* in both Asia and the West. On the contrary, it sounds very close to the buildup of intestinal gas, which even Westerners seem quite familiar with. Nothing better elaborates this surprising conception of *qi* than the illustration (Figure 6.2) with which Dr. Chuang explained the detrimen-tal health effects of taking a nap right after lunch. As this illustration depicts how gaseous bubbles are blocked within the stomach when a person lies down during a nap,[17] her main concern here is clearly the gaseous waste stored in the intestines.

It was through a series of personal tragedies that Dr. Chuang discov-ered the pathogenic role of intestinal, gaseous *qi*. Recalling how she had developed the crucial insight into the correlation between *qi* and disease, she traced this discovery back to the tragic time when she lost both her father and husband to cancer. When comparing these two cancer victims whom she had been able to observe intimately, Dr. Chuang found a series of sharp contrasts as well as an intriguing common point between them. To begin with, her father had been overweight. Busy with his job as an herbalist, he had often skipped lunch and tended to take his meals in a rush. After retiring

---

17. Chuang, *Zenyang shenghuo bu shengqi*, 143.

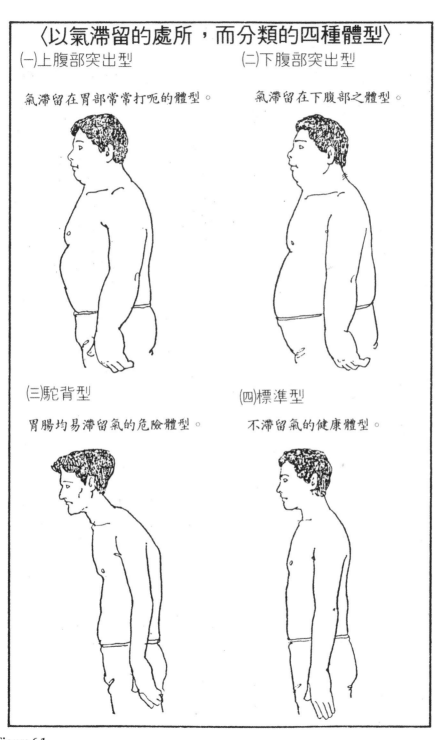

Figure 6.1

The four body types as defined by the stagnation of *qi* in Chuang Shu Chih, *How to Live without Generating Qi*, 58.

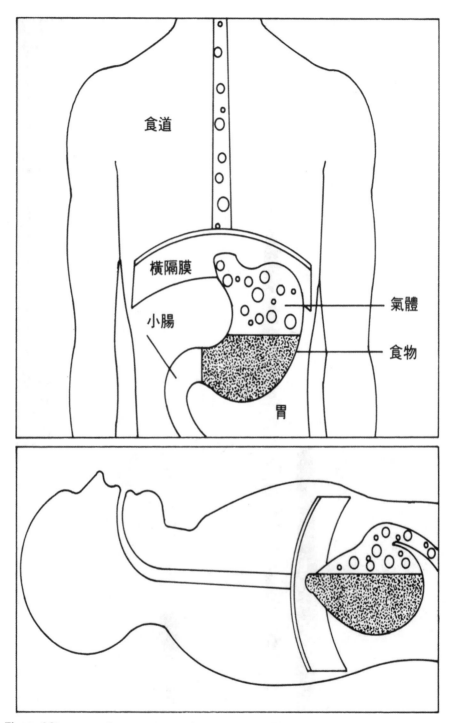

Figure 6.2

Movements of *qi* in two contrasting body positions in *How to Live without Generating Qi*, 143.

from work in the evening, he had indulged himself with huge amounts of meat, greasy and fatty dishes, garlic, chili peppers, and sweets. Although her father had snored a lot during sleep and suffered from constipation, he had almost never suffered from colds. Her husband, in sharp contrast, had been short and thin, and had had a rather small appetite. Instead of meaty dishes, he had liked raw vegetables and foods that were sour in taste. Often feeling exhausted and complaining about sore shoulders, he had suffered from colds almost constantly.[18]

While they had thus been very different in terms of body figures, food preferences, appetites, and health complaints, especially in regards to catching colds, Chuang's father and husband had shared one thing in common: they had both passed gas with remarkable intensity and frequency. Her overweight father had burped so frequently in public that he had caused her embarrassment; similarly, her husband had passed gas all the time and in such quantities that his children had made fun of him saying, "Papa is again playing fire-crackers." Observing this salient commonality, Dr. Chuang wondered "whether their *qi* somehow related to their being victims of cancer." Preoccupied with this thought, in her medical survey she asked her patients to report any problems with flatulence and burping, which finally led her to establish the crucial link between *qi* accumulations and cancer.[19]

Chuang Shu Chih claimed to have discovered that the crucial link between *qi* accumulation and fatal diseases was food. This "discovery" should not have surprised many Taiwanese who were familiar with traditional dietary therapy; they should have sensed from her description that her father and her husband were begging for trouble because of their specific, and arguably unhealthy, food cravings. Being overweight, her father should have increased his intake of sour dishes and vegetables, but instead he had craved and indulged in "heating foods," that is, salty, greasy, and spicy meats. In contrast, her skinny husband had apparently suffered from "cooling conditions" and frequently caught colds, but had nevertheless preferred "cooling foods," namely cold vegetables and sour dishes, instead of meat and poultry. While Dr. Chuang did not spell this fact out in her confessional statement, their two distinct tastes for food stand for the fundamental dichotomy between heating and cooling food in traditional Chinese dietary therapy. And the two contrasting concepts of "heating" (*re* 熱) and "cooling" (*liang* 涼 or *han* 寒), as Eugene N. Anderson points out, in fact "developed

---

18. Chuang Shu Chih, *Zhongguo xingyi jiankang fa* [Chinese-style health management] (Taipei: Zhongyang ribao she, 1991), 63–65.
19. Chuang, *Zenyang shenghuo bu shengqi*, 20–21.

from a medieval fusion of Chinese ideas of Yang and Yin with Hippocratic-Galenic humoral medicine introduced from the Near East."[20]

Drawing on this deep-seated conceptual tradition of dietary therapy, Chuang Shu Chih amplified the key role of taste in disease formation. As illustrated by this pair of contrasting cases, once an abnormal body type had taken shape, it attained a life of its own by way of the person's taste preference, leading to a vicious cycle: People with excessive qi tended to develop a pathogenic craving for certain foods that in turn lead to more such accumulation of qi within their bodies. While this feedback cycle might sound similar to the idiom "you are what you eat," in a crucial sense Dr. Chuang's doctrine departs decisively from this once-commonsensical understanding of the relationship between food and the self. Instead of assuming, "What tastes good to you is good for you," she used her family tragedies to argue the opposite, namely, "What tastes good to you is what causes disease." To break this vicious cycle, she emphasized, people had to refrain from following their cravings and instead start to deliberately choose foods on the basis of the knowledge of their own body type.

Since everyone knows how difficult it is to change a person's taste for food, *How to Live without Generating Qi*, the title of another of Dr. Chuang's books, became a question worth taking seriously. In the preface, Chuang presented three cardinal principles of life cultivation: the healthiest people have no qi; people with average health have qi but are capable of releasing it; and the least-healthy people have qi and are incapable of releasing it.[21] Thanks to her instructions, many of her Taiwanese readers started developing a new awareness concerning how often they passed gas, burped, or experienced flatulence. A useful window into this otherwise hidden process of embodiment can be found in Dr. Chuang's Mailbox, a weekly Taiwanese newspaper column that she hosted for two years, from November 1991 to November 1993.[22] Every week, Dr. Chuang used this forum to answer questions raised by readers who were anxious to know about their own health conditions. Among 120 exchanges, collected and later published as a book under the same title, she advised one-fifth (around 24 cases) to reduce flatulence, even though many of them had not asked about this problem. In about 10 cases, the inquirers reported having a problem with passing gas and burping; some were also worried about the bad smell of this gas.[23] Most revealingly, some of her readers thereafter reported recognizing the previously unregistered comforts associated with these mundane and everyday physiological func-

20. Eugene N. Anderson, "Folk Nutritional Therapy in Modern China," in *Chinese Medicine and Healing: An Illustrated History*, ed. T. J. Hinrichs and Linda L. Barnes (Cambridge, MA: Belknap Press of Harvard University Press, 2013), 159.

21. Chuang, *Zenyang shenghuo bu shengqi*, 14.

22. Chuang Shu Chih, *Zhuang boshi xinxiang* [Dr. Chuang's mailbox] (Taipei: Qingfeng chubanshe, 1999).

23. Chuang, *Zhuang boshi xinxiang*, 38, 96, 99, 102, 107, 112.

tions. In short, Dr. Chuang apparently succeeded in making some of her followers feel *qi* as a salient sensation in their own bodies.

But this is a very unusual understanding of *qi* that might even strike some people as amusing. It is neither the vital energy people nowadays associate with the concept of *qi* in traditional Chinese medicine (TCM), nor the breath exercise of *qigong*. While these popular understandings of *qi* are also important to Dr. Chuang, most saliently in her Cosmic Gymnastics, the concept of *qi* she relied on here to classify body types is quite different. This *qi* has nothing to do with either the respiratory system or spirituality but everything with the digestive system and an embarrassing corporeality. Since the digestive system is the channel through which *qi* is presumably generated, circulated, accumulated (Figure 6.1), and blocked (Figure 6.2), this conception of *qi* helps people to connect the sensation of *qi* within their bodies with the food they consume. Chuang Shu Chih thus presented to her audience an unusually mundane conception of *qi*, because she needed it to elevate the everyday activity of food consumption into a crucial practice for health maintenance.

Food as Poison and Medicine

What made Chuang Shu Chih famous in Taiwan in the first place was precisely her teachings on dietary therapy (*shiliao* 食療), the practice of using food as medicine. From 1986 to 1999, her first Chinese book, *What Is the Healthiest Way to Eat?*, sold more than 400,000 copies.[24] A follow-up was published in 1991, entitled *Eating This Way Is the Healthiest Way*. Besides providing guidelines for a balanced lifestyle and instructions for Cosmic Gymnastics in the first 40 pages, these two books consist of a 300-page collection of recipes, accompanied by detailed explanations of their therapeutic effects.

In case the reader now wonders why food is so important to medicine in China, one reason is perhaps that food is simply this important to Chinese culture in general. "Few other cultures are as food oriented as the Chinese," asserts K. C. Chang in the pioneering study *Food in Chinese Culture*.[25] While Chang might have overemphasized the uniqueness of the Chinese case, the role of food indeed stands out in the following small but revealing episode. When public health experts were modifying the World Health Organization Quality of Life Index to adapt it to the experience of the Taiwanese people, they decided to add the following question to the questionnaire: "Can you always get the food that you would like to eat?" The food question is one of only two questions that Taiwanese experts added to the questionnaire,

---

24. Chuang Shu Chih, *Zenyang chi zui jiankang* [What is the healthiest way to eat?] (Taipei: Wenjin she, 1986).
25. K. C. Chang, introduction to *Food in Chinese Culture: Anthropological and Historical Perspectives*, ed. K. C. Chang (New Haven: Yale University Press, 1977), 9.

the other one being related to having "face" and feeling respected.[26] Many Taiwanese people would agree, I think, that delicious food is indeed essential to one's quality of life.

More importantly, as Chang points out, "[t]he overriding idea about food in China—in all likelihood an idea with solid, but as yet unrevealed, scientific backing—is that the kind and amount of food one takes is intimately relevant to one's health. . . . Food therefore is also medicine."[27] Elaborating on this substantial link, if not identity, between medicine and food, the anthropologist Judith Farquhar returns to the far distant past, to the famous myth that Shennong, the sage king, tasted one hundred herbs when he founded Chinese pharmacy. As a result, "pharmaceutical classification is presented as reflecting actual tastes of substances in the materia medica corpus."[28] The combination of the five *wei* (flavors) has to be carefully considered when preparing both mouth-watering dishes and effective drug formulas. No wonder Dr. Chuang paid such close attention to her father's and husband's tastes of food! Because of the long tradition of dietary therapy in the history of Chinese medicine, foods and drugs were not clearly differentiated in Chinese medicine until the twentieth century.

Against this historical context, it is noteworthy that in 1999 the Taiwanese government promulgated the Health Foods Control Act, which was designed to transcend the dichotomized division between food and drugs. This law deliberately created a new legal category of health foods (*jiankang shipin* 健康食品), clearly distinguished from the international concept of dietary supplements, which is referred to in Chinese with a term that literally translated as "health-protecting foods" (*baojian shipin* 保健食品). Unlike dietary supplements, which is treated as a subcategory of food in most countries, following the lead of the United States, the foods referred to as health foods in Taiwan are regulated in a more rigorous way, modeled on the regulation of drugs. As the legislator behind the new legislation reasoned, the rationale was that Taiwanese people in fact use these foods as efficacious drugs to cope with serious health problems, and the companies producing them also actively promote them as such. Therefore, it is a governmental responsibility to make sure that these "foods" live up to the high standard expected for drugs, most specifically to ensure that the official certification of health foods is "duly supported by scientific assessment and testing of their health care effects or by academic principles that they are harmless and carry definite, steady health care effects" (Heath Foods Control Act). By way of creating a new

---

26. These two questions can be found on the World Health Organization Quality of Life Taiwan Version as questions 28 (food) and 27 ("face" or being respected). I first heard about this interesting piece of information in a lecture by the epidemiologist Rongde Wang but would like to thank Yiping Lin for her help in getting a copy of the actual document.

27. K. C. Chang, introduction, 9.

28. Judith Farquhar, *Appetites: Food and Sex in Post-socialist China* (Durham, NC: Duke University Press, 2002), 65.

legal category, this law effectively ensured that health foods is a category that is independent from and equal to the two major categories of food and drug.[29] In light of the governmental promulgation of such a unique law in Taiwan, the popularity of Dr. Chuang's doctrine is by no means an isolated phenomenon. Instead, her doctrine at once drew on, transformed, and reinforced the living tradition of dietary therapy in East Asia.

With the help of traditional dietary therapy, Dr. Chuang valorized the domestic routine of preparing food into a knowledge-intensive process of health management. It is crucial to note in this context that her teachings on dietary therapy are not based upon the general idea that food has some health benefits, an idea with which even modern nutritional science agrees. Instead, she used her own personal tragedies to argue for the allegedly "traditional" but now quite radical idea that daily food is capable of causing cancer. To emphasize this little-registered danger of food consumption, she included the following strongly worded confession in many of her books:

> I often think that I killed my father. Why do I have this thought? Is it because I was not a filial and obedient daughter? No, absolutely not. I loved my father very much. It was exactly my love that caused most harm to him. No matter how busy I was, I prepared for him his favorite dishes and never served anything that he disliked. At that time, I never imagined that what he liked most could have caused his illness, and what he disliked could have been the best medicine. I used to spend the whole day in the kitchen and never realized that I was simply preparing one plate of "poison" after another. This was indeed an "ignorant love."[30]

To make sense of this confession, several points need to be elaborated: First of all, in terms of the therapeutic efficacy of food, what her personal tragedies meant to testify was more its capacity to cause fatal illness than its capacity to bring health. While it might sound a bit far fetched to modern ears that inappropriate food intake can constitute a direct cause of cancer, the foundational insight of Chinese dietary therapy is indeed the idea that daily food can cause serious illness. In his *Beiji qianjin yaofang* 備急千金藥方 (Prescriptions worth a thousand in gold for urgent need), the eminent practitioner and scholar Sun Simiao 孫思邈 (581–682) devoted a whole volume to dietary treatment (*shizhi* 食治), which is considered the first and foundational text of Chinese dietary therapy.[31] On the one hand, Sun advocated the

---

29. An Chin-Chih, "Jiuming xiancao huo Shengji lingyao: Lingzhi de kexue, shichang yu liaoxiao zhengzhi" [Miraculous herb or biotechnological drug: Science, market, and the efficacy politics of *lingzhi*] (PhD diss., Department of Sociology, National Taiwan University, 2016).

30. Chuang Shu Chih, *Zheyang chi zui jiankang* [This is the healthiest way to eat] (Taipei: Guanghe chubanshe, 1995), 17.

31. Chen Yuan-peng, "*Chuantong shiliao gainian yu xingwei de chuanyan: Yi 'qianjin, shizhi' wei hexin de guancha*" [Traditional food and healing: The Shih-chih chapter in Sun Szu-miao's *Ch'ien-chin yao-fang*], *Bulletin of the Institute of History and Philology*, Academia Sinica 69 (1998): 765–825. Ute Engelhardt, "Dietetics in Tang China and the First Extant Works of

use of food to cure illness because the effects of foodstuffs are less dangerous than drugs. According to him, only when dietary therapy fails should a
physician turn to drugs. On the other hand, as Ute Engelhardt points out, the
crucial innovation of Sun's work lies in its emphasis on the underregistered
danger of foods. Among the 160 kinds of foods analyzed in this volume,
Sun Simiao included sixty "nutritional interdictions" (shijin 食禁). In fact,
he made the number of nutritional interdictions the organizing principle of
the volume, beginning with the section on fruits, which includes the fewest
prohibitions.[32] To summarize, while urging physicians to cure illness with
food, he simultaneously strove to highlight the great danger involved in the
careless and unconscious consumption of foods, which have strong effects
and therefore can cause great danger to one's health.

Drawing on this traditional insight first formulated by Sun, Chuang Shu
Chih went so far as to call food "poison" to make an important, but very
different, argument. As a matter of fact, Chuang and Sun held the same view
that food can both cause illness and cure it. But they argued for this view
from opposite directions because of their very different audiences. As Sun
and his contemporaries took for granted the efficacy of food, he warned of
the dangers involved in the unconscious consumption of foods. In contrast,
Chuang's modern readers generally do not believe that food can be as efficacious as medicine. To challenge their belief that food is inefficacious, she
first used her own personal tragedies to argue for the point that food—if
inappropriately consumed over a long period of time—can cause fatal illness
and thus have the same effect as "poison." From here she went on to argue
that appropriate efficacious foods are capable of preventing the formation
of abnormal body types as well as curing illness. To summarize, as much as
food is believed to be capable of causing cancer, it should be equally capable
of serving as a powerful tool for coping with it.

More importantly, the health effects of food—both good and bad—are
not an inherent quality of that material entity, but rather a relative quality
that results from the match or mismatch between the food and the specific
person who consumes it. According to Dr. Chuang, herein lies the defining
difference between modern nutritional science and Chinese dietary therapy.
While the former emphasizes that some foods are intrinsically healthy and
others harmful, the latter holds the principle of yi li yi hai (一利一害, literally "benefit for one, harm for the other"), namely that the same food can
bring health benefits to one person while causing harm to another.[33] This
principle explains why the question of body type is listed eminently at the
very beginning of Dr. Chuang's questionnaire. Because the medical efficacy

Materia Dietetica," in *Innovation in Chinese Medicine*, ed. Elisabeth Hsu (Cambridge:
Cambridge University Press, 2001), 173–91.
32. Engelhardt, "Dietetics in Tang China," 181.
33. Chuang, *Zheyang chi zui jiankang*, 8.

of any single dish is specific to individual body type, with few dishes being generally healthy regardless of body type, knowing one's own body type constitutes the necessary precondition for any appropriate application of dietary therapy.

Finally, as each food functions like a double-edged sword, constituting both the major cause of and a powerful tool for coping with cancer, preparing food in the kitchen becomes comparable to handling effective drugs, and more importantly dangerous "poisons," in the "family pharmacy" (*jiating yaoju* 家庭藥局).[34] By criticizing herself as practicing "ignorant love," Dr. Chuang thus highlighted the key role of knowledge in food preparation and thereby the moral responsibility of the food provider to equip him- or herself with such knowledge. With this realization, she elevated cooking from a routine chore into a knowledge-intensive process of preparing individually tailored medicine for each family member. As suggested by the many recipes included in her books, the person in charge of meals should carefully prepare individualized foods to help alleviate the specific symptoms that each of the family members might be suffering from. For people believing that daily food can serve effectively as both medicine and poison, Dr. Chuang was absolutely right: the family member in charge of cooking should view him- or herself as a "family pharmacist."

Upgrading the Housewife to the Family Pharmacist

Although Chuang Shu Chih's regimen encouraged people to "be your own physician," the role of "family pharmacist" was created exclusively for women, especially housewives. The first chapter of her first Chinese best-seller, *What Is the Healthiest Way to Eat?*, is entitled, "You Control the Key to the Health of Your Whole Family," while the fifth chapter is entitled, "Are You a Qualified Pharmacist in Your Family Pharmacy?"[35] As the Chinese written language uses different characters for the masculine and feminine forms of "you," it is clear here that she is specifically addressing a female audience in the titles of these two chapters. Because of the book's popularity among housewives, in the second edition, published eight years later in 1994, the publisher changed the title of the first chapter to "Housewives Control the Key to the Health of the Whole Family." Unlike other forms of alternative medicine, which as a rule demand moral responsibility from the patient him- or herself, Dr. Chuang urges housewives to take responsible for the health of the whole family.

It is intriguing that Chuang Shu Chih and her Taiwanese publishing company did not focus on housewives as the target audience right from the

---

34. Ibid., 45.
35. Chuang, *Zenyang chi zui jiankang*, 45.

beginning. This marketing strategy should have been immediately obvious because it was housewives who had made her a popular writer and health consultant in Japan in the early 1970s. Her first best seller in Japan, *A Youth-Preserving Lifestyle and Diet*, was published by Friends of Housewives (*Shufu no tomo* 主婦の友), the publishing house that published one of the earliest, and most long-lasting, Japanese women's magazines with the same title. Being the first Japanese magazine to set its sights on young married women as its readership, *Friends of Housewives* quickly became the most popular Japanese women's magazine, reporting a monthly circulation of 600,000 in 1931.[36]

In fact, the Japanese term *shufu* was coined in 1876, only decades before the birth of this famous magazine in 1917. While the Chinese characters for *shufu* (*zhufu*) originally meant "primary wife," this term has now been used to translate into Japanese—and later Chinese—the English concept of housewife.[37] As many scholars have pointed out, the rise of the social role of housewife is an essential aspect of global modernity. The emergence of this role is inseparable from the rise of a pattern of gendered division of labor, with the husband working outside the family and the wife taking charge of "housework." In comparison to previous periods, moreover, modern housework became particularly demanding because it was ushered into existence by the joint forces of an idealized image of the home and the rising expectations of domestic life. As it grew into an ever-expanding list of tasks, including the preparation of three meals a day, high standards of domestic hygiene, children's education, and so on, housework demanded the wife's full devotion and thereby constituted the identity of the housewife.[38]

While echoing the global emergence of housewife, the concept of *shufu* was deliberately created in Meiji Japan to confine a new kind of woman within the family, namely one who had received formal education for the first time in the history of East Asia. In terms of this ideological function, the concept of *shufu* was closely related to the well-known trans–East Asian ideological construct of "good wife, wise mother" (*ryōsai kenbo* 良妻賢母 in Japanese, *xianqi liangmu* 賢妻良母 in Chinese).[39] It is worth pointing out that the concept of "good wife, wise mother" had once served as a progressive idea for East Asian women. When the term was first coined in the late nineteenth century, it offered the crucial rationale for providing a formal

---

36. Barbara Sato, *The New Japanese Woman: Modernity, Media and Women in Interwar Japan* (Durham, NC: Duke University Press, 2003), 95.
37. Sato, *New Japanese Woman*, 79.
38. Ochiai, *Japanese Family System in Transition*, 26–36.
39. Shizuko Koyama, *Ryōsai Kenbo: The Educational Idea of "Good Wife, Wise Mother" in Modern Japan* (Leiden and Boston: Brill, 2013); Jin Jungwon [Chen Zhengyuan], *Cong Dongya kan jindai Zhongguo funü jiaoyu: Zhishi fenzi dui "xianqi liangmu" de gaizao* [An East Asian perspective on women's education in modern China: Reform "wise wife and good mother" by the intellectuals] (Taipei: Daoxiang chubanshe, 2005).

education for women, first in Japan and later in China and Korea. The rationale expressed by this term was that it takes an educated "wise mother" to help educate the nation's children, especially boys.[40] Until this day, children's education is ranked as one of the top responsibilities for East Asian mothers. While the exact term *ryōsai kenbo* fell into disuse in Japan after 1945 because of its association with the discredited ideology of the prewar imperial state, the idea remained influential in postwar Japan at least into the late 1980s.[41] Against this ideological background, there were three rounds of "housewife debates" that took place in the mass media of postwar Japan.[42] As late as the 1990s, Japanese historians still strongly criticized *Friends of Housewives* for "reinforcing a vision of the 'ideal wife' whose identity is compatible with a 'family state.'"[43]

In practice, however, the social role of *shufu* also brings to Japanese housewives a certain degree of power within the family. Literally meaning "female master," the concept of *shufu* placed wives in the position of being more or less fully in charge of the family domain, including the important task of managing the husband's salary and organizing the family's financial investments.[44] Therefore, "[i]n contrast with American housewives of the 1950s, who performed the work of housekeeping and child-raising but deferred to their husbands in matters of finances, children's education, and the family's social network, the Japanese housewife role has always been more encompassing."[45] More importantly, Japanese housewives perceive their domestic work as important because it is indeed socially valued. As Merry White insightfully points out, rarely do you hear a Japanese woman say, "I am *just* a housewife."[46] As some Japanese women have continued to embrace the identity of *shufu*, the term has survived as the title for this historic magazine into the twenty-first century.

In light of the genealogy of the Japanese concept of *shufu* as well as the specific context of *Friends of Housewives*, Chuang Shu Chih's concept of the "family pharmacist" apparently followed the well-established strategy of valorizing the knowledge of the housewife. To help married women to serve as—and to consider themselves—the female master of their households, women's magazines like *Friends of Housewives* urged Japanese housewives to acquire knowledge in many fields of family life: accounting, hygiene,

40. Koyama, *Ryōsai Kenbo*, 29.
41. Kathleen S. Uno, "The Death of 'Good Wife, Wise Mother'?" in *Postwar Japan as History*, ed. Andrew Gordon (Berkeley: University of California Press, 1993), 303.
42. Ochiai, *Japanese Family System in Transition*, 23–27.
43. Sato, *New Japanese Woman*, 83.
44. Merry White, "The Virtue of Japanese Mothers: Cultural Definitions of Women's Lives," *Daedalus* 116(3) (1987): 153.
45. Amy Borovoy, *The Too-Good Wife: Alcohol, Codependence, and the Politics of Nurturance in Postwar Japan* (Berkeley: University of California Press, 2005), 105.
46. White, "Virtue of Japanese Mothers,"153.

nutrition, scientific motherhood, and so on. Among these fields of knowledge, health-related articles were a regular feature in all popular mass women's magazines but were especially frequent in *Friends of Housewives*.[47] To assist these educated women to view themselves as knowledgeable female masters, "[e]ven the increasingly elaborate recipes [from such publications], though symbols of domesticity, imparted 'special' knowledge to housewives, making them 'expert' in their private spheres."[48] While Japanese women's magazines have long fashioned housewives as "experts" in the modern science of nutrition, Dr. Chuang's dietary therapy further valorized their domestic "expertise," elevating their knowledge about food into the determining factor for coping with life-threatening diseases.

More than equipping housewives with new expertise, however, Dr. Chuang's teachings on dietary therapy placed a heavy moral responsibility on their shoulders. Certainly, holding housewives responsible for the health of the whole family did not begin with Dr. Chuang. According to anthropologist Margaret Lock's observations in the 1980s, Japanese housewives in general regarded themselves as being responsible for the health of all family members. Their sense of responsibility as caretaker was so strong that when they themselves became more than mildly ill, they often opted to return to their own parents, to relax and recover under the care of their mothers.[49] To spell out more clearly what is special about the way that Chuang Shu Chih imposed responsibility upon housewives, let us recall the striking opening sentence of her confession: "I often think that I killed my father." Here, she is not referring to her responsibility of promoting health, but to her responsibility in creating the fatal threats with her labor of love.

If daily food could cause such serious harm, it follows that the person in charge of cooking for the household has to take responsibility for controlling this threat. Moreover, just like Chuang's own father and husband, male family members were generally not only ignorant of this threat but would often blindly eat their way into cancer because of their pathogenic food cravings. Since they could not be trusted to handle this fatal risk to their own health, a self-identified "female master" had to shoulder this responsibility for them. When Dr. Chuang spoke to her female followers in this confession, she addressed them as fellow mothers and housewives. She urged them to view themselves as enlightened and knowledgeable "family pharmacists," to actively put into practice this seemingly mundane knowledge on preparing foods. By doing so, they would help protect their family members from falling victim to their own tastes in food as well as to their ignorance. As a Taiwanese informant pointed out to me, she became interested in Dr.

---

47. Sato, *New Japanese Woman*, 100.
48. Ibid., 103.
49. Margaret Lock, *East Asian Medicine in Modern Japan* (Berkeley: University of California Press, 1988), 80.

Chuang's regimen because she agreed wholeheartedly that housewives should take care of the health of the whole family. This informant has been a loyal follower of her teachings for more than a decade, owning seven copies of her most popular book.

Once housewives have accepted Chuang Shu Chih's ideas, they might still spend their day in the kitchen slicing cabbage and cooking rice, but they can view themselves as preparing medicine and making an essential contribution to the family. By the same token, however, as housewives embrace the exalted role of "family pharmacist," they have little choice but to assume their responsible place in the family pharmacy, namely, the kitchen.

"True Women of Taiwan"

In addition to the exalted role of family pharmacist, Chuang Shu Chih offered two other important resources to her female followers for the construction of their self-identities.

First, instead of pathologizing the female body, Chuang's writings celebrate the major transformations in the course of women's lives—puberty, pregnancy, and menopause—as privileged opportunities for bodily rejuvenation. Calling them "women's three springs" (*nüren de sanchun* 女人的三春), Dr. Chuang went so far as to use this phrase as a book title.[50] While menopause often signifies physical degradation and arouses anxiety in Western women,[51] Dr. Chuang considers it a valuable opportunity for physical rejuvenation. It is worth pointing out that if we were to contextualize this concept within the history of obstetrics and gynecology in China, her elevation of these three life events into valuable "springs" constitutes a revolutionary break with—if not a betrayal of—the tradition of Chinese medicine. Far from being a special endowment from nature, these three life events are generally associated with pathological phenomena; to this day, they characterize the difficulties of "women's diseases," to be treated by the specialty of gynecology that first took shape in the Song dynasty (960–1279).[52] It appears that as Chuang Shu Chih fashioned her regimen for a predominantly female audience, she transformed what had traditionally

---

50. Chuang Shu Chih, *Nüren de sanchun* [Women's three springs] (Taipei: Shibao chubanshe, 2005).

51. Margaret Lock, *Encounters with Aging: Mythologies of Menopause in Japan and North America* (Berkeley: University of California Press, 1993).

52. Charlotte Furth, *A Flourishing Yin: Gender in China's Medical History, 960–1665* (Berkeley: University of California Press, 1999). With the exception of dietary therapy, the most popular aspect of Chuang's regimen concerns "sitting out the month" (*zuoyuezi* 坐月子) after delivering a baby. In response to popular demand, Chuang's granddaughters launched a commercial service that delivers dishes cooked according to her recipes to families after childbirth. Partially helped by Chuang's reputation, "sitting out the month" has returned as a huge business opportunity and distinctive feature of Taiwanese medical culture.

been thought of as the vulnerable phases in women's lives into privileged, health-enhancing opportunities for women.

Second, Dr. Chuang presented herself as a role model for her female followers. In the public's perception, she is physically associated with her popular regimen; it is no exaggeration to say that her regimen is one with her public persona. Because her inspiring life story is included in most of the books she has authored, many of her readers know as much about her biography as about her health advice. Her books and interviews often include pictures in which she is personally demonstrating her Cosmic Gymnastics or the correct postures for walking, sitting, giving massages, and preparing dishes. As a result, her inspiring life story, her cultivated elegance, even her daily routines have taken on an exemplary tone. Having followed Chuang Shu Chih through her daily routine, one female Taiwanese journalist concluded that it felt like witnessing an educational film about how to live an elegant and healthy life.[53] Since Dr. Chuang is such a prominent representation of her own regimen, following the regimen has become virtually inseparable from identifying with her.

The pair of images above can illuminate certain details concerning Chuang's public persona. In the first image (Figure 6.3), which is taken from one of her Japanese books, Dr. Chuang is shown as an elegant woman wearing a *qipao*, a dress that had become the standard formal dress in China in the 1920s.[54] Since Dr. Chuang was appealing to the authority of traditional Chinese medicine in her Japanese publications, she foregrounded the "Chinese-ness/Taiwanese-ness" of her regimen and her persona in Japan. In her writings, the terms "Chinese" and "Taiwanese" can be used interchangeably in many contexts. For example, while one of her Japanese books is entitled *The Chinese-Style Mobile Medicine and Health Maintenance*, its preface does not hesitate to foreground the Taiwanese folk practices included in it.[55] When Chuang's foundation for cancer prevention held its annual meeting in Tokyo in the late 1990s, she still required all staff to dress in *qipao* and posters to be written in Chinese.[56] Again, since *qipao* had become popular in China in the 1920s and in Taiwan in the 1930s,[57] wearing this style of clothing did not entail a hard choice for her between her Taiwanese and Chinese identity. In addition to revealing her sense of identity, the point of her self-representation was to highlight its foreignness to Japan.

---

53. Xu Fangju, "Zhuang Shuqi," 87.
54. Antonia Finnane, "What Should Chinese Women Wear? A National Problem," *Modern China* 22(2) (1996): 106–15.
55. Chuang, *Zhongguo xingyi jiankang fa*, 13.
56. Chuang, *Zhuang Shuqi huiyilu*.
57. Wu Chihao, "Yangfu, hefu, taiwanfu: Irzhi shiqi Taiwan duoyuan de fuzhuang wenhua" [Western attire, Japanese kimono, and Taiwanese clothing: The multicultural hybridity of Taiwan clothing during the Japanese colonial period], *Xinshixue* [New History] 26(3) (2015): 102–9.

Figure 6.3

Image of Chuang Shu Chih on the back cover of her Japanese book, *Pregnancy Brings You Beauty and Health* (1983)

莊淑旂 そうしゅくき●医学博士

1920年　中華民国台北市の医家の家に生まれる　父と夫をガンで失い　それ以来ガン撲滅と　女性の真の健康のために長年にわたって研究を続けガンの予防に大きな成果をあげている　現在　国際家族防癌協会の代表として活躍中　著書に『ガンにならない・体験の本』(潮文社)『青春を長もちさせる生活と食事』(主婦の友社)『生理痛・生理不順は必ず治る』(PHP研究所)

莊淑旂・台北市人

　日本慶應大學醫學博士，中華民國中醫師。現任日本國際家族防癌連合會會長、青峯社會福利事業基金會董事長、國際家族防癌總會創辦人。

Figure 6.4

Image of Chuang Shu Chih on the back cover of her Chinese book published in Taiwan, *What Is the Healthiest Way to Eat?* (1986)

Ironically, some of Dr. Chuang's medical doctrines such as abdominal diagnosis, for example, clearly originated in Japanese-style *kampō* medicine, and to this day many Taiwanese women trust Japanese patent medicines that incorporate traditional medicinal formulas. To cope with menstrual disorders, for example, many Taiwanese women take Chūjōtō 中將湯, which, as Susan Burns's article in this volume points out, was created by a Japanese pharmaceutical company in the early twentieth century and sold all over its colonies. In light of the fact that Japan has its own traditional *kampō* medicine, we need more research to understand why in the 1970s Japanese housewives were enthusiastic to learn the wisdom of traditional Asian medicine from a self-fashioned Chinese/Taiwanese woman.

When Dr. Chuang started promoting her regimen in Taiwan in the 1980s, her immediate success owed much to her association with Japan. She was promoted as the author of multiple bestsellers in Japan and personal physician of some Japanese celebrities. For example, the caption under Figure 6.4, taken from her first Chinese best seller in Taiwan, introduces her as the personal physician of the Japanese Crown Princess Michiko. The second chapter of this book consists of a Chinese translation of a Japanese article entitled "Crown Princess Michiko's Beauty Secrets," in which Dr. Chuang's regimen is credited for the crown princess's remarkable improvement in health. More importantly, as revealed by the catchy term "beauty secret," Dr. Chuang's Japanese background made her a role model not only in terms of health but also in terms of beauty and elegance. Even though this chapter has been eliminated from later editions of this book, in the Taiwanese context, Chuang Shu Chih's credibility and image remained closely connected with her background in Japan.

In other words, the creation of Dr. Chuang's public persona involved a three-way back-and-forth borrowing of cultural symbols among Taiwan, Japan, and China. Dressed in *qipao*, she sold the medical wisdom of traditional China to Japanese housewives. As a PhD from Keio University and a personal physician to Princess Michiko, she returned to Taiwan with the prestige and aesthetics associated with contemporary Japan. Clearly, what made this three-way trading possible was not the similarities or shared "tradition" among these three nations but rather their perceived differences, which she exploited, consciously or unconsciously, by placing them opposite each other.

Instead of being perceived as either Chinese or Japanese, however, Chuang Shu Chih was celebrated as one of the true women of Taiwan (*Taiwan zhen nüren* 台灣真女人) when she came back to her home country in the late 1980s. As such, she was selected as one of the main figures in a Taiwanese TV series entitled *True Women of Taiwan* in 1998. Instead of praising her for representing the conventional virtues of housewives, this Taiwanese TV program focused on her legendary career and celebrated it as an embodiment of

Taiwanese female perseverance. This symbolic event reveals a serious but little-noted tension between what Dr. Chuang preaches to her female followers and what she represents in the Taiwanese public perception. Having crafted the role of family pharmacist, she urges her followers, both Japanese and Taiwanese, to take responsibility for the health of the whole family, devoting time and energy to the task of cooking. Nevertheless, the special characteristics that caused her to be celebrated as a living example of the *True Women of Taiwan* have little to do with the virtues of the Japanese *shufu*. On the contrary, her celebrated achievements at times required her to make choices that would be extremely painful for any ordinary family, not the least for its female master.

To overcome the seemingly insurmountable obstacles in pursuing her advanced degree in Tokyo, for example, Chuang had to leave behind four of her five children with her mother in Taiwan. When the Japanese publisher Friends of Housewives promoted her as "a gentle and elegant mother of five children" in the caption under her picture on the cover of her first Japanese best seller,[58] it certainly did not mention the fact that, for almost nine years, she had not had an opportunity to see four of them. During these years, whenever Chuang could not bear the feeling of missing her children, she climbed to the top of her office building and weep alone. In her memoir, she recalls a heartbreaking conversation with her younger son. Deeply disappointed with her as an absent mother, her son once said to her face that he would like to marry a woman who is both deaf and mute so that she would cook for him every day and wait at home for his return from work.[59] No other accusation could have been more ironic or painful for one who advocated the idea of an involved kitchen pharmacist. Despite the fact that this cruel statement was meant to hurt her feelings and therefore should not be taken literally, Dr. Chuang's son agreed with her on one crucial point: among the responsibilities of a housewife, nothing is more fundamental than cooking. Regardless of her intentions, a serious tension remains between the gendered role of family pharmacist that she preaches to housewives and the persona of an iron-willed career woman that her life story represents to the Taiwanese public. Once put together, however, this pair of roles, while painfully conflicting in appearance, perhaps serves as a more flexible and thus better resource for Taiwanese women to individually tailor and adapt to their unique needs, circumstances, and aspirations.

---

58. Chuang Shu Chih [Shukuki Soo], *Seishun o nagamochisaseru seikatsu to shokuji* [A youth-preserving lifestyle and diet] (Tokyo: Shufu no tomo sha, 1970).
59. Chuang, *Zhuang Shuqi huiyilu*, 307.

Conclusion and the Question Unanswered

Since the focus of this paper has been food, I would like to begin its conclusion by situating this focus within the relationship between gender and medicine in East Asia, the central theme of this volume. To state the most obvious, the case of Chuang Shu Chih reconfirms a general impression that food is much more essential to East Asian motherhood than to its counterpart in the West. Nevertheless, this phenomenon might simply reflect a higher significance of food in East Asia in general and therefore might not be specifically connected to gender. Recall the revealing fact that one of the two questions that Taiwanese scholars added to the Quality of Life Questionnaire to express their local interests asks about food. As such, it is no wonder that Taiwanese housewives place more weight on food than do housewives in the West. Nevertheless, the difference in their attitude toward food is much more than just quantitative; it involves qualitatively different conceptions of food.

Few people would have taken note had Dr. Chuang advocated to housewives merely the general idea that some foods have health benefits. Housewives around the globe, including in East Asia, have long learned this idea from modern nutrition and have been eagerly applying this knowledge when preparing dishes for their families. While Dr. Chuang's dietary therapy certainly borrows from modern nutritional science, her doctrine is distinctively different because it is built upon and foregrounds the fatal threats posed by daily food to the human body. This unusual conception of food has profound implications for the gendered identities that Chuang Shu Chih constructed for housewives.

It was this unusual conception of food that justified the seemingly exaggerated role of "kitchen pharmacist" for housewives. Since these self-motivated "female masters of the family" cannot bear the thought of leaving unaddressed such a salient threat to the health of their beloved family, they have to take seriously the question that Dr. Chuang posed: "Are you a qualified family pharmacist?" Not surprisingly, this radical notion of food is also the most "traditional." When Sun Simiao wrote his foundational text on dietary treatment in the seventh century, he very much emphasized the danger of the ignorant or unconscious consumption of these generally efficacious foods and included many "nutritional interdictions."[60] Sun's insights have remained relevant ever since and manifested, for example, in the famous *Complete Compendium of Countless Treasures* (*Wanbao quanshu* 萬寶全書) in Ming to Qing China. This popular encyclopedia devotes a whole section to detailing numerous daily foods as being "harmful" to health. The popularity of Chuang Shu Chih's doctrine reveals that many of her followers still believed this traditional insight without being aware of how unusual it is in our modern age to compare daily foodstuffs to life-threatening drugs.

---

60. Engelhardt, "Dietetics in Tang China," 181.

In this sense, her Taiwanese followers are indeed quite different from house-wives in the West, because this unusual notion of food as alternately poison or medicine made them feel justified, and obligated as well, to view them-selves as "kitchen pharmacists."

Having spelled out this radical feature of Chuang Shu Chih's teachings on dietary therapy, I would like to return to the third question raised in the introduction, namely, the gender-related consequences of valorizing food as medicine and housewives as family pharmacists. Despite Chuang's inspiring life story and her well-intended efforts to empower housewives, it is easy to view her dual valorization as simply a new development of the tired patri-archal strategy of confining women to housework. The danger is too salient to dismiss: By assigning a time-consuming household task to housewives, she urged them to take responsibility for the health of the whole family and might make them feel guilty for feeding family members "poisons" if they failed to prepare dishes individually tailored to each member. On top of that, her teachings might mislead her readers to overestimate tremendously the practical value of this new housework when they follow her teachings to address various serious illnesses by means of food.

This salient danger in turn reveals two crucial reasons for the appeal of her ideas to Japanese and Taiwanese housewives. First of all, in comparison to biomedical knowledge, her teachings are far more evocative by celebrating women's agency in the production of knowledge and health. When house-wives appropriate biomedical knowledge—nutritional science, domestic hygiene, and scientific motherhood—in their role as female masters of the household, they have to learn the knowledge, often in a more simplified and popular format, from professional scientists and physicians. This makes them more or less passive receivers of this professional knowledge. In sharp contrast, Dr. Chuang's dietary therapy is information that was authored by a housewife for her fellow housewives. Although Chuang Shu Chih fashioned herself as a guardian of the traditional wisdom of East Asian medicine, she authored important new knowledge for her female followers. In addition to the slogan of "Women's Three Springs," she articulated a novel notion of *qi* as circulating neither in the meridian channels nor in the respiratory system but in the digestive system. In comparison to other popular and often high-minded understandings of *qi*—as vital energy, spirituality, or breath exercise in *qigong*—her notion of *qi* is remarkably corporeal and humble; it is directly connected with people's food intake and the mundane sensations of flatu-lence and belching. This humble conception of *qi* nevertheless does a great job in elevating the value of food and the status of food producers in main-taining health. To exaggerate a bit, this *qi* is a conceptual tool that Chuang Shu Chih created for herself and her followers; it is designed to support their belief that daily dishes, carefully prepared by them, are much more signifi-cant and efficacious than conventionally conceived.

Moreover, Dr. Chuang's teachings on dietary therapy stand not only outside the territory of biomedicine but also of state-sanctioned, professional Chinese medicine. As Taiwanese women have always used daily food to cope with health problems, much traditional knowledge about dietary therapy has been transmitted mainly, if not exclusively, within this nonofficial, female network. For example, Four Agent Decoction (Siwutang 四物湯), perhaps the most widely used herbal formula in Taiwan, has been transmitted literally as a recipe for a bowl of "soup" from mothers to daughters across kitchen tables to aid with the establishment and maintenance of regular menstrual cycles. By equating food with medicine, Dr. Chuang celebrates housewives' agency in authoring, transmitting, implementing, and embodying this knowledge on preparing food as well as on creating health.

In addition to celebrating women's agency, Chuang's writings might appeal to housewives because of their potential to challenge the hierarchy between women's housework and the biomedical profession and, by extension, that between domestic knowledge and public knowledge. Precisely because her dietary therapy has not been sanctioned by science and biomedicine, it promises to these housewives a revolutionary valorization of their knowledge and labor within the kitchen. Just imagine for a moment this scenario: If a man comes to believe that daily food has helped him or a beloved family member recover from cancer or any other serious illness for which modern biomedicine offers little help, he is bound to feel regret for underestimating the value of his wife's knowledge and housework. And this imaginary scenario is not completely without basis; many famous and powerful men—Wang Yongqing, to cite an example—and women have indeed adopted her doctrine, openly offering their testimony to support her. When housewives read about this public testimony or find evidence of improvement in their own bodies, they have good reasons to believe that what they have learned is by no means a method of self-deception. Instead, they might come to view themselves as guardians of a valuable tradition of knowledge, a tradition that has been ignored by mainstream, professional, male-dominated modern society. To fully evaluate the consequences of valorizing housewives as family pharmacists, we eventually have to address the fundamental question that I have yet to address: Can food really be effectively used as medicine?[61]

---

61. This is a question that I consider fundamental to this story but am unfortunately unable to address in this chapter. The way in which any scholar or reader of Chuang's books answers this question is bound to influence his or her evaluation. To provide a comparable case, I would like to call attention to the role that diet plays in Margaret Lock's famous comparative study of menopause in Japan and America. In her argument for the concept of "local biologies," she suggests that diet, especially soybeans, "*may be* one part of the cultural repertoire that contributes to the low symptom reporting of hot flashes on the part of Japanese women." Margaret Lock and Patricia Kaufert, "Menopause, Local Biologies, and Culture of Aging," *American Journal of Human Biology* 13 (2001): 500, emphasis mine.

Part III

Potent(ial) Virility: Labor, Migration, and the Military in the Construction of Masculinity

The chapters by Leung, Chiang, and DiMoia explore how labor requirements, military cultures, and demographic policies shaped, and in turn, were shaped by shifting and competing visions of masculinity, influenced by changing medical authorities and legitimacy of colonial powers and postcolonial nation-states. Leung explores the growing number of "weak" male migrant laborers and soldiers (notably Chinese and Japanese) plagued by beriberi/*jiaoqi*/*kakké* increasingly framed as a "deficiency" disease in the early twentieth century. She highlights anxieties and concerns over the supposed "failures" of East Asian masculinity and female fertility in this modern biomedical framing of the disease. The normative physiology of postcolonial Taiwanese men and the involvement of the military in its reproduction, analyzed by Chiang in the Cold War case of "the Chinese Christine," continued to shape expressions of anxiety over masculinity well into the latter half of the twentieth century. East Asian military culture remains significant for DiMoia's study of (South) Korean masculinity, where he investigates the role of vasectomy as an integral part of family planning in the late 1960s. South Korean men were called upon to volunteer for this physiological procedure as part of their "duty" to the nation in addition to their military service, yet "continued potency," as propagated by the state, was an ongoing concern to their masculinity.

7
Weak Men and Barren Women

Framing Beriberi/*Jiaoqi*/*Kakké* in Modern East Asia, ca. 1830–1940

Angela Ki Che Leung

Introduction*

Beriberi, a disease "discovered" by Dutch doctors in Batavia in the nineteenth century, was key to the construction of the new "nutritional science" in the early twentieth century.[1] Defined as a potentially fatal nervous degeneration disorder due to the deficiency of vitamin B1 (thiamine), it is still believed to be prevalent in rice-eating regions where the diet is based on polished rice, from which the thiamine-rich seed coat has been removed.[2] Since its being framed in biomedical terms in the late 1920s, beriberi, curiously translated in East Asia by the names of an ancient disorder, *jiaoqi* 腳氣 in Chinese, and *kakké* in Japanese (both meaning literally "leg-*qi*," highlighting the conspicuous symptom of weak legs), indicating recognized kindship between the historical and modern ailments,[3] has been studied and analyzed

* This chapter is a partial output of project no. 745613, The Construction of Nutritional Knowledge in Modern China (ca. 1850–1950), 2014–2017, funded by the Hong Kong Research Grants Council. I am grateful to participants of the two workshops in 2009 and 2013, and especially to Ruth Rogaski, for their pertinent comments and suggestions on earlier versions of this chapter.
1. Christiaan Eijkman (1858–1930) fed chicken with white rice in the East Indies in the late nineteenth century to develop the theory, and British chemist Frederick Hopkins (1861–1947) further elaborated on the chemical composition of vitamins. Both men obtained the Nobel Prize in 1929 for their study on vitamins. See Kenneth Carpenter, *Beriberi, White Rice, and Vitamin B: A Disease, a Cause, and a Cure* (Berkeley: University of California Press, 2000), 102–4.
2. See, for example, the definition of beriberi in *The Bantam Medical Dictionary*, Third Revised Edition, prepared by the editors of Market House Books Ltd. (New York: Bantam Books, 2000), 52: "A nutritional disorder due to deficiency of vitamin B1 (thiamin). It is widespread in rice-eating communities in which the diet is based on polished rice, from which the thiamine-rich seed coat has been removed."
3. There is occasional confusion about the contemporary use of the Chinese term *jiaoqi*, which is sometimes used erroneously or locally to mean athlete's foot or gout. We exclude such meanings of the term in this chapter.

mostly in terms of dietetics, especially rice eating, even in historical contexts where polished rice did not exist.[4]

This ultimate biochemical explanation of beriberi as a major milestone in the construction of nutritional science[5] was in fact juxtaposed on evolving framing processes of beriberi/jiaoqi/kakké within different medical traditions throughout the colonial period in East Asia, in different languages.[6] While European scientists were discovering, experimenting, and speculating on what they saw as a new disease in Asia that they finally linked to the consumption of a modern food product, polished white rice, Asian doctors were puzzled by the "reemergence" of an old ailment amply described in classical medical treatises as one caused by the penetration of damp in the body. Colonial governments were concerned with the disease as they saw in it a major threat to economic productivity. As an author of an early report on beriberi in Hong Kong wrote, quoting "an old resident" of the colony: "The prosperity of this Colony largely depends on the sturdy shoulders of the Hong Kong coolie."[7] For East Asian society, on the contrary, the noticeable weakening male bodies coined by the Chinese term "sick men of East Asia,"[8] in crowded, industrializing, and stressful urban centers infested with "modern" diseases such as tuberculosis, syphilis, and beriberi, accounted for its inferiority compared to the West. The modern Asian beriberi/jiaoqi/kakké epidemic fully encapsulated the anxiety on this "observable" diminished

---

4. Notably an article by Lu Gwei-Djen and Joseph Needham in 1951 in *Isis* 42 (1951): 13–20, "A Contribution to the History of Chinese Dietetics," based on a chapter of Lu's PhD dissertation in chemistry on beriberi submitted in 1939. The recent work on Japanese *kakké* by Alexander Bay also accepts such a kinship with beriberi. See his *Beriberi in Modern Japan: The Making of a National Disease* (Rochester, NY: University of Rochester Press, 2012).

5. Michael Worboys, "The Discovery of Colonial Malnutrition between the Wars," in *Imperial Medicine and Indigenous Societies*, ed. David Arnold (Manchester: Manchester University Press 1988), 208–25.

6. Beriberi is an excellent example of the futility of writing the "biography" of a disease, as eloquently argued by Roger Cooter in *Writing History in the Age of Biomedicine* (with Claudia Stein, New Haven: Yale University Press, 2013), chapter 7. It is impossible to do retrospective diagnosis to verify claimed cases of beriberi of which East Asian and European experts had very different conceptual tools to formulate explanations at different historical moments. The Asian epidemic emerged as mysteriously as it disappeared in the twentieth century. On the contrary, the study of the different framing processes of beriberi/jiaoqi/kakké in this period, an approach proposed by Charles Rosenberg ("Disease in History: Frames and Framers," *Milbank Quarterly* 67[1] [1989]: 1–15) reveals how the epidemic became an actor in a "complex social situation" (10), affecting personal lifestyle, therapeutic methods, and the design of public health strategies in East Asia.

7. R. M. Gibson, "Beriberi in Hong Kong, with Special Reference to the Records of the Alice Memorial and Nethersole Hospitals and with Notes on Two Years' Experience of the Disease," manuscript, March 16, 1900, p. 4.

8. For the formulation of this expression, see Yang Ruisong, "Xiangxiang minzu chiru: Jindai Zhongguo sixiang wenhua shang di 'Dongya bingfu'" [Imagined national humiliation: "Sick men of East Asia" in modern Chinese thought and culture], *Guoli Zhengzhi Daxue lishi xuebao* 23 (May 2005): 1–44.

masculinity linked especially to the military,[9] a phenomenon discussed in depth, but from another perspective, in John DiMoia's and Howard Chiang's chapters in this volume.

Doctors of competing medical traditions in colonial Asia, despite differences in approach and premises, agreed that beriberi's main victims were Asian men even though this gender difference could not be fully accounted for in physiological terms. The social framing of the epidemic thus became important for making the ailment comprehensible. Conflicting explanations proposed by experts from different medical traditions made the beriberi/ *jiaoqi*/*kakké* phenomenon one of the most puzzling and elusive epidemic experiences in modern East Asia while they at the same time unraveled layers of individual and collective anxieties in a rapidly changing world, articulated most effectively in terms of the health of the gendered body.

The Emerging Asian Pandemic: A Male Disease

It was in modern institutions with high concentrations of young men that Western medical doctors working in colonial Asia first noticed this unfamiliar "Asian" disease, in the mid-nineteenth century. The British doctor Malcolmson published one of the first books on beriberi in 1835 based on his observations on the impact of the disease on native troops in Northern Circars in the late 1820s.[10] Later in the 1860s, Dutch scientists, including C. Eijkman, began systematic study of beriberi in Batavia, with the British and the Americans getting more involved in research from the beginning of the twentieth century.[11] The first regional alert of a beriberi epidemic outbreak took place in 1860 in Sungaiselan, where one-eighth of the miners were reported to be sick and one-third of the sick died. In the following year, the disease caused 700 deaths in Belitung. In the 1890s in Bangka hundreds of workers died each year of the disease that accounted for 5 percent death rate of the total force of about 12,000 workers, many of them Chinese.[12] The situation continued to be serious in the early twentieth century in Java. The

---

9. The close link between beriberi and the military in East Asia is best represented by the Japan case; see Alexander Bay, "Beriberi, Military Medicine, and Medical Authority in Prewar Japan," *Japan Review* 20 (2008): 111–56.

10. He noted that in 1827, twenty-eight out of eighty-eight deaths in native troops, and twenty out of fifty-two deaths in 1830 were due to beriberi, see J. G. Malcomson, *A Practical Essay on the History and Treatment of Beriberi* (Madras: Vepery Mission Press, 1835), 11–26.

11. Carpenter, *Beriberi, White Rice, and Vitamin B*, chapters 1, 3, 5, and 6. Duan Simmons, "Beriberi, or the 'Kakké' of Japan," *China Imperial Maritime Customs Medical Reports*, Special Series no. 2, 19th issue, for the half-year ended March 31, 1880 (Shanghai: Statistical Department of the Inspectorate General), 41.

12. Mary F. S. Heidhues, *Bangka Tin and Mentok Pepper: Chinese Settlement on an Indonesian Island* (Singapore: Institute of Southeast Asian Studies, 1992), 61–65.

number of cases treated between 1901 and 1924 fluctuated between 840 and 7,719.[13]

Similar epidemics among Chinese tin miners were also observed in the Federated Malay States at the turn of the century.[14] By 1905, beriberi was reported to be the most prevailing disease in Malaya, representing one-fifth of all hospital cases, with 2,215 cases and 330 deaths (whereas there were 2,109 malaria cases with 173 deaths).[15] Leonard Braddon's (state surgeon of the Federated Malay States) famous report on the disease in 1907 in the Malay States showed that the epidemic was particularly prevalent among the Chinese male adult population with a case incidence of 40/1,000 in 1901.[16] Reports on other Southeast Asian countries, including the Philippines, Siam, and French Indochina, all recorded rapidly increasing numbers of beriberi patients.[17] Victor Heiser, director of health for the Philippine Islands in the 1910s, estimated in 1913 that there were 100,000 deaths in Asia per year due to beriberi.[18]

In Japan, despite consistent attention given to kakké in kampō texts back in the eighteenth century,[19] the ailment became globally visible only in the late nineteenth century. The American doctor Duane Simmons was one of the first Western doctors who observed the epidemic in Japan in the 1870s and wrote a report in 1880 based on his observation in the Government

---

13. C. D. Langen, "The International Control of Beriberi," Far Eastern Association of Tropical Medicine (FEATM) Transactions of 6th Biennial Congress, Tokyo, 1925, 70–71.
14. Hamilton Wright, "An Enquiry into the Etiology and Pathology of Beri-Beri," *Journal of Tropical Medicine* (June 1, 1905): 161–62; a more complete study of the epidemic in the Malay States is Herbert Durham's "Notes on Beriberi in the Malay Peninsula and on Christmas Island (Indian Ocean)," *Journal of Hygiene* (1904): 112–55.
15. "Malay States Medical Report for the Year 1905," *Journal of Tropical Medicine and Hygiene*, January 1, 1907, p. 9.
16. Leonard Braddon, *The Cause and Prevention of Beri-Beri* (London and New York: Rebman, 1907), 3–4.
17. Edward Vedder, captain medical corps of the US Army in Manila wrote a report in 1913 that between 1895 and 1902, there were 57,025 admissions of beriberi patients in thirty-one district hospitals, of whom 8,990 died, see E. Vedder, *Beriberi* (New York: William and Wood, 1913), 17. Siam was another epidemic region. The principle medical officer reported in 1913 that of a total of 500 conscripts in the Police School at Bangkok, 444 developed beriberi within two months and were sent home on a month's leave. He also observed an increasing epidemic trend of beriberi from 1913 to 1929, with 852 recorded cases in 1913 and 3,871 in 1929, see H. C. Highet, "The Sequelae of Beriberi," Far Eastern Association of Tropical Medicine (FEATM), Comptes rendus de travaux du 3e congrès biennal tenu à Saigon 1913, 255. Gaide (general surgeon of colonial troops in Indochina) and Bodet (deputy general inspector), "Le beriberi en Indochine," Far Eastern Association of Tropical Medicine (FEATM) Transactions of the 8th Congress held in Siam, 1930, 104.
18. Victor Heiser, "Beri-beri. An Additional Experience at Culion," Far Eastern Association of Tropical Medicine (FEATM) Comptes rendus de travaux du 3e congrès biennal tenu à Saigon 1913, 371.
19. See my chapter, "Japanese Medical Texts in Chinese on Kakké in the Tokugawa and Early Meiji Periods," in *Antiquarianism, Language, and Medical Philology*, ed. Benjamin A. Elman (Leiden: Brill, 2015), 163–85.

Hospital in Yokohama and also in private and consulting native practices in both Yokohama and Tokyo. He noted 660 conscripts affected with beriberi were admitted to military and naval hospitals in Tokyo in 1875, representing 3.8 percent of the whole force of 17,000, not counting those victims whose symptoms were milder and not sent to the hospital.[20] The increasingly alarming epidemic was made known to the world after the publication of the medical report on the navy in 1901 on the First Sino-Japanese War of 1894–1895 showing that, in the 1880s, almost one-third of the navy was infected with the disease. The eventual control of the epidemic by the implementation of diet change narrated in the report was an exemplary epidemiological study in the up-and-coming Western biochemical tradition.[21]

In China, the modern *jiaoqi* epidemic was first revealed in a monograph on the ailment in 1887 by a Cantonese doctor working in British Hong Kong, Zeng Chaoran 曾超然. This work, entitled *Jiaoqi chuyan* 腳氣芻言 (Preliminary words on *jiaoqi*) was a recognized medical work in modern China,[22] and remarkable in situating the epidemic, still framed largely in classical terms, in the modern and global context of Asia. It was based on notes of the author's clinical practice during his tenure as in-house doctor and teacher at the charitable Tung Wah Hospital, opened in 1872, that provided Chinese medical treatment for the Chinese population in the British colony.[23] This work indicates an emerging *jiaoqi* epidemic since probably the 1870s among Chinese men living or transiting in Hong Kong that British doctors were not aware of. Prominent figures in tropical medicine such as Patrick Manson (1844–1922) and his protégé James Cantlie (1851–1926) working in Hong Kong did not begin to observe actual beriberi patients until 1887, when Alice Memorial Hospital, the first Western charitable hospital for the Chinese, was established.[24] In fact, British bacteriologists in Hong Kong, having little contact with Chinese patients, were totally misinformed about the situation and claimed in 1905 that the disease was not endemic in Hong Kong or in China, only to contradict themselves two years later when statistics from

---

20. Simmons, "Beriberi, or the 'Kakké' of Japan," 41, 70.

21. Baron Saneyoshi and Shigemichi Suzuki, *The Surgical and Medical History of the Naval War between Japan and China during 1894–1895* (Tokyo: Tokio Print, 1901), 450–78, on *kakké*.

22. This book was reedited many times subsequently, by the Cantonese army in the last years of the Qing dynasty and in the Republican period. Republican medical journals also reproduced and commented on large parts of it. Xie Guan considered the book the most important in the modern period on *jiaoqi* (see note 38).

23. Encouraged by the British colonial government, the hospital was established and financed by Chinese business elites to take care of Chinese inhabitants, who distrusted biomedicine practiced in the Civil Hospital. On its history, see Elizabeth Sinn, *Power and Charity: Chinese Merchant Elite in Colonial Hong Kong* (Hong Kong: Oxford University Press, 1989).

24. Patrick Manson said in 1888, "It was not until last year, when the Alice Memorial Hospital was opened, that the general medical practitioners of Hong Kong had a proper opportunity to see and study native diseases and that we began to learn a little definite about our endemic Beri-beri." See R. M. Gibson, "Beriberi in Hong Kong," 2.

local Chinese hospitals became accessible to them.[25] According to such data, from 1897 to 1906 the number of beriberi patients increased from 173 (with 102 deaths) to 517 (with 257 deaths).[26] The situation deteriorated with time up to the 1920s: while 562 and 736 deaths were recorded in 1907 and 1908, the numbers peaked to 1,744 and 1,192 in 1925 and 1926 for the whole of Hong Kong, amounting to about 5 percent of the colony's total deaths recorded.[27] The mortality in a Chinese hospital in Canton appeared to be lower: 76 of 701 (implying an annual figure of more than 1,000) inpatients died in the second half of year 1929, but this mortality was second only to tuberculosis.[28]

Chinese, Japanese *kampō*, and Western medical experts of the period all took note of the overwhelming proportion of male patients in this regional pandemic. Duane Simmons, who wrote for the China Imperial Maritime Customs Service, observed in 1880 that, in Japan, the few women who had the disease were pregnant.[29] Leonard Braddon in Malaysia, Gaide and Bodet, military surgeons in Indochina, C. Langen, a German doctor, and Noel Davis, assistant health officer in Shanghai, observing the beriberi epidemics respectively in Malaya, Indochina, Java, and Shanghai, also stressed that patients were predominantly young, able-bodied, and male.[30] The first British colonial doctors reporting on beriberi in Hong Kong's Alice Memorial Hospital provided more precise information on the unusual male/female ratio: the percentage of male to female beriberi cases was 95.72 percent to 4.28 percent (of a total of 1,476 patients in 1888–1889), while the usual proportion of male to female patients in attendance was 4 to 1.[31] A later survey in Shanghai in 1934 showed a similarly lopsided ratio of 8 to 1.[32] In other

---

25. William Hunter, "The Incidence of Disease in Hong Kong," *Journal of Tropical Medicine* (May 1, 1905): 130; Hunter, "The Prevalence of Beriberi in Hong Kong," *Journal of Tropical Medicine and Hygiene* 10(16) (August 5, 1907): 265–71.

26. Meanwhile, mortality of malaria decreased from 571 (191 deaths) to 248 (96 deaths) according to the "Report of the Inspecting Medical Officer to the Tung Wah Hospital, 1906," sessional paper (Hong Kong, 1907), 463. The medical officer was Dr. Thomson.

27. "Vital statistics," *Hong Kong Administrative Report 1908* (Hong Kong: Government Printer, 1908), 12; "Public Health," *Hong Kong Administrative Report 1927* (Hong Kong: Government Printer, 1927), 22. These figures confirmed those given to Dr. Edward Vedder of the US Army in the Philippines, see Vedder, *Beriberi*, 13–16. These works provides the most comprehensive epidemiological situation of beriberi in Asia.

28. *Fangbian Yiyuan tongji huikan* [Collection of statistics of the Expediency Hospital], 1929, section "yi'an." That year tuberculosis claimed 117 lives of the 320 inpatients.

29. Simmons, "Beriberi, or the 'Kakké' of Japan," 43.

30. Braddon, *Cause and Prevention of Beri-Beri*, 256, 278; Gaide and Bodet, "Le beriberi en Indochine"; Langen, "International Control of Beriberi"; Noel Davis, "Observations on Beriberi in Shanghai," Far Eastern Association of Tropical Medicine (FEATM) Transactions of the 2nd Biennial Congress, Hong Kong, 1912, 23–30. He observed the cases in the prison (with 33.3 percent mortality), police recruits, a tramway company, where only men were observed, and a charitable organization for young girls.

31. Gibson, "Beriberi in Hong Kong," 18.

32. B. S. Platt and S. Y. Gin, "Some Observations on a Preliminary Study of Beriberi in Shanghai," Far Eastern Association of Tropical Medicine (FEATM) Transactions of the 9th Congress, Nanking, China, October 2–8, 1934 (Nanking: National Health Administration,

words, even considering the sociological factors accounting for the higher number of male patients in hospitals observed for any disease, the male/ female proportion for beriberi in this period was still unusually high. At the same time, medical experts of the different traditions also noted the relation between the pandemic and a rapidly urbanizing, industrializing, and globalizing Asia.

Jiaoqi/Kakké Modern: A New Old Ailment?

Kampō doctors of Tokugawa Japan were probably the first to consciously explain *kakké* in the context of a profoundly transformed human ecology brought about by a changing political economy. Despite the claimed affinity of the modern Japanese epidemic with early medieval *jiaoqi* recorded in Chinese medical classics, *kakké* was considered not exactly the same as *jiaoqi* but a "modern" version of the old disease. Taki Motokata 多紀元堅 (1795–1857) stressed in 1853 the mutative character of *kakké* by highlighting the possibility that, just as modern *kakké* was different from what it was in the past, *kakké* in the future might very well be different again.[33] The elusiveness of *kakké* was further elaborated by Nakano Yasuaki 淺田昌春 (1813–1894) and Asada Sōhaku 淺田惟常, director of the Hakusai byōin in 1878, who published the *General Treatise on Kakké* (*Kakké gairon* 脚氣概論) in 1879, where they developed the idea that *kakké* changed with time and place:

> In our country, the disease had existed for a thousand years. . . . In later time, when the four seas were in great turmoil with incessant warfare, we rarely heard of the disease again. In recent years, [this illness] re-emerges. The clinical patterns are similar to those described in Jin/Tang medical classics. The analyses are also similar. This is due to changing time and customs. We are in a different era.[34]

The authors seemed to imply here that *kakké* was a disease of prosperity and peace as it disappeared during wars and political turmoil and reappeared in modern Japan just as real *jiaoqi* was endemic in prosperous Tang China. Moreover, these *kampō* doctors highlighted the fact that the *kakké* in modern times was characterized by its prevalence in the warmer seasons between summer and autumn, affecting mostly the young and able-bodied male, features that were not noted in medieval Chinese classics on *jiaoqi*.[35]

1935), 407–8. This study was based on the fifty thousand outpatients of the Lester Chinese Hospital.

33. Taki Motokata, *Zatsubyō Kōyō* [Broad essentials on various diseases], 1853 (Beijing: Renmin weisheng chubanshe, 1983), 120.

34. Nakano Yasuaki and Asada Sōhaku, *Kakké gairon* [General treatise on *kakké*], 1879, Huanghan yixue congshu 1936. (Shanghai: Zhongyi xueyuan chubanshe, 1993), 5.

35. Ibid., 5–6.

The connection between *kakké* and Japanese modern urbanity was spelled out most strongly by Imamura Ryō 今村亮 in his 1878 work *Kakké shinron* 腳氣新論 (A new discussion on *kakké*) where he explained the notion of "wind-toxin," *fūdoku* 風毒, by evoking a new element: toxic air buried beneath urban ground:

> Wherever the land is lowly and damp, with dense populations and over-whelming human activities, where people do not even have enough place to stand on, the *ki* of the ground, not being able to dissipate freely, would cause this disease. Why then does it emerge only in the spring and summer? It is because [during this season] the *ki* of the ground is on the rise and as it gets blocked [by human masses and activities on the ground], the obstructed steaming process would produce a toxic *ki*.

In this toxic urban environment, he thought, "[d]iseases are complex, their changes are multiple. There are modern diseases that did not exist in the past, such as cholera. And those that became more prominent than in the past, such as *kakké*."[36]

Chinese doctors' writing on *jiaoqi* in the nineteenth and early twentieth centuries did not articulate as precisely as *kampō* authors on the modern characteristics of the ailment, but they did not fail to explain the disease in a changing global context. Chinese doctors were sensitive to the living environment of their patients, mostly male migrants working in coastal metropolises such as Shanghai and Hong Kong, or in Southeast Asia.[37] Xie Guan 謝觀 (1885–1950), an influential doctor in the Shanghai district, like many of his contemporaries, was convinced that the "reemergence" of this old disease was in fact the "reintroduction" of the ailment to China from Southeast Asia.[38] This point was statistically supported by a 1928 list of patients to be repatriated to Canton showing that more than one-third were transients having stayed in Hong Kong for less than two years, many from Southeast Asia.[39] While Hong Kong was already considered a place with bad "water and soil," Southeast Asia was worse. A Chinese doctor residing in Hong

---

36. Imamura Ryō, *Kakké shinron* [New treatise on *kakké*] (Edo: Keigyōkan edition, 1878), preface, 2a, 3a.

37. The above-mentioned Zeng Chaoran of the Hong Kong Tung Wah Hospital noted the prevalence of the disease in South China and Southeast Asia in the 1880s. See his *Jiaoqi chuyan*, 11b–13a; Ding Fubao, the famous popular medical writer at the turn of the century highlighted the epidemic in Japan, Shanghai, and the Guangdong regions in his 1910 edited volume on beriberi. See his 1910 work, *Jiaoqi bing zhi yuanyin ji liaofa* [Causes and treatment of the *jiaoqi* ailment] (Shanghai: Wenming shuju, 1910), preface, 3.

38. Xie Guan, *Zhongguo yixue yuanliu lun* [On the root of Chinese medicine] (Shanghai: Chengzhai yishe, 1935), 47. Xie, commenting on Zeng Chaoran's 1887 book, stated that the disease disappeared in China after the Song dynasty and was "reintroduced" in China from overseas, a view already implied in Zeng's book.

39. Donghua Hospital Archives (DHA). Letter from the Donghua Hospital to the Colony's Medical Officer, February 16, 1933, 432–38. Out of seventy-five listed, twenty-nine were either passing through Hong Kong or were residing in Hong Kong for less than two years.

Kong refused to take up a position offered by a Kuala Lumpur hospital in 1920 because, as he explained in the letter to the hospital, "The 'water and soil' of the Southern Ocean [Malaya] is not as stable as that in Hong Kong[;] most [who go to Malaya] will develop *jiaoqi* and bone pain."[40] This concern underlies the great anxiety vividly expressed in popular songs and ballads lamenting Chinese migrants' wretched lives in Southeast Asia.[41] The sick Chinese migrant worker at that time usually sought repatriation—that is, leaving the place where he fell ill—as a preferred therapeutic move.

The repatriation of sick Chinese migrants in the colonial period was thus not simply a colonial policy to get rid of nonproductive workers, but a medical strategy based on the belief shared by Europeans, Japanese, and Chinese of the time that the patient should leave the location where he fell sick. While the Japanese therapeutic strategy of *tenchi* 轉地 (to change site) meant moving patients to higher, dryer ground, the Chinese version, sometimes expressed as *zhuan shuitu* 轉水土 (to change "water and soil") implied being repatriated to their native place. Four patients of the ten cases described by Zeng in his 1887 book returned to their native towns in Guangdong in the late nineteenth century upon the recommendation of the doctor. Beginning no later than 1903–1904 and until the early 1940s, the Tung Wah Hospital in Hong Kong where Zeng had worked began to organize regular shipments of repatriated migrants sick with *jiaoqi* from Southeast Asia, Latin America and Hong Kong itself to Canton to be treated in charitable hospitals, the most important of which was the Fangbian Hospital 方便醫院 (Expediency Hospital, established in 1899).[42] News on these public health strategies derived from the modern understanding of *jiaoqi* in Chinese East Asia, was frequently covered by public printed media in the early twentieth century.[43]

---

40. DHA, 1919–1920 Waijie laihan [Letters received], 130-B19/20-214, pp.172–73, Doctor Yu Baochu to the Tung Wah Hospital refusing to take the position in Tongshan Hospital in Kuala Lumpur as arranged by the two hospitals.

41. I would like to thank Wilt Idema for drawing my attention to a genre of modern Hakka and Minnanese Songs and Ballads about Overseas Migration (*Guofan ge* 過番歌) from late imperial and early Republican China that highlight the dread of catching all kinds of strange diseases in the southern seas.

42. DHA, Minutes of the Board Meeting of the Tung Wah Hospital on January 26, 1904, recorded board members' appreciation of sending *jiaoqi* patients back to Guangdong as they thought that the sick would have a better chance of cure or survival, notably the Guangji and Fangbian Hospitals. Patients were first shipped to Canton via the West River and, later in the twentieth century, taken by the Canton-Kowloon train. The Tung Wah Hospital, as a major charitable organization for Hong Kong and overseas Chinese since 1871, paid the Fangbian Hospital for accommodating patients repatriated by the Tung Wah. See also *Xianggang Donghua Sanyuan bainian shilüe* [One hundred years of history of the three Tung Wah Hospitals in Hong Kong] (Hong Kong: Tung Wah Hospital, 1970), 58.

43. Some Shanghai medical journals reported such operations as early as the 1910s, e.g., *Medical World* (*Yixue shijie* 醫學世界), no. 22, 1913, p. 62, reported the shipment of forty-seven patients from Tung Wah Hospital to the Fangbian Hospital in Canton. A major Chinese newspaper in Hong Kong, *Huazi ribao* 華字日報, for example, reported in 1928 that "[s]ome of the immigrants in Hong Kong could not adjust to the local 'water and soil' (*shuitu* 水土)

At the same time, white rice was being proposed by Western scientists as the main culprit of this modern Asian disease. Being the traditional Asian staple transformed by modern technology and spread by global trade that accentuated rural-urban dichotomy, rice was a natural suspect when the disease was linked to a bad food.[44] Dr. C. D. de Langen of the Medical School in Batavia noted in his article for the 1925 Congress of the Far Eastern Association of Tropical Medicine (FEATM) that beriberi there "rarely occurs in the interior, but is chiefly confined to the large towns, the plantations, industrial centres, prisons[,] etc." He explained that as only rice for export from British India, French Saigon, and Siam in the region was mechanically and thoroughly milled for easier transportation, storage, and good market value, it was natural that the epidemic mainly occurred in urbanized, coastal Java where such rice was consumed.[45] Similarly, the *jiaoqi* and *kakké* epidemics in China and Japan were reported by Chinese and Japanese experts to concentrate first in Westernized coastal metropolises such as Hong Kong, Canton, Shanghai, Tokyo, Kyoto, and Osaka from the nineteenth century onward. With the improvement in transportation that facilitated human migration, circulation of goods, and colonization, the disease was described to be spreading inland and to places where it was believed to have been nonexistent, such as Taiwan, Korea, Australia, and even Manchuria, in the twentieth century.[46] The movement of beriberi / *jiaoqi* / *kakké* simply followed the trajectories of polished rice as a modern commodity.

By the late 1920s, Chinese doctors increasingly internalized the biochemical framing of *jiaoqi* to articulate the difficulty of living in a modern world. Jiang Zhenxun 姜振勛, a doctor practicing in Shanghai in the 1920s and 1930s and a popular medical writer, took up the new vitamin B1 theory and concluded that "the prevalence of *jiaoqi* in recent years is a result of progress in material civilization," meaning fine food processing with modern engineering. However, the way to prevent the disease, he continued, was not to give up modern civilization, as this was neither feasible nor reasonable, but to modify the lifestyle so that material progress would not go against the body. He did not prescribe giving up consuming white rice but picked up recommendations from classical medical and life-nourishing texts such as moderation in sex, work, and diet, and sanitary living environments. Like

---

and develop *jiaoqi*. Recently the ship Daxing travelling between the colony and Wuzhou had taken more than ten patients" (June 27, 1928). The destination of the passengers was normally Canton via Wuzhou.

44. On this problem in Canton, see Seung-Joon Lee's recent study, "Taste in Numbers: Science and the Food Problem in Republican Guangzhou, 1927–1937," *Twentieth-Century China* 35(2) (April 2010): 81–105.

45. Langen, "International Control of Beriberi," 69–71.

46. This narrative of the spread of beriberi was quite commonly given in popular medical periodicals in the 1930s in China. For example, Chi Zheng, "Jiaoqi bing" [The *jiaoqi* ailment], *Minzong yibao* (1931): 12, especially p. 13.

Ding Fubao 丁福保 (1874–1952), the popular medical writer in Shanghai with Japanese training and editor and translator of a 1910 text on *jiaoqi* originally in Japanese, Jiang recommended moderation, restraint, and discipline of the old "life-nourishing" tradition to counter the challenge of a modern world of excess, overabundance, overexertion, and great stress.[47]

A Disease of Asian Male: Decadent or Deprived?

As a disease thought to be brought about by modern technology in a new global economy, beriberi / *jiaoqi* / *kakké* was not considered one of deprivation at the beginning. The epidemic was associated for several decades with wealth, new opportunities, and urban lifestyle, and with them, all the stress, decadence, and immorality in a "poisonous" urban environment. Traditional *jiaoqi* / *kakké* etiology in East Asia readily underpinned this framing.

Kampō doctors were the first to articulate the link between affluence, urban men, and *kakké*. Imamura's emphasis on the toxic environment of new urbanized centers made the point most clearly. In his 1861 text, he noted the prevalence of the epidemic especially in metropolitan centers such as Edo, Kyoto, and Naniwa (Osaka), concluding that the epidemic was the result of the hedonistic and decadent lifestyle of wealthy urban men. He further explained that the main cause for the wealthy to fall ill was essentially internal: excessive food and sex depleted the body of its primodial *ki* (*genki* 元氣), making it receptive to external pathogens[48] that he now called *utsudoku* 欝毒, a compressed severe toxin buried deep underground, especially in crowded urban centers.[49] Imamura pushed the "internal" cause argument further to highlight the moral aspect of *kakké* etiology. In modern Japanese metropolises, urban men in their prime indulging in excessive sex and lavish lifestyles were the main victims of the illness, while women, children, and the elderly, not being able to enjoy such excessive bodily pleasures, were spared. He provided statistics to prove his point: urban well-to-do males made up 80–90 percent of *kakké* patients.[50]

Modern Chinese doctors were also sensitive to this characteristic of *jiaoqi* patients. The above-mentioned Zeng Chaoran writing in Hong Kong in the 1880s, and Zhou Xiaonong 周小農 (1876–1942), a famous practitioner in Wuxi in the first decades of the twentieth century, presented cases uniquely of men. Zeng provided the age and native place of all of his ten male patients, all from the Pearl River Delta, ranging from age eighteen to thirty.

47. Jiang Zhenxun, "Jiaoqi qian shuo" [Brief note on *jiaoqi*], *Xinyi yu shehui huikan* 1 (1928): 208–11.
48. Imamura Ryō, *Kakké kōyō* [Essentials on *kakké*] (Edo: Keigyōkan edition, 1861), 3b.
49. Ibid., 1b–2b.
50. Ibid., 3b–4a. Imamura also stressed that roughly half of the victims (50–60 percent) were attacked by *kakké* while suffering from other diseases.

He also provided information on their background or occupations, lifestyle, and physical appearance that were considered to have some bearing on the disorder: two students who rarely left their desk, one accountant who never exercised, one without occupation but leading a leisurely life. Three of his patients were described as "robust," or even opulent (*zhuangsheng* 壯盛), one of whom being a good drinker and eater. Two of them were returning emigrants from Southeast Asia. In other words, the typical patient was a young man of comfortable situation, physically inactive in some white-collar occupation, living or arriving in Hong Kong from Southeast Asia, often with a deceptively sturdy appearance.

Zhou Xiaonong's nine cases were about Shanghai men traveling to Wuxi to get treatment from him. Other than a fireman, the patients were either intellectuals (students, writers) or merchants (one in the iron business, a couple of shopmen, including one in the hotel business). Except for an older patient aged fifty-six, all the patients were young. Like Zeng's patients, quite a few of these Shanghai dwellers were described as excessively indulgent in food and drink. One was observed to be masturbating too much. For both Zeng and Zhou, the typical *jiaoqi* patient was an urban young male with an unhealthy lifestyle, undisciplined in diet and sex. Zhou, however, put more weight on the bad natural environment (*shuitu*) of Shanghai, city par excellence of new immigrants, as a cause:

> The coastal areas of Shanghai are damp . . . causing the disease. People from other provinces are not aware of this and do not pay attention. I have worked in the police bureau for three years as a doctor . . . and know that in the lowly areas of Pudong and Jiangwan, policemen . . . often contracted this disease. Then many young men in the commercial sector also fell ill and did not understand why.[51]

Similarly, all the five *jiaoqi* cases included in a compilation of medical cases by "renowned national [traditional] doctors" (1929) involved male patients; two fell sick because of too much food, alcohol, and sex, the others were victims of an overly damp, toxic environment. The compiler of the book, He Lianchen 何廉臣 (1861–1929), like Zhou, made a special comment on Shanghai as a lethal place for new settlers.[52] Popular medical writings in the early twentieth century generally stressed the vulnerability of healthy young men to different epidemiological hazards, including *jiaoqi*, in big cities where they recently settled. During the war, Chongqing, a city for refugees

---

51. Zhou Xiaonong, *Zhou Xiaonong yi'an* [Medical cases of Zhou Xiaonong] (Hong Kong: Commercial Press, 1971), 198.

52. He Lianchen, ed., *Quanguo ming yi yan'an leibian* [Selected medical cases (showing medical efficiency) by famous doctors in the nation], 1929 (Taipei: Xuanfeng chubanshe 1971), *juan* 4: 36a–41b, his comment on p. 38a.

including civil servants, students, workers, and soldiers, also became endemic with *jiaoqi*.[53]

Deprivation, however, gradually displaced affluence as the leading explanation of the disease, even though men remained as main victims. With this shift, the issue of class differences took a new turn. Chinese and Japanese doctors began to produce epidemiological studies that showed the vulnerability of laboring men. Omori in a paper presented at the 1925 Congress of Far Eastern Association of Tropical Medicine stated that *kakké* spread from students and merchants to the lower working classes, particularly afflicting hard physical workers such as soldiers and other laborers. The disease targeted the young, "especially those whose lymphatic systems are enlarged."[54] In China, the above-mentioned Shanghai doctor Jiang Zhenxun made the observation in the 1930s that most victims were factory workers, soldiers, and students who were new arrivals in the city, some of whom sometimes mistook their illness to be syphilis.[55] Wu Lien-teh (1879–1960), director of the Manchurian Plague Prevention Service, reported in 1925 based on information from a Shanghai hospital that of the 28 patients treated, more than half (15) were soldiers, the others including shopmen, a cook, a detective, a tailor, a clothier, an actor, and a penmaker, apparently all males of the working classes.[56] Benjamin S. Platt (1903–1969), an English physiologist working at the Henry Lester Institute in Shanghai in the early 1930s, had a much larger database. He reported in 1934 that the Lester Chinese Hospital treated some 50,000 beriberi patients, with a male/female ratio of 8 to 1, of whom half were artisans, one-third laborers, and the rest sailors, students, and shop assistants.[57] In the 1930s, biomedical nutritionists in China did a series of studies on industrial health in Shanghai to show the deficient diets of workers. A 1936 report, for instance, showed that vitamin B was deficient in 80 percent in juvenile factory workers and recommended the consumption of brown unpolished rice and an increase in the use of animal fats.[58]

53. Chao Yafeng, in "Jiaoqi laza" [Miscellaneous comments on *jiaoqi*], *Fuxing Zhongyi* 2(4) (1941), noted that many businessmen, workers, shop apprentices, and employees freshly arriving in Shanghai from the countryside easily fell victim to the disease. See Zhang and Wu, "Chongqing zhongyang yiyuan jiaoqi bing ershiba li zhi linchuang baogao" [Clinical report on the 28 *jiaoqi* cases at the Central Hospital of Chongqing], *Huaxi yixun* 5(1) (1948): 19.
54. Kenta Omori, "Studies on the Cause and Treatment of Beri-Beri in Japan," Far Eastern Association of Tropical Medicine (FEATM) Transactions of 6th Biennial Congress, Tokyo, 1925: 183, 186, 200.
55. Jiang Zhenxun, "Er ge jiaoqi bingli" [Two cases of *jiaoqi*], *Xinyi yu shehui huikan* 2 (1934): 257–58.
56. J. W. H. Chun and Lien Teh Wu, "Beri-Beri Control from an Administrative Standpoint," Far Eastern Association of Tropical Medicine (FEATM) Transactions of 6th Biennial Congress, Tokyo, 1925, 157.
57. Platt and Gin, "Some Observations on a Preliminary Study of Beriberi in Shanghai," 407.
58. Lee Wei Yung, Eric Reid, and Bernard Read, "Industrial Health in Shanghai, China, III: Shanghai Factory Diets Compared with Those of Institutional Workers," *Chinese Medical*

In Republican China, as in Japan since the late nineteenth century, *jiaoqi* as a symbol of weak male bodies was increasingly considered a serious national security problem, especially in the South. In the 1920s and 1930s observations and studies on *jiaoqi* began to be done in military units and published in military medical journals, increasingly with biomedical theory and methodology.[59] Throughout the 1930s, *jiaoqi* patients treated in the Guangdong Military Hospital represented already more than 15 percent of hospitalized soldiers in the internal medicine section. In the immediate prewar years, one of the first full-length biomedical monographs on *jiaoqi* / beriberi in China by Yang Shen 楊紳, a Japan-trained doctor working in the hospital of the Nanking Military Police, was published, based on the epidemiological study on the disease in the hospital, where 58 percent of patients, all young males, naturally, suffered from *jiaoqi*.[60] By 1937 when the war broke out, the military hospital in Shaoguan of Guangdong Province was reorganized into one specialized in *jiaoqi* treatment.[61] By this time *jiaoqi* was increasingly described in the media to be a disease of young men having to work excessively hard as soldiers, workers, and laborers in shops, plantations, factories, schools, and other modern institutions.[62] After the war, excessive physical exertion that burned more thiamine than ingested, rather than the consumption of white rice, had become the main explanation for the high morbidity of Guangdong soldiers with beriberi.[63]

Racial differences in beriberi, unexplained in the early period, also became accountable with deprivation as the main cause. In the nineteenth century, British colonial doctors in South Asia shared the observation but did not explain the fact that it was mostly Asian males who fell victim to the disease, while Westerners seemed to be spared.[64] By the late 1910s, when

---

59. There were a number of articles on the disease in the army of Zhejiang province in the 1920s, especially in *Guangji yikan* 廣濟醫刊 in Hangzhou; in the 1930s, the military medical journals of the Guangxi military school, *Guangxi jianshe yixue yuekan* 廣西健社醫學月刊, and of the Guangdong military, *Guangdong junyi zazhi* 廣東軍醫雜誌, and the journal of the Zhongshan Medical School in Guangzhou, *Zhongshan yibao* 中山醫報, published a number of research articles on the *jiaoqi* problem in the provincial armies in southern China.
60. Yang Shen, *Jiaoqi lun* [On *jiaoqi*] (Nanking: Military Police Hospital, 1933).
61. Li Zhaoshi, "Jiaoqi bing zhi guofang guan" [Looking at *jiaoqi* from the national defense point of view], *Guangxi Jianshe yixue yuekan* 1(3) (1937): 33–34; "Zu jiaoqi yiyuan" [Organizing a *jiaoqi* hospital], *Huazi ribao* [Chinese Mail], April 17, 1937.
62. Chi, "Jiaoqi bing," 11–13.
63. Zhu Shihui and Chen Airen, "Guangzhou jundui zhi jiaoqi bing" [The *jiaoqi* disease in the Cantonese army], *Zhongshan yibao* 3 (5–6) (1948): 10.
64. This view was held by the Europeans since John Malcomson's book in 1835. In this early text on beriberi, Malcomson, assistant surgeon in Madras, reported that the ethnic groups most vulnerable to beriberi were the "Mussulmauns (Indian Muslims). The next amongst the Gentoos (Hindus) and Malabars (Southern Indians); the next amongst the Rajpoots (Indian warrior classes); and lastly of all amongst the Parrias (the untouchables). . . . The Mussulmauns are, of all the natives, the most addicted to luxurious living on the coast; and have been accustomed to the use of much animal food and spices." He also noted

the deficient white rice theory was emerging,[65] European doctors and scientists found an explanation for racial difference, or for the "Asian-ness" of beriberi: deficiency diseases are practically nonexistent among modern civilized Europeans, for, when living on the ordinary mixed diet of civilization, it is difficult to avoid getting an adequate amount of each separate vitamin. It is where the diet is more simple, as is the case with those of many Eastern races, that the risk of deficiency disease becomes proportionately greater.[66] The view that rice-based Asian diets were universally "more simple" and thus deficient gradually took hold among many Western nutritionists in the twentieth century.[67] By the mid-1920s, in popular biomedical writings in China, this explanation was gradually internalized. It was falling in line with the idea that the disease was prevalent mostly among the darker races, while Westerners, whose diets were believed to be superior, with greater diversity of foods, were spared.[68] One Chinese article published in a serious medical journal in 1939 listed ten characteristics of modern *jiaoqi* and the first was that "it is rare among Westerners, but common among East Asians." Without providing statistics and admitting that the real cause of beriberi remained obscure, the same article continued to emphasize the vulnerability also of the laboring classes, of people living in collectives, and those emigrating out of China. This popular framing of beriberi reflected the rapidly growing currency of the deficiency theory that targeted the socially and economically deprived and racially inferior.[69]

---

reports showing that Europeans troops were only rare and occasional victims of the disease, though he conceded that "I have reason to believe that some cases occurred in the European regiment, but if so, they are returned under other names [dropsies and palsies]." Malcolmson, *Practical Essay on the History and Treatment of Beriberi*, 41–42, 26.

65. Casimir Funk's contribution to the deficiency theory in the period was critical; see his "The Etiology of the Deficiency Diseases," *Journal of State Medicine* 20 (1912) where he states that "[t]he deficiency diseases break out in countries where a certain unvarying diet is partaken of for long periods" (341).

66. H. Click and E. Hume (Lister Institute of Preventive Medicine), "The Distribution among Foodstuffs of the Substances Required for the Prevention of Beriberi and Scurvy," *Journal of the Royal Army Medical Corps* 29 (July–December 1917): 123.

67. See Worboys, "Discovery of Colonial Malnutrition between the Wars."

68. David Arnold shows with the Indian example how rice, associated with nutritional poverty, was to account for negative racial stereotypes, even though beriberi was not a serious epidemic there. See his "British India and the 'Beriberi Problem' 1798–1942," *Medical History* 54 (2010): 312.

69. Liu Shusen, "Jiaoqi zhi yanjiu" [The study of *jiaoqi*], *Xin yiyao kan* 74 (1939): 16. In an earlier article, the author Min Yuquan categorically noted that the disease was rare among Europeans and Americans but more common among the yellow and dark races. See his "Jiaoqi bing yufang fa" [Preventive measures against *jiaoqi*], *Yiyao pinglun* 54 (1931): 19. See also Wu Zhiming, "Jiaoqi zai Yuandong" [Beriberi in the Far East], *Xiandai yulin* 19 (1939): 41.

What Women Got Sick: The Mother and the Whore?

Considered socially inactive by nature, Asian women originally were thought to have been spared in the modern beriberi epidemic. Just like traditional Chinese and Japanese *kampō* experts, biomedical doctors began by considering women vulnerable only when their bodies were under the stress of reproduction, their main social duty. Simmons noted that, in Japan in the 1870s, few women had beriberi, "except during pregnancy and a short time after confinement. It shows itself soon after the middle of gestation, in the wet form of the disease, and culminates at its completion. . . . Dr. Stuart Eldridge informs me that in Hokodadi, while he had charge of the Government Hospital there, *kakké* was very prevalent and fatal among pregnant women." This seemed to fit Simmons's belief that beriberi is "distinctly a specific disease related to the condition of anemia" that British doctors had noted in India.[70] This explanation was highly compatible with the classical one for female *jiaoqi* or *kakké* in China and Japan, established no later than the twelfth century when medicine for women became a separate field of study. The ailment was described as not only affecting reproducing women but especially a serious cause of infertility.[71] This classical explanation for female *jiaoqi* centering on women's reproductive functions remained valid throughout the premodern period in East Asia.[72]

Later, at the turn of the century, when eating polished white rice was emerging as the cause, the reasons for women affected by beriberi required a different set of explanations, first to satisfy the "decadent" assumption. W. L. Braddon, pointing out in his influential 1907 text the "special incidence of beriberi" on the well-fed, suggested that the vigorous and strong naturally ate rice in "quantities absolutely greater" than did the lean, explaining why they more easily contracted the disease. Based on this observation, he

---

70. Simmons, "Beriberi, or the 'Kakké' of Japan," 50. Victor Heiser later in the Philippines also observed the vulnerability of reproducing women to the disease by studying infantile beriberi. See note 18.

71. See Charlotte Furth, *A Flourishing Yin: Gender in China's Medical History, 960–1665* (Berkeley: University of California Press, 1999). See also Hilary Smith, "Foot *Qi*: History of a Chinese Medical Disorder" (PhD diss., University of Pennsylvania, 2008).

72. Chen Ziming 陳自明 (1190–1270) in his milestone publication of *Furen daquan liangfang* (All-inclusive good prescriptions for women 婦人大全良方, 1237) , thus framed the *jiaoqi* disorder: "Men get it because of depleted Kidney that makes them vulnerable to Wind and Dampness; while women get it because of depleted *qi* of the Womb vessel, making them vulnerable to Wind toxin." He also considered female *jiaoqi* closely linked to infertility. Chen Ziming's female version of *jiaoqi* linked to Blood and reproduction became a focus of debate in later medical discussions on the disease. Zhu Xiu 朱橚 (?–1425), author of the influential *Recipes for General Relief* (*Puji fang* 普濟方, 1406) of the early Ming distinguished between reproductive women and virgins as victims of *jiaoqi*: the former fell sick because of blood depletion, the latter because of blood stagnation. Most late imperial doctors tended to argue that women patients should be treated differently because of their unique reproduction function and their particular emotionality.

concluded that fewer women got the disease because, in general, they ate less rice than men. However, "I have noticed that amahs (who feed themselves, and can afford to buy plenty of rice), the Chinese wives of Eurasians, and Straits-born Chinese 'babas' (wet nurses) are particularly prone to the malady. This is also true of prostitutes. All these classes eat rice in excess."[73]

H. Durham writing in 1904 on the disease in the Malay Peninsula and on Christmas Island off the shore of Java concurred: Chinese women with beriberi could mostly be observed in brothels; "beriberi is very far from common, notwithstanding that they (the women patients) live herded together; on the other hand, their employment is fairly lucrative and they follow where money is plentiful; it may be supposed that they are not usually stinted in food." Similarly, he said, the rare Japanese female beriberi patients in the Malay States were also mostly prostitutes.[74] Noel Davis, assistant health officer of Shanghai, observing the beriberi epidemic in various institutions in the city in 1912, chose to gather data from the new jail; the police force; Shanghai Tramway Company's native employees, where only younger men were present; and the homes of Door of Hope Rescue Society, where girls "rescued" from brothels were interned, showing the close association made by Western doctors between female beriberi and prostitution in this period.[75] For these early biomedical experts working in Asia, polished white rice was a bad luxury food that few women could afford. The rare Asian women patients of beriberi, if they were not reproducing, must therefore be prostituting themselves to satisfy their gluttony in white rice.

Ding Fubao, the popular medical writer and publisher active in Shanghai in the first decades of the twentieth century, well versed in traditional medicine and a prolific translator of Japanese *kampō* and biomedicine texts, reasoned on the same line in his 1910 compilation on *jiaoqi*, "Men have predisposing causes (*suyin* 素因), due to their special lifestyle. . . . [T]hey have predisposing causes, but not women, due to their different lifestyles,"[76] implying that respectable women, perceived as idle and disconnected from public and economic activities were less vulnerable than working men, even though they were of the weaker sex.[77]

It was Liao Wenren (Ryō Onjin 廖溫仁, 1893–1936), a Japan-trained Chinese doctor in Japanese Taiwan, who provided a complete explanation on female *kakké* based on their somatic makeup subsuming their more

73. Braddon, *Cause and Prevention of Beri-Beri*, 256.
74. Durham, "Notes on Beriberi," 122, 125.
75. Davis, "Observations on Beriberi in Shanghai," 28. He noted that the jail had the most cases (134), twenty-six cases were found among the girls in 1910, a few more than those in the police force and Tramway Company.
76. Ding, *Jiaoqi bing zhi yuanyin ji liaofa*, part 2, 29, 36.
77. Many popular articles confirmed this view: Zhu and Chen, "Guangzhou jundui zhi jiaoqi bing," 10; Liu Shusen, "Jiaoqi zhi yanjiu," 16; Kuang Heling, "Ru'er jiaoqi bing" [*Jiaoqi* ailment of babies], *Zhongshan yibao* 6(5–6) (1951): 8.

noticeable social roles: women were less vulnerable to *kakké* as they did not normally have the occasion to indulge in excessive food and alcohol, as men did in their prime. They normally would not suffer from a stomach corroded by damp, a direct cause of the disease. Women, however, would contract the disease under two exceptional circumstances: when they were reproducing or if they indulged in excessive sex, like prostitutes. The pregnancy of the rare female *kakké* victims, according to Ryō, blocked not only blood and *ki* but also fluid flow in their lower burner, causing the lower limbs to swell. As for the case of prostitutes, he quoted the famous doctor Taki Motokata: prostitutes were depleted in the lower body because of excessive sex, making them vulnerable to the sudden, upward, and fatal "heart attack" (*shōshin* 衝心) of *kakké*. Ryō thus provided a neat set of explanations based only on the makeup of the female sexual and reproductive body.[78]

Ryō's explanation of the way *kakké* attacked the woman either as mother or whore was a modern version of the East Asian classical account of *jiaoqi* in the twelfth century that focused only on the reproductive woman. This modern version articulates a new and profound anxiety on the prostitute as a public, working woman in modern, global Asia. Limiting the explanation of the ailment to the prostitute's somatic makeup, dismissing the social factor of immoral wealth and white rice gluttony once proposed by biomedical doctors, Ryō was confirming vital somatic vulnerabilities of the prostitute to this "modern" disease, caused not by too much bad food but by excessive sexual activity.

Ryō's explanation was formulated at the time of the consolidation of the deficiency theory, which was also wartime. Deprivation or excessive physical exertion was increasingly given more weight as a cause of the epidemic in Asia. Thus, working women did end up being counted in the epidemiologic statistics. Omori reported in 1925 that the disease was most prevalent among first soldiers, then laborers, factory girls (spinning girls), and students.[79] The Chinese doctor Zhu Qian (朱潛), studying pregnant women infected with beriberi in 1933, also noted their different occupations: of the thirty-eight cases he studied in Guangdong province, ten clearly belonged to the laboring classes, fourteen were of unknown occupations or interned in social institutions, with only three belonging to the well-to-do classes. Other than noticing the great fatigue of eight of them, he also indicated the possible association of the disease with other health issues such as syphilis, opium smoking, and alcoholism, hinting that some of these women were

---

78. Ryō Onjin, "Tōyō kakké byō kenkyō" [Research on Japanese *kakké*] 1932 ed. (Kyoto, doctoral dissertation, 1928), 299–303.
79. Omori, "Studies on the Cause and Treatment of Beri-Beri in Japan," 186. The statistics were said to be collected at the beriberi clinic at the Tokyo Imperial University by Dr. Baelz (no date given; Baelz left Japan in 1905). Omori claimed that statistics taken by him in 1921 and 1922 at his own hospital at Keio University were in agreement with the Baelz data.

actually prostitutes.[80] In a sense, prostitutes represented the extreme case of working women.

Qu Shaoheng 瞿紹衡, a famous Western-trained obstetrician working in Shanghai in the 1930s, was one of the first and rare experts who perceived women's social role and its relation to the disease differently. He stressed the importance of the exceptional hardship that women were facing because of the war: many lost their homes, not having a regular place to live in the crowded city, and having instead to work hard to sustain the family. Their body was highly "stressed" and became vulnerable to the epidemic in miasmatic Shanghai.[81] His explanation clearly shows that the white rice theory did not convince him as a sufficient cause for beriberi, in disagreement with Western biomedical doctors working in Asia.[82]

Conclusion

Modern East Asian populations familiar with the classical *jiaoqi*/*kakké* traditions first searched for causes of the epidemic in the rapidly changing living environment: miasmatic cities with excessive damp and warmth generated by human density, activities, and rivalry. As they saw it, man, especially able-bodied man, the main actor in the arenas of work and war in modern East Asia, was the natural victim of the epidemic. Before the 1930s when the vitamin B1 theory, adorned with a Nobel Prize won in 1929, came out triumphant, diagnostic assemblages of beriberi/*jiaoqi*/*kakké* worked together to frame East Asia as an unhealthy natural and human environment that damaged Asian men's physical prowess, diminished their bravery and economic productivity, and reduced women's fertility. The beriberi epidemic was thus the high price of modernity that Asian societies were paying with their bodies and health. The unique East Asian therapeutic strategies of removing patients from the site of sickness, either to a more "healthy" place or especially back to their native place from where they had emigrated to work, expressed the understanding of the epidemic as being rooted in a modern, global, and alienating context. To get cured required leaving that global stage and retiring to a private space or home, or going back to the

---

80. Zhu Qian, "Jiaoqizheng yu funü fenmianqi de guanxi" [Relationship between *jiaoqi* and women during pregnancy], *Guangji yuekan* 19(8) (1933): 3–9, especially p. 5.
81. Qu Shaoheng, "Renchen yu *jiaoqi*" [Pregnancy and *jiaoqi*], *Xin yiyao kan* 69 (1938): 38–39.
82. For example, Cort reported from Siam in 1930 that pregnant women there got the disease because, "according to an old and still strongly observed custom, the diet of a woman for the month following childbirth consists of only rice and dried fish," or "almost exclusively, a glutinous rice." E. C. Cort, "Sporadic Beriberi in Chiengmai, Siam," Far Eastern Association of Tropical Medicine (FEATM) Transactions of the 8th Biennial Congress, Siam, 1930, 98. Another report on beriberi of mother and child in Burma also attributed the cause to the heavy proportion of rice in their diet, despite the fact that they also had a reasonable portion of vegetable, meat, and fruit. See S. Postmus, "Beriberi of Mother and Child in Burma," *Tropical and Geographical Medicine* 10 (1958): 363–69.

traditional ideal mode of life of moderation in desire, food, and sex. Like *feilao* 肺癆 (lung-exhaustion), or tuberculosis, beriberi was an Asian modern old disorder par excellence, with classical diagnostic categories engaging with an uncompromising health-threatening modernity.[83]

As beriberi research gradually became a key to the development of biochemical nutritional science after squeezing out competing diagnostic concepts such as germs, miasma, overcrowding, poor drainage, lack of sunshine, contagion, toxic foods, and the like,[84] vitamin theory came out triumphant in the late 1920s. Thiamine (B1) was singled out as the necessary substance for healthy nerves and for beriberi prevention. This groundbreaking discovery that formed the basis of this new science eliminated the miasmatic theory tied to a locality as a cause and did away with the factor of somatic makeup that was central to Asian traditional diagnostic systems. Beriberi could have been a disease independent of place and race. However, the specific link made all along between deficiency and the consumption of polished white rice put East Asia and Asians right back into the controversy on beriberi, now defined as an unfortunate product of an inferior Asian diet, seen as simple and monotonously rice based. The white rice theory also gained explanatory power on the relative vulnerability to the disease along racial, class, and gender lines. The immoral aspects of this modern Asian "junk food," polished white rice—as a mechanized modern commodity in lucrative global capitalist ventures—also stigmatized some of the beriberi victims: indulgent, able-bodied, urban men and gluttonous prostitutes who desired too much white rice in the earlier period, and ignorant and uneducated industrial workers in the latter period.

However, one should note that, unlike Western biochemical experts of nutritional science, East Asian biomedical doctors' take on thiamine deficiency was interestingly different and understated. Instead of incriminating white rice as a bad food, and thus promoting the taxing of regional rice trade as an international policy to curb beriberi as did Western scientists,[85] Chinese doctors focused more on deficiency theory by emphasizing the

---

83. It may be interesting to compare *jiaoqi*/beriberi with *feilao*/tuberculosis described in Sean Lei's "Weisheng weihe bu shi baowei shengming" [Why is hygiene not about protecting life?], in *Diguo yu xiandai yixue* [Empires and modern medicine], ed. Li Shangren [Shang-Jen Li] (Taipei: Linking Publishers, 2008), 438–48, in which Lei contrasts the traditional "life-nourishing" approach toward *feilao* as an exhaustion, and the modern combative attitude toward tuberculosis as a germ-caused disease.
84. Carpenter, *Beriberi, White Rice, and Vitamin B*, 32–35, 44–45, 64–65, 84.
85. Despite the Americans' unilateral decision to ban the use of polished rice in all state institutions in the Philippines in May 1910 and the urging of other medical officers in the region to control the polished white rice trade in Asia, no collective decision was made by the FEATM for fear of popular discontent and opposition from rice traders. For David Arnold, "it was the cultural objection to banning or taxing white rice that seemed most conclusive." David Arnold, "Tropical Governance: Managing Health in Monsoon Asia, 1908–1938," Asia Research Institute, National University of Singapore, Working Papers Series, no. 116, 2009.

extreme physical exertion to explain the lack of thiamine. For them beriberi was not about how much rice that patients ate but about how much thiamine they could and should retain in their body with the increasingly demanding physical activities in the workplace and especially during wartime, a question that even postwar American nutritionists could not have answered.[86] For them, these young men's, and increasingly women's, bodies were not weakened or sterilized exactly by white rice but by, again, an increasingly stressful living and working environment in an uncertain world order.

The therapeutic solutions for biochemically framed beriberi became highly technical: to increase foodstuff rich in thiamine, to tax polished white rice, and, most importantly, to give "miraculous" thiamine injections developed in the late 1930s to prevent the ultimate fatal heart attack. The Hong Kong Tung Wah Hospital purchased a large amount of thiamine injections from Britain in September 1940, after which the board decided that from then on *jiaoqi* patients would be solely treated by Western medicine. The exclusion of Chinese medicine in the treatment of *jiaoqi* in this hospital, even though it claimed a 70 percent success rate,[87] was a significant step toward the complete ban of Chinese medicine in the hospital in 1945.[88]

---

86. The American *Nutrition Reviews* (Washington, DC) published many articles on the incomplete knowledge on thiamine deficiency in the postwar period reflecting the unresolved question in the late 1940s. See especially the 1947 issue, vol. 5, that posed the question, "What is the complete biochemical picture in beriberi?" (7), which remained without a satisfactory answer.
87. DHA, *Minutes of Board Meeting*, August 26, September 3, September 10, 1940.
88. The pressure of banning Chinese medicine came directly from the Hong Kong colonial government, DHA, *Minutes of Board Meeting*, September 10, 1940; Xian Yuyi and Liu Runhe, *Yishan xingdao* [Enhancing charity and practicing the way] (Hong Kong: Sanlian, 2006), 68–69.

8

Christine Goes to China

Xie Jianshun and the Discourse of Sex Change in Cold War Taiwan

Howard Chiang

An Episode of Transnational Spectacle

On August 14, 1953, the *United Daily News* (聯合報, *Lianhebao*) announced the striking discovery of an intersexed soldier, Xie Jianshun 謝尖順, in Tainan, Taiwan. The headline read "A Hermaphrodite Discovered in Tainan: Sex to Be Determined after Surgery."[1] By August 21, the press adopted a radically different rhetoric, now trumpeting that "Christine Will Not Be America's Exclusive: Soldier Destined to Become a Lady."[2] Considered by many as the "first" Chinese transsexual, Xie was frequently dubbed as the "Chinese Christine." This allusion to the contemporaneous American ex-GI transsexual celebrity Christine Jorgensen, who received her sex reassignment surgery in Denmark and became a worldwide household name immediately afterward due to her personality and glamorous looks, reflected the growing influence of American culture on the Republic of China at the peak of the Cold War.[3] Within a week, the characterization of Xie in the Taiwanese press changed from an average citizen whose ambiguous sex provoked uncertainty and anxiety throughout the nation, to a transsexual icon whose fate indisputably contributed to the global staging of Taiwan on a par with the United States. Centering on the making of Xie Jianshun's celebrity, this chapter argues that the publicity surrounding her transition worked as a pivotal fulcrum in shifting common understandings of transsexuality, the role of medical science, and their evolving relation to the popular press in

---

1. "Nanshi faxian yinyangren jiangdong shoushu bian nannü" [A hermaphrodite discovered in Tainan: Sex to be determined after surgery], *Lianhebao* [United Daily News], August 14, 1953, no. 3.
2. "Burang Kelisiding zhuanmei yuqian dabing jiang bianchen xiaojie" [Christine will not be America's exclusive: Soldier destined to become a lady], *Lianhebao*, August 21, 1953, no. 3.
3. On Christine Jorgensen, see Joanne Meyerowitz, *How Sex Changed: A History of Transsexuality in the United States* (Cambridge, MA: Harvard University Press, 2002). For the coverage of the Jorgensen story in Iran, see Afsaneh Najmabadi, *Professing Selves: Transsexuality and Same-Sex Desire in Contemporary Iran* (Durham, NC: Duke University Press, 2013).

mid-twentieth-century Sinophone culture.[4] Undergirding this volume is the central theme of competition for biomedical advancement in various postwar East Asian societies. The ascendance of Xie into the limelight—epitomizing what Francesca Bray calls "the biological turn" in the introduction of this volume—precisely captures the driving forces of such forms of competition crucial to the shaping of scientific modernity in 1950s Taiwan.

The feminization of the Chinese Christine became a national story in Taiwan at a pivotal juncture in the making of Cold War East Asia. Predating the Jinmen shelling crisis of August 1958, this episode of sex transformation commanded public attention at the conclusion of the Korean War (1950–1953) and the nascent "liberating Taiwan" campaign (1954–1955) on the Mainland. The Chinese Communist Party's (CCP) involvement in the Korean and First Indochina Wars further consolidated the US-Guomindang (GMD) alliance and amplified the longstanding CCP-GMD tensions, while achieving what historian Chen Jian identifies as Mao's aspiration for continuing the momentum of his communist revolution at home and abroad.[5] Between 1951 and 1965, Taiwan received a steady annual support of US$100 million from the United States. American interest in stabilizing Taiwan's military system and economic growth was folded into the USAID Health Program drafted and distributed in 1954. In the next two decades, American guidance and recommendations would gradually replace the Japanese model and play a central role in shaping the long-term public health policy and priorities in Taiwan.[6] Meanwhile, the CCP and the US-backed GMD engaged in repeated confrontations across the Taiwan Strait in the 1950s, thereby making this area one of the main "hot spots" of the Cold War. It was within this historical context of postcolonial East Asian modernity—providing the conditions for such mimetic political formations as the Two Koreas and the Two Chinas— that the mass circulation press introduced the story of Xie Jianshun to readers in Taiwan. This chapter offers a preliminary glimpse of where the parallel contours of culture and geopolitics converged in early Cold War Taiwan.

---

4. By the Sinophone, I follow Shu-mei Shih's definition to refer to Sinitic-language cultures and communities outside of China or on the margins of the hegemonic productions of the Chinese nation-state or Chinese-ness. See Shu-mei Shih, *Visuality and Identity: Sinophone Articulations across the Pacific* (Berkeley: University of California Press, 2007); Shu-mei Shih, "The Concept of the Sinophone," *PMLA* 126(3) (2011): 709–18; and the essays collected in Shu-mei Shih, Chien-hsin Tsai, and Brian Bernards, ed., *Sinophone Studies: A Critical Reader* (New York: Columbia University Press, 2013). See also Howard Chiang and Ari Larissa Heinrich, eds., *Queer Sinophone Cultures* (New York: Routledge, 2013).
5. Chen Jian, *Mao's China and the Cold War* (Chapel Hill: University of North Carolina Press, 2001), 165–71.
6. Tsui-hua Yang, "Meiyuan dui Taiwan de weisheng jihua yu yiliao tizhi zhi xingsu" [US aid in the formation of health planning and the medical system in Taiwan], *Bulletin of the Institute of Modern History* 62 (2008): 91–139.

Dripping with national and trans-Pacific significance, Xie's experience made *bianxingren* 變性人 (transsexual) a household term in the 1950s.[7] She served as a focal point for numerous new stories that broached the topics of changing sex, human intersexuality, and other atypical conditions of the body.[8] People who wrote about her debated whether she qualified as a woman, whether medical technology could transform sex, and whether the two Christines were more similar or different. These questions led to persistent comparisons of Taiwan with the United States, but Xie never presented herself as a duplicate of Jorgensen. As Xie knew, her story highlighted issues that pervaded post–World War II Sinophone society: the censorship of public culture by the state, the unique social status of men serving in the armed forces, the limit of individualism, the promise and pitfalls of science, the relationship between military virility and national sovereignty, the normative behaviors of men and women, and the boundaries of acceptable sexual expression. Her story attracted the press, but the public's avid interest in sex and its plasticity prompted reporters to dig deep. As the press coverage escalated, new names and unfamiliar medical conditions grabbed the attention of journalists and their readers.[9] The kind of public musings about sex change that saturated Chinese culture earlier in the century now took center stage in Republican Taiwan.[10]

---

7. The word "transexual" was first coined by the American sexologist David Cauldwell in 1949. Cauldwell wrote, "When an individual who is unfavorably affected psychologically determines to live and appear as a member of the sex to which he or she does not belong, such an individual is what may be called a *psychopathic transexual*. This means, simply, that one is mentally unhealthy and because of this the person desires to live as a member of the opposite sex." David Cauldwell, "Psychopathia Transexualis," *Sexology* 16 (1949): 274–80. In 1966, endocrinologist Harry Benjamin used the word "transsexual" in his magnum opus, *The Transsexual Phenomenon* (New York: Julian Press, 1966). This book was the first large-scale work describing and explaining the kind of affirmative treatment for transsexuality that he had pioneered throughout his career. On the intellectual and social history of transsexuality in the United States, see Bernice L. Hausman, *Changing Sex: Transsexualism, Technology, and the Idea of Gender* (Durham, NC: Duke University Press, 1995); Meyerowitz, *How Sex Changed*.

8. In this chapter, I adopt the feminine pronoun when referring to Xie both generally and in the specific contexts after her first operation. I use the masculine pronoun to refer to Xie only in discussing her early media publicity, because she expressively refused sex reassignment before the first operation.

9. See Howard Chiang, "Gender Transformations in Sinophone Taiwan," *positions: asia critique* 25, no. 3 (2017): 527–63.

10. On the vibrant discourse of sex change in Republican China, see Frank Dikötter, *Imperfect Concepts: Medical Knowledge, Birth Defects, and Eugenics in China* (New York: Columbia University Press, 1998), 74–81; Howard Chiang, "The Conceptual Contours of Sex in the Chinese Life Sciences: Zhu Xi (1899–1962), Hermaphroditism, and the Biological Discourse of *Ci* and *Xiong*, 1920–1950," *East Asian Science, Technology and Society* 2(3) (2008): 401–30; Howard Chiang, "How China Became a 'Castrated Civilization' and Eunuchs a 'Third Sex,'" in *Transgender China*, ed. Howard Chiang (New York: Palgrave Macmillan, 2012), 23–66; Alvin Ka Hin Wong, "Transgenderism as a Heuristic Device: On the Cross-historical and Transnational Adaptations of the *Legend of the White Snake*," in Chiang, *Transgender China*, 127–58.

Discovering Xie

When the story of Xie first came to public spotlight, it established a direct reference to Jorgensen: "After the international frenzy surrounding the news of Miss Christine, the American ex-G.I. who turned into a lady after surgery, a *yin-yang* person [hermaphrodite] has been discovered at the 518 Hospital in Tainan." This opening statement reflects the popular tendency to conflate sex change surgery with the medical treatment of intersexed conditions in the 1950s. During the initial disclosure of Xie's biographical information, the *United Daily News* released an article suggesting that Xie had in fact been fully aware of his feminine bodily traits since childhood, but had kept it a secret until its recent "revelation" under the close attention of doctors in Tainan. A native of Chaozhou, Guangdong, the 36-year-old Xie joined the army when he was 16, lost his father at the age of 17, and lost his mother at 18. He came to Taiwan with the Nationalist army in 1949. "At the age of 20," the article continued, "his breasts developed like a girl, but he had hidden this secret when serving in the military rather successfully. It was finally discovered on the 6th of [August], upon his visit to the Tainan 518 Hospital for a physical examination due to regular abdominal pains and crams, by the chair of external medicine Dr. Lin. He has been staying at the hospital since the 7th [of August]."[11]

The initial national excitement focused on deciphering Xie's sex, sexuality, and gender. In their first impression of Xie, the public was given the opportunity to imagine his sexually ambiguous body with extensive somatic descriptions: "According to Dr. Lin, the abnormal bodily features of the *yin-yang* person include the following: protruding and sagging breasts, pale and smooth skin, soft hands, manly legs, squeaky and soft voice, a testicle inside the left lower abdomen but not the right, a closed and blocked reproductive organ, no [male] urinary tract, a urethra opening between the labia, a small symbolic phallic organ, and the capacity to urinate in the standing posture." Xie's "head appears to be normal, mental health is slightly below average, facial features are feminine, personality is shy, other bodily parts and dietary habits are normal." According to Dr. Lin Chengyi (林承一), a graduate of the Tokyo Zhaohe Hospital and the external medicine department of the Jingjing Medical School, Xie's first operation was scheduled to take place on August 20 and would involve the following three major steps: exploratory laparotomy (the opening of the abdominal cavity) to detect the presence of ovarian tissues; labia dissection to examine the vaginal interior, determine the length of the vagina, and confirm the presence (or absence) of the hymen; and finally, "if ovaries and vagina are found inside the womb, removing the penis can turn Xie into a woman; otherwise he becomes a man." From its premise that Xie intentionally concealed his biological femininity, to

---

11. "Nanshi faxian yinyangren."

its detailed description of Xie's physical makeup, and to its presentation of the criteria involved in Xie's sex determination (or transformation), the press operated as a cultural vehicle through which medical biases towards Xie's body could be expressed liberally. Through and through, Xie was *assumed* to be a biological woman trapped inside a male body, whose feminine-like features gradually revealed themselves under the fingertips of medical experts and in the eyes of the public.[12]

On the day following the public "discovery" of Xie, the media immediately signaled a radical departure of his experience from the familiar story of the American Christine. Whereas the American transsexual celebrity had a deep-seated desire to become physically transformed into a woman, the Republican Chinese soldier had an unshakable longing to remain a heterosexual man. The headline declared, "*Yin-Yang* Person Uncovers a Personal Past and Hopes to Remain a Man." The article stressed that "the *yin-yang* person Xie Jianshun is still in love with his lover of more than two decades—the rifle" and that he "personally desires to become a perfectly healthy man." Most tellingly, the paper disclosed Xie's heterosexual past by offering an account of his relationship experience with women, including graphic descriptions of his past sexual encounters. The *United Daily News* narrative reminded the reader of, rather than downplayed, Xie's physical defects: "At the age of seven, Xie fell sick. At the time, his penis was tied to his labia, but given his living situation in the countryside, going to a doctor for surgical intervention was not immediately feasible. His mother therefore simply tore them apart by hand. From that point on, he urinated from both secretion openings."[13]

According to the article, Xie's "unpleasant experience with his physiological abnormality" started at the age of twelve. That year, his grandmother introduced him to a girl, whom he was arranged to marry. Although he was just a child, his fondness for the girl grew by day. One day, when no adult was in the house, he initiated an intercourse with the girl but ultimately failed because of his "biological defect." They ended up getting around the problem "by using their hands." Since then, Xie "acquired the habit of masturbation without the ability to produce sperm, being in a state of more physiological pain." After joining the army, he fell in love with another girl. Her father even accepted their marriage proposal. This seemingly positive news, however, upset Xie. Given his "physiological shortcomings," Xie wanted to avoid leading the girl into an unhappy union. At the time, he still did not have the courage to come clean about his reproductive problems.

---

12. Ibid.
13. "Yinyangren xisu wangshi yuan cishen chengwei nan'er" [The hermaphrodite reveals his/her past: Hopes to remain a man], *Lianhebao*, August 15, 1953, no. 3.

He therefore ran away from the girl and the relationship, a decision some writers interpreted as "a comedy of marriage escape."[14]

The most significant message that this biographical synopsis seems to convey is squarely concerned with his (forthcoming) sex determination or transformation. Will Xie turn into a man or a woman? What does *he* want? The article ended with a confident note: "He firmly hopes to remain male, to be able to return to the army and pick up the rifle again" to "defeat mainland China and eliminate the communists."[15] Indeed, the paper mentioned in passing that Xie "experiences 'sexual' desire when interacting with women, but none towards men."[16] Construed as a respectable citizen of the Republican state, Xie was heterosexualized and masculinized as a national subject fulfilling his duty, even as he faced the possibility of being stripped of his manliness within a week. At least for a brief moment, Xie was able to articulate through the mainstream press his desire of *not* wanting to change his sex. And it was the first time that readers heard his voice. The remark, "If my biology does not allow me to remain a man but forces me to become a woman, what else can I do?" marked the first appearance of his opinion in the press. On the second day of his media exposure, readers started to sympathize with Xie and considered him, unlike the American Christine, a rather normal, however unfortunate, heterosexual man.

If doctors and reporters hastened to purport a clear picture of Xie's hidden sex and normative sexuality, they tried to uncover his gender orientation in a more cautious fashion. As soon as the 518 Hospital scheduled Xie's first "sex change surgery," the relevant experts proposed a plan to determine Xie's gender self-awareness. They sent a group of women nurses to mingle with Xie five days before the operation. Given Xie's longtime career involvement in the military, "the hospital considers his previous social interactions with men insufficient for determining how Xie feels deep down inside as man- or woman-like. In preparing for Xie's sex reassignment surgery, a number of 'attractive' nurses were asked to keep Xie company and chat with him on August 15." Through Xie's interaction with these nurses, it was hoped that "a better understanding of his/her inner sense of self as a man or woman could be reached by drawing on the clues from his emotions and facial expressions, which should reflect his inner sense of self." It is worth noting that neither the medical profession nor the popular press locked him into a particular gender persona at this juncture. Despite their assumptions about Xie's biological hidden (female) sex, doctors at the 518 Hospital actually believed that they had adopted a more careful and "objective" approach to determining his psychological gender. And despite its covert announcement

---

14. Ibid.
15. Ibid.
16. "Nanshi faxian yinyangren."

of his heterosexuality, the press refrained from reaching any conclusion yet about Xie's gendered sense of self.[17]

The First Operation

The first turning point in the framing of Xie Jianshun's story in both medical and popular discourses came with his first operation. Again, the press collaborated with Xie's physicians closely and kept the public informed about their progress. On August 20, the day of Xie's first operation, *United Daily News* published a detailed description of the surgical protocols scheduled for three o'clock that afternoon: "The operation scheduled for today involves an exploratory laparotomy, followed by a careful examination of his lower cavity to detect the presence of uterus and ovary. If Xie's reproductive anatomy resembles that of a typical female, a second operation will follow suit as soon as Xie recovers from this one. In the second operation, the presently sealed vaginal opening will be cut open, and the vaginal interior will be examined for symptoms of abnormality. If the results of both operations confirm that Xie has a female reproductive system, the final step involves the removal of the symbolic male genital organ on the labia minora, converting him into a pure female. Otherwise, Xie will be turned into a pure male."[18]

By bringing the reader's eyes "inward" toward Xie's internal anatomical configurations, the press repeated the epistemological claims of the medical operation intended for the determination of Xie's sex. Step by step, the newspaper article, presumably relying on the information provided by Dr. Lin and his team, told its reader the surgical procedures and criteria for the establishment of Xie's female sex. Yet no symmetrical explanation was given for establishing a male identity for Xie. The narrative only concluded with the brief remark, "Otherwise, Xie will be turned into a pure male." One wonders what would happen then if Xie's interior anatomy was found to be drastically different from the normal female sex. What were the doctors planning to do then with his "sealed vaginal opening"? If Xie could be transformed into a "pure female" by simply cutting off his "symbolic male genital organ," what would turning him into a "pure male" entail? Would that also involve the removal of something? Or would that require the adding on of something else? Even if female gonads were found inside his reproductive system and the second operation followed suit, what happens next if his vaginal interior showed signs of anatomical abnormality? On what grounds would the doctors evaluate the resemblance of his vagina to that

---

17. "Yinyangren bianxing shoushu qian zhunbei hushi xiaojie qunyu tanxiao miqu xinli fanying ziliao" [Before the hermaphrodite's sex change operation: Chatting with nurses to reveal psychological data], *Lianhebao*, August 16, 1953, no. 3.

18. "Yinyangren Xie Jianshun jinkaidao biancixiong" [Hermaphrodite Xie Jianshun: Sex determined today through surgery], *Lianhebao*, August 20, 1953, no. 3.

of an average woman at this stage? To what degree could his vagina deviate from the internal structure of a "normal" vagina before it is considered too "abnormal"? The newspaper passage answered none of these questions. Under the pretense of keeping its readers informed, it actually imposed more assumptions (and raised more questions) about Xie's "real" sex. By the day of his first operation, the medical and popular discourses congruently prepared the lay public for a sensational outcome of this unprecedented sex change episode in Chinese culture. Xie's sex was arguably already "determined" and "transformed" before the actual surgery itself. This reciprocated the ambiguity surrounding the purpose of his first operation: Was its goal the determination or transformation of his sex?

On the following day, the Taiwanese public confronted a lengthy coverage of Xie's surgery in the news billed "Soldier Destined to Become a Lady." This echoed the headline of the New York *Daily News* front-page article that announced Christine Jorgenson's sex change surgery back in December 1952, "Ex-GI Becomes Blonde Beauty." The *United Daily News* piece included a more telling subtitle: "The *Yin-Yang* Person's Interior Parts Revealed Yesterday after Surgery: The Presence of Uterus and Ovaries Confirmed." From this point on, Xie was frequently dubbed as the "Chinese Christine." Whereas reporters had always used either the masculine pronoun "he" (*ta* 他) or both the masculine and the feminine pronouns (*ta* 他 [她]) during the first week of press coverage, they changed to the feminine pronoun entirely to refer to Xie in all subsequent writings. In his discussion of Xie's operation, Dr. Lin asserted that "Xie Jianshun should be converted into a woman in light of his physiological condition" and that this procedure would have "a 90 percent success rate." The article described Xie's first surgery with remarkable detail:

> Xie's operation began at 3:40pm yesterday. Dr. Lin Chengyi led a team of physicians, including Le Shaoqing and Wang Zifan, and nurses, including Jin Ming. Because this is the first clinical treatment of an intersexed patient in Taiwan, Dr. Lin permitted out-of-town doctors and news reporters to observe the surgical proceeding in the operating room with a mask on. After anesthesia, Dr. Lin cut open the lower abdominal area at 3:50 and examined its interior parts. The operation ended successfully at 4:29, with a total duration of 39 minutes. It also marked a decisive moment for determining the sex of the *yin-yang* person Xie Jianshun.[19]

This excerpt thus brought the reader back to the clinical setting of Xie's surgery, thereby reinforcing Xie's status as an object of medical gaze even after the surgery itself. Ultimately, this careful textual restaging of Xie's medical operation translated its *clinical* standing into a glamorized *cultural* phenomenon in postwar Taiwan.

---

19. "Burang Kelisiding zhuanmei yuqian."

Xie's growing iconicity as a specimen of cultural dissection also hinged on the detailed public exposure of the surgical findings. According to the press coverage:

> After a thirty-minute inspection of the [lower] abdominal region, the *yin-yang* person is confirmed female given the presence of ovarian tissues. The uterus is 6cm long and 3.5cm wide, which is similar to the uterus size of an unpenetrated virgin, but slightly unhealthy. Not only are the two ovaries normal, the existence of Fallopian tubes is also confirmed. Upon physical inspection prior to the surgery, no testicle can be detected on the lower right abdominal region and only an incomplete testicle can be found on the left. Because Xie Jianshun once had chronic appendicitis, her appendix is removed during this operation. The five viscera are identified as complete and normal. Based on the above results, have [the doctors] decided to perform a [sex change] surgery on Xie Jianshun? The answer is with 90 percent certainty.
>
> According to what her physician in charge, Dr. Lin, told the reporters following the operation, the [sex] transformation surgery will take place in two weeks after Xie Jianshun has recovered from this exploratory laparotomy. The procedure for converting [him] into female begins with the cutting open of the presently closed *labia majora* and *labia minora*. After that, a close inspection of [her] vagina will be necessary to see if it is healthy and normal. Anyone with a uterus has a vagina. After both the *labia majora* and *labia minora* have been split open and the symbolic phallic organ has been removed from the latter, [Xie]'s transformation into a pure woman will be complete.[20]

Based on these descriptions alone, the reader was able to join Dr. Lin's medical team and examine Xie's physical body, not unlike what happened on the previous day at the 518 Hospital. This narrative even made it possible to anticipate and imagine a future for this unprecedented medicalized sex change in Chinese culture. Although one type of interrogation was conducted in the "private" (closed) space of the operation room and the other was carried out in the "public" (open) domain of printed publications, medical science and the popular press ultimately converged as mutually reinforcing sites for the anatomization of Xie's sex transformation. One policeman could not hide his excitement. He publicly declared his admiration for Xie and interest in dating her after the operation.[21]

As the outcome of Xie's first operation attracted growing publicity, the press further aligned itself with the medical profession by keeping Xie in a public "closet." This "closet" was characterized in a way different from what gay and lesbian scholars have typically conceived to be the staple features of queer lives in the past: hidden, secretive, and "masked."[22] Instead

---

20. "Shoushu shunli wancheng gaizao juyou bawo" [Surgery successfully completed: Alteration is feasible], *Lianhebao*, August 21, 1953, no. 3.
21. "Yinyangren yiyou zhiyin" [Hermaphrodite already has an admirer], *Lianhebao*, August 24, 1953, no. 4.
22. On the significance of cultural concealment in American gay history, see John D'Emilio, *Sexual Politics, Sexual Communities: The Making of a Homosexual Minority in the United States*

of concealing one's (homo/bi)sexuality in public, Xie's closet allowed the public to hide his transsexuality from himself. Following the surgery, to quote the exact words in the *United Daily News*, "'Miss' Xie Jianshun opened her eyes and looked with a slightly painful expression at her surrounding visitors. But she seems to be in a good psychological state. While not a single word has slipped out of her mouth, and although she has not consulted the doctors about the outcome of her surgery, she is at present oblivious of her fate—that she is destined to become a lady." When a photo of the surgical proceeding and a photo of Xie became available for the first time in public on August 22, the news of future medical plans to change his sex (including female hormonal therapy) still remained unknown to Xie (see Figure 8.1).[23] Xie was finally "brought out of the closet" nine days after the exploratory laparotomy, which many deemed a success.[24] On the afternoon of August 29, Dr. Lin discussed the result of the surgery with Xie, and, being the last person to know about his fate, Xie agreed to cooperate in all subsequent medical procedures that would eventually lead to a complete sex reassignment.[25] Prior to that, by maintaining his sex change operation as a secret from Xie himself, both the doctors involved in his case and the press that reported on it generated a public "closet" that delineated a cultural division between the desire of the transsexual individual and the desire of others. Only in this case, however ironically, Xie, the transsexual, had once expressed his *reluctance* to change sex.

Why did the medical team not inform Xie of its decision immediately following the operation? As Dr. Lin explained it, his colleagues learned from the nurses that Xie expressed great anxiety about turning into female after having lived as a man for more than thirty-six years. Given his strong desire to remain biologically male, Dr. Lin's team was afraid that, if Xie found out about their decision to convert his sex so abruptly, he would commit suicide, which was implicated in his earlier conversations with the nurses.[26]

(Chicago: University of Chicago Press, 1983); George Chauncey, *Gay New York: Gender, Urban Culture, and the Making of the Gay Male World, 1890–1940* (New York: Basic Books, 1994); John Laughery, *The Other Side of Silence: Men's Lives and Gay Identities: A Twentieth-Century History* (New York: Henry Holt, 1998); Martin Meeker, "Behind the Mask of Respectability: Reconsidering the Mattachine Society and Male Homophile Practice, 1950s and 1960s," *Journal of the History of Sexuality* 10(1) (2001): 78–116; Martin Meeker, *Contacts Desired: Gay and Lesbian Communications and Community, 1940s–1970s* (Chicago: University of Chicago Press, 2006). For an analytical rendition of the "closet" more salient to the history of trans-sexuality, see David Serlin, "Christine Jorgensen and the Cold War Closet," *Radical History Review* 62 (Spring 1995): 136–65.

23. "Xie Jianshun kaidaohou zuori qingkuang zhenchang" [Xie Jianshun's operation proceeded normally yesterday], *Lianhebao*, August 22, 1953, no. 3.
24. "Yinyangren daokou chaixian" [The hermaphrodite's stitches removed], *Lianhebao*, August 28, 1953, no. 3.
25. "Yinyangren Xie Jianshun tongyi gaizao nüxing" [Hermaphrodite Xie Jianshun agreed to be turned into a woman], *Lianhebao*, August 30, 1953, no. 3.
26. "Shoushu shunli wancheng."

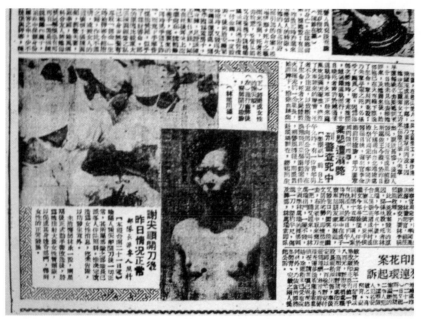

Figure 8.1
Photo of Xie Jianshun after the first operation. Source: *Lianhebao*, August 22, 1953.

Although the doctors attempted to uncover Xie's gender orientation (by sending a group of "attractive" women nurses to socialize with him) just a few days before the first operation, the surgical outcome—reinforced by the sensationalist tone of the press—nonetheless suggested that for them biology trumped psychology.[27] Despite the fact that Xie's condition was really a case of human intersexuality, the doctors insisted time and again that they were surgically transforming his sex.

From the beginning, the exploratory laparotomy operation lacked a clear objective. Although the doctors announced their attempt to determine Xie's sex based on his internal anatomical configurations, they repeatedly proposed a series of surgeries to be performed on Xie's body and called them "sex transformation" operations. After the exploratory laparotomy, bolstered by the breathtaking accounts that stormed the newspapers nationwide, they successfully maintained a "public closet" that prevented Xie from intervening their plan to change his sex. Xie's refusal to be transformed into a woman shifted from public knowledge to an open secret. The doctors continued to push for an opposite surgical outcome, and, as the journalistic sensationalism surrounding his ambiguous medical condition accumulated, they behaved as vanguards of medical science in the Republic of China by hinting at their ability to alter Xie's sex just like the doctors abroad. In the shadow of

---

27. "Yinyangren bianxing shoushu qian zhunbei."

Christine Jorgensen, the construction of Xie Jianshun's (trans)sexual identity was driven less by his self-determination and more by the cultural authority of the surgeons involved and the broader impact of the mass circulation press.

The Chinese Christine

Nine months after the New York *Daily News* announced the sex change surgery of Jorgensen, readers in postwar Taiwan were told that they, too, had their own "Chinese Christine." A newspaper article titled "The Chinese Christine" provides a poignant cross-cultural comparison of the two transsexual icons.[28] The writer, Guan Ming, began by describing Jorgensen's situation in the United States, noting the substantial measure of fame and wealth that her sex-change surgery had brought her. Guan also rightly noted how the Jorgensen story became harder to "sell" when news of her incomplete female anatomy went public. (Jorgensen did not undergo vaginoplasty until 1954, and, prior to that, many physicians considered Jorgenson's sex change unsuccessful.) Indeed, after Jorgenson returned from Denmark, American journalists soon questioned her surgically transformed sex. *Time* declared, "Jorgenson was no girl at all, only an altered male," and *Newsweek* followed suit.[29]

In contrast, Guan observed, "Our 'Chinese Christine,' Xie Jianshun, has turned into a 100 percent biological woman, succeeding the 'incomplete female' Christine Jorgensen." Unlike the American celebrity, Xie was inclined to continue living as a man, "let alone earning money [with a dazzling transsexual embodiment]." Guan added that Xie was even "afraid of losing his privilege to stay [in the military] after sex reassignment." Based on these differences, the author concluded, Jorgensen's transformation generated an international sensation in part because of her "opportunistic inclinations" and the "widespread curiosity in society"; Xie's sex change operations, in contrast, proceeded as a proper medical solution for a congenital bodily defect. "But no adequate social resources were yet available for people like Xie," wrote Guan.[30] At the time of expressing his views, Guan of course could not anticipate the kind of spiritual and financial support that Xie would eventually receive from various military units in southern Taiwan on a sporadic basis.[31] More problematically, Guan had mistaken Xie's

---

28. Guan Ming, "Zhongguo Kelisiding" [The Chinese Christine], *Lianhebao*, September 1, 1953, no. 6.
29. Joanne Meyerowitz, "Sex Change and the Popular Press: Historical Notes on Transsexuality in the United States, 1930–1955," *GLQ: A Journal of Lesbian and Gay Studies* 4(2) (1998): 159–87, on pp. 173–74.
30. Guan, "Zhongguo Kelisiding."
31. See "Nanbu junyou fenshe weiwen Xie Jianshun" [Soldiers from the southern station console Xie Jianshun], *Lianhebao*, September 4, 1953, no. 3; "Zenkuan Xie Jianshun buwang

first exploratory laparotomy operation for a full sex transformation surgery. He also overlooked the convention among experts in the Western medical profession, in the years before Jorgensen, to declare sex change surgeries as acceptable treatment for intersexed conditions.[32]

Nonetheless, Guan's comparison of the two transsexual icons nicely illustrates how sexualized bodies circulating in the early Cold War–era public milieu represented an ambivalent platform on which claims about national similarities (e.g., between the United Sates and the Republic of China) could simultaneously infuse broader claims about cultural (and perhaps even civilizational) divergence between "China" and the West.[33] On the one hand, by systematically referring to Xie as the "Chinese Christine," Taiwanese journalists and public commentators interpreted her medical condition and Jorgensen's transsexual experience as more similar than different. On the other hand, they brought Xie's intention to remain biologically male to full public disclosure and, at one point, even suggested the possibility that Xie may be a "true" hermaphrodite and Jorgensen only a "pseudo" one.[34] For Guan in particular, whereas the global reputation of Jorgensen's transsexuality could be attributed to the social norms of "opportunistic" thinking and curiosity in the West, Xie's publicity in postwar Taiwan reflected the ethical responsibility of Chinese doctors to provide proper care for exceptional medical conditions. In either case, the popular press portrayed Xie's condition and her sex change surgery as a rare and important event in medical science, thereby modeling such advancement in postwar Taiwan after the latest surgical breakthrough in Western biomedicine. In this way, the story of Xie Jianshun helped to situate Taiwan on the same global horizon as the United States.[35]

abingjie" [Donating to Xie Jianshun: Never forget the female soldier], *Lianhebao*, September 21, 1953, no. 4; "Xie Jianshun xiaojie jiang beilai kaidao" [Miss Xie Jianshun coming to Taipei for surgery], *Lianhebao*, October 29, 1953, no. 3; "Wei qiuzheng shengli yi diding yinyang" [To validate physiology and yin or yang], *Lianhebao*, December 5, 1953, no. 3.

32. See Anne Fausto-Sterling, *Sexing the Body: Gender Politics and the Construction of Sexuality* (New York: Basic Books, 2000); Meyerowitz, *How Sex Changed*; Alison Redick, "American History XY: The Medical Treatment of Intersex, 1916–1955" (PhD diss., New York University, 2004); Christina Matta, "Ambiguous Bodies and Deviant Sexualities: Hermaphrodites, Homosexuality, and Surgery in the United States, 1850–1904," *Perspectives in Biology and Medicine* 48(1) (2005): 74–83.

33. For theoretical considerations of the problem of civilizationalism, see Samuel Huntington, "The Clash of Civilizations?" *Foreign Affairs* 72(3) (1993): 22–49; Kuan-Hsing Chen, "Civilizationalism," *Theory, Culture & Society* 23(2–3) (2006): 427–28. For another example of the Xie-Jorgensen comparison, see "Hebi ruci feijing" [Why go through so much trouble], *Lianhebao*, March 26, 1954, no. 3.

34. "Xie Jianshun jue laibei kaidao xinan yinü nanding duankan erci shoushu" [Xie Jianshun has decided to relocate to Taipei for surgery: Sex determination depends on the second operation], *Lianhebao*, November 27, 1953, no. 3.

35. Guan, "Zhongguo Kelisiding."

Despite the prevailing tendency to compare the two transsexual icons, Xie reacted to her unforeseen publicity in a manner radically different from that of the glamorous American Christine. Whereas Jorgensen enjoyed her international fame, collaborated with various media agents to help shape it, and took other deliberate measures to promote it, Xie did not seize the press coverage of her genital surgery as an opportunity to boost her own reputation. To Xie, the popular rendition of her body as a valuable medical specimen and a concrete ground for US-Taiwan idiosyncratic comparison were less important than her desire to be treated properly and resume a normal and healthy life. Little did Xie realize that the significance of her celebrity came not only from the direct comparisons with Jorgensen, but also from the underlying similarities between the evolving perceptions of transsexuals in the popular imagination (due to her publicity) and the subsequent flood of other stories in Taiwan. Both the Christine analogy and the surfacing of other similar sex change stories in Taiwan were, in many ways, inflected by the global reach of the Jorgensen narrative. As the nominal label of "Chinese Christine" suggests, "the power behind the culture of U.S. imperialism comes from its ability to insert itself into a geo-colonial space as the imaginary figure of modernity, and as such, the natural object of identification from which the local people are to learn."[36]

The Second Operation

As the Republican government officials took a more serious interest in her case, Xie resisted their top-down decisions. Xie's second operation was initially scheduled to take place within two weeks after the first, but the only news that reached the 518 Hospital four weeks after the exploratory laparotomy was a state-issued order to transport her to Taipei. The reporters wrote, "In order to ensure Xie's safety, and in the hope that a second operation will be carried out smoothly, it has been decided that she will be relocated to Taipei. After being evaluated and operated upon by a group of notable doctors in a reputable hospital, [Xie's sex change] will mark a great moment in history." Xie refused, however. She immediately wrote to bureaucrats to express her preference for staying in Tainan and being operated upon there again.[37]

To her dismay, Xie paid a price for challenging the authorities. They neglected her and delayed her operation for at least three weeks following her request. The press reappeared as a viable venue for voicing her dissent. On October 17, Xie disclosed the anxiety she had developed from her last

---

36. Kuan-Hsing Chen, *Asia as Method: Toward Deimperialization* (Durham, NC: Duke University Press, 2010), 177.

37. "Xie Jianshun gaizao shoushu huo jianglai Taibei kaidao" [Xie Jianshun's alteration surgery might take place in Taipei], *Lianhebao*, September 24, 1953, no. 3.

menstrual experience, which occurred roughly a month ago. "Given her vaginal blockage, wastes could only be discharged from a small [genital] opening, leading to extreme abdominal pains during her period," an article with the title "The Pain of Miss Xie Jianshun" explained. Since another menstrual cycle was just right around the corner, she urged Dr. Lin, again, to perform a second operation as promptly as possible. But Dr. Lin despairingly conceded that he must receive a formal response from the central government before he could initiate a second surgical attempt. All he could do at this point, as one might have expected, was to re-forward Xie's second request to the higher officials and wait.[38] At the end of the month, Xie's former captain, Fu Chun 傅純, paid her a visit, bringing her $300 to help her get by during this difficult period.[39]

By late November, the prolonged waiting and the accumulated unanswered requests forced Xie to agree reluctantly to relocate to Taipei. The newspapers announced the fifth of the following month as the date of her arrival and the Taipei No. 1 General Hospital as her second home. A medical authority from the Taipei hospital anticipated their takeover of Xie's case: "In light of Xie's biology, there should be no leap of faith in how successful the second operation will be in completing Xie's transition. The only thing that remains to be determined is whether Xie is a fake or true hermaphrodite. This can be accomplished by taking a sample from one of Xie's incomplete testes and determine whether it could produce semen." The doctor reinforced the popular perception of Xie's condition as an extraordinary phenomenon of nature by labeling it "truly rare in the world's medical history."[40]

In early December, the *United Daily News* announced "Chinese Christine Coming to Taipei Today for Treatment," and many gathered around the Taipei main station that day expecting to greet the transsexual celebrity in person.[41] Despite the great measure of patience and enthusiasm with which her Taipei fans waited, the papers reported on the following day, on December 6, that their hopes ended up in despair: Xie's anticipated relocation failed to materialize, which disappointed those who were eager to witness the legendary transsexual icon. Journalists reported that "Xie's Taipei trip might have been canceled or postponed due to unknown reasons" but offered no estimation of her new arrival date.[42] To the public's dismay, it would be at least six more weeks before Xie quietly showed up at the No. 1 General Hospital in Taipei.

The media had heretofore functioned as a key buffer among the medical professionals, Xie Jianshun, and the Taiwanese public. The national dailies in

---

38. "Xie Jianshun xiaojie de yintong" [The pain of Miss Xie Jianshun], *Lianhebao*, October 17, 1953, no. 3.
39. "Xie Jianshun xiaojie jiang beilai kaidao."
40. "Xie Jianshun jue laibei kaidao."
41. "Wei qiuzheng shengli yi diding yinyang."
42. "Zhongguo Kelisiding zuori wei beilai" [The Chinese Christine did not arrive at Taipei yesterday], *Lianhebao*, December 6, 1953, no. 3.

particular served as the primary means through which readers could learn Xie's thoughts and opinions. Those who followed her story closely relied mainly on the press for the ins and outs of her medical treatment. Recall that doctors even allowed news reporters to witness the first exploratory laparotomy operation and, afterward, publicly disclosed their decision to turn Xie into a woman before telling Xie herself. Similarly, Xie considered the press as the most immediate (and perhaps reliable) way to publicize her desire to remain biologically male before the operation and her unwillingness to leave Tainan afterward. Almost without the slightest degree of hesitation, both Xie and her physicians readily collaborated with journalists to escalate the initial scoop of media reporting into a nationwide frenzy.

Although the reporters continued to clamor, the coverage took a dip near the end of 1953. In 1954, only three articles in the *United Daily News* and none in either the *China Daily News* (中華日報, *Zhonghua ribao*) or the *Taiwan Shin Sheng Daily News* (台灣新生報, *Taiwan xinshengbao*) followed up on Xie's situation. After the cancellation of her December trip, the first update on Xie's health condition came in as late as mid-February 1954. It was only by that point that her reticent move to Taipei on January 16 was revealed to the public. The name of her new surgeon in charge at the No. 1 General Hospital was Jiang Xizheng 姜希錚. Yet, despite the surprising news that Xie was now in Taipei, the closest impression one could gain from reading this article was a description of the hospital room in which she was staying: "Xie Jianshun's room features simple decorations, with one bed, a tea table, a long table, and a chair. There is a window at the end of the room, but the curtains are almost always closed in order to prevent strangers from taking a peek at [her] secrets."[43] What these words reflected was not only the physical distance between Xie and any curious-minded visitors at the hospital; these words also captured the metaphorical distance between Xie and the readers who found it increasingly difficult to gather information about her situation and the concrete plans for her second operation based on the newspaper reports alone. Even as the *United Daily News* indicated that Xie was now taking hormones so that she was closer to becoming "the second Christine," it failed to identify who exactly provided that information and the degree of its reliability.[44]

The long silence in the press coverage might suggest that the public's interest in Xie's story had begun to wane. However, the next *United Daily News* article, which appeared roughly a month later in mid-March, indicated otherwise and put forth a more plausible explanation:

---

43. "Xie Jianshun bingfang shenju jingdai shoushu ding yiyang" [Xie Jianshun residing in the hospital room: Waiting for sex-determination surgery], *Lianhebao*, February 15, 1954, no. 3.
44. Ibid.

The hospital has been especially secretive about the exact location of her room so as to avoid unsolicited visits from intrusive strangers. Meanwhile, perhaps as a result of her male-to-female transformation, Xie Jianshun has become increasingly shy in front of strangers, so she has asked the hospital staff not to disclose any further information about her treatment to the public while she is hospitalized. Deeply concerned with her psychological wellbeing, the doctors agreed as a matter of course.[45]

In other words, the dip in the press coverage had less to do with the public's declining interest in Xie, than with a mutual agreement between Xie and her attending physicians to refrain from speaking to journalists and reporters. This constituted the second turning point in the evolving relationship between the medical profession and the reporting of Xie's sex change in the mass media. The popular press no longer played the role of a friendly mediator among the public, the doctors, and Xie herself. To both Xie and her medical staff after the first operation, the publicity showered on them seemed to impede rather than help their plans. Xie, in particular, might have considered the authorities' indifference toward her earlier request to stay in Tainan as a consequence of nationwide media coverage, thereby holding her prolonged waiting against the reporters. Apart from a brief comment about how Xie displayed "more obvious feminine characteristics" post hormonal injections, the March *United Daily News* article included no new information on her situation.

As the voice of the newspaper accounts became increasingly speculative, and as the mediating role of the press gradually receded to the background, to the readers, available information about Xie's second operation proved to be less certain and more difficult to ascertain. The tension between the reporters and those who tried to protect Xie from them peaked around late June, when the *United Daily News* reported on Xie's story for the third and final time in 1954. The article opened with a sentence that mentioned only in passing Xie's "more 'determinant' operation performed recently at the No. 1 General Hospital." Framed as such, Xie's "second" operation was barely publicized, and even if readers interpreted this line to mean that Xie had undergone a second operation, the doctors withstood giving an update on it. When the reporters consulted Xie's medical team on June 24, they were met with a persistent reluctance to respond to any questions and to permit visitation rights for nonmedical personnel. A staff at the No. 1 General Hospital was even quoted for saying, "We are not sure if Xie Jianshun is still staying with us at this hospital."[46]

---

45. "Xie Jianshun youju daibian yijue de titai jiaorou" [Xie Jianshun secluding herself and becoming feminized], *Lianhebao*, March 18, 1954, no. 3.

46. "Xie Jianshun jiju nü'ertai qinsi mantou fenbaimian youju mishi yizeng xiu" [Xie Jianshun appears extremely feminine], *Lianhebao*, June 25, 1954, no. 5.

In contrast to the sensationalist tone and mundane details that dominated the discussion of Xie's first surgery, the way that the media discussed
the second operation was less fact oriented and more congested with sup-
positions. The major newspapers glossed over any information that would
support the claim that Xie had become more feminized after relocation.
Despite the best intentions of the hospital staff to distance the media people
from Xie,

> A journalist has conducted an investigation inside the hospital and found
> signs that suggest that Xie Jianshun has become more lady-like and that she
> is undergoing an accelerated metamorphosis. . . . Despite the high surveil-
> lance under which Xie Jianshun is monitored, sometimes her face can still
> be seen. According to an individual who claims to have seen Xie Jianshun in
> person lately, it is difficult to discern whether Xie Jianshun has transformed
> into a woman completely. Nonetheless, based on what he saw, Xie's hair
> has grown longer, and her face has become paler and smoother. The general
> impression one would get from looking at Xie now is that Xie Jianshun has
> transformed into a woman gradually over time.[47]

Not only did this account fail to mention what the second operation entailed,
it only *surmised* the outcome based on some unknown secondary source.
Unlike the step-by-step recounting of the surgical protocols involved in the
first operation, the doctors' strategy for pursuing Xie's bodily transformation in the immediate future remained opaque.

Transformation Complete

The mysterious aura surrounding Xie Jianshun's fate did not last long. The
public's avid interest finally pushed medical experts to step up and come
clean about Xie's situation. In January 1955, a newspaper article with the
headline, "Xie Jianshun's Male-to-Female Transformation Nearly Complete:
The Rumor of Surgical Failure Proved to be False," shattered any doubts
about the stunted progress in Xie's physical change. After the first operation,
given the way that Xie's doctors had intentionally refrained from leaking
any word to the press, the public was left with an unclear impression of
what was going on inside the hospital specifically and how Xie was doing
more generally. Rumor soon had it that the doctors' long silence meant Xie's
transition was ultimately unsuccessful. According to the article, the cause of
this rumor "can be traced to an incident reported last month in Tainan of a
yin-yang person. The general public's memory of Xie was refreshed by this
story of the *yin-yang* person in Tainan, and as a result of this reminder, the
public began to revisit the question of whether Xie had succeeded in being
transformed into a woman." In an attempt to dispel any doubts, doctors

47. Ibid.

from the No. 1 General Hospital were quoted for confirming that "the rumor is definitely false." They clarified that "Xie Jianshun's sex transformation has in fact proceeded rather successfully and is reaching its final stages." Xie, the doctors promised, "is living a perfectly healthy life." But when the reporters requested to speak to Xie in person, they were turned away and were told by the hospital staff that this kind of request "could only be fulfilled with a permit from the state authorities."[48]

The initial upsurge of the renewed interest in Xie survived only briefly. It would take another eight months—after the doctors had performed Xie's "third" and final operation—before her name would make headlines again.[49] On August 31, 1955, the *United Daily News* carried an extended front-page article with the headline, "A New Chapter in the Nation's Medical History: The Success of Xie Jianshun's Sex Change Surgery."[50] On the following day, the newspapers teased the public by announcing that "The Details of Xie Jianshun's Sex Change Operations Will Be Publicized Shortly." According to Xie's physician in charge, "Contrary to a number of fabricated claims, Xie Jianshun's final operation took place very smoothly on the morning of August 30. With respect to the protocols and results of this decisive surgery, the medical team promises to release all of the relevant information in a formal report in due course." The papers glossed over the aim of this operation with the succinct words "to unclog her Fallopian tubes," the obstruction of which had caused her periodic discomfort for months. Apparently, Xie felt dizzy after the operation but recovered by the next morning. The representatives from the No. 1 General Hospital explained that both Xie's own request and the uniqueness of her case constituted their main reasons for holding off on disclosing the clinical details underpinning her case. Since Xie had explicitly asked the medical staff to abstain from speaking to journalists and reporters, the doctors assumed the responsibility of protecting her privacy from media exposure. On the other hand, the doctors believed that her sex change operations "promise to mark an important medical breakthrough in the country," so they wanted to be extra careful in making any kind of public statement. Silence seemed to be the best demonstration of their precaution before the final verdict.[51]

48. "Xie Jianshun younan biannü shoushu yi jiejin chenggong" [The surgery of Xie Jianshun's male-to-female transformation almost complete], *Lianhebao*, January 9, 1955, no. 3.

49. I put the word "third" in quotation marks here (and only here), because the official report released later in the year will contradict this count and indicate that this was actually Xie's fourth operation. See below.

50. "Woguo yixue shishang de chuangju Xie Jianshun bianxing shoushu chenggong" [A new chapter in the nation's medical history: The success of Xie Jianshun's sex change surgery], *Lianhebao*, August 31, 1955, no. 1.

51. "Xie Jianshun biangxing shoushu jingguo duanqi zhengshi gongbu" [The details of Xie Jianshun's sex change surgery to be publicized shortly], *Lianhebao*, September 1, 1955, no. 3.

On the following day, the papers declared "the success of Xie Jianshun's sex change surgery," pitching it as "a fact that can no longer be shaken." Although the staff at the No. 1 General Hospital pledged to disclose the surgical specifics in the near future, readers in Taiwan had already learned a great deal on the day following the operation. Xie's popularity first skyrocketed two years ago, in August 1953, when doctors, scientists, the press, and the lay public "discovered" her. Despite the detailed coverage of her first operation, or because of it, Xie and the people in her immediate circle became much quieter in their dealing with reporters. As its media coverage began to thin out in 1954, the Xie story grew more and more mysterious, while other stories of uncommon body morphology abounded in the press.[52] Even the timing and completion of her second operation were never thoroughly announced until this point. The pertinent newspaper article now clarified that, in the months following her first operation, Xie not only resisted relocating to Taipei but ardently opposed changing her sex. The second operation eventually took place in April 1954, and it involved "the removal of the two symbolic male gonads." After the second operation, Xie "began to develop stronger female sexual characteristics," which included the enlargement of her breasts and the onset of regular menstruation. Because Xie's reproductive system lacked a full vaginal canal, her periodic menses caused regular discomfort when excreted with urine through the urethra. As she "started to learn how it feels to be a woman," these physiological reorientations made her more reluctant to identify as a woman. After wrestling with the idea of relocating to Taipei, she struggled with and eventually failed to convince her surgeons not to transform her sex.[53]

Amid a world of uncertainties brought about by World War II and its immediate aftermath, the media used the metaphor of the Cold War to depict Xie's relationship with the doctors. If the rough timing of the second operation were true, sixteen months had elapsed before Xie entered her recent surgery. To quote the exact words used to frame this extended period of time, "[T]he Cold War between Xie Jianshun and the hospital lasted until April 5 of this year." What got frozen during this period was not only Xie's reaction to the decisions made by her physicians in charge, but also the overall fate of her medical treatment (or sex transformation). Distinguishing her ambition from the intent of her doctors, Xie requested a second relocation to a different hospital, but her request was ultimately denied. What "ended this Cold War," according to the newspapers, was a letter that she wrote to the president, Chiang Kai-Shek, in which she expressed her disdain

52. Chiang, "Gender Transformations in Sinophone Taiwan."
53. "Xie Jianshun de nü'erjing qi xumei busheng xiunao huai jilü jingnian fangjie" [Xie Jianshun's anxiety about menstruation problems finally resolved], *Lianhebao*, September 2, 1955, no. 3.

toward how the doctors handled her case and the absence of adequate nutri-tion administered at the hospital.[54]

In response to the letter, the Ministry of National Defense sent two rep-resentatives to the No. 1 General Hospital to resolve the tension between Xie and the doctors. Xie's complaint about how she was mistreated at the hospital, they found out, was a misleading "expression of her wrong set of mind." They told her that the regular cramps that she experienced were due to the menstrual periods, which typified the bodily experience of the female reproductive system. In order to alleviate this somatic (and not psychologi-cal) discomfort, the doctors needed to construct a functional vaginal canal for her. Ultimately, the two National Defense representatives succeeded in persuading Xie to accept the doctors' advice and complete her sex transfor-mation with one final surgery. The newspapers speculated that "perhaps it is due to her prejudice against the hospital staff, or perhaps it is due to her loyalty to the military, she agreed to a third operation after contemplating for only ten minutes or so."[55] The year-long "Cold War" thus ended with the direct intervention of not the medical experts but state authorities. Whereas, according to historian Elaine May, the contemporaneous structural norms of American families helped offset the nation's domestic and foreign politi-cal insecurities, Cold War's metaphoric power, as evident in the example of Xie's transsexuality, was diffused in the public discussion of sexually mal-leable bodies in the context of postwar Taiwan, situated on the fringes of China and Chineseness.[56]

Before the doctors released their official report of Xie's case, details of the third operation and its influence on Xie were already openly discussed by those in her immediate circle. The new surgeon in charge, Zhang Xianlin 張先林, for example, uninhibitedly expressed his view of the nature of Xie's latest operation. Whereas most peopled considered this operation the most critical and fate determining, Zhang regarded it merely as "a simple reconstructive surgery." Because Xie's reproductive system was already confirmed female, according to Zhang, the operation involved the enhancement of her female biology by "removing her symbolic phallic organ" and, more importantly, "the construction of an artificial menstrual canal," which would allow her to release menses normally. The operation, which Zhang considered to be a breeze, began at eight o'clock in the morning and ended at ten after nine.[57] To assess the effect of the operation on Xie, the doctors vowed to administer an X-ray examination in two weeks.[58] When the *United Daily News* in Taiwan

---

54. Ibid.
55. Ibid.
56. See Elaine Tyler May, *Homeward Bound: American Families in the Cold War Era* (New York: Basic Books, 1988).
57. "Xie Jianshun de nü'erjing."
58. "Xie Jianshun bianxing shoushu hou yishi liangzhou hou kexue yan quansheng" [Doctors will examine Xie Jianshun's body scientifically two weeks after sex change operation],

and the *Kung Sheung Daily News* in Hong Kong published half-nude photos of the "post-op" Xie on September 8, representatives from the No. 1 General Hospital quickly dismissed them as a sham.[59] As a sign of their interest in looking after Xie's psychological well-being, within three weeks after the operation, the Ministry of National Defense awarded Xie 1,000 New Taiwan Dollars to help her defray the cost of purchasing new feminine attire.[60] This generous sum offered Xie greater freedom in constructing a social image— and a new sense of self—that aligned cogently with her new biological sex.

On October 28, 1955, the *United Daily News* carried a front-page story that finally proclaimed "The Completion and Success of Xie Jianshun's Sex Change Operation."[61] The story continued on page 3, which contained a full-length official report on Xie's medical treatment released by the No. 1 Army Hospital. The official report revealed numerous aspects of the Xie story that overthrew earlier speculations. Of these revelations, the most surprising was probably the fact that Xie's most recent operation was actually her fourth and not her third operation. Recall that Xie's second operation received little publicity in the previous year. By June 1954, from reading the scattered newspaper accounts, interested readers could gain a vague impression that doctors in Taipei had performed a second surgery on her, but its date, nature, and purpose lacked transparency. According to this official report, however, Xie's second operation, which was also an exploratory laparotomy but with the additional step of removing parts of her male gonadal tissues, took place on April 10, 1954. Based on the samples extracted from her body during this operation, the doctors confirmed Xie's status as a true hermaphrodite, meaning that she had both ovarian and testicular tissues in her gonads. The doctors also clarified that by that point, her "testicular tissues were already deteriorating and unable to generate sperm," but her "ovarian tissues were still functional and able to produce eggs." In light of a stronger presence of female sexual characteristics, the medical team performed a third operation on August 26, 1954. After the surgery, Xie's penis was replaced by an artificial vaginal opening. All of this happened more than a year prior. Taking place on August 30, 1955, Xie's most recent and fourth genital surgery was simply a vaginoplasty. Now with "a normal woman's vaginal interior," Xie Jianshun's "transformation from a soldier into a lady is now indisputable."[62]

Lianhebao, September 3, 1955, no. 3.

59. "Xie Jianshun luoxiong zhaopian zhengshi xi gongpin" [Xie Jianshun's half-nude photo: A hoax], *Lianhebao*, September 10, 1955, no. 3.

60. "Banfa yingbianfei qianjin zeng hongzhuang" [Awarding Xie for building her new feminine look], *Lianhebao*, September 21, 1955, no. 3.

61. "Lujun diyi zongyiyuan xuanbu Xie Jianshun shoushu chenggong" [No. 1 Hospital announces the completion and success of Xie Jianshun's sex change operation], *Lianhebao*, October 28, 1955, no. 1.

62. "Sici shoushu yibianerchai Xie Jianshun bianxing jingguo" [Male to female transformation after four surgeries: The sex change experience of Xie Jianshun], *Lianhebao*, October 28, 1955, no. 3.

Brought to light by the report, Xie's personal triumph encapsulated the postwar fears and hopes about the possibilities of medical science.[63]

On the same day, the second page of *United Daily News* included the sixteenth installment of "The Story of Miss Xie Jianshun," a biography of Xie that had been serialized daily since October 13.[64] The concluding installment appeared on November 18, which meant that for more than a month, Taiwanese readers were exposed to Xie's life story with familiar moments and surprising details.[65] This extended exposure seemed to reflect the fact that the Xie story continued to sell even two years after the initial frenzy. No less significant, again, was the similarity in the marketing strategies of the Taiwanese and American presses. The stylistic objective of "The Story of Miss Xie Jianshun" closely resembled that of the series "The Story of My Life," which appeared in *American Weekly* three days after Jorgensen returned to the United States from Denmark. Jorgensen's series was billed as "the story all America has been waiting for," which would have been an equally appropriate description for the Xie installments with a nominal substitution of the word "Taiwan" for "America."[66] But the two series bore significant differences as well. Whereas the first-person confessional format of the American version gave Jorgensen a chance to convey her own voice, the third-person observational tone of the Taiwanese version allowed the writer, Yi Yi 憶漪, to narrate Xie's experience with a unique voice that was at once authoritative and yet absorbing. This mode of narration, of course, built on the earlier public image of Xie, who had been constantly portrayed as a nationally and transnationally significant figure but never for reasons acknowledged by herself. Although Jorgensen's full-length personal memoir was eventually published in 1967 and its film adaptation released in 1970, by that point Xie had lost all contact with the press and faded from the public sphere.[67] The final media blitz surrounding the Xie story occurred in the late 1950s, during which it was reported that Madame Chiang Kai-shek had visited her in Taipei and that she had begun working at the Ta Tung Relief

---

63. For voices that challenged the propriety and authority of the official report, pointing out that its explicit content was too invasive of Xie's privacy and that its "scientific" tone did not pay sufficient attention to Xie's post-op psychology, see, respectively, "Fabiao Xie Jianshun mimi weifan yishifa buwu shidangchu" [Publicizing Xie Jianshun's secret goes against the legal regulation of medicine], *Lianhebao*, October 29, 1955, no. 3; and "He yi wei Xie Jianshun" [How to console Xie Jianshun], *Lianhebao*, October 29, 1955, no. 3.

64. Yi Yi, "Xie Jianshun xiaojie de gushi" [The story of Miss Xie Jianshun], *Lianhebao*, October 13, 1955, no. 3; Yi Yi, "Xie Jianshun xiaojie de gushi" [The story of Miss Xie Jianshun], *Lianhebao*, October 28, 1955, no. 2.

65. Yi Yi, "Xie Jianshun xiaojie de gushi" [The story of Miss Xie Jianshun], *Lianhebao*, November 18, 1955, no. 2.

66. Quoted in Meyerowitz, *How Sex Changed*, 65.

67. Christine Jorgensen, *Christine Jorgensen: A Personal Autobiography* (San Francisco: Cleis Press, 2000 [1967]); *The Christine Jorgensen Story*, directed by Irving Rapper (Los Angeles: United Artists, 1970).

Institute for Women and Children (*Datong furu jiaoyang yuan* 大同婦孺教養院) under the new name Xie Shun 謝順 after *nine*, not four, surgeries.[68] Ever since the birth of "the Chinese Christine," the comparison of Xie to Jorgensen had intrigued, satisfied, and resonated with observers time and again, but never without its limits.

Conclusion

In their initial diagnoses of Xie, doctors frequently spoke of a hidden "female" sex. In contrast, the press provided a cultural space for him to articulate a past heterosexual romantic life and the desire of *not* wanting to change his sex in a masculinist voice. Early on, both medical and popular discourses adhered to a neutral position in discussing his psychological gender. Both discourses were fundamentally reoriented by the time of his first operation. The pre-op coverage of the details of his first surgery only foreshadowed a highly sensational outcome—the characterization of Xie as the "Chinese Christine," the first transsexual in Chinese society. By elevating Xie's iconic status as both the object of medical gaze and the specimen of (trans)cultural dissection, medical and popular discourses foreclosed any space of epistemic ambiguity concerning Xie's "innate" sex, gender, and sexuality. Many believed that Xie was destined to become a woman. Or, more aptly put, he became nothing but a transsexual star like the American Christine. In the following two years, the press covered Xie less and less, and began to report more widely on other surprising accounts of unusual bodily conditions. After her fourth surgery in May 1955, Xie's popularity as the first transsexual in Chinese culture, on top of these other pathological "symptoms" of postcolonial modernity, helped establish the global significance of Taiwan vis-à-vis the neocolonial hegemony of the United States.

In the spirit of marking out "a space in which unspoken stories and histories may be told, and to recognize and map the historically constituted cultural and political effects of the cold war,"[69] this chapter has raised a series of interrelated questions that challenge the various categorical assumptions that continue to haunt a "China-centered perspective."[70] Was Xie Jianshun's

---

68. "Xiri dabing tongzhi jianglai fulian huiyuan" [Former soldier comrade: A future member of women's association], *Lianhebao*, October 10, 1956, no. 3; "Yishi chuangzao nüren wunian duding qiankun" [Doctors building a woman: Sex determined in five years], *Lianhebao*, September 4, 1958, no. 4; "Xiri shachang zhanshi jinze jingru chuzi" [Former battle warrior: A present quiet virgin], *Lianhebao*, September 17, 1958, no. 4; "Xiaoyangnü Fu Xiuxia zhu Tatong Jiaoyangyuan" [Little girl Fu Xiuxia boarding Ta Tong Relief Institute], *Lianhebao*, June 7, 1959, no. 3; "Xie Jianshun guanxiongfu" [Xie Jianshun adjusting to feminine psyche], *Lianhebao*, November 11, 1959, no. 4.

69. Chen, *Asia as Method*, 120.

70. For a historiographical rendition of the "China-centered perspective," see Paul A. Cohen, *Discovering History in China: American Historical Writing on the Recent Chinese Past*, new ed. (New York: Columbia University Press, 2010 [1984]).

transsexuality "Chinese" or "American" in nature? Transsexuality in whose sense of the term? Was it a foreign import, an expression (and thus internalization) of Western imperialism, or a long-standing indigenous practice in a new light? How can we take the Republican state's administrative relocation in the late 1940s seriously? Is it possible to speak of a "Republican Chinese modernity" that challenges the familiar socialist narrative of twentieth-century Chinese history? Which China was alluded to by the Chinese-ness of the label "Chinese Christine"? In the yet-to-appear discourse of Taiwanese nativism, did the Republican regime exemplify settler colonialism, migration, immigration, or diaspora? To better comprehend the historical context, we might also ask "Is the [GMD] regime a government in exile (which would mean that it resides abroad), a regime from another province, a defeated regime, or simply a Cold War regime?"[71] Evidently, the complexity of the history far exceeds the common terms used to describe the historical characteristics of postwar Taiwan. To call the GMD a regime from the outside or a colonial government only partially accounts for its proto-Chineseness or extra-Chineseness, and precisely because of the lack of a precedent and analogous situation, it is all the more difficult to historicize, with neat categorical imperatives or ways of periodization, the social backdrop against which and the epistemic condition under which people began to talk about the first Chinese transsexual.

It is interesting to note that in the context of the 1950s, the Chinese term *bianxingren* carried almost none of the psychopathological connotations that distinguished its English counterpart, *transsexual*. This probably reflected the relatively late involvement of Taiwanese psychiatric experts in dealing with patients diagnosed with *bianxing yuzheng* (變性慾症, transsexualism).[72] In this regard, the national spotlight on the male-to-female (MTF) transsexual Jiang Peizhen 江佩珍 in 1981 opened a new chapter in the history of transsexuality in Taiwan that lies beyond the scope of this chapter (which concerns specifically its emergence). According to Jiang's psychiatrist and past superintendent of the Tsyr-Huey Mental Hospital in Kaohsiung County, Dr. Wen Jung-Kwang 文榮光, the story of Jiang Peizhen made a huge impact on enhancing the public awareness of transsexualism in Taiwan in the early 1980s. Her case pushed doctors, especially the psychiatrists, to come to terms with patients requesting sex reassignment or showing symptoms of gender identity disorder, and to consult the Harry Benjamin Standards of Care that had been adopted by American medical and psychological experts

---

71. Chen, *Asia as Method*, 154.
72. Hsu Su-Ting, "Bianxingyuzheng huanzhe bianxing shoushu hou de shenxin shehui shiying" [The physical, psychological and social adaptation among transsexuals after sex reassignment surgery: A study of six cases] (MA thesis, Kaohsiung Medical University, 1998).

since 1979.[73] Personal testimonies of transsexuals attested to the breadth, significance, and cultural reach of the Jiang story. Miss Lai 賴, a former MTF patient of Wen, noted how the possibility of sex reassignment surgeries was brought to her attention only by the time of the media coverage of Jiang.[74] In the 1980s, Xie Jianshun and her surgeons had disappeared altogether from the public sphere, and this seemed to confirm that one era had ended. For the new generation of transsexuals and doctors like Miss Lai and Wen, the hero(ine) from the 1980s onward was Jiang.[75]

Nevertheless, the saga of Xie Jianshun and other sex change reports that sprung up in the Taiwanese press exemplify the emergence of transsexuality as a form of modern sexual embodiment in Chinese-speaking society. Xie's story, in particular, became a lightning rod for many post–Second World War anxieties about gender and sexuality, and called dramatic attention to issues that would later drive the feminist and gay and lesbian movements in the decades ahead.[76] In a different way, these unprecedented stories of bodily transformation bring to light a genealogy that exceeds, even subverts, familiar historicizations of Taiwan's postcoloniality. They illustrate the ways in which the Chinese community in Taiwan inherited a Western biomedical epistemology of sex from not only the Japanese colonial regime (a conventional reading of Taiwan's colonial past), but also, more importantly, the intellectual complexity of the earlier scientific globalism that characterized the Republican period on the Mainland.[77] This genealogy from Republican-

73. Personal interview with Jung-Kwang Wen on March 20, 2008.
74. Personal interview with Miss Lai on March 22, 2008. I thank Dr. Wen for introducing me to Miss Lai.
75. See Josephine Ho, ed., *Kuaxingbie* [Transgender] (Jungli, Taiwan: National Central University Center for the Study of Sexualities, 2003); Liu Dao-Jie, "Biannan biannü bian bian bian" [Transsexualism and sex-reassignment surgery in Taiwan] (MA thesis, National Taiwan University, 1993). For a thick ethnographic study of contemporary transgender embodiment in Taiwan, see Josephine Ho, "Embodying Gender: Transgender Body/Subject Formations in Taiwan," *Inter-Asia Cultural Studies* 7(2) (2006): 228–42.
76. Yu Hsin-ting, "Taiwan zhanhou yiduanxing/shenti de guansu lishi: Yi tongxinglian han yinyangren weilie, 1950s–2008" [Regulating deviant sexualities and bodies in Taiwan, 1950s–2008: The cases of homosexuality and hermaphrodites] (MA thesis, Kaohsiung Medical University, 2009). It is interesting to note that Xie was never described as a "human prodigy" (*renyao* 人妖) in the Taiwanese press. On the history of this concept in postwar Taiwan, see Howard Chiang, "Archiving Peripheral Taiwan: The Prodigy of the Human and Historical Narration," *Radical History Review*, no. 120 (2014): 204–25.
77. On the legacy of Japanese colonialism in the healthcare system of postwar Taiwan, see, for example, Michael Shiyung Liu, "Zhanhou Taiwan yiliao yu gongwei tizhi de bianqian" [The transformation of medical care and public health regime in postwar Taiwan]. *Huazhong shifan daxue xuebao* 49(4) (2010): 76–83; Fu Daiwie, *Yaxiya de xinshenti: Xingbie, yiliao yu jindai Taiwan* [Assembling the new body: Gender/Sexuality, medicine, and modern Taiwan] (Taipei: Socio Publishing, 2005). On scientific globalism in Republican China, see Frank Dikötter, *Sex, Culture and Modernity in China* (Honolulu: University of Hawai'i Press, 1995); Danian Hu, *China and Albert Einstein: The Reception of the Physicist and His Theory in China, 1917–1979* (Cambridge: Harvard University Press, 2005); Frank Dikötter, *The Age of Openness: China before Mao* (Berkeley: University of California Press, 2008); Sigrid

era scientific modernity to postwar Taiwanese transsexuality, connected via the Sinitic language but also made possible culturally by the migration of over 1 million people from the Mainland in the late 1940s, underscores the ways in which the Nationalist government regained sovereignty in Taiwan beyond a monolithic framing of Japanese postcolonialism.[78] Parallel to British colonial Hong Kong, Taiwan experienced the highly institutionalized establishment of Western biomedical infrastructure under Japanese occupation.[79] In the 1950s, when Mao "nationalized" Chinese medicine in continental China, both Taiwan and Hong Kong represented the most advanced regions in modern Western medicine situated on the geo-margins of the Sinosphere.[80] Adding to its catalytic role in the transmission of Western biomedical knowledge and practice, British colonialism was instrumental for establishing Hong Kong as a more permissive cultural space when other

---

Schmalzer, *The People's Peking Man: Popular Science and Human Identity in Twentieth-Century China* (Chicago: University of Chicago Press, 2008); Chiang, "The Conceptual Contours of Sex in the Chinese Life Sciences"; Howard Chiang, "Epistemic Modernity and the Emergence of Homosexuality in China," *Gender and History* 22(3) (2010): 629–57; Tong Lam, *A Passion for Facts: Social Surveys and the Constructions of the Chinese Nation-State, 1900–1949* (Berkeley: University of California Press, 2011); Thomas Mullaney, *Coming to Terms with the Nation: Ethnic Classification in Modern China* (Berkeley: University of California Press, 2011); Grace Yen Shen, *Unearthing the Nation: Modern Geology and Nationalism in Republican China* (Chicago: University of Chicago Press, 2013); Bridie Andrews, *The Making of Modern Chinese Medicine* (Vancouver: University of British Columbia Press, 2014); Sean Hsiang-lin Lei, *Neither Donkey nor Horse: Medicine in the Struggle over China's Modernity* (Chicago: University of Chicago Press, 2014); and the essays in Jing Tsu and Benjamin A. Elman, eds., *Science and Technology in Modern China, 1880s–1940s* (Leiden: Brill, 2014).

78. For a detailed study of the Nationalist migration from mainland China to Taiwan, see Meng-Hsuan Yang, "The Great Exodus: Sojourn, Nostalgia, Return, and Identity Formation of Chinese Mainlanders in Taiwan, 1940s–2000s" (PhD diss., University of British Columbia, 2012).

79. See Michael Shiyung Liu, "1930 niandai rizhi shiqi Taiwan yixue de tezhi" [Taiwanese medicine during Japanese occupation in the 1930s], *Taiwan shi yanjiu* 4(1) (1998): 97–147; Michael Shiyung Liu, "Building a Strong and Healthy Empire: The Critical Period of Building Japanese Colonial Medicine in Taiwan," *Japanese Studies* 23(4) (2004): 301–13; Fan Yan-qiu, *Jibing, yixue yu zhimin xiandaixing: Rizhi Taiwan yixueshi* [Diseases, medicine, and colonial modernity: History of medicine in Japan-ruled Taiwan] (Taipei: Daw Shiang Publishing, 2006); Michael Shiyung Liu, *Prescribing Colonization: The Role of Medical Practice and Policy in Japan-Ruled Taiwan* (Ann Arbor, MI: Association for Asian Studies, 2009); Hui-yu Caroline Ts'ai, *Taiwan in Japan's Empire-Building: An Institutional Approach to Colonial Engineering* (New York: Routledge, 2009). Although the activities of the Canadian missionary George E. Mackay represent an effort to introduce modern Western biomedicine to Taiwan before Japanese colonialism, many critics have pointed out its limited role in the formation of Taiwan's modernity. On Mackay's activities, see Fu, *Yaxiya de xinshenti*, chapter 2. On the issue of Mackay's representativeness, see Daiwie Fu, "How Far Can East Asian STS Go? A Position Paper," *East Asian Science, Technology and Society* 1(1) (2007): 7.

80. On the nationalization of Chinese medicine in early communist China, see Kim Taylor, *Chinese Medicine in Early Communist China, 1945–1963: A Medicine of Revolution* (New York: Routledge, 2005). For a recent study of "the Sinosphere" vis-à-vis Japan, see Joshua A. Fogel, *Articulating the Sinosphere: Sino-Japanese Relations in Space and Time* (Cambridge, MA: Harvard University Press, 2009).

parts of mainland China were strictly governed by a socialist state.[81] These historical factors thus allowed for the immense media publicity showered on Xie Jianshun and sex change more broadly. Together, the rapid technology transfer of Western biomedicine and the availability of a fairly open social and cultural milieu enabled the Sinophone articulation of transsexuality to emerge first and foremost across the postcolonial East Asian Pacific Rim.

81. John M. Carroll, *A Concise History of Hong Kong* (Lanham, MD: Rowman and Littlefield, 2007), 140–66. For examples of queer cultural production in Hong Kong in the 1960s, see Weixing shiguan zhaizhu, *Zhongguo tongxinglian mishi* [The secret history of Chinese homosexuality], 2 vols. (Hong Kong: Yuzhou chuban, 1964 and 1965). Scholars have begun to reconceptualize the history of love, intimacy, and sexuality in socialist China, but most revisionist readings are limited to discussions of heteronormative desires. See Men Yue, "Female Images and National Myth," in *Gender Politics in Modern China: Writing and Feminism*, ed. Tani Barlow (Durham, NC: Duke University Press, 1993), 118–36; Harriet Evans, *Women and Sexuality in China: Female Sexuality and Gender Since 1949* (New York: Continuum International Publishing Group, 1996); Wendy Larson, "Never So Wild: Sexing the Cultural Revolution," *Modern China* 25(4) (1999): 423–50; Emily Honig, "Socialist Sex: The Cultural Revolution Revisited," *Modern China* 29(2) (2003): 153–75; Yunxian Yan, *Private Life under Socialism: Love, Intimacy, Family Change in a Chinese Village, 1949–1999* (Stanford: Stanford University Press, 2003); Everett Zhang, "Rethinking Sexual Repression in Maoist China: Ideology, Structure, and the Ownership of the Body," *Body and Society* 11(3) (2005): 1–25.

9
Providing Reassurance and Affirmation

Masculinity, Militarization, and Refashioning a Male
Role in South Korean Family Planning, 1962 to the late
1980s

John P. DiMoia

Conflicting Messages (1973)

By the early to mid-1970s, nearly a decade after the introduction of a vigorous
family planning (FP) campaign (1964) in South Korea, efforts headed by
the Planned Parenthood Federation of Korea (PPFK) and its international
partners were just beginning to settle into a routine cycle of practice.[1] A host
of actors—from high-level demographers and social scientists to members
of Mothers' Clubs and the target population, rural villagers—mobilized and
distributed birth control technologies (intrauterine devices [IUDs]), birth
control pills, condoms, and contraceptive foam) to reach as many sectors
of society as possible, with rural residents increasingly the focus of attention, especially as FP became subsumed under the rubric of the emerging
Saemaul Undong (New Village movement).[2] Limitations of literacy and a
weak communications infrastructure continued to hinder outreach, and
planners of the program had recognized this development late in the preceding decade (1968), mobilizing the Mothers' Clubs specifically to provide
villagers with direct access to critical information through human contact,
preferably an individual known to them through existing social networks
within the village hierarchy.[3]

---

1. The Planned Parenthood Federation of Korea (PPFK), *The 10 (Ten)-Year History of Family
    Planning in Korea* (Seoul, 1976). See also Eunkyoung Bae, *Human Reproduction in the Korean
    Modernity* (Seoul: Sigan-yeohaeng, 2012), especially for Bae's critical reading from a Korean
    feminist perspectives.
2. For the original focus on rural residents, Dr. Jae-mo Yang of Yonsei University carried out
    the Koyang Study: Sook Bang, Man Gap Lee, and Jae-mo Yang, "A Survey of Fertility and
    Attitude toward Family Planning in Rural Korea," *Yonsei Medical Journal* 4(1) (December
    1963): 77–102. FP preceded the New Village movement but gradually became absorbed
    within the scope of the new program over the course of the early 1970s.
3. Mothers' Clubs first began operations in 1968, although, arguably, they had a precedent in
    the formation of similar groups in preceding decades. See Sonja Myung Kim, "Contesting
    Bodies: Managing Population, Birthing, and Medicine in Korea, 1876–1945" (PhD diss.,

In keeping with the emphasis on ease of access and basic forms of communication, the majority of the materials and publicity associated with FP provided highly visual contents, with text offered almost exclusively in hangul, the Korean script used for everyday communication, as opposed to the more sophisticated, literary *hanja* (Chinese characters).[4] With this approach, PPFK hoped to send a comforting message of convenience, urging greater control of one's life by having fewer children and raising each with a greater share of household income. To make these aims comprehensible, the social science informing FP was often idealized in the rural villager's mind, with the birth control pill associated specifically with the rising and setting of the sun (daily cycle), and future earnings linked to additional bags of rice (agricultural equivalence) that a family might purchase.[5]

Within this idealized dynamic of communication between the PPFK and the state on the one hand, and South Korean villagers on the other, there remained many points of tension, and this observation holds true particularly in terms of the use of birth control technologies provided through FP. There were many instances of dropouts in the mid-1960s IUD campaigns (1964–1968). One example saw rural women accepting the use of the Lippes loop initially, only to withdraw from the program shortly thereafter, citing a wide variety of physical and psychological symptoms.[6] In fact, the sharp decline in "acceptors," as characterized by the program, was one of the major factors informing the creation of the new clubs that targeted village women. Another key issue lay with patterns of communication in families, as males continued to function, at least nominally, as the head of household, wanting to direct or participate in any decision making. The role of the male, in other words, remained undefined and very much in transition, as the state sought new ways to extend the appeal of its message.

In a society undergoing rapid change, with large numbers of people migrating to cities, and with industrial jobs beginning to replace agrarian

---

University of California, Los Angeles, 2008). For an account of village life, see Vincent S. R. Brandt, *An Affair with Korea* (Seattle: University of Washington Press, 2015), an ethnography of an East Coast fishing area undergoing rapid transition in 1966.

4. For example, *Happy Home*, which began its publication and distribution in 1968, appeared exclusively in hangul, and its cover page featured an explicit reference appealing to its target demographic, rural residents.

5. This type of concern was not unique to Korea and can easily be found in RAC (Rockefeller Archive Center) materials for related FP sites like Taiwan. Taiwan (especially the city of Taichung) served as a model for South Korea in the early 1960s, and Japan also played an active role in shaping Korean FP.

6. "Family Planning and Workers Creed," in PC FC # 61, Population Council, Accession #2, Rockefeller Archive Center (RAC), p. 1. This document explained to FP workers that they might have to advise acceptance of IUD technology to a female user whose body would reject it and rationalized the pain in terms of the larger goals of the program. See Chikako Takeshita (University of California, Riverside) on the international history of the IUD: *The Global Biopolitics of the IUD: How Science Constructs Contraceptive Users and Women's Bodies* (Cambridge, MA: MIT Press, 2011).

forms of labor, the role of the male was no longer entirely clear.[7] On the surface, the dominant male image was one embodying conspicuous strength and vitality, the message of a state promoting an aggressively anti-Communist ethic, and one also requiring military conscription. Moreover, South Korea had recently chosen to participate in the Vietnam War (1965–1973), signaling its intent through the dispatch of medical and logistical support forces as early as September 1964.[8] At the same time, though, this outwardly aggressive, largely conventional message was challenged by the social science language of family planning, which requested that husbands engage with their wives in joint decision making and, more importantly, indicated that they might need to curb their sexual activity, or at the very least, redirect its intent. The idea that Korean men should voluntarily limit their desire to father children was quite radical and needed careful presentation to gain acceptance.

One possible way to mobilize popular support behind the desired goal of male participation in FP involved the mobilization of celebrities as part of the campaign, and this style of publicity began to appear in sponsored publications starting in the early 1970s. The magazine *Happy Home* (rendered in Korean as 가정의벗, literally, "Friend of the home") first appeared in 1968, with substantial financial support from Sweden International Development Agency underwriting its publication costs.[9] By the following decade, a typical ad might include a famous athlete or a popular figure, with one such effort invoking the singer Kim Yong Man (김용만) and his deliberate choice to participate in family planning.[10] While the ad did not specify the means by which Mr. Kim had achieved his goal, it carefully noted his singular child and depicted father and child standing together prominently in the foreground, making to all appearances a happy family. Here the emphasis rested less on the masculinity of the central figure but more on his willing sacrifice, eagerly complying with collective goals, despite his obvious social status.

Certainly, this style of appeal represented one alternative, but it did not offer any immediate plan of action, something practical that Korean men could do to show their willingness to participate. From the inception of the national FP campaign in 1964, condoms were included on the "menu" of available birth control items, but this scheme had only a limited degree of success. Still, the major thrust of FP continued to rest with the types of birth

---

7. Valerie Gelézeau, *Ap'at'ŭ Konghwaguk: P'ŭrangsŭ chiri hakcha ka pon Han'guk ŭi ap'at'ŭ* [On the republic of apartments] (Seoul: Humanitas Press, 2007).

8. Frank Baldwin, Diane Jones, and Michael Jones, *America's Rented Troops: South Koreans in Vietnam* (Philadelphia: American Friends Service Committee, 197–). The September 1964 date marks the arrival of the first Korean MASH unit based at Vung Tau (Southeast Coast, close to Saigon), taking place prior to the subsequent arrival of troops in 1965.

9. *Happy Home*, largely visual and offered in hangul, was targeted specifically to the concerns and aspirations of rural residents.

10. *Happy Home*, Special Collections, Yonsei University Library.

control technologies—the Lippes loop (1964), the pill (1968), contraceptive foam—that could easily be distributed to women and then tracked, with the cost of these items partially subsidized by a range of international partners.[11] If South Korean men were to participate actively, a different approach was needed, and indeed, this issue was not unique to the Republic of Korea (ROK); eliciting a male response was frequently a topic of discussion within international family planning circles.

In the South Korean case, family planning dates back to the early 1960s, with Park Chung Hee (1961–1979) mandating the introduction of a campaign at the national level from 1962 and the distribution of birth control technologies from 1964. This is not to forget precedents established during the lengthy period of Japanese colonial rule (1910–1945), and, indeed, a small subset of missionary interests continued to advocate for such a program during the later stages of President Rhee Syngman's administration (1948–1960) following the Korean War (1950–1953).[12] If Park's decision to move forward was not necessarily "new," at least in the strictest sense, it fit nicely within a corresponding set of regional and international interests that urged the adoption of such schemes for developing nations. For East Asia more broadly, both Japan and Taiwan preceded the ROK in setting up their own programs, and the Taiwanese program in particular, especially with its model based at Taichung, informed a great deal of the early Korean policy-making.[13] With international partners such as the Population Council funding the distribution of new birth control technologies, these early programs in East Asia were largely quantitative in their conception: the technologies would be distributed to women ("acceptors"), their use tracked,

11. International partners for South Korean FP included the Population Council (Rockefeller), the Ford Foundation, Sweden International Development Agency, Japanese assistance through JOICFP (Japan Organization for International Cooperation in Family Planning), and any number of university-based demography centers, especially the Population Studies Center at the University of Michigan, famous for its work in Taiwan, under the leadership of Dr. Ron Freedman. For the international story of funding patterns and outreach to Asia, see Matthew Connelly, *Fatal Misconception: The Struggle to Control World Population* (Cambridge, MA: Harvard University Press, 2007).

12. Sonja Kim, "Contesting Bodies." The timeline for the Korean FP campaign at the national level covers: (1) the 1960s (1962–1970, development and expansion), (2) the consolidation stage taking place during much of the 1970s, and (3) the scaling down/reshaping in the late 1980s, with recognition that the replacement rate had already been passed early in the decade (1983). See Warren C. Robinson and John A. Ross, eds., *The Global Family Planning Revolution: Three Decades of Population Policies* (Washington, DC: IBRD: 2007). See especially Chapter 11, "The Korean Breakthrough," for the standard narrative, and p. 178 contains a concise (1961–1975) time line of major developments.

13. Ronald Freedman, *Family Planning in Taiwan: An Experiment in Social Change* (Princeton: Princeton University Press, 1969). Freedman's group at the University of Michigan was important for Taiwan and South Korea. For more on the Taiwan FP program, see the PhD dissertation of Yuling Huang, State University of New York–Binghamton, and, for Japan, see the work of Aya Homei, "Modernising Midwifery: The History of a Female Medical Profession in Japan, 1868-1931" (PhD diss., Manchester University, 2003).

and an expected decline in fertility would follow, with the entire scheme coded in the language of modernization theory.[14] Implicitly, the governing assumption of the planners, whether domestic or international, was to focus on a rural, female population as the primary means to achieve change.

From behavioral modification to bodily intervention: Refashioning the message

This chapter takes as its focus the related questions of how and why Korean men came to form a substantial part of the FP campaigns by the early to mid-1970s, precisely at a later, transitional stage in Korean FP, a time when masculinity, male gender roles, and the popular image of the Korean male were in the process of being openly challenged and dramatically reshaped. From the hypermasculine Korean male associated with his participation in the Vietnam War, a deliberate embrace of anti-Communist, patriotic values, to the "industrial warriors" associated with rapid ROK economic growth, Korean boys, young men, and adult males faced increasing pressure to conform and adapt their behavior to a range of socially prescribed roles.[15] At the same time, the FP program, nearly a decade into its tenure, encouraged the channeling of reproductive energies to other pursuits and provided a range of incentives, among these financial and housing, to elicit a greater percentage of participation.[16] In other words, the Korean male received a contradictory set of messages from the state and its affiliated actors, simultaneously encouraged to be strong and virile—especially while fighting, living, and working abroad—while also taking a much more responsible stance, one of caution, reflection, even nurturing, when at home.[17]

More specifically, the second part of this ethic was made possible through a set of new medical interventions, with the condom maintained as an available item through the late 1960s, but one soon to be replaced by a more convenient surgical option: vasectomy first began to appear as an option or voluntary choice roughly midway through the decade, and we will consider its implications through the central figure of Dr. Lee Hee Yong (이희

---

14. The KAP (Knowledge Attitude Practice) surveys conducted in many countries embody this theme. The idea was that villagers would inevitably practice family planning once educated about it (knowledge causes a change in attitude and thereby leads to the adoption of new forms of practice).

15. The term "industrial warriors" may apply to Korean women working in factories, especially in the textile industry, but I am referring here to the male side of the story, especially during Korea's economic transition from the 1960s onward.

16. The types of incentives will be discussed briefly in the section "The Home Reserve Army Meets (Male) Family Planning."

17. Working abroad for Korean men also became a realistic option with the first construction ventures in Southeast Asia (Thailand, Vietnam) during the late 1960s and later in the Middle East in the 1970s (Saudi Arabia, Iran, Iraq).

영) of Seoul National University Hospital (SNUH), one of its major advocates and practitioners.[18] Operating on a wide range of subjects, Dr. Lee sought not only to master the procedure and its immediate post-op complications, but also to understand the particular constellation of physical and psychological symptoms that he might expect to encounter. Moreover, as his patient base grew, he developed an increasing confidence in the procedure as a quick and efficient means to remediate the issue of South Korean family size, recognizing that this option could give men greater control over their lives through an effective impediment to pregnancy.

If Dr. Lee's efforts focused almost exclusively on the surgical procedure itself as a craft and, specifically, how to perform the operation more capably and effectively, he could not carry his project much beyond the immediate confines of Seoul National University Hospital. For this to happen, the procedure had to become an essential part of the social fabric of FP, and the message needed to be disseminated at the mass level. Certainly male FP formed a small part of the program from its inception (1962–1965), with projected goals set for voluntary vasectomy, but this effort proved a much harder sell than the comparable distribution of IUDs and birth control pills. In its promotional materials, the PPFK and its public health partners required a simple message capable of convincing males that the procedure was both effective and routine, not something to be overly concerned about. Moreover, the message openly embraced a contradiction by the early 1970s, emphasizing the effectiveness of birth control, while also assuring the prospective patient of his undiminished virility and masculinity.[19]

Two related measures made possible the dramatic transformation of the public image of vasectomy over the course of a decade. First, when Dr. Lee considered the psychological effects of the surgery, his aim was not simply a concern over his patients' immediate welfare. Instead, it invoked a much longer history in which vasectomy was linked to notions of criminality and a lack of mental fitness. In perfecting the surgery, therefore, Dr. Lee sought to establish its appropriateness for a much wider patient base, rendering it useful as a birth control method. Second, if the aim of normalization could be accomplished, the burden of FP practice would become much easier, a task to be handled through bodily modification to the male organ. Reassuring the male patient of his ongoing potency, the campaign shifted its attention to the incentives attached to the procedure, making the decision a relatively easy one. This procedure would not require extensive self-discipline or a

---

18. Dr. Lee published a significant number of studies in the *Korean Journal of Urology* beginning in the early 1960s.

19. While I have been unable to locate video-related materials for the vasectomy campaigns, I have heard numerous apocryphal stories from Korean academics about the use of cigarettes in the popular imagery (TV commercials) to suggest the ease of the surgery, as well as undiminished potency.

significant change to one's routine: the task could be accomplished with a minimum of pain and very little expenditure of time.

To be fair, however, the message was not necessarily an easy sell even in its refashioned version. The numbers of voluntary vasectomy in the 1960s tended to remain low, and the procedure was also not without controversy, conflated in the popular imagination with castration and, equally, associated with criminal or deviant behavior. For Dr. Lee, challenging this larger set of associations would have to wait, as his primary interest lay with mastering the surgery as a form of practice and considering its psychological effects upon the patient base. What made a difference in finally moving vasectomy to the center, ultimately, was the heated ideological context of the late 1960s and early 1970s, especially as the effects of the demographic transition taking place began to make their presence known. State FP planners, eager to continue this trend and still fearing a reversal, sought new ways to expand the demographics beyond the initial target of a female, rural population base.

Moreover, the mechanisms by which this reformulated message was distributed would soon find an effective means, as South Korea's standard policy of military conscription offered a convenient vehicle for FP pedagogy, potentially reaching all males at a relatively young age. The formation of the Home Reserve Army (*yebigun* 예비군) in April 1968 captured a distinct audience with a uniquely patriotic fervor, as these soldiers were mobilized in the aftermath of two related incidents.[20] First, North Korean commandos mounted a night assault on the South Korean Blue House in January 1968, famously coming within several hundred meters of the site; and, later that same year, an attack took place on two East Coast border towns.[21] In April, the ROK created the Home Reserve, a civil defense force, with the stated aim of protecting the domestic sphere, while also mobilizing the entire population against North Korea. In this context, the FP education offered to young ROK soldiers held a message binding the individual to the nation, asking him for great personal sacrifice, even after being decommissioned and returning to civilian life.

Through this joint combination of pragmatism and patriotism, the choice soon became a preferred option among Korean men, increasing in its popularity in the early to mid-1970s, and going on to reach a peak in the heated, ideological atmosphere of the early to mid-1980s. As with circumcision, another practice common to Korean males, the decision to opt for this choice was likely motivated less by a careful evaluation of the biomedical criteria involved, and more by the growing support infrastructure, in addition to

---

20. http://www.yebigun1.mil.kr/. Accessed March 14, 2014.
21. Ibid.

accompanying peer pressure.[22] By the mid to late 1980s, voluntary steriliza-tion of this type made up more than 10 percent of the Korean male demo-graphic for FP, with much of this activity linked to military service and the subsequent transition to civilian life.[23] The paradox of a strident masculinity linked to a convenient surgical option captures the curious, hybrid character of emerging South Korean modernity, with ease and access serving to high-light the defining features of its elusive appeal.

Constructing Urology: Refining Surgical Practice and Medical Professionalization (1957 to late 1960s)

Adapting international biomedical models

Prior to considering the target population, it helps to recognize that the South Korean medical community was undergoing its own series of trans-formations following the experience of the Korean War (1950–1953). From a limited profession open to only an elite few during the colonial period (1910–1945), biomedicine began to provide more opportunities with the war, both in terms of hands-on clinical experience brought through combat, and also in terms of overseas scholarship and professional opportunities. Following the war, hospital facilities like those based at SNUH and Yonhi College received extensive sources of international financial assistance to be put toward the purchase of new equipment and to augment existing medical pedagogy, still based heavily on Japanese imperial models.[24] The decade following the war brought large numbers of foreign medical personnel to Seoul as part of the rebuilding process, with Seoul National University forming a joint relation-ship with the University of Minnesota, one of the key areas centering on the exchange of surgical specialization.[25]

In fact, the Department of Surgery at SNUH did not possess specific areas of specialization late in the 1950s, although this would change rapidly as visiting Minnesota personnel began to teach and perform a series of demonstration surgeries.[26] Two areas in particular, thoracic surgery and neu-rosurgery, gained a good deal of attention under the leadership provided

---

22. Genaro Castro-Vazquez, *Male Circumcision in Japan* (New York: Palgrave Macmillan, 2015), 170–71.

23. These figures peaking in the mid-1980s suggest a highly effective bureaucracy, without any single causal or explanatory factor.

24. Neil L. Gault, "Korea—a New Venture in International Medical Education," *University of Minnesota Medical Bulletin* 33 (November 1961): 73–85.

25. "How the U Helps Seoul University Rebuild after the Ravages of War," *Minnesotan* 10(3) (December 1956): 3–7, 11, 14–15.

26. These surgeries generally took place between about 1957 and 1960, as Minnesota faculty members sought to convey surgical techniques to their Korean counterparts. At the same time, Korean doctors and nurses were training in Minneapolis. The two sides of this project came together after 1962 in Seoul.

respectively by Drs. George Schimert and Lyle French, with Korean surgeons taking over these programs early in the following decade.[27] For a young surgeon like Lee Hee Yong, this was an extremely exciting time to become a medical practitioner, with professional opportunities to build a career and develop new forms of practice taking place much more rapidly than had been possible previously. In the *Korean Journal of Urology*, which began publication in 1960, the first references to vasectomy appeared in 1961, coinciding with the growth of the new field and, more specifically, corresponding to the frenzy of clinical activity taking place at the hospital.[28]

At this early stage, vasectomy formed only one small part of family planning, and the specifics of working out the procedure involved a good deal of work on animal subjects, more readily available and much easier to experiment with than human subjects.[29] Indeed, this form of practice was not unique to South Korea, and, moreover, other surgical programs at the hospital followed a similar pattern, with the thoracic surgery program developing its cardiac surgery efforts by exploring cross-circulation techniques with dogs.[30] Even though different groups emphasized highly specific sets of surgical techniques, the hospital maintained a single General Surgery Department for bureaucratic purposes, meaning that doctors shared a common home and likely had the opportunity to share their experiences outside of the operating theater. The close of the Minnesota Project (1954–1962), which came in 1962 when the new government of Park Chung Hee declined to renew the exchange relationship, did not end these efforts; in fact, Korean medicine continued to learn and develop its ambitions well into the decade.[31]

Even prior to the official start of the national FP program (1964), there were efforts to conduct pilot studies for some portion of its techniques, and this holds true for vasectomy, which first became available through a government subsidy in 1962.[32] From this point forward, the Department of Urology at SNUH needs to be distinguished from the FP campaigns per se, as the latter proceeded to move much more rapidly in expanding its coverage, even as the former group sought to provide as safe and painless an experience as possible. Of course, this implies the possibility of conflict between the two agendas, so we need to be conscious that many of the vasectomies performed under the FP banner took place in rural villages under less than ideal

27. The 9th Meeting of the William T. Peyton Society, Honoring the Contributions of Lyle A. French, Saturday August 27, 2005, McNamara Alumni Center, Minneapolis, Minnesota.
28. http://kjurology.org/, accessed March 14, 2014.
29. H. Y. Lee, "Clinical Studies on the Influences of Vasectomy," *Korean Journal of Urology* 7(1) (1966): 11–29.
30. This work took place under the direction of Dr. Young-Gyun Lee of the Thoracic Surgery program at SNUH.
31. Most of the surgical subspecialties at SNUH would begin to claim their labels as of the late 1960s and the early 1970s.
32. H. Y. Lee, "Clinical Studies on the Influences of Vasectomy," 17.

circumstances.[33] Mobile vans began to convey reproductive technologies and follow-up visits to many villages from 1966, and this network was likely the first point of contact for many of the would-be volunteers.[34] In short, the controlled, sterile experience at SNUH remained quite distinct from that of rural Korea, where much of the actual work of FP was taking place. The material realities of clinical practice in South Korea were based on a limited set of tools, with local clinics and facilities frequently used as a contingency measure.

Keeping this distinction in mind, surgical conditions at the hospital improved throughout the decade because of both the greater depth of knowledge acquired by Korean doctors and the various forms of material assistance provided by foreign partners. In the absence of the departed Minnesota partners, doctors from Seoul National University had access to other international collaborators and their new approaches. First, Minnesota had introduced a system of residents, clerks, and interns late in the previous decade (1957–1959), and, at least in theory, the working environment for junior practitioners was now less hierarchical and much more collaborative.[35] Certainly opportunities for clinical experience were much greater than had been possible two decades earlier, when students could only watch anatomy demonstrations, with little or no chance to gain hands-on practice. Moreover, the creation of a National Medical Center (국립의료원), another project initiated following the Korean War, meant that a large number of Scandinavian doctors and nurses worked in Seoul for much of the decade, departing only in the late 1960s (1958–1971).[36]

For the vasectomy procedure, work with animals (rats, dogs) continued through the middle of the decade, and human subjects came into the picture as well (1962–1965), with two distinct streams of patients noted upon intake: (1) those paying out of pocket for the procedure and (2) those willingly accepting the benefits of the government-subsidized program.[37] While their motivations may have shared a similar basis, the conspicuous

---

33. This coincided with the emphasis on rural areas beginning in 1966. "Korea, Family Planning Program—Historical Review," in "Paul Hartman, 1967–1968," Box 26/FC, Population Council, Accession #2, RAC.

34. Paul Hartman's accounts of this activity are quite vivid in describing the work of FP in improvised outdoor conditions or temporarily arranged structures such as a tent or hut.

35. William F. Maloney, "Report of Observations as Adviser in Medicine," July 1, 1956; Edmund B. Flink, "Report and Recommendations on Teaching and Research in Internal Medicine," February 1, 1958; E. P. Brown, "Report of Observation and Activities as Adviser in Medicine," January 24, 1959; Glenn R. Mitchell, "Report on the Seoul National University Hospital," 1958; James H. Matthews, "Final Report of Observations and Recommendations," November 7, 1958, all in Special Collections, University of Minnesota. In total, eleven Minnesota advisers spent time in Seoul.

36. *The National Medical Center in Korea: A Scandinavian Contribution to Medical Training and Health Development, 1958–1968* (Oslo: Universitetsforlaget, 1971).

37. H. Y. Lee, "Clinical Studies," 17.

economic differences between these two groups introduce the obvious question concerning the role of class. In addition, what appears consistently in this and a series of follow-up studies is an emphasis on the immediate psychological effects of the procedure and its implications for any subsequent forms of treatment. Phrases like "psychological instability" and references to a decrease in sexual desire raised concerns about post-op effects, and there was already a need for a presurgical consult at this early stage, a meeting designed to allay any concerns on the part of the subject.[38] As noted previously, these concerns likely reflect a much older history in which the procedure was linked with notions of curbing criminal behavior.

As we have seen, the subject population varied widely according to the two different schemes, suggesting at least some element of class implicit to the government's subsidy scheme. Moreover, it is possible to offer some basic generalizations about demographics. Members of the self-funded, or "private," patient group, tended to self-identify with "commerce" as their primary means of employment and were typically married for slightly longer than a decade before seeking a medical consultation.[39] In other words, these were Korean men with a fairly successful, or at least steady, career, with a growing family, who were seeking to limit or control their family size in the future. In contrast to this first group of about 15,000 men, the subsidy patients were generally more diverse and outnumbered the private group by a ratio of approximately 4 to 1 (60,000).[40] Both groups averaged in their early forties in terms of age, with the subsidy group having on average more children. From the perspective of the FP planners, the need for the program was obvious, with even the private group having between four and five children per household.

If the evaluative language used to address these two populations upon intake proves fascinating in itself, the situation becomes even more interesting when we examine how the procedure was characterized and then repackaged as a convenient form of surgery to this target public. As noted previously, a pre-op consultation was considered routine as a screening procedure, especially to check for signs of excessive concern or possible psychological issues. The chief motivation at this point was to assure patients of the safety and reliability of the procedure, along with its convenience and relative ease. In the first half of the decade, therefore, the analogy used to accomplish this task offered a comparison between the male body and a watermelon: "seminal fluid of the vasectomized and non-vasectomized man might be compared with watermelon with seed and without seed."[41] The comparison to the fruit was designed to provide reassurance of their absolute

---

38. Ibid., 25.
39. Ibid., 18.
40. Ibid., 19.
41. Ibid., 17. This analogy and its use was Dr. Lee's own creation.

equivalence, especially following the surgery: "the size, color, shape, smell, sweetness etcetera are quite the same [with] each other."[42]

Although we should not read too much into the selection of the watermelon as the basis of comparison, it does suggest an appeal directed at the subsidy group, rather than the private patients, with its conjoined emphasis on agriculture and botany. Historian Tae-ho Kim of Hanyang University has pointed out the introduction of the seedless watermelon in the South Korean context, a development associated with the scientist and botanist Woo Jang-Choon in the postwar period.[43] Dr. Woo used this seedless watermelon specifically to demonstrate the power of modern biological science following the Korean War. In effect, along with its obvious appeal and widespread popularity, the seedless watermelon likely held a particular form of nationalist appeal to South Koreans, making Dr. Kim's analogy plausible. Finally, along with this loose analogy, the early vasectomy project also placed a particular emphasis on time: "It will take about one cigarette smoke (ten to twenty minutes) to complete the operation."[44] In both cases, the stress on a combination of ease, convenience, and practicality suggests a procedure that was being prepared for introduction to a wider audience.

The emphasis on ease and convenience also underscores the troubling reality of a procedure that remained very much in process throughout the decade. That is, there was a conspicuous gap between what doctors acknowledged privately about their work in progress and the stable image they mobilized publicly as part of the FP campaigns. For his own part, Dr. Lee continued to develop his interest in refining the surgery, even as he explored other options simultaneously. Beginning in the mid-1960s (1966), he started to perform vasovasostomy (reversal of vasectomy) on a trial basis, operating on an extremely limited number of patients, certainly in comparison to his vasectomy population.[45] This pursuit indicates an interest in all matters concerning fertility, and it also hints at anxieties within the program, as Dr. Lee recognized that not every patient would be satisfied, and some might want to pursue alternatives.

Tensions within the Program: (1) Material Lack and (2) Expertise in Process

This last observation anticipates the availability of a larger program, including the required medical infrastructure, a set of doctors fully trained to handle the procedure, and the presence of sufficient support personnel.

---

42. Ibid.
43. Personal communication, Tae-ho Kim, Hanyang University.
44. H. Y. Lee, "Clinical Studies," 16.
45. H. Y. Lee, "A Twenty Year Experience with Vasovasostomy," *The Journal of Urology* 136(2) (September 1986): 413–15.

As noted earlier, Dr. Lee was in the process of making the transition from working with animals to working with humans when the subsidy program began in 1962, and he continued to refine his practice throughout the decade. Vasectomy was by no means a complete or fully regulated surgical procedure in the Korean context, and it remained very much a work in progress, with the subsidy program essentially mirroring the work of a clinical trial conducted on a national scale. The first half of the decade a total of 497 doctors enrolled as part of the subsidy program, training them to perform the surgery on a contractual basis, with each procedure providing a fee of 500 won upon referral.[46] Although the majority of these doctors "were not specialists in urology or surgery," they assumed the burden of the task to the best of their ability.[47]

The site(s) at which these doctors performed their work does not receive attention, although this concern, too, should fall within the scope of our inquiry. In terms of region and geography, the program's official claim was that "[doctors] [we]re distributed evenly throughout the country," meaning that access was likely not an issue.[48] At the same time, it is reasonable to speculate about differences in quality with respect to site location, especially in terms of relative proximity to a major urban area.[49] Certainly by 1966, with the use of mobile vans, it is easy to find accounts of a vasectomy being performed in a rural area on a strictly outpatient basis, with doctors using either a temporary structure (e.g., a tent or hut) or a local building temporarily transformed into a mobile clinic.[50] The scaling up to a national program severely strained the material infrastructure of the PPFK for its birth control distribution program, and it is only fair to make similar estimates about the structures in place for the male side of the program, especially as this dimension did not receive major emphasis.

Moreover, the psychological side of the surgery placed an additional strain on available resources, both in terms of the need for a pre-op consultation and also in terms of subsequent follow-up work. At the program's inception, the consultation was used to perform preliminary screening work, as well as to provide a baseline form of public education, informing patients about the procedure to follow. As outlined previously, a special point of emphasis here was the relatively benign nature of the procedure, as well as further clarification about how it differed from the act of castration, with both of these measures meant to reassure the prospective client. Despite this proactive stance, however, the program found that vasectomy tended to correlate with a host of psychological symptoms, including among these

---

46. H. Y. Lee, "Clinical Studies," 17. This was the equivalent of about US$2.00.
47. Ibid.
48. Ibid.
49. The urban-rural divide for the relative distribution of doctors in Korea has a lengthy history.
50. Again, Hartman's accounts as an FP representative in country capture this.

some forms of depression and anxiety. Classifying this cluster of behaviors under the broad category "sterilization neurosis," Dr. Lee and his colleagues argued that the best solution at this point was an even more careful pre-screening regimen, that is, seeking to remove from the demographic those likely to develop such issues.

Even with these precautions, and with an increased scrutiny of possible subjects at intake, the program still found that psychological and physical complaints continued to accumulate through the mid-1960s. In his publications, Dr. Lee had to acknowledge that "male sterilization can often have a profound emotional impact," noting further that "there is an element of self-destruction through self-castration by its equivalent sterilization, and there are invariably deeper and usually unconscious reasons for the operation."[51] Moreover, the differences between the two patient groups remained conspicuous, although Dr. Lee attributed this less to a nuanced understanding of class, and more to the "low education and low income of the subsidized group."[52] Surprisingly, he admitted the problems associated with medical training and infrastructure, critiquing the "unsatisfactory operative technique of the designated doctors." This last remark appears to be less that of a specialist guarding his area of expertise and is perhaps more typical of the growing pains encountered as the program began to take on national implications.

The strains that the Vietnam War placed on the nation's nascent medical infrastructure at about this time may also have played a role, with doctors and medical personnel included among those sent to the theater. For the first time since the Korean War, families had to experience the trauma of a returning loved one sealed in a coffin, and the sight of such bodies, while not yet entirely familiar, became a little less strange. At the same time, the need for blood, plasma, and related supplies also became critical, and blood drives targeting specific populations—housewives, college students—became quite common by the second half of the decade.[53] In other words, the Korean medical system experienced severe strains on its capabilities. Although family planning was a national priority, it is not surprising that the training for this specific type of surgery was not very extensive.

Where vasectomy would soon become useful, however, was at the return end of this cycle, with the resumption of civilian life. Here, as soldiers returned home with thoughts of family and employment, the ROK military politely informed them of the possible choices and options available. From the early 1970s through the 1980s, as FP continued enthusiastically until at least sometime midway through the decade, Korean males typically received

51. H. Y. Lee, "Clinical Studies," 27.

52. Ibid.

53. *Seoul Through Pictures*, vol. 4, *Seoul, to Rise Again* (Seoul: The City History Compilation Committee of Seoul, 2005), 57–59.

a one-hour lecture before decommission, with the offer of reduced reserve duty in the future.[54] As we will see in the next section, this was not the only incentive scheme provided, and a range of housing choices and education schemes also figured at the height of ROK militarization in the early 1970s. If vasectomy had played only a small role in its first decade (1962–1973), its role expanded considerably as a means of mass education, tied to the Vietnam context and the corresponding creation of the Home Reserve. Of course, many males did not choose this option, but the lectures and materials provided soon became a common part of military experience, leaving behind many memories and apocryphal stories.

At the same time, Dr. Lee continued his surgical program beyond the decade, continuing to perfect the surgery, and especially seeking to minimize any associated discomfort, as well as to speed up the recovery process. Working with both animal and human subjects, he sought to develop techniques that could deal with the newer problems cropping up, such as the persistence of potency following surgery, a surprisingly common issue stemming from a number of possible scenarios. As we leave Dr. Lee and turn our attention to the complex social world of the Korean military, we should recognize the basic paradox here: an effort to embrace vasectomy, an essentially incomplete procedure, at a time coinciding with heightened nationalism. The typical recruit was asked to sign on for a period of several years, guided by heightened aggression, before returning to civilian life and, thereafter, forsaking the same set of values.

The hypermasculine ideal and nation building (1968–1973)

It also helps to recall the ideological culture of the late 1960s to understand the context for this controlled form of aggression, which was not tied to Vietnam alone. Fears of a North Korean intervention were quite realistic for this time, and the number of border incidents taking place along the demilitarized zone (1965–1968) is now believed to be linked to a North Korean testing of the ROK's defense capabilities.[55] In the recently reissued memoir, *An Affair with Korea* (2015), anthropologist Vincent S. R. Brandt recalls his time as a participant-observer in Sokp'o, a West Coast fishing village situated along the Yellow Sea.[56] According to Brandt's account, the microworld of the village was highly controlled, and when he traveled by bus to return to Seoul, he frequently found himself observed by security agents, who often sat alongside him in a conspicuous fashion.[57] It was nothing he had done but

---

54. PPFK, *10 (Ten)-Year History of Family Planning in Korea*, 91.
55. While there is no official label for this activity, some scholars now refer to it as a "Second Korean War" or, alternately, as the "Korean DMZ Conflict" (1966–1969).
56. Brandt, *Affair with Korea*.
57. Ibid.

his simple presence as a foreign resident in rural Korea that attracted this special notice.

This palpable sense of unease reached a peak in early 1968, when North Korean agents crossed the border and attempted to assassinate President Park Chung Hee, a failed attempt that caused a national sense of alarm. In the short term, the security apparatus described previously spent the next several months tracking down the scattered members of the North Korean team. Following this, the government needed to find some means of monitoring domestic events, and this led to the creation of the Home Reserve, in effect mobilizing the entire population against future North Korean incursions, and providing an excuse for additional political mobilization. If South Korea was already a militarized nation, the late 1960s and early 1970s represents a peak in this style of hypermasculine behavior, as the nation's citizens supported a substantial commitment to Vietnam, while also backing the reduction of domestic freedoms under the conjoined banners of patriotism and security.

Along with the package of masculine ideals embodied in military service, the Vietnam experience also helped to reshape attitudes about one's body, especially in terms of a growing familiarity with available forms of Western medical care. To a certain extent, military training serves as a baseline for almost any society in which conscription crosses class and regional lines, placing a diverse set of individuals in a common form of training. Ideally, this method results not only in camaraderie in the short term but also in greater identification with the nation over the long term. For South Korea, the health care available in the military for much of this period was equal to, or better than, that available to all but the most elite back home. The exposure soldiers received while serving to the related ideas of physical fitness, maintenance, and upkeep were new to many, at least as presented in a biomedical fashion. Moreover, the available treatment when injured or sick was unfamiliar in a nation where *hanuihak* (traditional practice) still represented the preference for many through the late 1960s. In a surprising way then, the violent encounter of Vietnam likely promoted a much greater awareness and receptivity toward biomedical alternatives.

The Home Reserve Army Meets (Male) Family Planning (1973–late 1980s)

The creation of the Home Reserve did not radically alter the circumstances with respect to FP and males, initially. The PPFK and its international partners continued to target a male demographic through the late 1960s, encountering many of the same issues previously mentioned. As for the overall climate of militarization, the Home Reserve fit quite nicely within a broader pattern of the military permeating nearly every aspect of South

Korean life, extending well beyond the boundaries of the army. For example, Korean students were quite accustomed to performing military-style drills as part of their daily lives, and this style of mobilization reached even those at a relatively young age. The creation of a new graduate institution, KAIS (Korea Advanced Institute of Science), in 1971 required a new approach to the issue of military service.[58] Those receiving admission found their formal military obligations waived, as they were deemed to be doing "science for the nation," regarded as an alternative form of service.[59] Still, it is quite easy to find images from the institute's early years featuring daily military drills, as even aspiring scientists and engineers needed to stay fit and prepared.[60]

This relationship did not change until 1973, when the reserves began to be targeted as one of the primary means for new FP pedagogy, given the appeal of a captive audience and the opportunity to reach nearly all males. During the intervening period (1968–1973), the ROK had begun its withdrawal from the Vietnam War, with international and domestic events shaping a climate of increased tension. US president Richard Nixon's 1969 speech, later characterized as the Guam Doctrine, called for America's Asian partners to assume a greater role in tackling the issue of self-defense, and certainly this is how the speech was received in South Korea. Domestically, 1971 also witnessed an extremely close presidential election, with President Park narrowly retaining his position and then responding by suspending the constitution and claiming supreme power, invoking the so-called Yusin (Renewal) state. In other words, the quiet retreat from Vietnam did not necessarily reduce the intense climate of military preparedness, and Park used this atmosphere to mobilize the nation with an even greater measure of resolve.

Along with this heated politics, the medical climate for vasectomy was better prepared by the early 1970s in terms of accommodating a potentially larger subject population. Internationally, vasectomy holds a much longer history in its association with criminality and mental fitness, and, in fact, its use as a birth control method did not really begin until the first decade of the postwar period. For South Korea, similarly, there was a corresponding trend in mandating sterilization for those deemed mentally unfit, and this history runs roughly parallel with FP through much of this period. In creating a larger infrastructure to handle the procedure, Dr. Lee and his colleagues were not only working out the surgery as a form of practice but also working to place vasectomy in a separate conversation of its own, decoupling it out from these previous pejorative associations. Only then could the surgery be

---

58. KAIS not only involved military training at the daily level, but many of its early graduates concentrated on studying the use of new weapons systems and military equipment.
59. In effect, studying was deemed equivalent to national service.
60. These pictures can be seen in any of the annual volumes celebrating the history of KAIST.

offered to a national demographic, one potentially affecting a large segment of the male population.

The early 1970s witnessed several new measures placed in force almost simultaneously, with their combined power making vasectomy a much more appealing option. First, as noted, the pedagogy for the procedure was linked directly with the military and the act of separation from armed service (1973), capturing an enormous population at a critical point in their lives. A similar measure extended to other populations of interest, including industrial sites and low-income areas, making it possible to read these gestures collectively as possessing some degree of a eugenic component, even if expressed only implicitly. Second, at the national level, the FP program began a group specific to voluntary sterilization from 1975 (Korea Association for Voluntary Sterilization), providing an additional push to the campaign, which had previously represented only a minor part of FP planning.[61] This is critical, as many acceptors later noted that interaction with a representative was the primary determining factor in shaping their personal decision.

Targeting the reserve forces (1973–)

For FP specifically, this activity translated as an enormous bonus, allowing the concentration of its resources and the ongoing mobilization of the agenda as a major part of the nation's economic and social planning. South Korea was just beginning to exhibit genuine signs of its economic growth, especially in terms of achieving middle-class aspirations; and the general trends of increased migration to urban areas, the corresponding transition to apartment living, and the growth of a consumer culture showed no signs of waning in the short term.[62] Strictly speaking, the first high-rise apartments—meaning new units in buildings with six floors and no elevators—had begun to appear as early as the first half of the 1960s, but the following decade is more clearly associated with an advance in the quality of life, especially with the emergence of megacomplexes in the southern half of Seoul.[63] While such opportunities were out of the reach of many, these goals and aspirations were strategically incorporated as part of the FP mobilization, allowing families to imagine how they might live, thereby neatly translating national goals into the concrete realization of individual dreams.

Beginning in 1973, the male component of FP, which had continued to operate with two populations in mind, private and subsidized, made a

---

61. H. Y. Lee, "The Role of a National Association for Voluntary Sterilization in the National Family Planning Program," Association for Voluntary Sterilization of the Asian Regional Conference on Voluntary Sterilization, Taipei, May 10–12, 1975 (Taipei, July 1975), 222–25.
62. See Gelézeau's *Republic of Apartments* (French, Korean) for a wonderful take on the effects of apartment living.
63. The second half of the 1970s marked the arrival of the more affluent areas south of the river.

dramatic shift with its rapid incorporation into reserve training pedagogy. Although there is no mention of the withdrawal from Vietnam in the literature, the overlap of these two developments certainly meant a greater number of soldiers returning to the domestic sphere and the unique opportunity to target this population with a carefully formulated message. As part of reserve training, therefore, FP received permission to offer all soldiers on reserve duty a one-hour lecture on the benefits of family planning, with an explicit message tying vasectomy to a range of possible incentives.[64] While some of these aims varied over the length of the program, the most common incentives included appeals to one's free time and to future life goals for the family unit. The first of these often translated into a release from future service: consent to the operation meant a rapid transition to civilian life, while others needed to continue to serve on a reserve basis.

The transition to a focus on the reserves in the early 1970s was in many ways a necessity for the FP program, as in comparison to the other options, vasectomy had historically lagged behind, proving the least favored birth control choice over the duration of the 1960s.[65] The basic appeal to reservists, therefore, needed a careful refashioning, along with the newer material and lifestyle aspirations to be discussed shortly. D. E. Park discusses this critical shift in the article "How Korea Turned the Tide of Male Indifference," noting that the campaigns became more than simply an introduction to vasectomy and included a much more comprehensive vision of sex education and family life.[66] Moreover, the campaigns emphasized the liberation of women as a core part of the message, stressing the obligation of Korean men to aid their wives in the family mission.[67] This theme in particular represented something new for the Korean context and appealed to comparative gender roles in a way that had not been explored previously.

In terms of its infrastructure, the program also had to devote additional resources as part of the transition. The initial effort conducted in 1973, for example, produced a total of 395 vasectomies, a promising beginning based almost solely on a one-hour introductory lecture to reserve soldiers. From this point forward, the PPFK and related partners began to expand the scope of the effort, with the preparation of additional materials, including a basic textbook, and a trained corps of lecturers to work in conjunction with the Ministry of National Defense. No longer regarded as a minor component of military training, family planning and sex education became firmly integrated into ROK military life during the decade of the 1970s, thereby

---

64. I have been able to track down only the housing incentives via documents, while there remain many other apocryphal stories from the period.
65. Condom use also lagged behind the distribution of the IUD and birth control pills.
66. D. E. Park, "How Korea Turned the Tide of Male Indifference," *People* 13(1) (1986): 22–23.
67. Park's account cites the "liberation of women" as a prominent theme.

reaching almost the entire male population under the age of thirty-five.[68] In sharp contrast to the efforts of Dr. Lee in the previous decade, the program was not restricted to a single hospital site, nor was it in any way experimental or tentative in its ambitions.

Among the incentives included in the early years of renewed focus was a directive designed to appeal specifically to the lifestyle ambitions of the returning soldier. With the construction of new apartment complexes south of the river (1975), volunteers consenting to a vasectomy were granted a higher place in the waiting list, and news of this policy revision made its way into the popular press.[69] Although it is not clear whether the policy was intended as a one-off—which is highly likely—or, instead, formed part of a larger strategy to accommodate returnees, the effects were palpable in a society where many held such aspirations. PPFK had frequently used images of thatched or similar types of housing in its mid-1960s campaigns, contrasting it with the newer forms of housing just becoming available. *Happy Home* went even further, taking its representatives for visits into new apartments, offering a colorful, visual display to the prospective apartment dweller. Now the vasectomy made the transition to apartment life a reality, allowing acceptors to bypass the lengthy queue in the wait for such a desirable space.

In popular memory, this gesture, and along with it, relief from further reserve training, remains the dominant impression, with family planning potentially opening the door to a wealth of free time and, moreover, better housing in which to spend it. There remain a host of associated incentives in memory—access to better schools and similar appeals to child welfare or childcare schemes—although it is difficult to track the specifics of these programs, some of which have to remain apocryphal or perhaps just specific to particular regions.[70] In any case, the mid-1970s renewed appeal to the vasectomy, along with the creation of a support infrastructure within the ROK military, meant the strengthening of ties between military and civilian life. The surgery, which had been heavily class based in the previous decade, could make some claim to reaching a wider demographic, insofar as military service was uniform, theoretically cutting across class and regional lines. At the same time, the program also began to reach beyond the reserve forces, aiming to get its pedagogy into other sites, including the introduction of family planning materials at the high school level and also reaching out to factory workers.[71]

If this mid-1970s moment marks the beginning of the vasectomy's "return," it does not necessarily represent its high point, which came only in

---

68. This activity would continue well past the 1970s, however.
69. References to apartments appeared in the *Korea Herald*, among others, and made it into both the Korean- and English-language press.
70. These claims have to be regarded as apocryphal for now.
71. PPFK, *The 10 (Ten)-Year History of Family Planning in Korea.*

the following decade of the 1980s. The decision to mobilize FP to the Home Reserve required time in which to achieve a proper buildup and, as indicated above, the devotion of additional resources and personnel. In particular, a team of trained lecturers was soon incorporated within the military, providing a standard form of training, keeping the program on message to each new batch of trainees.[72] Along with the original one-hour lecture dating to 1973, subsequent efforts involved regular exposure to FP, with supplemental instructional materials including pamphlets, leaflets, and flip charts.[73] The problem associated with the original program, the availability and reliability of surgeons, was also addressed as the surgery became a common form of practice. By the late 1970s, the efforts attached to the Home Reserve were beginning to pay dividends, with military personnel making up an increasingly large portion of the total number of volunteers.

Before turning to these figures, it is worth pausing to consider how and why the renewed program could be so surprisingly effective, particularly in contrast to the prior 1960s effort, which had a much smaller impact. In part, the basic infrastructural issues had been addressed, and the ability to handle male clients in bulk now represented a realistic possibility. The bureaucracy established within the larger goals of PPFK meant a self-sustaining impulse in some sense, one that would continue to promote FP's goals enthusiastically, even as South Korea had met its population goals and fell below the replacement rate sometime early in the 1980s. This trend was true not just of vasectomy but also in general, meaning that birth control technologies continued to be distributed well into the 1990s. Even more than this factor, though, was the sheer effectiveness of mass mobilization achieved through militarization, with uniform military conscription bringing a large, young, and eager demographic to receive the message.

In many ways, this last period of military rule (1980–1987) in South Korea saw its most fervent embrace of anti-Communist ideology and practice, even as dramatic change was to come within a decade.[74] The National Security Law remained very much in force, meaning that expressions of public dissent were generally regarded as unfavorable, labeled a form of left-wing activity. In the nation's public schools, anti-Communist education continued to provide a highly ideological form of indoctrination, with North Koreans depicted as inhuman, unworthy of equal treatment or regard. In such a climate, military service was no mere sinecure but, rather, a further means of achieving a degree of homogeneity and conformity. In this sense,

---

72. D. E. Park, "How Korea Turned the Tide of Male Indifference," 22.
73. Ibid.
74. Choe Sang-Hun, "Korean County Achieves Its Goal: Less Control, More Babies," *New York Times*, November 28, 2015, accessed March 28, 2016, http://www.nytimes.com/2015/12/01/world/asia/korean-county-achieves-its-goal-less-birth-control-more-babies.html?_r=0. The article opens with historical background on how village workers were asked to establish quotas for tubectomies and vasectomies.

the "consent" of these Korean young men has to be read in this context, certainly as shaped and guided in part by the forces of the state, even as choice remained an option, at least nominally.

Success with the reserves?

To some extent, the renewed success of the mobilization by the early 1980s was merely the logical outcome of the accumulation of sufficient bureaucratic expertise: the elements, once set in place, represented the proper functioning of a massive system. At the same time, the new figures were startling, certainly in comparison with nearly two decades earlier; and, moreover, the percentage of military members making up a significant percentage of the overall pool of vasectomy acceptors grew rapidly as well. If the first fifteen years of the program (1962–1976) had witnessed roughly 20,000 procedures a year, the figures would increase dramatically after 1977, and by early in the next decade, the range was between 50,000 to 100,000 surgeries per year.[75] Of these, roughly one-third of acceptors consisted of military members, new recruits who heard the message and volunteered for the surgery and its associated package of benefits. If communicating its message in a popular form was this convenient and effective, the program might easily have taken such an approach at an earlier stage.

In other words, it is not enough to follow the simple path of the program to achieve its aims successfully without offering some form of speculation about what was going on culturally. For one, the achievement of these high figures took place just about the time the nation needed to think seriously about reversing course, as the replacement rate had already been surpassed. Along with this historical irony, we can add the mobilization associated with the Chun Doo Hwan period (1981–1987), as national leaders ramped up the spirit of patriotism and participation in the aftermath of Park's death (1979), even as protests and student resistance reached an all-time high by the middle of the decade. Here it may help to recall the disproportionate percentage of rural residents in the military and their voting patterns in national elections. That is, the more conservative soldiers tended to come from these areas and, arguably, were more receptive to the state's message via family planning. More than ever, vasectomy was a concrete means to demonstrate one's patriotic fervor, particularly as the nation appeared to be at risk.

For the duration of the decade, the numbers remained consistently high, with figures reaching as high as slightly more than 120,000 in an exceptional year, and with the low never falling below a range of between 25,000 to 30,000 cases annually. Again, recall that the target figures for the 1960s typically set a figure of 20,000 subjects, often falling short of this aim. Similarly,

---

75. PPFK, *The 10 (Ten)-Year History of Family Planning in Korea.*

the percentage of subjects drawn from the military stayed at a high rate, generally comprising about a third of the overall group of acceptors. If this picture suggests a well-established and effective mobilization, it also hints at the degree of ideological fervor—and perhaps the pressure placed upon commanding officers—standard for the period. This in no way suggests that the Park years were easy, but the Chun (1981–1987) years achieved a new and heightened sense of crisis, with the numbers surpassing not only the replacement rate but also continuing beyond the political transition of 1987, with the return to a presidential election.

In terms of its relationship to family planning, vasectomy also holds a certain ambiguity, as does FP in general for this period. Although there is now acknowledgement that the replacement rate was surpassed at some point in the early 1980s, birth control technologies continued to be distributed, and the 1990s is sometimes referred to as the "fourth decade of family planning" in the literature. In other words, a clear and stark break with existing practice was lacking, and the efficient bureaucracies that had been set up performed quite well beyond the point of any useful returns. One of the earliest signs of an alternative approach dates to 1996, with the introduction of the first "quality and welfare" campaigns in South Korea, recognizing the need for attention to a better quality of life for mothers. If the intervention of the Asian financial crisis put a damper on the new effort, this type of project—emphasizing some combination of access to childcare, education for children, and more opportunities for working mothers—has dominated the conversation in the most recent fifteen to twenty years, corresponding with the eventual turn to a pronatal outlook.

FP Transition and Its Legacy (1996–)

Even prior to the formal changes taking place within FP, a number of men questioned the surgery on the basis of their dissatisfaction, along with the symptoms of discomfort they experienced. It is not surprising then that some members of this population began to request a reversal of the procedure, and this type of procedure, too, had to be worked out, with the first vasectomy reversals dating to the late 1970s, approximately two decades after the initial wave of enthusiasm.[76] From the perspective of a specialist like Dr. Lee Hee Yong, this development represented a mere technicality, something to be worked out and approached almost strictly as a medical problem. To the historian, however, it offers a problematic, even if not outright, opposition to the program and is perhaps indicative of larger changes taking place. The hypermasculinity associated with the Home Reserve and its campaigns was

---

76. Dr. Lee's clinical research on the vasovasostomy procedure dates to the mid-1960s, so the later date refers to the surgery becoming more widely available to the public.

beginning to wane, and Korean society was starting to take on a new set of priorities with the shift to democratization, even as military conscription remained a feature of male life.

Where the echoes remain interesting is between two vastly different sets of campaigns—the mid-1970s vasectomy efforts as documented here, and the mid-1990s "quality and welfare" campaigns—in the common figure of the working woman. For an Organisation for Economic Co-operation and Development country with its powerful economy and social aspirations, South Korea still ranks surprisingly low on many international indices for gender equality, economic transparency, and work opportunities. This was perhaps even more true in the mid-1990s, when "globalization" became the byword of the Kim Young-Sam administration (1992–1997), the first ROK president to be elected freely with no association or formal ties to the military government for much of the preceding three decades (1961–1987). At this moment, the ROK decided to increase working opportunities for women, especially by relieving them of some of the burden of childcare or similar responsibilities that might tie them to the home. Two decades later, these ideas are still being debated in Korean society, with increasing the percentage of women in the workplace mobilized explicitly as a goal by the Park Geun-hye government.[77]

It should not be surprising, after all, that gender relations involve a complex negotiation between male and female partners, and this is particularly true of the most recent FP efforts in South Korea, now grouped under the recent rubric of Saero-Maji, an emerging campaign dating to the early twenty-first century. Explicitly pronatalist in its character and typically rendered in English as "new beginning" or "new rendezvous," the Saero-Maji scheme aims to tackle several issues in tandem: access to childcare, working opportunities for women, and the problem of a rapidly aging population.[78] In its rhetoric and publicity materials, however, the plan elides almost any connections with prior campaigns, meaning that the historical relationship I have posited here can be established only by examining the points of comparison. Just as women were mobilized in the 1970s as beneficiaries of a family unit to be reduced in size, they are now being mobilized as valuable contributors to the Korean workforce, with the state providing subsidies to make this possible, even while encouraging growth in family size. Although the logic is a very different one, with a different aim, the object remains surprisingly stable, thereby placing the male category in question as well.

The Saero-Maji campaigns certainly deserve another essay in their own right, but, for now, suffice it to say that the male figures depicted in the

---

77. Perhaps it is more accurate to say that certain civil society groups mobilize these figures.
78. http://momplus.mw.go.kr/main.do, accessed on March 14, 2014.

publicity materials tend to overlap substantially with the desired father of an earlier era. To be fair, the tough exterior is lacking, as is immediate the Cold War military context, but still we see a Korean father who provides for and is capable of achieving almost anything on behalf of his children. Perhaps most importantly, he now willingly embraces his nurturing side, participating eagerly in childcare and sharing parental responsibilities equally with his partner, who more than likely works outside the home. My point here is not to argue that the most recent campaign has anything hidden or subliminal to it but simply to point out its relationship with a much longer historical trajectory, one in which Korean males have been asked to assume a wide variety of roles in succession. If the antinatal campaigns envisioned a sacrifice for the nation, similarly, the present-day efforts ask for even more energy and time devoted to the family, portraying the aims here in terms of personal enrichment for one's spouse, as well as possible national gains, if this last goal has to remain elusive and abstract.

To characterize the Saero-Maji campaigns in a somewhat different vein, in terms of more recent ROK politics, the debates and negotiations that started in the Kim Young-Sam and Kim Dae-Jung administrations concerning the quality of family life have only recently been translated into a set of material social policies. In other words, the legacy of three successive postdemocratization presidential administrations—Kim (1993–1997), Kim (1998–2002), and Ro (2003–2007)—had to be passed on to two more recent presidents, both of whom have been identified with a style favoring large business interests and primarily economic concerns. To put it more briefly, the campaigns reflect a series of negotiated compromises, an attempt to provide the state with a calculus to enable the possibility of working mothers and access to childcare, while recognizing the conspicuous reality of an increasingly competitive, neoliberal environment in contemporary South Korea. Families will have their chances calculated according to a point system, a mathematics scheme endorsed by the state.

The results of this pronatalist vision remain very much uncertain, although, to date, the government does not seem to have succeeded in achieving its vision. South Korean women continue to have children, but, increasingly, they have just one child, with the campaign specifically targeting its incentives and seeking to promote the critical move to a second child. For the male, his place within this scheme remains, as suggested earlier, one requiring a much higher degree of flexibility than in the past. The comforting certainty associated with military service (conscription) and personal sacrifice (vasectomy) that typified much of militarized life has been replaced with a wider range of options in a pronatal world. If FP consciously sought the goal of the nuclear family, with a reduction in size from the extended family of the village, Saero-Maji actually shares a number of the same goals. However, Saero-Maji acknowledges that fathering/parenting carries an individual male into a more complex set of social relations with his wife and children, and his duties are no longer merely economic, that of serving as a provider, but also one of nurturing his children and, equally, proving a space and opportunity for his wife to accomplish her personal goals, especially professional ones. In crowded, neoliberal South Korean cities, with the majority of families continuing to live in apartments, it will be interesting to see how this dynamic plays out.

If Saero-Maji appears much more subtle in its incentives, it still reflects a top-down government scheme in the end, indicating that South Korea has not changed as dramatically as some would have it, even following democratization. If the emphasis on vasectomy marked an initial move away from overt behavior modification in favor of bodily intervention, the newer campaigns in the most recent decade continue to embody a social science approach, with education and childcare provisions deemed sufficient to attract notice from the target demographic. And, once again, the male role has continued to undergo potential change, with the ongoing appeals to aid women by bringing them into, thereby making them a more equal part of, the workforce. The hypermasculine ideal of the early 1970s has given way to a much more subdued, progressive vision of a Korean male who is nurturing and caring, both in terms of his family and also in terms of the contribution he is willing to make to society.

Bibliography

Adrian, Stine Willum. "Sperm Stories: Policies and Practices of Sperm Banking in Denmark and Sweden." *European Journal of Women's Studies* 17(4) (2010): 393–411.

An Chin-Chih 安勤之. "Jiuming xiancao huo shengji lingyao: Lingzhi de kexue, shichang yu liaoxiao zhengzhi" 救命仙草或生技靈藥：靈芝的科學、市場與療效政治 [Miraculous herb or biotechnological drug: Science, market, and the efficacy politics of *lingzhi*]. PhD diss., Department of Sociology, National Taiwan University, 2016.

Anderson, Eugene N. "Folk Nutritional Therapy in Modern China." In *Chinese Medicine and Healing: An Illustrated History*, edited by T. J. Hinrichs and Linda L. Barnes, 259–60. Cambridge, MA: Belknap Press of Harvard University Press, 2013.

Anderson, Warwick. "Asia as Method in Science and Technology Studies." *East Asian Science, Technology and Society: An International Journal* 6(4) (2013): 445–51.

Andrews, Bridie. *The Making of Modern Chinese Medicine*. Vancouver: University of British Columbia Press, 2014.

Arnold, David, ed. "British India and the 'Beriberi Problem' 1798–1942." *Medical History* 54 (2010): 312.

———. *Imperial Medicine and Indigenous Societies*. Manchester: Manchester University Press, 1988.

———. "Tropical Governance: Managing Health in Monsoon Asia, 1908–1938." Asia Research Institute, National University of Singapore, Working Papers Series, no. 116, 2009.

Arrighi, Giovanni, Takeshi Hamashita, and Mark Selden, eds. *The Resurgence of East Asia: 500, 150 and 50 Year Perspectives*. London and New York: Routledge, 2003.

ART Clinics Inspection Commision of the Korean Society of Obstetrics and Gynecology (ACIC-KSOG) 대한산부인과학회 인공수태시술의료기관 심사소위원회. "Hangook Bojosaengsicksoolui Hyeonhwang 1994" 한국 보조생식술의 현황1994 [Current status of ART in Korea for 1994]. *Daehan Sanbooingwa Hakhoejee* 대한산부인과학회지 [Korean journal of obstetrics and gynecology] 41(1) (1998): 236–52.

———. "Current Status of ART in Korea, 1995." *Korean Journal of Obstetrics and Gynecology* 42(4) (1999): 681–703. (In Korean)

———. "Current Status of ART in Korea, 1996." *Korean Journal of Obstetrics and Gynecology* 42(2) (1999): 231–53. (In Korean)

———. "Current Status of ART in Korea, 1997." *Korean Journal of Obstetrics and Gynecology* 42(10) (1999): 2151–75. (In Korean)

———. "Current Status of ART in Korea, 1998." *Korean Journal of Obstetrics and Gynecology* 44(10) (2001): 1883–99. (In Korean)

———. "Current Status of ART in Korea, 1999." *Korean Journal of Obstetrics and Gynecology* 45(10) (2002): 1700–17. (In Korean)

———. "Current Status of ART in Korea, 2000." *Korean Journal of Obstetrics and Gynecology* 46(10) (2003): 1888–904. (In Korean)

———. "Current Status of ART in Korea, 2001." *Korean Journal of Obstetrics and Gynecology* 47(12) (2004): 2285–302. (In Korean)

———. "Current Status of ART in Korea, 2002." *Korean Journal of Obstetrics and Gynecology* 48(12) (2005): 2777–96. (In Korean)

———. "Current Status of ART in Korea, 2003." *Korean Journal of Obstetrics and Gynecology* 49(12) (2006): 2480–97. (In Korean)

———. "Current Status of ART in Korea, 2004." *Korean Journal of Obstetrics and Gynecology* 50(12) (2007): 1615–39. (In Korean)

ART Committee of Korean Society of Obstetrics and Gynecology (AC-KSOG) 대한산부인과학회 보조생식술소위원회. "Hangook Bojosaengsicksoolui Hyeonhwang, 2005" 한국 보조생식술의 현황 2005 [Current status of ART in Korea, 2005]. *Korean Journal of Obstetrics and Gynecology* 51(12) (2008): 1421–47.

———. "Current Status of ART in Korea, 2006." *Korean Journal of Obstetrics and Gynecology* 52(12) (2009): 1212–38. (In Korean)

———. "Current Status of ART in Korea, 2007." *Korean Journal of Obstetrics and Gynecology* 53(12) (2010): 1052–77. (In Korean)

———. "Current Status of ART in Korea, 2008." *Korean Journal of Obstetrics and Gynecology* 54(12) (2011): 741–63. (In Korean)

Asahi shimbunsha 朝日新聞社. *Zen Nihon kara erabaretaru kenkō yūryōji sanbyakunin* 全日本から選ばれたる健康優良児三百人 [Three hundred healthy children selected from all over Japan]. Tokyo: Asahi shimbunsha, 1930.

Asai Haruo 浅井春夫, Murase Yukihiro 村瀬 幸浩, and Itō Satoru 伊藤 悟, eds. *Nihon no otoko wa dokokara kite, doko e ikunoka* 日本の男はどこから来て、どこへ行くのか [Japanese men: Where did they come from, and where are they going]. Tokyo: Jūgatsusha, 2001.

Bae, Eunkyoung. *Human Reproduction in the Korean Modernity*. Seoul: Sigan-yeohaeng, 2012.

Baeltz, Erwin. *Die koerperlichen Eigenschaften der Japaner* [The physical properties of the Japanese]. Yokohama: Deutsche Gesellschaft für Natur- und Voelkerkunde Ostasiens, 1882.

Baldwin, Frank, Diane Jones, and Michael Jones. *America's Rented Troops: South Koreans in Vietnam*. Philadelphia: American Friends Service Committee, 1970–1977.

Bailey, Paul J. *Gender and Education in China: Gender Discourses and Women's Schooling in the Early Twentieth Century*. London and New York: Routledge, 2007.

Bang, Sook, Man Gap Lee, and Jae-mo Yang. "A Survey of Fertility and Attitude toward Family Planning in Rural Korea." *Yonsei Medical Journal* 4(1) (December 1963): 77–102.

Bantam Medical Dictionary. Third Revised Edition. Prepared by the editors of Market House Book Ltd. New York: Bantam Books, 2000

Barnes, Trevor. "What Regional Studies Might Have Been: Cold War American Social Science." *Regional Studies* 47(3) (2013): 461–64.

Barney, Sandra. "Accessing Medicalized Donor Sperm in the US and Britain: An Historical Narrative." *Sexualities* 8 (2005): 205–20.

Bay, Alexander. "Beriberi, Military Medicine, and Medical Authority in Prewar Japan." *Japan Review* 20 (2008): 111–56.

———. *Beriberi in Modern Japan: The Making of a National Disease*. Rochester, NY: University of Rochester Press, 2012.

Belsky, J. "Family Experience and Pubertal Development in Evolutionary Perspective." *Journal of Adolescent Health* 48(5) (May 2011): 425–26.

Belsky, J., L. D. Steinberg, R. M. Houts, S. L. Friedman, G. DeHart, E. Cauffman, G. I. Roisman, B. L. Halpern-Felsher, and E. Susman. "Family Rearing Antecedents of Pubertal Timing." *Child Development* 78(4) (July 2007): 1302–21.

———. "Infant Attachment Security and the Timing of Puberty: Testing an Evolutionary Hypothesis." *Psychological Science* 21(9) (September 2010): 1195–2011.

Benjamin, Harry. *The Transsexual Phenomenon.* New York: Julian Press, 1966.

Bennett, Paula, and Vernon Rosario, eds. *Solitary Pleasures: The Historical, Literary and Artistic Discourses of Autoeroticism.* New York: Routledge, 1995.

Blank, Robert. "Regulation of Donor Insemination." In *Donor Insemination: International Social Science Perspectives*, edited by Ken Daniels and Erica Haimes, 131–50. Cambridge: Cambridge University Press, 1998.

Bornstein, Kate. *Gender Outlaw: On Men, Women, and the Rest of Us.* New York: Routledge, 1994.

Borovoy, Amy. *The Too-Good Wife: Alcohol, Codependence, and the Politics of Nurturance in Postwar Japan.* Berkeley: University of California Press, 2005.

Boston Women's Collective. *Our Bodies, Ourselves.* Boston: New England Free Press, 1971.

Braddon, Leonard. *The Cause and Prevention of Beri-Beri.* London and New York: Rebman, 1907.

Brandt, Vincent S. R. *An Affair with Korea.* Seattle: University of Washington Press, 2015.

Bray, Francesca. "Becoming a Mother in Late Imperial China: Maternal Doubles and the Ambiguity of Fertility." In *Chinese Kinship: Contemporary Anthropological Perspectives*, edited by Susanne Brandstädter and Gonçalo D. Santos, 181–203. London: Routledge, 2008.

———. "The Chinese Experience." In *Medicine in the Twentieth Century*, edited by John V. Pickstone and Roger Cooter, 717–36. Amsterdam: Harwood Academic Publishers, 2000.

———. *Technology and Gender: Fabrics of Power in Late Imperial China.* Berkeley: University of California Press, 1997.

Brekke, Ole Andreas, and Thorvald Sirnes. "Biosociality, Biocitizenship and the New Regime of Hope and Despair: Interpreting 'Portraits of Hope' and the 'Mehmet Case.'" *New Genetics and Society* 30(4) (2011): 347–74.

Brown, E. P. "Report of Observation and Activities as Adviser in Medicine." Special Collections, University of Minnesota, January 24, 1959.

Brumberg, Joan Jacobs. *The Body Project: An Intimate History of American Girls.* New York: Random House, 1997.

Bu, Luping, Darwin H. Stapleton, and Ka-che Yip. "Marketing Women's Medicines: Gender, OTC Herbal Medicines and Medical Culture in Modern Japan." *Asian Medicine* 5 (2009): 146–72.

———, eds. *Science, Public Health and the State in Modern East Asia.* New York: Routledge, 2012.

Cao Fei 曹非, ed. *Chuzhong shiyong shengli weishengxue* 初中實用生理衛生學 [Practical physiology and hygiene for junior highs]. Reviewed by Chen Lieguan 陳烈光. 1928. Changsha: Fenfengguan, 1948.

Caprio, Mark E. "Assimilation Rejected: The Tong'a ilbo's Challenge to Japan's Colonial Policy in Korea." In *Imperial Japan and National Identities in Asia, 1895–1945*, edited by Li Narangoa and Robert Cribb, 129–45. London: Routledge, 2003.

Carel, Jean-Claude, and Juliane Léger. "Precocious Puberty." *New England Journal of Medicine* 358 (2008): 2366.

Carmeli, Yoram S., and Dapnha Birenbaum-Carmeli. "Ritualizing the 'Natural Family': Secrecy in Israeli Donor Insemination." *Science as Culture* 9(3) (2000): 301–24.

Carpenter, Kenneth. *Beriberi, White Rice, and Vitamin B: A Disease, a Cause, and a Cure.* Berkeley: University of California Press, 2000.

Carroll, John M. *A Concise History of Hong Kong.* Lanham, MD: Rowman and Littlefield, 2007.

Castro-Vazquez, Genaro. *Male Circumcision in Japan.* New York: Palgrave Macmillan, 2015.

Cauldwell, David. "Psychopathia Transexualis." *Sexology* 16 (1949): 274–80.

Cernada, G., T. H. Sun, M. C. Chang, and J. F. Cai. "Taiwan's Population and Family Planning Efforts: An Historical Perspective." *International Quarterly of Community Health Education* 27(2) (2006): 99–120.

Chang Che-chia 張哲嘉. "Funü zazhi zhong de yishi weisheng guwen" 婦女雜誌中的醫事衛生顧問 [The medical advisory column in the *Ladies' Journal*]. *Research on Women in Modern Chinese History* 12 (2004): 145–68.

Chang, K. C. "Introduction," *Food in Chinese Culture: Anthropological and Historical Perspectives*, edited by K. C. Chang, 3–21. New Haven: Yale University Press, 1977.

Chang, Kyung-Sup. *South Korea under Compressed Modernity: Familial Political Economy Transition.* Abingdon and New York: Routledge, 2010.

Chang, Ming-Yang 張明揚. "Rengong shengzhifa de zhengyixing huati diaocha baogao" 人工生殖法的爭議性話題調查報告 [Survey result to the controversial assisted reproduction law]. *Taiwan Endometriosis Association Journal* 中華民國子宮內膜異位症婦女協會會刊 8(4) (2001): 3–8.

Chang, Ying-Hua, Tu Hsu-Hao, and Lia Pei-Shan. *Taiwan Social Change Survey 2012.* Taipei: Academia Sinica, 2013.

Chao Yafeng 巢亞豐. "Jiaoqi laza" 腳氣拉雜 [Miscellaneous comments on *jiaoqi*]. *Fuxing Zhongyi* 復興中醫 2(4) (1941): 37–39.

Chauncey, George. *Gay New York: Gender, Urban Culture, and the Making of the Gay Male World, 1890–1940.* New York: Basic Books, 1994.

Chen, Jian, *Mao's China and the Cold War.* Chapel Hill: University of North Carolina Press, 2001.

Chen, Kuan-Hsing. *Asia as Method: Toward Deimperialization.* Durham, NC: Duke University Press, 2010.

———. "Civilizationalism." *Theory, Culture & Society* 23(2–3) (2006): 427–28.

Chen Qitian 陳啟天. *Jindai Zhongguo jiaoyushi* 近代中國教育史 [History of education in modern China]. Taipei: Zhonghua shuju, 1970.

Chen Yongguan 陳用光. 1908. *Shengli weishengxue* [Physiology] 生理衛生學. Shanghai: Kexuehui bianjibu, 1911.

Chen Yuan-peng 陳元朋. "Chuantong shiliao gainian yu xingwei de chuanyan: Yi 'qianjin, shizhi' wei hexin de guancha" 傳統食療概念與行為的傳衍——以〈千金·食治〉為核心的觀察 [Traditional food and healing: The Shih-chih chapter in Sun Szu-miao's *Ch'ien-chin yao-fang*]. *Bulletin of the Institute of History and Philology, Academia Sinica* 中央研究院歷史語言研究所集刊 69 (1998): 765–825.

Chen Yucang 陳雨蒼, ed. *Chuji zhongxue shengli weishengxue* 初級中學生理衛生學 [Physiology and hygiene for junior highs]. Revised by Xue Deyu 薛德焴. Nanjing and Ganzhou: Zhengzhong shuju, 1936.

———, ed. *Chuzhong weisheng* 初中衛生 [Hygiene for junior highs]. Revised by Xue Deyu 薛德焴. Shanghai and Nanjing: Zhengzhong shuju, 1935.

———, ed. *Shengli weisheng* 生理衛生 [Physiology and hygiene]. Revised by Zhou Jianren 周建人. 2nd ed. Changchun: Northeast Xinhua bookstore, 1949.

Chen Ziming 陳自明. *Furen daquan liangfang* 婦人大全良方 [All-inclusive good prescriptions for women]. 1237.

Cheng Hanzhang 程瀚章. *Chuzhong weisheng jiaoben* 初中衛生教本 [Junior high hygiene textbook]. Shanghai: Dadong shuju, 1933.

———. *Chuzhong weishengxue* 初中衛生學 [Hygiene for junior highs]. Edited by Liu Huaizhu 劉懷翥. Emended by Zhou Zhongqi 周宗琦. Shanghai: Beixin shuju, 1933.

———. *Weishengxue* 衛生學 [Hygiene]. Shanghai: Commercial Press, 1933.

Cheng Shijie 成士杰. *Shengli weisheng* 生理衛生 [Physiology and hygiene]. Tianjin: Baicheng shuju, 1932.

Chi Zheng 池正. "Jiaoqi bing" 腳氣病 [The *jiaoqi* ailment]. *Minzhong yibao* 民眾醫報 (1931): 11–13.

Chiang, Howard Hsueh-Hao. "Archiving Peripheral Taiwan: The Prodigy of the Human and Historical Narration." *Radical History Review* 120 (2014): 204–25.

———. "The Conceptual Contours of Sex in the Chinese Life Sciences: Zhu Xi (1899–1962), Hermaphroditism, and the Biological Discourse of *Ci* and *Xiong*, 1920–1950." *East Asian Science, Technology and Society: An International Journal* 2(3) (2008): 401–30.

———. "Epistemic Modernity and the Emergence of Homosexuality in China." *Gender and History* 22(3) (2010): 629–57.

———. "Gender Transformations in Sinophone Taiwan." *positions: asia critique* 25, no. 3 (2017): 527–63.

———. "How China Became a 'Castrated Civilization' and Eunuchs a 'Third Sex.'" In *Transgender China*, edited by Howard Chiang, 23–66. New York: Palgrave Macmillan, 2012.

Chiang, Howard, and Ari Larissa Heinrich, eds. *Queer Sinophone Cultures*. New York: Routledge, 2013.

Chick, H., and E. Hume (Lister Institute of Preventive Medicine). "The Distribution among Foodstuffs of the Substances Required for the Prevention of Beriberi and Scurvy." *Journal of the Royal Army Medical Corps* 29 (July–December 1917): 123.

Choi, Y.-M. 최영민, T.-G. Yoon 윤태기, E.-G. Min 민응기, D.-W. Han 한동운, J.-H. Hwang 황정혜, D.-Y. Lee 이동률, J.-J. Jun 전진현, J.-W. Kim 김정욱, J.-R. Lee 이정렬, G.-H. Lee 이경훈, and S.-A. Choi 최승아. *2010 Nyeondo Naneem Booboo Jeewonsaeop Gyeolgwabunseock Meet Pyeongga* 2010 년도 난임부부지원사업 결과분석 및 평가 [Analysis and evaluation of the result of national supporting program of infertile couples in 2010]. Seoul: Ministry of Health and Welfare, and Seoul National University Hospital, 2011.

Chōsen sōtokufu 朝鮮総督府 [Korea Governor-General]. *Chōsen bōeki nenpyō* 朝鮮貿易年表 [Chōsen table of shipping and trade]. 1910–1945.

———, ed. *Chōsen hōrei shūran* 朝鮮法令集覽 [Select collection of Chōsen laws]. Gansho shoten, 1915.

———. *Chōsen sōtokufu tōkei nenpō* 朝鮮總督府統計年報 [Korea governor-general annual report and statistics]. 1936.

———. *Showa 5-nen kokuzei chōsa* 昭和5年国勢調査 [1930 national census]. Vol. 1. 1931.

The Christine Jorgensen Story. Directed by Irving Rapper. Los Angeles: United Artists, 1970.

Chuang Shu Chih 莊淑旂 [Shukuki Soo]. *Hao pengyou yu ni* 好朋友與你 [A good friend and you]. Taipei: Wenjin she, 1989.

———. *Jiankang de yitian* 健康的一天 [A healthy day]. Taipei: Zhongyang ribao she, 1993.

———. *Nüren de sanchun* [Women's three springs] Taipei: Shibao chubanshe, 2005.

———. *Seishun o nagamochisaseru seikatsu to shokuji* 青春を長もちさせる生活と食事 [A youth-preserving lifestyle and diet]. Tokyo: Shufu no tomo sha, 1970.

———. *Zenyang chi zui jiankang* 怎樣吃最健康 [What is the healthiest way to eat?]. Taipei: Wenjin she, 1986.

———. *Zenyang chi zui jiankang* 怎樣吃最健康 [What is the healthiest way to eat?]. 2nd edition. Taipei: Wenjin she, 1994.

———. *Zenyang shenghuo bu shengqi* 怎樣生活不生氣 [How to live without generating qi]. Taipei: Zhongyang ribao she, 1990.

———. *Zheyang chi zui jiankang* 這樣吃最健康 [This is the healthiest way to eat]. Taipei: Guanghe chubanshe, 1995.

———. *Zhongguo xingyi jiankang fa* 中國行醫健康法 [Chinese style health management]. Taipei: Zhongyang ribao she, 1991.

———. *Zhuang boshi xinxiang* 莊博士信箱 [Dr. Zhuang's mailbox]. Taipei: Qingfeng chubanshe, 1999.

———. *Zhuang Shuqi huiyilu* 莊淑旂回憶錄 [Memoir of Chuang Shu Chih]. Taipei: Yuanliu chubanshe, 2001.

Chun, J. W. H., and Lien Teh Wu. "Beri-Beri Control from an Administrative Standpoint." Far Eastern Association of Tropical Medicine (FEATM) Transactions of 6th Biennial Congress, Tokyo, 1925.

Ciaro, David. *Advertising Empire: Race and Visual Culture in Imperial Germany.* Cambridge, MA: Harvard University Press, 2011.

Clarke, Adele, and Virginia Olesen. "Revising, Diffracting, Acting." In *Revisioning Women, Health, and Healing*, edited by Adele Clarke and Virginia Olesen, 3–48. New York: Routledge, 1999.

Cochran, Sheldon. *Chinese Medicine Men: Consumer Culture in China and Southeast Asia.* Cambridge, MA: Harvard University Press, 2006.

Cohen, Paul A. *Discovering History in China: American Historical Writing on the Recent Chinese Past.* New ed. 1984. New York: Columbia University Press, 2010.

Committee for ART, Korean Society of Obstetrics and Gynecology (CA-KSOG). "Current State of ART in Korea, 2009." *Obstetrics & Gynecology Science* 56(6) (2013): 353–61.

Conklin, Edwin Grant. *Heredity and Environment in the Development of Men.* Princeton: Princeton University Press, 1915.

Connelly, Matthew. *Fatal Misconception: The Struggle to Control World Population.* Cambridge, MA: Harvard University Press, 2007.

Cook, Rebecca J., Bernard M. Dickens, and Mahmoud F. Fathalla. *Reproductive Health and Human Rights: Integrating Medicine, Ethics, and Law.* Oxford and New York: Oxford University Press, 2003.

Cooper, Davina. *Power in Struggle: Feminism, Sexuality and the State.* Buckingham: Open University Press, 1995.

Cooter, Roger, and Claudia Stein. *Writing History in the Age of Biomedicine.* New Haven: Yale University Press, 2013.

Corea, G. *The Mother Machine: Reproductive Technologies from Artificial Insemination to Artificial Wombs.* New York: Harper and Row, 1985.

———. "The Reproductive Brothel." In *Man-Made Women: How New Reproductive Technologies Affect Women*, edited by G. Corea, R. D. Klein, J. Hanmer, H. B.

Holmes, B. Hoskins, M. Kishwar, J. Raymond, R. Rowland, and R. Steinbacher. London and Melbourne: Hutchinson, 1985.

Cort, E. C. "Sporadic Beriberi in Chiengmai, Siam." Far Eastern Association of Tropical Medicine (FEATM) Transactions of the 8th Biennial Congress, Siam, 1930.

Crawfurd, John. "On the Connexion between Ethnology and Physical Geography." *Transaction of the Ethnological Society of London* 2 (1863): 4–23.

———. "On the Physical and Mental Characteristics of the European and Asiatic Races of Man." *Transaction of the Ethnological Society of London* 5 (1867): 58–81.

Cwiertka, Katarzyna J. *Japanese Cuisine: Food, Power and National Identity*. London: Reaktion Books, 2006.

Daejonilbo 대전일보. "Chungcheong 11 Gae Jidgaechae Sanbooingwa Boonmanseal Eeopseo" 충청 11개 지자체 산부인과 분만실 없어 [There is no delivery room in 11 Chungcheong counties]. October 18, 2013.

Dai Ren 戴仁 [Jean-Pierre Drege]. *Shanghai Shangwu Yinshuguan, 1897–1949* 上海商務印書館 1897–1949 [La commercial press de Shanghai 1897–1949]. Translated by Li Tongshi 李桐實. Beijing: Commercial Press, 2000.

Daniels, Ken, and Karyn Taylor. "Formulating Selection Policies for Assisted Reproduction." *Social Science and Medicine* 37(12) (1993): 1473–80.

Davis, Kathy. *The Making of "Our Bodies, Ourselves": How Feminism Travels across Borders*. Durham, NC: Duke University Press, 2007.

Davis, Noel. "Observations on Beriberi in Shanghai." Far Eastern Association of Tropical Medicine (FEATM) Transactions of the 2nd Biennial Congress, Hong Kong, 1912.

D'Emilio, John. *Sexual Politics, Sexual Communities: The Making of a Homosexual Minority in the United States*. Chicago: University of Chicago Press, 1983.

Dikötter, Frank. *The Age of Openness: China before Mao*. Berkeley: University of California Press, 2008.

———. *The Discourse of Race in Modern China*. Stanford: Stanford University Press, 1992.

———. *Imperfect Concepts: Medical Knowledge, Birth Defects, and Eugenics in China*. New York: Columbia University Press, 1998.

———. *Sex, Culture and Modernity in China: Medical Science and the Construction of Sexual Identities in the Early Republican Period*. Honolulu: University of Hawai'i Press, 1995.

DiMoia, John P. *Reconstructing Bodies: Biomedicine, Health, and Nation Building in South Korea since 1945*. Stanford: Stanford University Press, 2013.

Ding Fubao. *Jiaoqi bing zhi yuanyin ji liaofa* 腳氣病之原因及療法 [Causes and treatment of the *jiaoqi* ailment]. Shanghai: Wenming shuju 1910.

Donghua Hospital Archives (DHA). Letter from the Donghua Hospital to the Colony's Medical Officer. February 16, 1933, pp. 432–38.

———. 1919–1920 Waijie laihan 外界來函 [Letters received]. 130-B19/20-214, pp. 172–73.

———. Minutes of the Board Meeting of the Tung Wah Hospital on January 26, 1904.

———. Minutes of Board Meeting, August 26, September 3, September 10, 1940.

Donghua Sanyuan bainian shilüe bianzuan weiyuanhui 東華三院百年史略編纂委員會. *Xianggang Donghua Sanyuan bainian shilüe* 香港東華三院百年史略 [One hundred years of history of the three Tung Wah Hospitals in Hong Kong]. Hong Kong: Tung Wah Hospitals, 1970.

Doyal, Lesley. *What Makes Women Sick: Gender and the Political Economy of Health*. New Brunswick, NJ: Rutgers University Press, 1995.

Du Yaquan 杜亞泉 and Ling Changhuan 凌昌煥, eds. *Gongheguo jiaokeshu shenglixue* 共和國教科書生理學 [Physiology textbook for the Republic]. 1914. Shanghai: Commercial Press, 1923.

Duara, Prasenjit. "Asia Redux: Conceptualizing a Region for Our Times." *Journal of Asian Studies* 69(4) (2010): 963–1029.

―――. *Rescuing History from the Nation: Questioning Narratives of Modern China.* Chicago: University of Chicago Press, 1995.

Duncan, David, ed. *The Life and Letters of Herbert Spencer.* Vol. 2. London: Methuen, 1908.

Durham, Herbert. "Notes on Beriberi in the Malay Peninsula and on Christmas Island (Indian Ocean)." *Journal of Hygiene* (1904): 112–55.

Edger, James Clifton. *The Practice of Obstetrics, Designed for the Use of the Students of Medicine and Practitioners.* Philadelphia: P. Blakiston's Son, 1903.

Elman, Benjamin A., ed. *Antiquarianism, Language, and Medical Philology.* Leiden: Brill, 2015.

Engelhardt, Ute. "Dietetics in Tang China and the First Extant Works of Materia Dietetica." In *Innovation in Chinese Medicine*, edited by Elisabeth Hsu, 173–91. Cambridge: Cambridge University Press, 2001.

EngenderHealth. *Contraceptive Sterilization: Global Issues and Trends.* New York: EngenderHealth, 2002.

Evans, Harriet. *Women and Sexuality in China: Female Sexuality and Gender since 1949.* New York: Continuum International Publishing Group, 1996.

"Family Planning and Workers Creed." In PC FC # 61, Population Council, Accession #2, Rockefeller Archive Center (RAC).

Fan, Fa-ti. "East Asian STS: Fox or Hedgehog?" *East Asian Science, Technology and Society: An International Journal* 1(4) (2007): 243–47.

Fan Yan-qiu 范燕秋. *Jibing, yixue yu zhimin xiandaixing: Rizhi Taiwan yixueshi* 疾病、醫學與殖民現代性：日治台灣醫學史 [Diseases, medicine, and colonial modernity: History of medicine in Japan-ruled Taiwan]. Taipei: Daw Shiang Publishing, 2006.

Fangbian Yiyuan tongji huikan 方便醫院統計彙刊 [Collection of statistics of the Expediency Hospital]. 1929.

Farquhar, Judith. *Appetites: Food and Sex in Post-socialist China.* Durham, NC: Duke University Press, 2002.

―――. "Market Magic: Getting Rich and Getting Personal in Medicine after Mao." *American Ethnologist* 23(2) (1996): 239–57.

―――. "Objects, Processes, and Female Infertility in Chinese Medicine." *Medical Anthropology Quarterly* 5(4) (1991): 370–99.

―――. "Problems of Knowledge in Contemporary Chinese Medical Discourse." *Social Sciences and Medicine* 20 (1987): 1013–21.

Farquhar, Judith, and Qicheng Zhang. *Ten Thousand Things: Nurturing Life in Contemporary Beijing.* New York: Zone Books, 2012.

Fausto-Sterling, Anne. *Sexing the Body: Gender Politics and the Construction of Sexuality.* New York: Basic Books, 2000.

Finnane, Antonia. "What Should Chinese Women Wear? A National Problem." *Modern China* 22(2) (1996): 99–131.

Firestone, Shulamith. *The Dialectic of Sex: The Case for Feminist Revolution.* New York: Bantam Books, 1971.

Flink, Edmund. "Report and Recommendations on Teaching and Research in Internal Medicine." Special Collections, University of Minnesota, February 1, 1958.

Fogel, Joshua A. *Articulating the Sinosphere: Sino-Japanese Relations in Space and Time.* Cambridge, MA: Harvard University Press, 2009.

Foucault, Michel. *The History of Sexuality.* Vol. 1. New York: Vintage Books, 1978.

Franklin, Sarah. *Embodied Progress: A Cultural Account of Assisted Conception.* London: Routledge, 1997.

Freedman, L. P., and S. L. Isaacs. "Human Rights and Reproductive Choice." *Studies in Family Planning* 24(1) (1993): 18–30.

Freedman, Ronald. *Family Planning in Taiwan: An Experiment in Social Change.* Princeton: Princeton University Press, 1969.

Frühstück, Sabine. *Colonizing Sex: Sexology and Social Control in Modern Japan.* Berkeley: University of California Press, 2003.

Fu Daiwie 傅大為. "How Far Can East Asian STS Go? A Position Paper." *East Asian Science, Technology and Society: An International Journal* 1(1) (2007): 1–14.

———. *Yaxiya de xinshenti: Xingbie, yiliao yu jindai Taiwan* 亞細亞的新身體：性別、醫療與近代台灣 [Assembling the new body: Gender/Sexuality, medicine, and modern Taiwan]. Taipei: Socio Publishing, 2005.

Fujime Yuki 藤目ゆき. *Sei no rekishigaku: Kōshō seido, dataizai taisei kara baishun bōshihō, yūsei hogohō taisei e* 性の歴史学：公娼制度、隨胎罪体制から売春防止法、優生保護法体制へ [History of sexuality: From the licensed prostitution and illegal abortion system to the Prostitution Prevention Act and the Eugenic Protection Act system]. Tōkyō: Fuji Shuppan, 1997.

Fukujō Komatarō 福城駒多朗. *Tsūzoku danjo eiseiron* 通俗男女衛生論 [Popular hygiene for men and women]. Tokyo: Shuppan kaisha, 1880.

Fukuzawa Yukichi 福沢諭吉. "Nihon fujin ron" 日本婦人論 [Theories on Japanese women]. *Jijishimpō*, June 4–12, 1885. Republished in *Fukuzawa Yukichi on Japanese Women: Selected Works*, translated and edited by Eiichi Kiyooka, 6–36. Tokyo: University of Tokyo Press, 1988.

Funk, Casimir. "The Etiology of the Deficiency Diseases." *Journal of State Medicine* 20 (1912): 341.

Furth, Charlotte. *A Flourishing Yin: Gender in China's Medical History, 960–1665.* Berkeley: University of California Press, 1999.

———. "Introduction: Hygienic Modernity in Chinese East Asia." In *Health and Hygiene in Chinese East Asia: Policies and Publics in the Long Twentieth Century*, edited by Angela Ki Che Leung and Charlotte Furth, 1–21. Durham, NC: Duke University Press, 2010.

Gaide, Laurent Joseph, and Henri Désiré M. Bodet. "Le beriberi en Indochine." Far Eastern Association of Tropical Medicine (FEATM) Transactions of the 8th Congress, Siam, 1930.

Galton, Francis. "Hereditary Talent and Character." *Macmillan's Magazine* 12 (1865): 157–66, 318–27.

Gault, Neil L. "Korea—a New Venture in International Medical Education." *University of Minnesota Medical Bulletin* 33 (November 1961): 73–85.

Gelézeau, Valérie. *Ap'at'ŭ konghwaguk: P'ŭrangsŭ chiri hakcha ka pon Han'guk ŭi ap'at'ŭ* 아파트 공화국：프랑스 지리 학자 가 본 한국 의 아파트 [On the republic of apartments]. Seoul: Humanitas Press, 2007.

Gibson, R. M. "Beriberi in Hong Kong, with Special Reference to the Records of the Alice Memorial and Nethersole Hospitals and with Notes on Two Years' Experience of the Disease." Manuscript, March 16, 1900.

Ginsburg, Faye D., and Rayna Rapp, eds. *Conceiving the New World Order: The Global Politics of Reproduction.* Berkeley: University of California Press, 1995.

Goss, John, and Terence Wesley-Smith. Introduction to *Remaking Area Studies: Teaching and Learning across Asia and the Pacific*, edited by Terence Wesley-Smith and John Goss, ix–xxvii. Honolulu: University of Hawai'i Press, 2010.

Gottschang, Suzanne Zhang. "Taking Patriarchy out of Post-partum Recovery." In *Transformations of Patriarchy in Contemporary China*, edited by Gonçalo Santos and Stevan Harrell. (Forthcoming).

Greenhalgh, Susan. "Biopower in East and Pacific Asia." In "Is There an Asian Biopolitics?" edited by Nicolas Langlitz, *BioSocieties* 6 (2011): 487–500.

———. *Cultivating Global Citizens: Population in the Rise of China*. Cambridge, MA: Harvard University Press, 2010.

———. *Just One Child: Science and Policy in Deng's China*. Berkeley: University of California Press, 2008.

Gu Shoubai 顧壽白. *Kaiming shengli weishengxue jiaoben* 開明生理衛生學教本 [Physiology and hygiene textbooks from Kaiming Bookstore]. Shanghai: Kaiming shudian, 1932.

———. *Xiandai chuzhong jiaokeshu shengli weishengxue* 現代初中教科書生理衛生學 [Modern junior high textbook of physiology and hygiene]. Shanghai: Commercial Press, 1923.

———. *Xinzhuan chujizhongxue jiaokeshu shengli weishengxue* 新撰初級中學教科書生理衛生學 [New composition of junior high physiology and hygiene textbook]. Shanghai: Commercial Press, 1926.

Gu Shusen 顧樹森, ed. *Xinzhi shenglixue jiaoben* 新制生理學教本 [Physiology textbook for new school system]. Reviewed by Wu Jiaxu 吳家煦. Shanghai: Zhonghua shuju, 1917.

Guan Ming 管明. "Zhongguo Kelisiding" 中國克麗斯汀 [The Chinese Christine]. *Lianhebao* 聯合報, September 1, 1953, no. 6.

Guo Renyuan 郭任遠. "Womende shenti zenme lai de ne" 我們的身體怎麼來的呢? [How did our body come about]. In *Chuzhong ziran kexue* 初中自然科學 [Natural science for junior highs]. Vol. 2. *Shengli zhi bu* 生理之部 [Physiology]: 1–20. 1926. Shanghai: Shijie shuju, 1930.

Ha, Jung-Ok. "Risk Disparities in the Globalization of Assisted Reproductive Technology: The Case of Asia." *Global Public Health: An International Journal for Research, Policy and Practice* 8(8) (2013): 904–25.

Habuto Eiji 羽太銳治. *Ippan seiyokugaku* 一般性慾學 [General sexology]. Tokyo: Jitsugyō no Nihonsha, 1920.

Haimes, Erica. "Recreating the Family? Policy Considerations Relating to the 'New Reproductive Technologies.'" In *The New Reproductive Technologies*, edited by Maureen McNeil, Ian Varcoe, and Steven Yearley, 154–72. New York: St. Martin's Press, 1990.

Hamashita, Takeshi. "Tribute and Treaties: Maritime Asia and Treaty-Port Networks in the Era of Negotiation: 1800–1900." In *The Resurgence of East Asia: 500, 150 and 50 Year Perspectives*, edited by Giovanni Arrighi, Takeshi Hamashita, and Mark Selden, 17–50. London and New York: Routledge, 2003.

Handwerker, Lisa. "The Consequences of Modernity for Childless Women in China: Medicalization and Resistance." In *Pragmatic Women and Body Politics*, edited by Margaret Lock and Patricia A. Kaufert, 178–205. Cambridge: Cambridge University Press, 1998.

———. "The Politics of Making Modern Babies in China: Reproductive Technologies and the 'New' Eugenics." In *Infertility around the Globe: New Thinking on Childlessness, Gender, and Reproductive Technologies*, edited by Marcia C. Inhorn and Frank van Balen, 298–314. Berkeley: University of California Press, 2002.

Happy Home. Seoul: PPFK, 1968–.

Haraway, Donna. "Situated Knowledges: The Science Question in Feminism and the Privilege of Partial Perspectives." *Feminist Studies* 14(3) (1988): 575–99.

Harding, Sandra. *Is Science Multicultural? Postcolonialisms, Feminisms, and Epistemologies*. Bloomington: Indiana University Press, 1998.

———. *The Science Question in Feminism*. Ithaca: Cornell University Press, 1986.

Hausman, Bernice L. *Changing Sex: Transsexualism, Technology, and the Idea of Gender*. Durham, NC: Duke University Press, 1995.

He Lianchen 何廉臣, ed. *Quanguo ming yi yan'an leibian* 全國名醫驗案類編 [Selected medical cases (showing medical efficiency) by famous doctors in the nation]. 1929. Taipei: Xuanfeng chubanshe 1971.

Heidhues, Mary F. S. *Bangka Tin and Mentok Pepper: Chinese Settlement on an Indonesian Island*. Singapore: Institute of Southeast Asian Studies, 1992.

Heiser, Victor. "Beri-Beri: An Additional Experience at Culion." Far Eastern Association of Tropical Medicine (FEATM) Comptes rendus de travaux du 3e congrès biennal tenu à Saigon, 1913.

Highet, H. C. "The Sequelae of Beriberi." Far Eastern Association of Tropical Medicine (FEATM) Comptes rendus de travaux du 3e congrès biennal tenu à Saigon, 1913.

Ho, Josephine. "Embodying Gender: Transgender Body/Subject Formations in Taiwan." *Inter-Asia Cultural Studies* 7(2) (2006): 228–42.

———, ed. *Kuaxingbie* 跨性別 [Transgender]. Jungli, Taiwan: National Central University Center for the Study of Sexualities, 2003.

Ho, Szu-Ying 何思瑩. "'Feifa' qingjingxia de kuer shengzhi: Taiwan nütongzhi de rengong shengzhi keji shizuo" 「非法」情境下的酷兒生殖：台灣女同志的人工生殖科技實作 [Queering reproduction in a prohibited context: Assisted reproductive technologies as utilized by Taiwan's lesbians]. *Nüxue xuezhi funu yu xingbie yanjiu* 女學學誌：婦女與性別研究 [Journal of Women and Gender Studies] 12 (2014): 53–122.

———. "Queer Reproduction: Lesbian Parenting Practice, Use of Reproductive Technology and Emotional Identity." MA thesis, National Taiwan University, 2008.

Hollick, Frederick. *Seishoku shizen shi: Ichi mei kon'in no* [The marriage guide, or The natural history of generation]. Translated by Oki Keijirō 隠岐敬治郎 and Ōnishi Naosaburo 大西直三郎. Tokyo: Shimamura Risuke, 1896.

Home Reserve. http://www.yebigun1.mil.kr.

Homei, Aya. "Birth Attendants in Meiji Japan: The Rise of the Biomedical Birth Model and a New Division of Labour." *Social History of Medicine* 19(3) (2006): 407–24.

———. "Midwives and the Medical Marketplace in Modern Japan." *Japanese Studies* 32(2) (2012): 275–93.

———. "Modernising Midwifery: The History of a Female Medical Profession in Japan, 1868–1931." PhD diss., University of Manchester, 2003.

Hong, Hyŏn-o. *Korea History of Pharmacy*. Seoul: Handok Yakŏp Chusikhoesa, 1972.

Hong Kong Administrative Report 1908. "Vital statistics." Hong Kong: Government Printer, 1908.

Hong Kong Administrative Report 1927. "Public Health." Hong Kong: Government Printer, 1927.

Honig, Emily. "Socialist Sex: The Cultural Revolution Revisited." *Modern China* 29(2) (2003): 153–75.

Houck, Judith A. *Hot and Bothered: Women, Medicine and Menopause in Modern America*. Cambridge, MA: Harvard University Press, 2006.

"How the U Helps Seoul University Rebuild after the Ravages of War." *Minnesotan* 10(3) (December 1956): 3–7, 11, 14–15.

Hsu Su-Ting 徐淑婷. "Bianxingyuzheng huanzhe bianxing shoushu hou de shenxin shehui shiying" 變性慾症患者變性手術後的身心社會適應 [The physical, psychological and social adaptation among transsexuals after sex reassignment surgery: A study of six cases]. MA thesis, Kaohsiung Medical University, 1998.

Hu, Danian. *China and Albert Einstein: The Reception of the Physicist and His Theory in China, 1917–1979*. Cambridge, MA: Harvard University Press, 2005.

Hua Wenqi 華文祺, ed. *Zhonghua zhongxue shengli jiaokeshu* 中華中學生理教科書 [Chinese Bookstore's physiology and hygiene textbook for junior highs]. Reviewed by Dai Kedun 戴克敦, Yao Hanzhang 姚漢章, and Lubi Kui 陸費逵. 18th ed. 1913. Shanghai: Zhonghua shuju, 1921.

Huazi ribao 華字日報 [Chinese Mail]. June 27, 1928.

———. "Zu jiaoqi yiyuan" 組脚氣醫院 [Organizing a *jiaoqi* hospital], April 17, 1937.

Human Fertilisation and Embryology Act (HFE) of 1990. Accessed March 1, 2014. http://www.legislation.gov.uk/ukpga/1990/37/contents.

Humphreys, S. C., ed. *Cultures of Scholarship*. Ann Arbor: University of Michigan Press, 1998.

Hunter, William. "The Incidence of Disease in Hong Kong." *Journal of Tropical Medicine* (May 1, 1905): 129–31.

———. "The Prevalence of Beriberi in Hong Kong." *Journal of Tropical Medicine and Hygiene* 10(16) (August 5, 1907): 265–71.

Huntington, Samuel. "The Clash of Civilizations?" *Foreign Affairs* 72(3) (1993): 22–49.

Hwang, Nami. "The Status and Performances of the National Support Program for Infertile Couples." *Health and Welfare Issue and Focus* 192 (2013): 1–8.

Imamura Ryō 今村亮. *Kakké kōyō* 脚氣鈎要 [Essentials on *kakké*]. Edo: Keigyōkan edition, 1861.

———. *Kakké shinron* 脚氣新論 [New treatise on *kakké*]. Edo: Keigyōkan edition, 1878.

Inhorn, Marcia C. *Cosmopolitan Conceptions: IVF Sojourns in Global Dubai*. Durham, NC: Duke University Press, 2015.

———. "'He Won't Be My Son': Middle Eastern Muslim Men's Discourses of Adoption and Gamete Donation." *Medical Anthropology Quarterly* 20(1) (2006): 94–120.

———. *Local Babies, Global Science: Gender, Religion, and In-vitro Fertilization in Egypt*. New York: Routledge, 2003.

———. "Making Muslim Babies: IVF and Gamete Donation in Sunni and Shi'a Islam." *Culture, Medicine, and Psychiatry* 30 (2006): 427–50.

Inhorn, Marcia C., and Daphna Birenbaum-Carmeli. "Assisted Reproductive Technologies and Culture Change." *Annual Review of Anthropology* 37 (2008): 177–96.

Inhorn, Marcia C., and Pasquale Patrizio. "Rethinking Reproductive 'Tourism' as Reproductive 'Exile.'" *Fertility and Sterility* 92(3) (2009): 904–6.

Institute for International Cooperation (IIC), Japan International Cooperation Agency (JICA). "Family Planning." In *Japan's Experiences in Public Health and Medical Systems*, 79–107. Tokyo: JICA, 2005.

Irving, Alan. "STS Perspectives on Scientific Governance." In *The Handbook of Science and Technology Studies*, edited by Edward J. Hackett, Olga Amsterdamska, Michael Lynch, and Judy Wajcman, 3rd ed., 583–607. Cambridge, MA: MIT Press, 2008.

Jackson, Stevi. "Gender, Sexuality, and Heterosexuality." *Feminist Theory* 7(1) (2008): 105–21.

Jackson, Stevi, Jieyu Liu, and Juhyun Woo, eds. *East Asian Sexualities: Modernity, Gender and New Sexual Cultures*. New York: Zed Books, 2008.

Ji Sihua 計泗華. *Chuzhong shengli weisheng zhidaoshu* 初中生理衛生學指導書 [Teachers' manual for junior high physiology and hygiene]. Shanghai: Shijie shuju, 1933.

Jiang Zhenxun 姜振勛. "Er ge jiaoqi bingli" 二個腳氣病例 [Two cases of *jiaoqi*]. *Xinyi yu shehui huikan* 新醫與社會彙刊 2 (1934): 257–58.

———. "Jiaoqi qian shuo" 腳氣淺說 [Brief note on *jiaoqi*]. *Xinyi yu shehui huikan* 新醫與社會彙刊 1 (1928): 208–11.

Jiaoyu zazhi 教育雜誌 [Education journal] 15, no. 8. Shanghai: Shanghai Commercial Press, 1923.

Jin Jungwon 陳姃湲 [Chen Zhengyuan]. *Cong Dongya kan jindai Zhongguo funü jiaoyu: Zhishi fenzi dui "xianqi liangmu" de gaizao* 從東亞看近代中國婦女教育：知識份子對「賢妻良母」的改造 [An East Asian perspective on women's education in modern China: Reform "wise wife and good mother" by the intellectuals]. Taipei: Daoxiang chubanshe, 2005.

Jo, Nam-Hun 조남훈, Il-Hyeon Kim 김일현, Mun-Hee Seo 서문희, and Yeong-Sik Jang 장영식. *Choigeuneoi Ingoojeongchaeck Donghyanggwa Jeonmang: Je 6 Cha 5 Gaenyeon Gaeheockeul Joongseemeuroo* 최근의 인구정책 동향과 전망: 제6차 5개년 계획을 중심으로 [Contemporary trends and prospects for population policy: The sixth Five-Year Plan]. Seoul: Korean Population and Public Health Research Center, 1989.

Johnson, Tina Phillips. *Childbirth in Republican China: Delivering Modernity*. Lanham, MD: Lexington Books, 2011.

Johnson, Tracy, and Elizabeth Fee. "Women's Participation in Clinical Research: From Protection to Access." In *Women and Health Research: Ethical and Legal Issues of Including Women in Clinical Studies*, edited by Anna C. Mastroianni, Ruth Faden, and Daniel Federman, 1–10. Washington DC: National Academy Press, 1994.

Jones, Gavin W. "Changing Marriage Patterns in Asia." Asia Research Institute Working Paper Series No. 131. 2010. Accessed July 28, 2015. http://www.ari.nus.edu.sg/wps/wps10_131.pdf.

Jones, Gavin, Paulin Tay Straughan, and Angelique Chan, eds. *Ultra-Low Fertility in Pacific Asia: Trends, Causes and Policy Issues*. London: Routledge, 2009.

Jones, Greta. "Women and Eugenics in Britain: The Case of Mary Scharlieb, Elizabeth Sloan Chesser, and Stella Browne." *Annals of Science* 52(5) (1995): 481–502.

Jorgensen, Christine. *Christine Jorgensen: A Personal Autobiography*. 1967. San Francisco: Cleis Press, 2000.

Judd, Dennis, and Keith Terrance Surridge. *The Boer War: A History*. London: I. B. Tauris, 2013.

Judge, Joan. "Meng Mu meets the Modern: Female Exemplars in Early Twentieth Century Textbooks for Girls and Women." *Jindai Zhongguo funüshi yanjiu* 近代中國婦女史研究 [Research on women in modern Chinese history] 8 (2000): 129–77.

Kahn, Susan Martha. *Reproducing Jews: A Cultural Account of Assisted Conception in Israel*. Durham, NC: Duke University Press, 2000.

Kaji Shigeo 加地成雄. *Sugi Kōji den* 杉亨二伝 [Biography of Sugi Kōji]. Tokyo: Aoi shobō, 1960.

Kaplan, L. J., and R. Tong. *Controlling Our Reproductive Destiny: A Technological and Philosophical Perspective*. Cambridge, MA: MIT Press, 1994.

Kawamura Kunimitsu 川村 邦光. "Onna no yamai, otoko no yamai" 女の病、男の病 [Women's illness, men's illness]. *Gendai shisō* 現代思想 21(7) (1993): 88–109.

Kecheng jiaocai yanjiusuo 課程教材研究所, ed. *Ershi shiji Zhongguo zhongxiaoxue kecheng biaozhun, jiaoxue dagang huibian* 20世紀中國中小學課程標準、教學大綱匯

編 [Collection of curricula directives and teaching guidelines for primary and secondary education in twentieth-century China]. Vol. 1, *Kecheng jiaoxue jihua juan* 課程教學計畫卷 [Planning for curricula and teaching]. Beijing: Renmin jiaoyu chubanshe, 2001.

Kim, Hoi-eun. *Doctors of Empire: Medical and Cultural Encounters between Imperial Germany and Meiji Japan.* Toronto: University of Toronto Press, 2014.

Kim, M.-H. 김명희, H.-C. Kwon 권혁찬, S.-J. Paik 백수진, C.-S. Park 박춘선, and G.-H. Lee 이경훈. *Naneembooboo Jeewonsaeup Gaeseonbangan Yeongoo* 난임부부 지원사업 개선방안 연구 [A study for the improvement of sub-fertility couple supporting program]. Seoul: Ministry of Health and Welfare, 2013.

Kim, S.-G. 김승권, Y.-K. Kim 김유경, H.-R. Kim 김혜련, J.-S. Park 박종서, C.-G. Son 손창균, Y.-J. Choi 최영준, Y.-W. Kim 김연우, G.-E. Lee 이가은, and A.-R. Yoon 윤아름. *2012 Nyeon Jeongook Choolsanyock Meet Gajeockbogeonbockjee Seeltaejosa* 2012년 전국 출산력 및 가족보건복지 실태조사 [The 2012 national survey on fertility, family health, and welfare in Korea.] Seoul: Korea Institute for Health and Social Affairs, 2012.

Kim, Sonja. "Contesting Bodies: Managing Population, Birthing, and Medicine in Korea, 1876–1945." PhD diss., University of California, Los Angeles, 2008.

———. "'Limiting Birth': Birth Control in Colonial Korea." *East Asian Science, Technology and Society: An International Journal* 2(3) (2008): 335–59.

Kim, Y.-K. 김유경, M.-J. Jin 진미정, Y.-J. Song 송유진, and G.-H. Kim 김가희. *Gagoo Gajeockeui Byeondonggwa Jeongchaeckjeock Daeungbangan Yeongoo* 가구 가족의 변동과 정책적 대응방안 연구 [Changes in family and household structures and social welfare policies]. Seoul: Korea Institute for Health and Social Affairs, 2013. Accessed February 4, 2014. https://www.kihasa.re.kr/html/jsp/publication/research/.

Ko, Dorothy. *Cinderella's Sisters: A Revisionist History of Footbinding.* Berkeley: University of California Press, 2005.

Kondō Mikio 近藤幹生. "Meiji chūki ni okeru gakurei mimanji no shūgakukinshi tsūtatsu ni kansuru kentō" 明治中期における学齢未満児の就学禁止通達に関する検討 [Study on prohibition of entering school notice for children pre-school age in the middle of the Meiji era]. *Nagano-ken tanki daigaku kiyō* 長野県短期大学紀要 60 (December 2005): 99–109.

———. "Meiji chūki ni okeru shūgaku nenrei no giron ni kansuru ichi kōsatsu." 明治中期における就学年齢の議論に関する一考察 [A study on school-age issues in the mid Meiji era]. *Nagano-ken tanki daigaku kiyō* 長野県短期大学紀要 59 (December 2004): 45–54.

"Korea, Family Planning Program—Historical Review." In "Paul Hartman, 1967–1968." Box 26/FC, Population Council, Accession #2, Rockefeller Archive Center (RAC).

Korea Institute for Health and social Affairs (KIHASA) 한국보건사회연구원. *2010 Nyeon Jeongook Choolsanyock Meet Gajeockbogeonbockjee Seeltaejosa* 2010년 전국 출산력 및 가족보건복지 실태조사 [The 2010 national survey on fertility, family health, and welfare in Korea]. 2010. Accessed January 24, 2014. http://kosis.kr/common/meta_onedepth.jsp?vwed=MT_CTITLE&listid=331_33101.

Korean Journal of Urology.

Koyama, Shizuko. *Ryōsai Kenbo: The Educational Idea of "Good Wife, Wise Mother" in Modern Japan.* Leiden and Boston: Brill, 2013.

Krieger, Nancy, and Elizabeth Fee. "Man-Made Medicine and Women's Health: The Biopolitics of Sex/Gender and Race/Ethnicity." In *Women's Health, Politics, and*

Power: Essays on Sex/Gender, Medicine, and Public Health, edited by Elizabeth Fee and Nancy Krieger, 11–29. New York: Baywood, 1994.

Ku, Yenlin. "The Changing Status of Women in Taiwan: A Conscious and Collective Struggle Toward Equality." *Women's Studies International Forum* 11(3) (1988): 179–86.

Kuang Heling 鄺賀齡. "Ru'er jiaoqi bing" 乳兒腳氣病 [*Jiaoqi* ailment of babies]. *Zhongshan yibao* 6(5–6) (1951): 8.

Kubo Kan 久保賢. "Arai Kotarō ryakuden" 新井厔太郎略伝 [An abbreviated biography of Arai Kotarō]. In *Zaisen Nihonjin yakugyō kaiko shi* 在鮮日本人薬業回顧史 [History of Japanese pharmaceutical industry in Korea], 377–80. Zaisen Nihonjin yakugyō kaikoshi hensankai, 1961.

Kubota Eisuke 久保田英助. "Kindai Nihon ni okeru kyōiku kara no 'seikyōyiku' haijo no kōzō—Meiji kōki no 'seiyaku kyōiku' ronsō to sono shakai haikei no bunkei wo tsūjite" 近代日本における教育からの「性教育」排除の構造—明治後期の「性慾教育」論争とその社会背景の分析を通じて [The removal of sex education in modern Japanese education—an analysis on the social background of late Meiji debates on sex education]. *Gakujutsu kenkyū (kyōiku: shōgai kyōiku gakuhen)* 学術研究 (教育 ~ 生涯教育学編) 53 (February 2005): 55–69.

Kure Shuzo 呉秀三. *Zhongxue shengli weisheng jiaokeshu* 中學生理衛生教科書 [Physiology and hygiene textbook for middle schools]. Translated by Hua Shenqi 華申祺 and Hua Wenqi 華文祺. 1906. Shanghai: Wenming shuju, 1912.

Kuriyama, Shigehisa. *The Expressiveness of the Body and the Divergence of Greek and Chinese Medicine*. New York: Zone Books, 1999.

Kuroki Shizuya 黒木静也, and Iida Senri 飯田千里. *Shikijō eisei tetsugaku: Jintai kairyō ron* 色情衛生哲学：人体改良論 [Philosophy of sexual hygiene: Theories on improving the body]. Tokyo: Tsūzoku eisei gakkai, 1906.

Kwon, Nayoung Aimee. "Translated Encounters and Empire: Colonial Korea and the Literature of Exile." PhD diss., University of California, Los Angeles, 2008.

Kwon, T. H. 권태환, T. H. Kim 김태헌, D. S. Kim 김두섭, K. H. Jun 전광희, and K. S. Eun 은기수. *Hangook Choolsanyock Byeoncheoneui Yeehae* 한국 출산력 변천의 이해 [Understanding Korea's demographic transition]. Seoul: Ilshinsa, 1997.

Lader, Lawrence. *Breeding Ourselves to Death*. New York: Seven Books, 1971.

Lam, Tong. *A Passion for Facts: Social Surveys and the Construction of the Chinese Nation-State, 1900–1949*. Berkeley: University of California Press, 2011.

Langen, C. D. "The International Control of Beriberi." Far Eastern Association of Tropical Medicine (FEATM) Transactions of 6th Biennial Congress, Tokyo, 1925.

Langlitz, Nicolas, ed. "Is There an Asian Biopolitics?" Books Forum Introduction, *BioSocieties* 6 (2011): 487–500.

Laqueur, Thomas W. *Solitary Sex: A Cultural History of Masturbation*. New York and London: Zone Books, 2003.

Larson, Wendy. "Never So Wild: Sexing the Cultural Revolution." *Modern China* 25(4) (1999): 423–50.

Laughery, John. *The Other Side of Silence: Men's Lives and Gay Identities: A Twentieth-Century History*. New York: Henry Holt, 1998.

Lee, Ellie, Jan Macvarish, and Sally Sheldon. "Assessing Child Welfare under the Human Fertilisation and Embryology Act 2008: A Case Study in Medicalization?" *Sociology of Health and Illness* 36 (2014): 500–15.

Lee, Gyoung Hoon, Hyun Jin Song, Kyu Sup Lee, and Young Min Choi. "Current Status of ART in Korea, 2010." *Conical and Experimental Reproductive Medicine* 42(1) (2015): 8–13.

Lee, H. Y. "Clinical Studies on the Influences of Vasectomy." *Korean Journal of Urology* 7(1) (1966): 11–29.

———. "The Role of a National Association for Voluntary Sterilization in the National Family Planning Program." Association for Voluntary Sterilization of the Asian Regional Conference on Voluntary Sterilization, Taipei, May 10–12, 1975. Taipei, July, 1975.

———. "A Twenty Year Experience with Vasovasostomy." *Journal of Urology* 136(2) (September 1986): 413–15.

Lee, Jen-der. "Gender and Medicine in Tang China." *Asia Major* 16(2) (2003): 1–23.

——— 李貞德. "Taiwan shengli weisheng jiaoyu zhong de xing, shengzhi yu xingbie (1945–1968)" 台灣生理衛生教育中的性、生殖與性別 [Sex and reproduction in physiology and hygiene textbooks of postwar Taiwan]. *Research on Women in Modern Chinese History* 22 (2013): 64–125.

Lee, Seung-Joon. "Taste in Numbers: Science and the Food Problem in Republican Guangzhou, 1927–1937." *Twentieth-Century China* 35(2) (April 2010): 81–105.

Lee, Wei Yung, Eric Reid, and Bernard Read. "Industrial Health in Shanghai, China, III: Shanghai Factory Diets Compared with Those of Institutional Workers." *Chinese Medical Association Special Report Series* 7 (1936): 21–22.

Lei, Sean Hsiang-lin. "Habituating the Four Virtues: Ethics, Family and the Body in the Anti-tuberculosis Campaigns and the New Life Movement." *Bulletin of the Institute of Modern History, Academia Sinica* 74 (2011): 133–77.

———. *Neither Donkey nor Horse: Medicine in the Struggle over China's Modernity.* Chicago: University of Chicago Press, 2014.

———. "Qi-Transformation and the Steam Engine: The Incorporation of Western Anatomy and the Re-conceptualization of the Body in Nineteenth Century Chinese Medicine." *Asian Medicine: Tradition and Modernity* 7(2) (2014): 319–57.

——— 雷祥麟. "Weisheng weihe bu shi baowei shengming" 衛生為何不是保衛生命? [Why is hygiene not about protecting life?]. In *Diguo yu xiandai yixue* 帝國與現代醫學 [Empires and modern medicine], edited by Li Shangren [Shang-Jen Li] 李尚仁, 438–48. Taipei: Linking Publishers, 2008.

Leung, Angela K. C. "Women Practicing Medicine in Pre-Modern China." In *Chinese Women in the Imperial Past: New Perspectives*, edited by H. Zurndorfer, 101–34. Leiden: Brill Academic Publishers, 1999.

Leung, Angela Ki Che, and Charlotte Furth, eds. *Health and Hygiene in Chinese East Asia: Policies and Publics in the Long Twentieth Century.* Durham, NC: Duke University Press, 2010.

Levenstein, Harvey. *Revolution at the Table: The Transformation of the American Diet.* Berkeley: University of California Press, 2003.

Lewis, Martin, and Kären Wigen. *The Myth of Continents: A Critique of Meta-geography.* Berkeley: University of California Press, 1997.

Li, Hung-hsi 李鴻禧. "Rengong shoujing de 'falu houyizheng': Cong shiguan ying'er tanqi (3) youshengxue guan yu nuquan yundongzhi 'fuzuoyong'" 人工授精的「法律後遺症」——從試管嬰兒談起 (三) 優生學觀與女權運動之「副作用」 [Legal "after effects" of artificial insemination: Eugenics and women's movement's "side effect"]. *Dangdai yixue* 當代醫學 [Contemporary medicine] 12 (1979): 96–102.

Li Zhaoshi 李兆時. "Jiaoqi bing zhi guofang guan" 腳氣病之國防觀 [Looking at *jiaoqi* from the national defense point of view]. *Guangxi Jianshe yixue yuekan* 1(3) 1937: 33–34.

Lianhebao 聯合報 [United Daily News]. "Banfa yingbianfei qianjin zeng hongzhuang" 頒發應變費 千金贈紅妝 [Awarding Xie for building her new feminine look]. September 21, 1955, no. 3.

———. "Burang Kelisiding zhuanmei yuqian dabing jiang bianchen xiaojie" 不讓 克麗絲汀專美於前 大兵將變成小姐 [Christine will not be America's exclusive: Soldier destined to become a lady]. August 21, 1953, no. 3.

———. "Fabiao Xie Jianshun mimi weifan yishifa buwu shidangchu" 發表謝尖順 祕密 違反醫師法 不無失當處 [Publicizing Xie Jianshun's secret goes against the legal regulation of medicine]. October 29, 1955, no. 3.

———. "Hebi ruci feijing" 何必如此費勁 [Why go through so much trouble]. March 26, 1954, no. 3.

———. "He yi wei Xie Jianshun" 何以慰謝尖順 [How to console Xie Jianshun]. October 29, 1955, no. 3.

———. "Lujun diyi zongyiyuan xuanbu Xie Jianshun shoushu chenggong" 陸軍第一 總醫院宣佈 謝尖順變性手術成功 [No. 1 Hospital announces the completion and success of Xie Jianshun's sex change operation]. October 28, 1955, no. 1.

———. "Nanbu junyou fenshe weiwen Xie Jianshun" 南部軍友分社 慰問謝尖順 [Soldiers from the southern station console Xie Jianshun]. September 4, 1953, no. 3.

———. "Nanshi faxian yinyangren jiangdong shoushu bian nannü" 南市發現陰陽人 將動手術辨男女 [A hermaphrodite discovered in Tainan: Sex to be determined after surgery]. August 14, 1953, no. 3.

———. "Shoushu shunli wancheng gaizao juyou bawo" 手術順利完成 改造具有把握 [Surgery successfully completed: Alteration is feasible]. August 21, 1953, no. 3.

———. "Sici shoushu yibianerchai Xie Jianshun bianxing jingguo" 四次手術易弁而 釵 謝尖順變性經過 [Male to female transformation after four surgeries: The sex change experience of Xie Jianshun]. October 28, 1955, no. 3.

———. "Wei qiuzheng shengli yi diding yinyang" 為求正生理 易地定陰陽 [To validate physiology and yin or yang]. December 5, 1953, no. 3.

———. "Woguo yixue shishang de chuangju Xie Jianshun bianxing shoushu chenggong" 我國醫學史上的創舉 謝尖順變性手術成功 [A new chapter in the nation's medical history: The success of Xie Jianshun's sex change surgery]. August 31, 1955, no. 1.

———. "Xiaoyangnü Fu Xiuxia zhu Tatong Jiaoyangyuan" 小養女傅秀霞 住大同教 養院 [Little girl Fu Xiuxia boarding Ta Tong Relief Institute]. June 7, 1959, no. 3.

———. "Xie Jianshun bianxing shoushu hou yishi liangzhou hou kexue yan quansheng" 謝尖順變性手術後 醫師兩週後 科學驗全身 [Doctors will examine Xie Jianshun's body scientifically two weeks after sex change operation]. September 3, 1955, no. 3.

———. "Xie Jianshun biangxing shoushu jingguo duanqi zhengshi gongbu" 謝尖順 變性手術經過 短期正式公佈 [The details of Xie Jianshun's sex change surgery to be publicized shortly]. September 1, 1955, no. 3.

———. "Xie Jianshun bingfang shenju jingdai shoushu ding yiyang" 謝尖順病房深 居 靜待手術定陰陽 [Xie Jianshun residing in the hospital room: Waiting for sex-determination surgery]. February 15, 1954, no. 3.

———. "Xie Jianshun de nü'erjing qi xumei busheng xiunao huai jilü jingnian fangjie" 謝尖順的女兒經 棄鬚眉不勝羞惱 懷積慮經年方解 [Xie Jianshun's anxiety about menstruation problems finally resolved]. September 2, 1955, no. 3.

———. "Xie Jianshun gaizao shoushu huo jianglai Taibei kaidao" 謝尖順改造手術 或將來台北開刀 [Xie Jianshun's alteration surgery might take place in Taipei]. September 24, 1953, no. 3.

————. "Xie Jianshun guanxiongfu" 謝尖順慣雄伏 [Xie Jianshun adjusting to feminine psyche]. November 11, 1959, no. 4.

————. "Xie Jianshun jiju nü'ertai qinsi mantou fenbaimian youju mishi yizeng xiu" 謝尖順極具女兒態 青絲滿頭粉白面 幽居密室益增羞 [Xie Jianshun appears extremely feminine]. June 25, 1954, no. 5.

————. "Xie Jianshun jue laibei kaidao xinan yinü nanding duankan erci shoushu" 謝尖順決來北開刀 係男抑女難定 端看二次手術 [Xie Jianshun has decided to relocate to Taipei for surgery: Sex determination depends on the second operation]. November 27, 1953, no. 3.

————. "Xie Jianshun kaidaohou zuori qingkuang zhenchang" 謝尖順開刀後 昨日情況正常 [Xie Jianshun's operation proceeded normally yesterday]. August 22, 1953, no. 3.

————. "Xie Jianshun luoxiong zhaopian zhengshi xi gongpin" 謝尖順裸胸照片 證實係贋品 [Xie Jianshun's half-nude photo: A hoax]. September 10, 1955, no. 3.

————. "Xie Jianshun xiaojie de yintong" 謝尖順小姐的隱痛 [The pain of Miss Xie Jianshun]. October 17, 1953, no. 3.

————. "Xie Jianshun xiaojie jiang beilai kaidao" 謝尖順小姐 將北來開刀 [Miss Xie Jianshun coming to Taipei for surgery]. October 29, 1953, no. 3.

————. "Xie Jianshun youju daibian yijue de titai jiaorou" 謝尖順幽居待變 益覺得體態嬌柔 [Xie Jianshun secluding herself and becoming feminized]. March 18, 1954, no. 3.

————. "Xie Jianshun younan biannü shoushu yi jiejin chenggong" 謝尖順由男變女手術已接近成功 [The surgery of Xie Jianshun's male-to-female transformation almost complete]. January 9, 1955, no. 3.

————. "Xiri dabing tongzhi jianglai fulian huiyuan" 昔日大兵同志 將來婦聯會員 [Former soldier comrade: A future member of women's association]. October 10, 1956, no. 3.

————. "Xiri shachang zhanshi jinze jingru chuzi" 昔日沙場戰士 今則靜如處子 [Former battle warrior: A present quiet virgin]. September 17, 1958, no. 4.

————. "Yinyangren bianxing shoushu qian zhunbei hushi xiaojie qunyu tanxiao miqu xinli fanying ziliao" 陰陽人變性手術前準備 護士小姐群與談笑 覓取心理反映資料 [Before the hermaphrodite's sex change operation: Chatting with nurses to reveal psychological data]. August 16, 1953, no. 3.

————. "Yinyangren daokou chaixian" 陰陽人 刀口拆線 [The hermaphrodite's stitches removed]. August 28, 1953, no. 3.

————. "Yinyangren Xie Jianshun jinkaidao biancixiong" 陰陽人謝尖順 今開刀辨雌雄 [Hermaphrodite Xie Jianshun: Sex determined today through surgery]. August 20, 1953, no. 3.

————. "Yinyangren Xie Jianshun tongyi gaizao nüxing" 陰陽人謝尖順 同意改造女性 [Hermaphrodite Xie Jianshun agreed to be turned into a woman]. August 30, 1953, no. 3.

————. "Yinyangren xisu wangshi yuan cishen chengwei nan'er" 陰陽人細訴往事 願此身成為男兒 [The hermaphrodite reveals his/her past: Hopes to remain a man]. August 15, 1953, no. 3.

————. "Yinyangren yiyou zhiyin" 陰陽人 已有知音 [Hermaphrodite already has an admirer]. August 24, 1953, no. 4.

————. "Yishi chuangzao nüren wunian duding qiankun" 醫師創造女人 五年篤定乾坤 [Doctors building a woman: Sex determined in five years]. September 4, 1958, no. 4.

————. "Zenkuan Xie Jianshun buwang abingjie" 贈款謝尖順 不忘阿兵姐 [Donating to Xie Jianshun: Never forget the female soldier]. September 21, 1953, no. 4.

———. "Zhongguo Kelisiding zuori wei beilai" 中國克麗絲汀 昨日未北來 [The Chinese Christine did not arrive at Taipei yesterday]. December 6, 1953, no. 3.

Liao, Ping-hui. "Print Culture and the Emergent Public Sphere in Colonial Taiwan, 1895–1945." In *Taiwan under Japanese Colonial Rule, 1895–1945*, edited by Liao Ping-hui and David Der-Wei Wang, 78–94. New York: Columbia University Press, 2006.

Lin Ben 林本. "Woguo chuzhong kecheng zhi yanjin" 我國初中課程之演進 [Development of junior high curricula in our country]. In *Jiaoyubu xiuding zhongxue kecheng biaozhun cankao ziliao* 教育部修訂中學課程標準參考資料 [Reference materials for revising secondary school directives by the Ministry of Education], vol. 2, edited by the Ministry of Education Department of Secondary Education, 36–59. 1960.

Lin, Shing-ting. "'Scientific' Menstruation: The Popularisation and Commodification of Female Hygiene in Republican China, 1910s–1930s." *Gender and History* 25(2) (2013): 294–316.

Lin, Sylvia Li-Chun. "Pink Pills and Black Hands: Women and Hygiene in Republican China." *China Review* 4(1) (Spring 2004): 201–27.

Lin Zhaogen 林昭庚, Chen Guangwei 陳光偉, and Zhou Peiqi 周珮琪. *Rizhi shiqi no Taiwan zhongyi, 1895–1945* 日治時期の臺灣中醫, 1895–1945 [On the evolution of traditional Chinese medicine in Taiwan under Japanese rule]. Taipei: Guoli Zhongguo yiyao yanjiusuo 國立中國醫藥研究所, 2011.

Liu Dao-Jie 劉道捷. "Biannan biannü bian bian bian" 變男變女變變變 [Transsexualism and sex-reassignment surgery in Taiwan]. MA thesis, National Taiwan University, 1993.

Liu, Michael Shiyung. "Building a Strong and Healthy Empire: The Critical Period of Building Japanese Colonial Medicine in Taiwan." *Japanese Studies* 23(4) (2004): 301–13.

———. *Prescribing Colonization: The Role of Medical Practices and Policies in Japan-Ruled Taiwan, 1895–1945*. Ann Arbor, MI: Association for Asian Studies, 2009.

——— 劉士永. "1930 niandai rizhi shiqi Taiwan yixue de tezhi" 1930年代日治時期臺灣醫學的特質 [Taiwanese medicine during Japanese occupation in the 1930s]. *Taiwan shi yanjiu* 臺灣史研究 4(1) (1998): 97–147.

———. "Zhanhou Taiwan yiliao yu gongwei tizhi de bianqian" 戰後台灣醫療與公衛體制的變遷 [The transformation of medical care and public health regime in postwar Taiwan]. *Huazhong shifan daxue xuebao* 華中師範大學學報 49(4) (2010): 76–83.

Liu Shusen 劉樹森. "Jiaoqi zhi yanjiu" 腳氣之研究 [The study of jiaoqi]. *Xin yiyao kan* 新醫藥刊 74 (1939): 16.

Lock, Margaret. *East Asian Medicine in Modern Japan*. Berkeley: University of California Press, 1988.

———. *Encounters with Aging: Mythologies of Menopause in Japan and North America*. Berkeley: University of California Press, 1993.

Lock, Margaret, and Patricia Kaufert. "Menopause, Local Biologies, and Culture of Aging." *American Journal of Human Biology* 13 (2001): 494–504.

Low, Morris, ed. *Building a Modern Japan: Science, Technology, and Medicine in the Meiji Era and Beyond*. New York: Palgrave Macmillan, 2005.

Lu Gwei-Djen, and Joseph Needham. "A Contribution to the History of Chinese Dietetics." *Isis* 42 (1951): 13–20.

Lu Xun 魯迅. *Rensheng xiangxiao* 人生象斅 [Learning of the human body]. In *Lu Xun yiwen quanji* 魯迅佚文全集 [Complete collection of Lu Xun's lost works], edited by Liu Yunfeng 劉雲峰, 100–258. Beijing: Qunyan chubanshe, 2001.

Lubi Kui 陸費逵. *Funü wenti zatan* 婦女問題雜談 [Miscellaneous talks on women]. Shanghai: Zhonghua shuju, 1925.

———. "Nannü gongxue wenti" 男女共學問題 [Issue of coeducation]. *Education Journal* 2(11) 1910: 5–7.

———. "Seyu yu jiaoyu" 色欲與教育 [Appetence and education]. *Education Journal* 3(9) (1911): 75–78.

Maeda Akiko 前田晶子 "Kindai Nihon no hattatsu gainen ni okeru shintairon no kentō" 近代日本の教育学と発達概念の展開 [Education and the idea of development in modern Japan]. *Kagoshima daigaku kyōiku gakubu kenkyū kiyō kyōiku kagaku hen* 鹿児島大学教育学部研究紀要 教育科学篇[Bulletin of the Faculty of Education, Kagoshima University, Studies in Education] 59 (March 2008): 283–95.

———. "Seichōron ni okeru hon'yaku goro no yakuwari: Jūhachi, jūkyū seiki Nihon no kosodate ron to shōni igaku ni chakumoku shite" 成長論における翻訳語彙の役割: 一八、一九世紀日本の子育て論と小児医学に着目して [The role of translated terms in child development: Focusing on child raising and pediatrics in the eighteenth and nineteenth centuries in Japan]. *Hitotsubashi ronsō* 一橋論叢 124(4) (October 2000): 547–53.

"Malay States Medical Report for the Year 1905." *Journal of Tropical Medicine and Hygiene*, January 1, 1907.

Malcolmson, J. G. *A Practical Essay on the History and Treatment of Beriberi*. Madras: Vepery Mission Press, 1835.

Maloney, William F. "Report of Observations as Adviser in Medicine." Special Collections, University of Minnesota, July 1, 1956.

Mao Zhengwei 毛震偉. *Weishengxue* 衛生學 [Physiology]. Shanghai: Commercial Press, 1936.

Marchand, Roland. *Advertising the American Dream: Making Way for Modernity, 1920–1940*. Berkeley: University of California Press, 1985.

Mascarenhas, M. N., T. Boerma, S. Vanderpoel, and G. A. Stevens. "National, Regional, and Global Trends in Infertility Prevalence since 1990: A Systematic Analysis of 277 Health Surveys." *PLOS Medicine* 9(12) (2012): 1–12.

Masuda Tajirō 増田太次郎. *Hikifuda ebira no fūzoku shi* 引札絵ビラの風俗史 [Fūzoku history of advertisements and posters]. Tokyo: Seiaibō, 1981.

Matta, Christina. "Ambiguous Bodies and Deviant Sexualities: Hermaphrodites, Homosexuality, and Surgery in the United States, 1850–1904." *Perspectives in Biology and Medicine* 48(1) (2005): 74–83.

Matsumoto Yasuko 松本安子. *Danjo seishoku kenzen hō* 男女生殖健全法 [Healthy reproductive method for men and women]. Tokyo: Chūō kangofu kai, 1900.

Matthews, James H. "Final Report of Observations and Recommendations." Special Collections, University of Minnesota, November 7, 1958.

May, Elaine Tyler. *Homeward Bound: American Families in the Cold War Era*. New York: Basic Books, 1988.

Meeker, Martin. "Behind the Mask of Respectability: Reconsidering the Mattachine Society and Male Homophile Practice, 1950s and 1960s." *Journal of the History of Sexuality* 10(1) (2001): 78–116.

———. *Contacts Desired: Gay and Lesbian Communications and Community, 1940s–1970s*. Chicago: University of Chicago Press, 2006.

Meiroku Zasshi 明六雑誌 [Journal of the Japanese Enlightenment]. Translated and introduction by William Reynolds Braisted, with the assistance of Adachi Yasushi and Kikuchi Yūji. Cambridge, MA: Harvard University Press, 1976.

Meng, Yue. "Female Images and National Myth." In *Gender Politics in Modern China: Writing and Feminism*, edited by Tani Barlow, 118–36. Durham, NC: Duke University Press, 1993.

Meyerowitz, Joanne. *How Sex Changed: A History of Transsexuality in the United States*. Cambridge, MA: Harvard University Press, 2002.

———. "Sex Change and the Popular Press: Historical Notes on Transsexuality in the United States, 1930–1955." *GLQ: A Journal of Lesbian and Gay Studies* 4(2) (1998): 159–87.

Miki Hiroko 三鬼浩子. "Josei zasshi ni okeru baiyaku kōkoku" 女性雑誌における売薬広告 [Pharmaceutical ads in women's magazines]. *Mediashi kenkyū* メディア史研究 13 (2002): 110–29.

Min Yuquan 閔玉泉. "Jiaoqi bing yufang fa" 腳氣病預防法 [Preventive measures against jiaoqi]. *Yiyao pinglun* 醫藥評論 54 (1931): 19.

Ministry of Health and Welfare (MOHW) 보건복지부. *2006 Nyeondo Booleem Booboo Jeewon Saeop Annae* 2006년도 불임부부지원사업안내 [Guidelines for the national support program for infertile couples 2006]. 2006.

———. *Guidelines for the National Support Program for Infertile Couples 2007*. 2007. (In Korean)

———. *2010 Nyeondo Gajock Geongang Saeop Annae* 2010년도 가족건강사업안내 [Guidelines for the family health services 2010]. 2010.

———. *Guidelines for the Family Health Services 2011*. 2011. (In Korean)

———. *Guidelines for the Family Health Services 2012*. 2011. (In Korean)

———. *2003 Nyeondo Moja Bogeon Saeop Annae* 2003년도 모자보건사업안내 [Guidelines for the maternal and child health services 2003]. 2003.

———. *Guidelines for the Maternal and Child Health Services 2004*. 2004. (In Korean)

———. *Guidelines for the Maternal and Child Health Services 2005*. 2005. (In Korean)

———. *Guidelines for the Maternal and Child Health Services 2006*. 2006. (In Korean)

———. *Guidelines for the Maternal and Child Health Services 2007*. 2007. (In Korean)

———. *Guidelines for the Maternal and Child Health Services 2008*. 2008. (In Korean)

———. *Guidelines for the Maternal and Child Health Services 2009*. 2009. (In Korean)

———. *Guidelines for the Maternal and Child Health Services 2013*. 2012. (In Korean)

———. *Guidelines for the Maternal and Child Health Services 2014*. 2013. (In Korean)

———. *Guidelines for the Maternal and Child Health Services 2015*. 2015. (In Korean)

Mishima Michiyoshi 三島通良. *Gakkō eisei torishirabe fukumeisho tekiyō* 学校衛生取調復命書摘要 [School hygiene investigative report conspectus]. Tokyo: Hakubunkan, 1895.

———. "Gakkō seito no shikijō mondai" 学校生徒の色情問題 [The question of sexual desires in school students]. *Jika zasshi* 児科雑誌 70 (1906): 95–104.

———. *Nihon kentai shōni no hatsuikuron* 日本健体小児の発育論 [The theory of healthy Japanese children's development]. Tokyo: Dai nihon tosho, 1902.

———. *Shengli weisheng xin jiaokeshu* 生理衛生新教科書 [New textbook for physiology and hygiene]. Translated by Sun Zuo 孫佐. Reviewed by Du Yaquan 杜亞泉 and Du Jiutian 杜就田. Revised by Ling Changhuan 凌昌煥. 1911. Shanghai: Commercial Press, 1923.

Mitchell, Glenn R. "Report on the Seoul National University Hospital." Special Collections, University of Minnesota, 1958.

Mittler, Barbara. *A Newspaper for China? Power, Identity, and Change in Shanghai's News Media, 1872–1912*. Cambridge, MA: Harvard University Asia Center, 2004.

Moore, Lisa Jean. *Sperm Counts: Overcome by Man's Most Precious Fluid*. New York: New York University Press, 2007.

Mullaney, Thomas. *Coming to Terms with the Nation: Ethnic Classification in Modern China*. Berkeley: University of California Press, 2011.

Murakami Seizō 村上清造. *Toyama-shi yakugyō shi* 富山市薬業史 [Pharmaceutical history of Toyama]. Toyama: Toyama-shi shōkōrōdōbu yakugyō kakari, 1975.

Najmabadi, Afsaneh. *Professing Selves: Transsexuality and Same-Sex Desire in Contemporary Iran*. Durham, NC: Duke University Press, 2013.

"Nakada Kōsaburō shi wo kakonde" 中田幸三郎氏を囲んで [A discussion with Nakada Kōsaburō]. In *Zaisen Nihonjin yakugyō kaiko shi* 在鮮日本人薬業回顧史 [History of Japanese pharmaceutical industry in Korea], 4–20. Zaisen Nihonjin yakugyō kaikoshi hensankai, 1961.

Nakano Yasuaki 岡田昌春 and Asada Sōhaku 淺田惟常. *Kakké gairon* 脚氣概論 [General treatise on *kakké*]. 1879, Huanghan yixue congshu 1936. Shanghai: Zhongyi xueyuan chubanshe, 1993, reprint.

Nakayama, Izumi. *Politics of Difference: Menstruation in Modern Japan* (manuscript in preparation).

———. "Posturing for Modernity: Mishima Michiyoshi and School Hygiene in Meiji Japan." *EASTS* 6(3) (September 2012): 355–78.

National Health Insurance Service 국민건강보험공단. *Geongang Boheom Tonggae* 건강보험통계 [National health insurance statistics]. 2005–2015. Accessed May 25, 2015. http://kosis.kr/wnsearch/totalSearch.jsp.

The National Medical Center in Korea: A Scandinavian Contribution to Medical Training and Health Development, 1958–1968. Oslo: Universitetsforlaget, 1971.

Nature 69(1798) (April 14, 1904).

Ninth Meeting of the William T. Peyton Society. Honoring the Contributions of Lyle A. French. August 27, 2005, McNamara Alumni Center, Minneapolis, Minnesota.

Nishi Amane 西周. "Naichi ryokō" 内地旅行 [Domestic travels]. *Meiroku zasshi* 明六雑誌 23 (December 1874): 1–7.

Noble, Jeanne, and Malcolm Potts. "The Fertility Transition in Cuba and the Federal Republic of Korea: the Impact of Organised Family Planning." *Journal of Biosocial Science* 28 (1996): 211–25.

Nukata Osamu 額田成. *Kodomo no shinchō wo nobasutameni dekiru koto—shōnika senmoni ga oshieru shokuji to seikatsu shūkan* 子どもの身長を伸ばすためにできること—小児科専門医が教える食事と生活習慣 [How to increase a child's height—a pediatrician's diet and lifestyle]. Tokyo: PHP kenkyūjo, 2004.

Nutrition Reviews. Version 5. Washington DC, 1947.

Ochiai, Emiko. *The Japanese Family System in Transition: A Sociological Analysis of Family Change in Postwar Japan*. Tokyo: LTCB International Library Foundation, 1996.

Oda Shūzo 小田俊三. *Gakkō katei tsūzoku eisei gaku* 学校家庭通俗衛生学 [Popular hygiene for home and school]. Osaka: Shinshindō shoten, 1930.

Ōkubo Takeharu 大久保健晴. *Kindai Nihon no seiji kōsō to Oranda* 近代日本の政治構想とオランダ [Modern Japanese political initiatives and Holland]. Tokyo: Tokyo University Press, 2010.

Ōkuma Shigenobu 大隈重信. *Taiyō* 太陽 [The sun]. Hakubunkan, 1913.

Ōkurashō 大藏省 [Ministry of Finance]. *Dai Nihon bōeki nenpyō* 大日本外国貿易年表 [Annual return of the foreign trade of the empire of Japan]. 1882.

Omori, Kenta. "Studies on the Cause and Treatment of Beri-Beri in Japan." Far Eastern Association of Tropical Medicine (FEATM) Transactions of 6th Biennial Congress, Tokyo, 1925.

Ong, Aihwa, and Stephen J. Collier, eds. *Global Assemblages: Technology, Politics, and Ethics as Anthropological Problems*. New York: Blackwell, 2005.

Ototake Iwazō 乙竹岩造. "Genji ōshū ni okeru seiyoku ni taisuru kyōiku oyobi inshu ni taisuru kyōiku no jōkyō ni kansuru hōkoku" 現時欧州ニ於ケル性慾ニ対スル教育及飲酒ニ対スル教育ノ状況ニ関スル報告 [A report on contemporary European sex and alcohol education]. *Kanpō* 7116 (1907): 566–68.

Otsubo, Sumiko. "The Female Body and Eugenic Thought in Meiji Japan." In *Building a Modern Japan: Science, Technology and Medicine in the Meiji Era and Beyond*, edited by Morris Low, 61–82. New York: Palgrave Macmillan, 2005.

Park, D. E. "How Korea Turned the Tide of Male Indifference." *People* 13(1) (1986): 22–23.

Park, Jin-kyung. "Corporal Colonialism: Medicine, Reproduction, and Race in Colonial Korea." PhD diss., University of Illinois at Urbana-Champaign, 2008.

Park, Seon-Young 박선영, Keuk-Kyoung Yoon 윤덕경, Bok-Soon Park 박복순, and Hye-Kyung Kim 김혜경. *Gajockeui Dayanghwaaei tareeun Gwanyeonbeopjae Jeongbee Yeongoo: Yeoseong Yieengwon Bojang Meet Chabyeolhaesoreul weehan Gwanyeonbeopjae Jeongbee Yeongoo* 가족의 다양화에 따른 관련법제 정비 연구: 여성인권보장 및 차별해소를 위한 관련법제 정비 연구 (II) [A study on the law for women's rights and elimination of discrimination (II): Focusing on the family]. Seoul: Korean Women's Development Institute, 2008.

Peterson, M. Jeanne. "Precocious Puberty in the Victorian Medical Gaze." *Nineteenth-Century Gender Studies* 4(2) (Summer 2008). http://www.ncgsjournal.com/issue42/peterson.htm.

Peterson, M. M. "Assisted Reproductive Technologies and Equity of Access Issues." *Law, Ethics and Medicine* 31 (2005): 280–85.

Petryna, Adriana. *Biological Citizenship: Science and the Politics of Health after Chernobyl*. Princeton: Princeton University Press, 2002.

Planned Parenthood Federation of Korea (PPFK). *The 10 (Ten)-Year History of Family Planning in Korea*. Seoul, 1976.

Platt, B. S., and S. Y. Gin. "Some Observations on a Preliminary Study of Beriberi in Shanghai." Far Eastern Association of Tropical Medicine (FEATM) Transactions of the 9th Congress, Nanking, China, October 2–8, 1934. Nanking: National Health Administration, 1935.

Pollitt, Katha. "The Strange Case of Baby M." *Nation*, May 23, 1987.

Postmus, S. "Beriberi of Mother and Child in Burma." *Tropical and Geographical Medicine* 10 (1958): 363–69.

Prescott, Heather Munro. *A Doctor of Their Own: The History of Adolescent Medicine*. Cambridge, MA: Harvard University Press, 1998.

Pyle, Kenneth. *The New Generation in Meiji Japan: Problems of Cultural Identity 1885–1895*. Stanford: Stanford University Press, 1969.

Qu Shaoheng 瞿紹衡. "Renchen yu jiaoqi" 妊娠與腳氣 [Pregnancy and *jiaoqi*]. *Xin yiyao kan* 新醫藥刊 69 (1938): 38–39.

Quételet, Adolphe. *Sur l'homme et le développement de ses facultés, ou Essai de physique sociale*. Paris: Bachelier, 1835, 2 volumes.

Rabinow, Paul. *French DNA: Trouble in Purgatory*. Chicago: Chicago University Press, 1999.

Rapp, Rayna. "One New Reproductive Technology, Multiple Sites: How Feminist Methodology Bleeds into Everyday Life." In *Revisioning Women, Health and Healing: Feminist, Cultural and Technoscience Perspectives*, edited by Adele E. Clarke and Virginia L. Olesen, 119–35. New York: Routledge, 1999.

———. *Testing Women, Testing the Fetus: The Social Impact of Amniocentesis in America*. New York: Routledge, 2000.

Redick, Alison. "American History XY: The Medical Treatment of Intersex, 1916–1955." PhD diss., New York University, 2004.

Reed, Christopher. *Gutenberg in Shanghai: Chinese Print Capitalism, 1876–1937.* Vancouver: University of British Columbia Press, 2004.

Repetto, Robert, Tai Hwan Kwon, Son-Ung Kim, John E. Sloboda, and Peter J. Donaldson. *Economic Development, Population Policy, and Demographic Transition in the Republic of Korea.* Cambridge, MA: Harvard University Press, 1981.

"Report of the Inspecting Medical Officer to the Tung Wah Hospital, 1906." Sessional Paper. Hong Kong, 1907.

Reproductive Medicine Committee of Korean Society of Obstetrics and Gynecology (RMC-KSOG) 대한산부인과학회 생식의학 소위원회. "Hangook Bojosaengsicksoolui Hyeonhwang" 한국 보조생식술의 현황 [Current status of ART in Korea]. *Daehan Sanbooingwa Hakhoe Hacksoolbalpyeo Nonmoonjeep* 대한산부인과학회 학술발표 논문집 [Conference proceedings of the Korean Society of Obstetrics and Gynecology] 75 (1995): 35–36.

Republic of Korea government 대한민국정부. *2011–2015 Jae 2 Cha Jeochoolsan Goryeongsahwae Gibongaehaeck: Saromajee plan 2015* 2011–2015 제2차 저출산 고령사회 기본계획: 새로마지 플랜 2015 [Second basic plan on low fertility and the ageing society in Korea, 2011–2015: Rolling plan 2015]. 2010.

Republic of Korea (ROC), Ministry of the Interior. *Taiwan-Fukien Demographic Fact Book.* Taipei: ROC Ministry of the Interior, 1988.

———. Marriage Status by Sex and 5-Year Age Group, 1989–2014. 2015. Accessed January 31, 2016. http://www.ris.gov.tw/zh_TW/346.

Richards, Thomas. *The Commodity Culture of Victorian England: Advertisement and Spectacle, 1851–1914.* Stanford: Stanford University Press, 1990.

Robinson, Warren C., and John A. Ross, eds. *The Global Family Planning Revolution: Three Decades of Population Policies.* Washington, DC: IBRD, 2007.

Rocha, Leon Antonio. "Xing: The Discourse of Sex and Human Nature in Modern China." *Gender and History* 22(3) (2010): 603–28.

Rogaski, Ruth. *Hygienic Modernity: Meanings of Health and Disease in Treaty-Port China.* Berkeley: University of California Press, 2004.

Rose, Nikolas, and Carlos Novas. "Biological Citizenship." In *Global Assemblages: Technology, Politics, and Ethics as Anthropological Problems,* edited by Aihwa Ong and Stephen J. Collier, 439–63. New York: Blackwell, 2005.

Rosenberg, Charles. "Disease in History: Frames and Framers." *Milbank Quarterly* 67(1) (1989): 1–15.

Rousseau, Julie. "Enduring Labors: The 'New Midwife' and the Modern Culture of Childbearing in Early Twentieth Century Japan." PhD diss., Columbia University, 1998.

Ruggie, Mary. *Marginal to Mainstream: Alternative Medicine in America.* Cambridge: Cambridge University Press, 2004.

Ryō Onjin 廖温仁. 1928. "Tōyō kakké byō kenkyō" 東洋脚氣病研究 [Research on Japanese *kakké*]. 1932 ed. Kyoto, doctoral dissertation, 1928.

Saero-Maji. http://momplus.mw.go.kr.

Saffron, Lisa. "Can Fertility Service Providers Justify Discrimination against Lesbians?" *Human Fertility* 5(2) (2002): 42–46.

Saitō Hikaru 斎藤光. *Hentai seiyoku non kenkyū: Kindai Nihon no sekushuaritii 3* 近代日本のセクシュアリティ [Sexuality in modern Japan: *Hentai* sexual desires and modern society]. Tokyo: Yumani shobō, 2006.

———. "'Onanie' kigō no keifu" 「オナニー」記号の系譜 [Genealogy of *onanie* sign]. *Kyōto seika daigaku kiyō* 京都精華大学紀要 31 (2006): 113–31.

———. "Psychopathia Sexualis no hatsu hon'yaku ni tsuite: Hōyaku no genten wa gencho dai nanhan ka" Psychopathia Sexualisの初邦訳について―邦訳の原典は原著題何版か？ [An original text of *Shikijōkyōhen* (色情狂編) 1894]. *Kyōto seika daigaku kiyō* 京都精華大学紀要 17 (1999): 72–91.

Sand, Jordan. *House and Home in Modern Japan*. Cambridge, MA: Harvard University Press, 2004.

Saneyoshi, Yasuzumi, Baron, and Shigemichi Suzuki. *The Surgical and Medical History of the Naval War between Japan and China during 1894–1895*. Tokyo: Tokio Print, 1901.

Sasaoka Shōzō 笹岡省三 and Kitabataki Takao 北畠孝夫. *Fujinbyōsha no kokoroe: Shikyūbyō chi no michi jitaku byōhō* 婦人病者の心得：子宮病血の道自宅病法 [Knowledge for those with women's diseases: Home remedies for the way of blood uterine disease]. Tokyo: Sasaoka Shōzō, 1910.

Sato, Barbara. *The New Japanese Woman: Modernity, Media and Women in Interwar Japan*. Durham, NC: Duke University Press, 2003.

Schiebinger, Londa. *Nature's Body: Gender in the Making of Modern Science*. Boston: Beacon Press, 1993.

Schmalzer, Sigrid. *The People's Peking Man: Popular Science and Human Identity in Twentieth-Century China*. Chicago: University of Chicago Press, 2008.

Schneider, M. Helen. *Keeping the Nation's House: Domestic Management and the Making of Modern China*. Toronto: UBC Press, 2011.

Seoul through Pictures. Vol. 4, *Seoul, to Rise Again*. Seoul: City History Compilation Committee of Seoul, 2005.

Serlin, David. "Christine Jorgensen and the Cold War Closet." *Radical History Review* 62 (Spring 1995): 136–65.

Shapin, Steven. "'You Are What You Eat': Historical Changes in Ideas about Food and Identity." *Historical Research* 87 (2014): 377–92.

Shapiro, Hugh. "Neurasthenia and the Assimilation of Nerves into China." 23rd International Symposium on the Comparative History of Medicine (Taniguchi Foundation) on "Toward a Medical Historiography for the 21st Century," Seoul National University, Medical College, Seoul, Korea, July 5–11, 1998. Accessed January 1, 2016. http://www.ihp.sinica.edu.tw/~medicine/conference/disease/shapiro.PDF.

———. "The Puzzle of Spermatorrhea in Republican China." *positions* 6(3) (Winter 1998): 551–95.

Shen, Grace Yen. *Unearthing the Nation: Modern Geology and Nationalism in Republican China*. Chicago: University of Chicago Press, 2013.

Shih, Shu-mei. "The Concept of the Sinophone." *PMLA* 126(3) (2011): 709–18.

———. "Theory, Asia and the Sinophone." *Postcolonial Studies* 13(4) (2010): 465–84.

———. *Visuality and Identity: Sinophone Articulations across the Pacific*. Berkeley: University of California Press, 2007.

Shih, Shu-mei, Chien-hsin Tsai, and Brian Bernards, eds. *Sinophone Studies: A Critical Reader*. New York: Columbia University Press, 2013.

Shimizu Tōtarō 清水藤太郎. *Nihon yakugakushi* 日本薬学史 [History of Japanese pharmacology]. Tokyo: Nanzandō, 1949.

Shin, Dongwon. "Hygiene, Medicine, and Modernity in Korea." *East Asian Science, Technology and Society: An International Journal* 3(1) (2009): 5–26.

Shin, In Sup, and Shin Kie Hyuk. *Advertising in Korea*. Seoul: Communication Books, 2004.

Shō Taihō 尚大鵬 [Shang Dapeng]. "Shinchō makki ni okeru shintaikan no keisei wo meguru nihon no eikyō ni kansuru kenkyū" 清朝末期における身体観の形

成を巡る日本の影響に関する研究 [Study of the Japanese impact on the formation of late Qing views of the body] *Heisei 17 nendo kenkyūhi hojokin kenkyū kekka hōkokusho* 平成17年度研究費補助金研究結果報告書 [2005 report for the research outcomes based on the grants-in-aid for research], March 28, 2006.

Simmons, Duane. "Beriberi, or the 'Kakké' of Japan." *China Imperial Maritime Customs Medical Reports*. Special Series no. 2, 19th issue, for the half-year ended March 31, 1880. Shanghai: Statistical Department of the Inspectorate General.

Sinn, Elizabeth. *Power and Charity: Chinese Merchant Elite in Colonial Hong Kong*. Hong Kong: Oxford University Press, 1989.

Smith, Hilary. "Foot *Qi*: History of a Chinese Medical Disorder." PhD diss., University of Pennsylvania, 2008.

Smith, Jennifer Lynne. "'Suitable Mothers': Lesbian and Single Women and the 'Unborn' in Australian Parliamentary Discourse." *Critical Social Policy* 23(1) (2003): 63–88.

Sōda Hajime 宗田一. *Nihon no dentōyaku: "Furusa" ga ima, totemo shinsen* 日本の伝統薬："古さ"がいま、とても新鮮 [Traditional medicine of Japan: "Old" is now, very fresh]. Tokyo: Shufu no tomo sha, 1989.

Sogabe Takao 曽我部孝雄. "Dainikigoro no omoide" 第二期頃の想い出 [Memories of the second period]. In *Zaisen Nihonjin yakugyō kaiko shi* 在鮮日本人薬業回顧史 [History of Japanese pharmaceutical industry in Korea], 373–76. Zaisen Nihonjin yakugyō kaikoshi hensankai, 1961.

Sohn, Anne-Marie. "Between the Wars in France and England." Translated by Arthur Goldhammer. In *History of Women in the West*, edited by Françoise Thébaud et al., 92–119. Cambridge, MA: Harvard University Press, 1996.

Song Chongyi 宋崇義. *Xinzhongxue jiaokeshu shengli weishengxue* 新中學教科書生理衛生學 [Physiology and hygiene textbook for new middle schools]. 1923. 35th ed. Shanghai: Zhonghua shuju, 1929.

Spallone, Patricia. *Beyond Conception: The New Politics of Reproduction*. London: Macmillan, 1989.

Stacey, Judith. *Unhitched: Love, Marriage and Family Values from West Hollywood to Western China*. New York: New York University Press, 2011.

Statistics Korea (National Statistical Office) 통계청. *2010 Nyeon Choolsaengtonggae* 2010년 출생통계 [Final results of birth statistics in 2010]. 2011. Accessed January 8, 2014. http://kostat.go.kr.

———. *Final Results of Birth Statistics in 2014*. 2015. Accessed November 24, 2015. http://kostat.go.kr. (In Korean)

———. *Joomindeungrock Yingoo Hyeonhwang 2013* 주민등록 인구 현황 2013 [Population statistics based on resident registration in 2013]. 2014. Accessed May 25, 2015. http://meta.narastat.kr/metasvc/index.do?orgId=101&confmNo=11026&kosis Yn=Y.

———. *2008 Sahwaejosa Bogoseo* 2008 사회조사보고서 [The 2008 report on the social survey]. 2008. Accessed January 23, 2014. http://kosis.kr/ups/ups_01List01. jsp?pubcode=KN.

———. *The 2010 Report on the Social Survey*. 2010. Accessed January 23, 2014. http:// kosis.kr/ups/ups_01List01.jsp?pubcode=KN. (In Korean)

———. *The 2012 Report on the Social Survey*. 2012. Accessed January 23, 2014. http:// kosis.kr/ups/ups_01List01.jsp?pubcode=KN. (In Korean)

———. *The 2014 Report on the Social Survey*. 2014. Accessed May 25, 2015. http:// kosis.kr/ups/ups_01List01.jsp?pubcode=KN. (In Korean)

Steele, Joel Dorman. *Shenglixue* 生理學 [Physiology]. Translated by Xie Honglai 謝洪賚. Shanghai: Commercial Press, 1904.

———. *Zhongxue shengli jiaokeshu* [Physiology for middle schools] 中學生理教科書. Translated by Ho Yushi 何燏時. Tokyo: Kyōkasho henyakusha, 1902.

Stengers, Jean, and Anne van Neck. *Masturbation: The History of a Great Terror*. New York: Palgrave, 2001.

Stern, Alexandra Minna, and Howard Merkel, eds. *Formative Years: Children's Health in the United States, 1880–2000*. Ann Arbor: University of Michigan Press, 2002.

Sugaya Akira 菅谷章. *Nihon iryō seidoshi* 日本医療制度史 [History of Japanese medical policies]. Tokyo: Hara shobō, 1976.

Sugiura Morikuni. "Mishima Michiyoshi 1–18" 三島通良. *Gakkō hoken kenkyū* [School health] 10(2)–12(12) (1968–1970).

———. *Wagakuni gakkō eisei no sōshisha Mishima Michiyoshi (jō)* 我が国学校衛生の創始者三島通良（上）[Mishima Michiyoshi, founder of our nation's school hygiene (part 1)]. Self-published, 1971.

Suh, Soyoung. "Korean Medicine between the Local and the Universal." PhD diss., University of California at Los Angeles, 2006.

Sun, Wanning. "Cultivating Self-Health Subjects: Yangsheng and Biocitizenship in Urban China." *Citizenship Studies* 19(3–4) (2015): 285–98.

Suzuki Akira 鈴木昶. *Nihon no denshōyaku* 日本の伝承薬 [Japanese folk medicine]. Tokyo: Yakuji nippōsha, 2005.

Suzuki, Shogo. *Civilization and Empire: China and Japan's Encounter with European International Society*. London: Routledge, 2009.

Taiwan Kyōikukai 台湾教育会, eds. *Taiwan kyōiku enkakushi* 台湾教育沿革史 [Historical background of Taiwanese education]. 1939. Taipei: Kotei shooku, 1973.

Taiwan sheng xingzheng zhangguan gongshu tongji shi 臺灣省行政長官公署統計室, ed. *Taiwan Sheng wushiyi nian lai tongji tiyao* 臺灣省五十一年來統計提要 [Taiwan 51-year statistical summary]. Taipei, 1946.

Taiwan sōtokufu 台湾総督府. *Taiwan hōrei shūran* 台湾法令輯覧 [Collection of Taiwan laws and ordinances]. Teikoku chihō gyōsei gakkai 帝国地方行政学会, 1918. Section 8: *Eisei keisatsu* 衛生警察 [Health police], 10–11.

Taiwan sōtokufu keimusho eiseika 台湾総督府刑務所衛生課. *Taiwan no eisei* 台湾の衛生 [Hygiene of Taiwan]. Taihoku: Taiwan sōtokufu, 1935.

Taiwan sōtokufu zaimukyoku zeimuka 臺灣總督府財務局稅務課 [Taiwan Governor-General, Financial Affairs Division, Revenue Division]. *Taiwan bōeki nenpyō* 臺灣貿易年表 [Annual return of the foreign trade of Taiwan]. 1898–1945.

Takashima Heisaburō 高島平三郎. *Taiiku genre* 体育原理 [Principles of physical education]. Tokyo: Ikueisha, 1904.

Takeshita, Chikako. *The Global Biopolitics of the IUD: How Science Constructs Contraceptive Users and Women's Bodies*. Cambridge, MA: MIT Press, 2011.

Takeuchi, Yoshimi. "Asia as Method." 1960. In *What Is Modernity? Writings of Takeuchi Yoshimi*, edited and translated by Richard F. Calichman, 149–66. New York: Columbia University Press, 2005.

Taki Motokata 多紀元堅. 1853. *Zatsubyō Kōyō* 雜病廣要 [Broad essentials on various diseases]. 1958. Beijing: Remin weisheng chuban she, 1983.

Tamagawa Shinmei 玉川信明. *Hangontan no bunkashi: Etchū Toyama no kusuriuri* 反魂丹の文化史―越中富山の薬売り [The cultural history of Hangontan: Medicine seller in Etchū Toyama]. Tokyo: Shōbunsha, 1979.

Tan Sitong 譚嗣同. *Renxue* 仁學 [On humanity]. Taipei: Taiwan Xuesheng shuju, 1998.

Tanaka Masato 田中昌人. "Bunmei kaikaki ni okeru hattatsu no gainen no donyū ni tsuite" 文明開化期における発達の概念の導入について [The introduction of the concept of development in the period of Bunmei kaika]. *Kyōto daigaku kyōiku* gakubu kiyō 京都大学教育学部紀要 [Bulletin of the Faculty of Education, Kyoto University] 34 (1998): 93–126.

———. "Rangaku ni okeru hattatsu no gainen no donyū ni tsuite (1–3)" 蘭学における発達の概念の導入について [The introduction of the concept of development in Dutch Studies]. Kyōto daigaku kyoiku gakubu kiyō 京都大学教育学部紀要 [Bulletin of the Faculty of Education, Kyoto University] 39–41, 1993–1994.

Tanaka, Stefan. "Childhood: Naturalization of Development into a Japanese Space." In Cultures of Scholarship, edited by S. C. Humphreys, 22–23. Ann Arbor: University of Michigan Press, 1998.

Taylor, Kim. Chinese Medicine in Early Communist China, 1945–1963: A Medicine of Revolution. New York: Routledge, 2005.

Terasaki Yasuhiro 寺崎康博. "Shokuminchi-jidai no Chōsen ni okeru kojin shohi shishutsu to suikei, 1913–1937" 植民地時代の朝鮮における個人消費支出と推計 [Individual consumption expenditures and estimates in Colonial Korea]. Nagasaki Daigaku Kyōyō Gakubu Kiyō 長崎大学教養学部紀要 24 (January 1984): 61–95.

———. "Taiwan Chōsen no shohi suijun." 台湾朝鮮の消費水準 [Consumption levels in Taiwan and Korea]. In Kyu Nihon shokuminchi keizai tokei: Suikei to bunseki 旧日本植民地経済統計：推計と分析 [Economic statistics from former Japanese colonies: Estimates and analyses], edited by Mizoguchi Toshiyuki and Umemura Mataji, 57–67. Tokyo: Tōyō keizai shinposha, 1988.

Terazawa, Yuki. "Gender, Knowledge, and Power: Reproductive Medicine in Japan, 1790–1930." PhD diss., University of California at Los Angeles, 2001.

———. "Racializing Bodies through Science in Meiji Japan: The Rise of Race-Based Research in Gynecology." In Building a Modern Japan: Science, Technology, and Medicine in the Meiji Era and Beyond, edited by Morris Low, 83–102. New York: Palgrave Macmillan, 2005.

Thompson, Charis. Making Parents: The Ontological Choreography of Reproductive Technologies. Cambridge, MA: MIT Press, 2005.

Thomsen, Hans, and Jennifer Purtle, eds. East Asian Visual Culture from the Treaty Ports to World War II. Chicago: Paragon Books, 2009.

Thorpe, Rachel, Samantha Croy, Kerry Petersen, and Marian Pitts. "In the Best Interests of the Child? Regulating Assisted Reproductive Technologies and the Well-Being of Offspring in Three Australian States." International Journal of Law, Policy and the Family 26(3) (2012): 259–77.

Tonga ilbo 東亞日報 [East Asia Daily]. February 22, 1925, June 3, 1927.

Ts'ai, Hui-yu Caroline. Taiwan in Japan's Empire-Building: An Institutional Approach to Colonial Engineering. New York: Routledge, 2009.

Tsu, Jing, and Benjamin A. Elman, eds. Science and Technology in Modern China, 1880s–1940s. Leiden: Brill, 2014.

Tsuge, Azumi. "How Society Responds to Desires of Childless Couples: Japan's Position on Donor Conception." Meijigakuin daigakuin shakaigakubu fuzokukenkyūsho nenpo [Bulletin of Institute of Sociology and Social Work, Meiji Gakuin University] 35 (2005): 21–34.

Tsurumi, E. Patricia. Japanese Colonial Education in Taiwan, 1895–1945. Cambridge, MA: Harvard University Press, 1977.

Turner, Bryan S. Medical Power and Social Knowledge. 2nd ed. London: Sage Publication, 1998.

United Marketing Research. "Survey on Same-Sex Marriage." United Daily, December 3, 2012. Accessed June 1, 2013. https://vision.udn.com/vision/story/7645/737364.

Uno, Kathleen S. "The Death of 'Good Wife, Wise Mother'?" In *Postwar Japan as History*, edited by Andrew Gordon, 293–322. Berkeley: University of California Press, 1993.

Vedder, Edward. *Beriberi*. New York: William and Wood, 1913.

Walthall, Anne. "Masturbation and Discourse on Female Sexual Practices in Early Modern Japan." *Gender and History* 21(1) (April 2009): 1–18.

Wang, Charlotte, Miao-Yu Tsai, Mei-Hsien Lee, Su-Yun Huang, Chen-Hung Kao, Nong-Nerng Ho, and Chuhsing Kate Hsiao. "Maximum Number of Live Births per Donor in Artificial Insemination." *Human Reproduction* 22(5) (2007): 1363–72.

Wang, Hsiu-yun. "How Did Our Bodies Become Your Body? Our Bodies Ourselves in Taiwan." Paper presented at the 12th meeting of the Taiwan Sociology Association, Tong-hai University, 2012. Accessed June, 2014. http://tsa2012.thu.edu.tw/20121125papers/A59.pdf.

Wang Jianshan 王兼善. *Shengli ji weishengxue* 生理及衛生學 [Physiology and hygiene]. 1914. Shanghai: Commercial Press, 1927.

Wang Xuefeng 王雪峰. *Jiaoyu zhuangxing zhijing: Ershi shiji shangban Zhongguo de xingjiaoyu sixiang yu shijian* 教育轉型之鏡：二十世紀上半中國的性教育思想與實踐 [Mirror of the education paradigm shift: Theories and practices of sex education in China in the early twentieth century]. Beijing: Shehui kexue wenxian chubanshe, 2007.

Wang Youpeng 王有朋, ed. *Zhongguo jindai zhongxiaoxue jiaokeshu zongmu* 中國近代中小學教科書總目 [Contents of textbooks for primary and middle schools in modern China]. Shanghai: Shanghai cishu chubanshe, 2010.

Wei Chunzhi 魏春芝, ed. *Shengli weishengxue* 生理衛生學 [Physiology and hygiene]. Revised by Jing Libin 經利彬. Beijing: Zhuzhe shudian, 1932.

Weinbaum, Alys Eve, The Modern Girl around the World Research Group, Lynn M. Thomas, Priti Ramamurthy, Uta G. Poiger, and Madeleine Yue Dong. *The Modern Girl around the World: Consumption, Modernity, and Globalization*. Durham, NC: Duke University Press, 2008.

Weixing shiguan zhaizhu 唯性史觀齋主. *Zhongguo tongxinglian mishi* 中國同性戀秘史 [The secret history of Chinese homosexuality]. 2 vols. Hong Kong: Yuzhou chuban, 1964 and 1965.

Wesley-Smith, Terence, and John Goss, eds. *Remaking Area Studies: Teaching and Learning across Asia and the Pacific*. Honolulu: University of Hawai'i Press, 2010.

White, Merry. "The Virtue of Japanese Mothers: Cultural Definitions of Women's Lives." *Daedalus* 116(3) (1987): 149–63.

Whittaker, Andrea. *Thai in Vitro: Gender, Culture and Assisted Reproduction*. New York: Berghahn, 2015.

Wikler, Daniel, and Norma J. Wikler. "Turkey-Baster Babies: The Demedicalization of Artificial Insemination." *Milbank Quarterly* 69(1) (1991): 5–40.

Winterson, Jeanette. *Why Be Happy When You Could Be Normal?* London: Jonathan Cape, 2011.

Wong, Alvin Ka Hin. "Transgenderism as a Heuristic Device: On the Cross-historical and Transnational Adaptations of the *Legend of the White Snake*." In *Transgender China*, edited by Howard Chiang, 127–58. New York: Palgrave Macmillan, 2012.

Worboys, Michael. "The Discovery of Colonial Malnutrition between the Wars." In *Imperial Medicine and Indigenous Societies*, edited by David Arnold, 208–25. Manchester: Manchester University Press 1988.

Wright, Hamilton. "An Enquiry into the Etiology and Pathology of Beri-Beri." *Journal of Tropical Medicine* (June 1, 1905): 161–62.

Wu Bingxin 吳冰心, ed. *Shiyong jiaokeshu shengli weishengxue* 實用教科書生理衛生學 [Practical textbook of physiology and hygiene]. Emended by Ling Changhuan. 1915. Shanghai: Commercial Press, 1926.

Wu, Chia-ling. "Have Someone Cut the Umbilical Cord: Women's Birthing Networks, Knowledge, and Skills in Colonial Korea." In *Health and Hygiene in Chinese East Asia*, edited by Angela Ki Che Leung and Charlotte Furth, 160–80. Durham, NC: Duke University Press, 2010.

———. "Managing Multiple Masculinities in Donor Insemination: Doctors Configuring Infertile Men and Sperm Donors in Taiwan." *Sociology of Health and Illness* 33(1) (2011): 96–113.

——— 吳嘉苓. "Shou wuming de xingbie, xingbiehua de wuming: Cong Taiwan 'buyun' nannü chujing fenxi wuming de xingbie zhengzhi" 受污名的性別、性別化的污名：從台灣『不孕』男女處境分析污名的性別政治 [Stigmatized gender and gendered stigma: The "infertile" men and women in Taiwan]. *Taiwan shehui xuekan* 台灣社會學刊 [Taiwanese Journal of Sociology] 29 (2002): 127–79.

Wu Chihao 吳奇浩. "Yangfu, hefu, taiwanfu: Irzhi shiqi Taiwan duoyuan de fuzhuang wenhua" 洋服、和服、臺灣服：日治時期臺灣多元的服裝文化 [Western attire, Japanese kimono, and Taiwanese clothing: The multicultural hybridity of Taiwan clothing during the Japanese colonial period]. *Xinshixue* 新史學 [New history] 26(3) (2015): 77–144.

Wu Fang-cheng 吳方正. "Luode liyou: Ershi shiji chuqi Zhongguo renti xiesheng wentide taolun" 裸的理由：二十世紀初期中國人體寫生問題的討論 [Questions concerning nude figure drawing in China at the beginning of the twentieth century]. *Xinshixue* 新史學 [New history] 15(2) (2004): 55–113.

Wu Zhiming 吳直明. "Jiaoqi zai Yuandong" 腳氣在遠東 [Beriberi in the Far East]. *Xiandai yulin* 19 (1939): 41.

Xian Yuyi 冼玉儀, and Liu Runhe 劉潤和. *Yishan xingdao* 益善行道 [Enhancing charity and practicing the way]. Hong Kong: Sanlian, 2006.

Xie Guan 謝觀. *Zhongguo yixue yuanliu lun* 中國醫學源流論 [On the root of Chinese medicine]. Shanghai: Chengzhai yishe, 1935.

Xu Fangju 許芳菊. "Zhuang Shuqi: Daziran de nü'er" 莊淑旂：大自然的女兒 [Chuang Shu Chih: Daughter of mother nature]. *Kangjian zazhi* [Common Health Magazine] 康健雜誌 41 (2002): 86–91.

Xu Huiqi 許慧琦. "Guoxinshenghuo, zuoxinnüxin: Xunzheng shiqi guomin zhengfu dui shidai nüxin xingxiang de suzao" 過新生活、做新女性：訓政時期國民政府對時代女性形象的塑造 [Living a new life, being a new woman: The image-making of the modern ideal woman by the KMT government in the Nanjing decade]. *Taidai wenshizhe xuebao* 台大文史哲學報 [Humanitas Taiwanica] 62 (2005): 277–320.

Xue Deyu 薛德焴. *Beixin shengli weisheng* 北新生理衛生 [Physiology and hygiene of Beixin Bookstore]. Shanghai: Beixin shuju, 1933.

———. *Chuzhong shengli weisheng* 初中生理衛生 [Physiology and hygiene for junior highs]. Shanghai: Xinya shudian, 1932.

———. *Chuzhong shengli weishengxue* 初中生理衛生學 [Junior high physiology and hygiene]. Shanghai: Zhongguo kexue tushu yiqi gongsi, 1949.

———. *Chuzhong weisheng* 初中衛生 [Junior high hygiene]. Shanghai: Xinya shuju, 1933.

Yamagishi Kenji 山岸鎌次. "Kaiko 50-nen" 回顧五十年 [Reviewing fifty years]. In *Zaisen Nihonjin yakugyō kaiko shi* 在鮮日本人藥業回顧史 [History of the Japanese pharmaceutical industry in Korea], 175–367. Zaisen Nihonjin yakugyō kaikoshi hensankai, 1961.

Yamamoto Takuji 山本拓司. "Kokuminka to gakkō shintai kensa" 国民化と学校身体検査 [Nationalization and school physical examinations]. Ōhara shakai mondai kenkyūjo zasshi 大原社会問題研究所雑誌 [Journal for the Ōhara Institute for Social Research] 488 (September 1999): 30–43.

Yan, Yunxian. Private Life under Socialism: Love, Intimacy, Family Change in a Chinese Village, 1949–1999. Stanford: Stanford University Press, 2003.

Yang, Meng-Hsuan. "The Great Exodus: Sojourn, Nostalgia, Return, and Identity Formation of Chinese Mainlanders in Taiwan, 1940s–2000s." PhD diss., University of British Columbia, 2012.

Yang Ruisong 楊瑞松. "Xiangxiang minzu chiru: Jindai Zhongguo sixiang wenhua shang de 'Dongya bingfu'" 想像民族恥辱：近代中國思想文化上的 "東亞病夫" [Imagined national humiliation: "Sick men of East Asia" in modern Chinese thought and culture]. Guoli Zhengzhi Daxue lishi xuebao 23 (May 2005): 1–44.

Yang Shen 楊紳. Jiaoqi lun 腳氣論 [On jiaoqi]. Nanking: Military Police Hospital, 1933.

Yang, Tsui-hua 楊翠華. "Meiyuan dui Taiwan de weisheng jihua yu yiliao tizhi zhi xingsu" 美援對台灣的衛生計畫與醫療體制之形塑 [US aid in the formation of health planning and the medical system in Taiwan]. Bulletin of the Institute of Modern History 中央研究院近代史研究所集刊 62 (2008): 91–139.

Yi Yi 憶漪. "Xie Jianshun xiaojie de gushi" 謝尖順小姐的故事 [The story of Miss Xie Jianshun]. Lianhebao 聯合報, October 13, 1955, no. 3.

———. "Xie Jianshun xiaojie de gushi" 謝尖順小姐的故事 [The story of Miss Xie Jianshun]. Lianhebao 聯合報, October 28, 1955, no. 2.

———. "Xie Jianshun xiaojie de gushi" 謝尖順小姐的故事 [The story of Miss Xie Jianshun]. Lianhebao 聯合報, November 18, 1955, no. 2.

Yip, Ka-che. Health and National Reconstruction in Nationalist China: The Development of Modern Health Services, 1928–1937. Ann Arbor: University of Michigan Association of Asian Studies, 1995.

Yixue shijie 醫學世界 [Medical world]. No. 22. 1913.

Yō Ki 姚毅. Kindai Chūgoku no shussan to kokka, shakai: Ishi, josanshi, sesseiba 近代中国の出産と国家・社会：医師、助産士、接生婆 [Childbirth and the nation/society in modern China: Doctors, delivery assistants, and midwives]. Tokyo: Kenbun shuppan, 2011.

Yomiuri Shimbun 読売新聞. May 29, 1941 (evening edition), 4.

Yonhap News 연합뉴스. "Gangwon Yeemsanboo Samangbee 32.1 Myeong, Jeongook Si Do Choigoo" 강원 임산부 사망비 32.1명, 전국 시도서 최고 [The maternal mortality ratio of Gangwon Province is 32.1, the highest among all Korean counties]. October 9, 2013.

Yoo, Theodore Jun. The Politics of Gender in Colonial Korea: Education, Labor, and Health. Berkeley: University of California Press, 2008.

Yoshi'i Tamio 吉井蒼生夫. "Seiō kindaihō no juyō to Mitsukuri Rinshō" 西欧近代法の受容と箕作麟祥 [Mitsukuri Rinshō and the reception of European modern law]. In Meiroku zasshi to sono shūhen: Seiyō bunka no juyō, shisō to gengo 明六雑誌とその周辺：西洋文化の受容、思想と言語 [Meiroku Journal and its environs: The reception, philosophy, and language of Western culture], edited by Kanagawa daigaku jimbungaku kenkyūjo 神奈川大学人文学研究所: 95–124. Tokyo: Ochanomizu bunko, 2004.

Yoshioka Shin 吉岡信. Edo no kigusuriya 江戸の生薬屋 [A pharmacy in Edo]. Tokyo: Seiaibō, 1995.

Yu Hsin-ting 余欣庭. "Taiwan zhanhou yiduanxing/shenti de guansu lishi: Yi tongxinglian han yinyangren weilie, 1950s–2008" 臺灣戰後異端性／身體的管束歷史：以同性戀和陰陽人為例, 1950s–2008 [Regulating deviant sexualities and bodies in Taiwan, 1950s–2008: The cases of homosexuality and hermaphrodites]. MA thesis, Kaohsiung Medical University, 2009.

Yu Xiaoyao 俞筱堯, and Liu Yanjie 劉彥捷, eds. *Lubi Kui yu Zhonghua shuju* 陸費逵與中華書局 [Lubi Kui and the Chinese Bookstore]. Beijing: Zhonghua shuju, 2002.

Yuan Shunda 袁舜達. *Chuzhong xin shengli weisheng* 初中新生理衛生 [New physiology and hygiene for junior highs]. Shanghai: Shijie shuju, 1936.

Yuan Yuan 袁媛. *Jindai shenglixue zai Zhongguo* 近代生理學在中國 [Modern physiology in China, 1851–1926]. Shanghai: Renmin chubanshe, 2010.

Yūsei shoin henshūbu 友生書院編輯部, ed. *Seinenki shōjo no kagakuteki kaibō* 青年期少女の科學的解剖 [Scientific dissection of a young woman]. Tokyo: Yūsei shoin, 1935.

Zeng Chaoran 曾超然. *Jiaoqi chuyan* 腳氣芻言 [Preliminary words on *jiaoqi*]. 1887.

Zhang Daqing. "P. B. Cousland—a Promoter for the Standardization of Medical Nomenclature." *China Historical Materials of Science and Technology* 22(4) (2001): 324–30.

Zhang, Everett Yuehong. "The Birth of *Nanke* (Men's Medicine) in China: The Making of the Subject of Desire." *American Ethnologist* 34(3) (2007): 491–508.

———. *The Impotence Epidemic: Men's Medicine and Sexual Desire in Contemporary China*. Durham, NC: Duke University Press, 2015.

———. "Rethinking Sexual Repression in Maoist China: Ideology, Structure, and the Ownership of the Body." *Body and Society* 11(3) (2005): 1–25.

Zhang Weihan 張維漢, and Wu Decheng 吳德誠. "Chongqing zhongyang yiyuan jiaoqi bing ershiba li zhi linchuang baogao" 重慶中央醫院腳氣病二十八例之臨床報告 [Clinical report on the 28 *jiaoqi* cases at the Central Hospital of Chongqing]. *Huaxi yixun* 華西醫訊 5(1) (1948): 19.

Zheng Mian 鄭勉, Gu Zhonghua 顧鍾驊, and Hua Fuxi 華阜熙, eds. *Chuzhong weisheng* 初中衛生 [Junior high hygiene]. Vol. 1. Revised by Hua Jucheng 華汝成. Shanghai: Zhonghua shuju, 1933–1934.

Zhou Jianren 周建人. *Xing Jiaoyu* 性教育 [Sex education]. Shanghai: Commercial Press, 1931.

Zhou Xiaonong 周小農. *Zhou Xiaonong yi'an* 周小農醫案 [Medical cases of Zhou Xiaonong]. Hong Kong: Commercial Press, 1971.

Zhu Maoting 朱茂庭. *Renti shengli weishengxue* 人體生理衛生學 [Physiology and hygiene of the human body]. Nanjing: Nanjing shudian, 1932.

Zhu Qian 朱潛. "Jiaoqizheng yu funü fenmianqi de guanxi" 腳氣症與婦女分娩期的關係 [Relationship between *jiaoqi* and women during pregnancy]. *Guangji yuekan* 廣濟月刊 19(8) (1933): 3–9.

Zhu Shihui 朱師晦, and Chen Airen 陳愛仁. "Guangzhou jundui zhi jiaoqi bing" 廣州軍隊之腳氣病 [The *jiaoqi* disease in the Cantonese army]. *Zhongshan yibao* 中山醫報 3(5–6) (1948): 10.

Zhu Xiu 朱橚. *Puji fang* 普濟方 [Recipes for general relief]. 1406.

Zhuan Weizhong 莊衛仲, and Gong Anyun 龔昂雲. *Chuzhong shengli weishengxue* 初中生理衛生學 [Physiology and hygiene for junior highs]. 1930. Shanghai: Shijie shuju, 1933.

Zhuang Wenkuang. "Ni shi laowai" 你是老外 [You are out-diner]. In *Taiwan diqu jiating shouzhi diaocha* 臺灣地區家庭收支調查 [Survey of Taiwanese family income]. Taipei: Directorate of Budget, Executive Yuan, Republic of China, Taiwan, 2006.

Contributors

Francesca Bray is a historian of science, technology, and medicine in China with a special interest in gender. Her publications on medicine and the body in China include "A Deathly Disorder: Understanding Amenorrhea in China" (in Bates, *Knowledge and the Scholarly Medical Traditions*, Cambridge University Press, 1995), "The Chinese Experience" (in Pickstone and Cooter, *Medicine in the Twentieth Century*, Harwood, 2000), "Becoming a Mother in Late Imperial China: Maternal Doubles and the Ambiguity of Fertility" (in Brandstädter and Santos, *Chinese Kinship*, Routledge, 2008), and *Technology, Gender and History in Imperial China: Great Transformations Reconsidered* (Routledge, 2013). She currently holds the chair of social anthropology at the University of Edinburgh.

Susan L. Burns is associate professor of Japanese history and East Asian languages and civilizations at the University of Chicago. She is the author of *Before the Nation: Kokugaku and Imagining of Community in Early Modern Japan* (Duke University Press, 2003) and the coeditor (with Barbara J. Brooks) of *Gender and Law in the Japanese Imperium* (University of Hawai'i Press, 2013). Her recent work on the history of medicine includes "Rethinking 'Leprosy Prevention': Entrepreneurial Doctors, Popular Journalism, and the Civic Origins of Biopolitics" (*Journal of Japanese Studies* 38, no. 2, Summer 2012), and "Marketing Health and the Modern Body: Patent Medicine Advertisements in Meiji-Taisho Japan" (in Thomsen and Purtle, *East Asian Visual Culture from the Treaty Ports to World War II*, Center for East Asian Arts, University of Chicago and Art Media Resources, 2009).

Howard Chiang is assistant professor of history at the University of California, Davis. He is the editor of *Transgender China* (Palgrave Macmillan, 2012), *Queer Sinophone Cultures* (Routledge, 2013, with Ari Larissa Heinrich), *Psychiatry and Chinese History* (Pickering and Chatto, 2014), *Historical Epistemology and the Making of Modern Chinese Medicine* (Manchester University Press, 2015), and *Perverse Taiwan* (Routledge, 2016, with Yin Wang). He is currently completing his first monograph, tentatively titled "After Eunuchs: Science, Medicine, and the Transformations of Sex in Modern China."

John P. DiMoia is a visiting researcher affiliated with Department III at the Max Planck Institute for the History of Science. His first book, *Reconstructing Bodies: Biomedicine, Health, and Nation-Building in South Korea since 1945*, was published by Stanford University Press in 2013. He is currently completing an edited volume, *Engineering Asia*, with Hiromi Mizuno of the University of Minnesota and Aaron S. Moore of Arizona State University.

Jung-ok Ha is research professor at the Institute for Gender Research, Seoul National University, South Korea. Her research interests include the global/local and gender politics of technology, women's health and bioethics, and feminist STS. She is currently working on the Science and Civilization in Korea Project, especially gender and science technology in the history of premodern and modern Korea.

Jen-der Lee is research fellow at the Institute of History and Philology, Academia Sinica, Taiwan. She examines legal and medical history from a gender perspective and teaches at several universities, including National Taiwan University. Most of her work focuses on early imperial China, but she has recently extended her interest to women's encounters with law and medicine in modern China and Taiwan. Her publications include two books, three edited volumes, and many articles.

Sean Hsiang-lin Lei is associate research fellow at the Institute of Modern History, Academia Sinica, Taiwan, and associate professor at the Institute of Science, Technology and Society (STS) at Yang-Ming University. He specializes in the history of medicine, including both biomedicine and traditional medicine, in modern China and Taiwan. His first book, *Neither Donkey nor Horse: Medicine in the Struggle over China's Modernity* (University of Chicago Press, 2014), seeks to understand how Chinese medicine was transformed from an antithesis of modernity into a potent symbol and vehicle for China's exploration of its own modernity.

Angela Ki Che Leung obtained her doctoral degree at the École des Hautes Études en Sciences Sociales, Paris. She is currently director and chair professor of the Hong Kong Institute for the Humanities and Social Sciences, University of Hong Kong. She has published articles in Chinese, French, and English on Chinese late imperial and modern history including a book in Chinese on philanthropic organizations in Ming-Qing China (1997). Her more recent publications include *Leprosy in China: A History* (Columbia University Press, 2009), *Health and Hygiene in Chinese East Asia in the Long*

20th Century (Duke University Press, 2010, coedited with Charlotte Furth). Her present research interests include the beriberi question in colonial Asia, the construction of nutritional knowledge, and related food technology in modern China. She was elected Academician of the Academia Sinica, Taiwan in 2010.

Izumi Nakayama is honorary assistant professor and research officer at the Hong Kong Institute for the Humanities and Social Sciences, University of Hong Kong. Her research interests include history of the body, medicine, and technology with a special focus on gender. Her current projects examine the histories of menstruation, breastfeeding, and infertility in Japan and East Asia.

Chia-ling Wu is professor of sociology at the National Taiwan University. Her recent publication studies women's risk negotiation of new reproductive technologies, the making of multiple embryo transfer regulation, and architectural design for the post-disaster reconstruction. Her current research projects examine the risk governance of multiple embryo transfer in Taiwan, Japan, and South Korea.

Index